T★34
SHOCK
THE SOVIET LEGEND IN PICTURES

FRANCIS PULHAM AND **WILL KERRS**

FONTHILL

Fonthill Media Language Policy

Fonthill Media publishes in the international English language market. One language edition is published worldwide. As there are minor differences in spelling and presentation, especially with regard to American English and British English, a policy is necessary to define which form of English to use. The Fonthill Policy is to use the form of English native to the author. Francis Pulham was born and educated in Brighton, England; therefore, British English has been adopted in this publication.

Fonthill Media Limited
Fonthill Media LLC
www.fonthillmedia.com
office@fonthillmedia.com

First published in the United Kingdom and the United States of America 2021

British Library Cataloguing in Publication Data:
A catalogue record for this book is available from the British Library

Copyright © Francis Pulham and Will Kerrs 2021

ISBN 978-1-78155-846-1

Typeset in Minion Pro 10pt on 13pt
Printed and bound in England

CONTENTS

ACKNOWLEDGEMENTS

This publication would not have been possible without the help of some close friends and colleagues.

Greatest thanks to my co-author, Will Kerrs, for his continuous hard work writing, editing, and proofreading the book with me.

Special thanks to Mark Rethoret for his assistance with technical details and for his fantastic technical drawings. Special thanks to Jaycee 'Amazing Ace' Davis for drawing the colour profiles.

Thanks to Leo Guo for translating Chinese sources and providing some additional consultancy on our Chinese T-34s section, and thanks to Gareth Lynn Montes for his additional consultancy on our Spanish Civil War section.

Thanks to Sergey Lotarev for information on the 8th and 12th Tank Divisions, and to the 'Nemirov-41' team for tank locations.

Thanks also to Stan Lucian for his proofreading, and to Alex Pulham for assistance taking measurements of T-34s.

Additional thanks to Maxim Kolomiets, Sergey Lotarev, Andery Firsov, Stan Lucian, Jiří Zahradník, Ed Okun, Will Kerrs, and Przemysław Skulski for kindly allowing us to use photographs from their private collections in this book.

Additional thanks also to the members of the following Facebook study groups for their comments: 'Francis Pulham Books', 'The T-34 Interest Group', 'Spanish Civil War Vehicles—Tanks, armoured cars, and aircraft', and 'Chinese Civil War Vehicles—Tanks, Armoured Cars, and Aircraft'.

This book would also not have been possible without the generosity of people who helped kickstart this book through Kickstarter.com. A total of £1,000 was raised for the pictures and technical drawings in this book. These people are £5: Tony Moseley. £10: Ian Wilcox, Georgios Tzouganakis Fougatsakis, and Kim Sweeney. £20: Craig Moore. £25: Duane Warnecke, Alex Smith, Paul Mutton, Andrey Firstov, Thomas Munk, Stan Lucian, Luc Belanger, Peter Samsonov, Bas Slaats, Tim Roberts, and Marcus Hock. £50: Vladimir Cervienka, Volkan Alkan, Jacob Burnett, Sonny Butterworth, Lorenzo Dutto, Will Kerrs, Helen Pulham, Nathaniel MacDonald, and Gary Hoyt. £100: Paul Timms.

INTRODUCTION

The T-34 medium tank is one of the most iconic weapons ever to have entered the battlefield. It is a tank that is often characterised as having 'won the Second World War', but the T-34 also took part in dramatic post-war triumphs. However, it was also a weapon of various oppressors. Indeed, while many view the T-34 as a symbol of Soviet might, greater numbers still view it as a weapon of conquest. Perhaps as infamous as the AK-47 assault rifle, the myths and legends around the T-34 are almost as incredible as the truth about the tank. While beyond obsolete today, the T-34 still roams the battlefields of various modern conflicts such as the Yemeni Civil War (2015–present), but perhaps fortunately, the T-34 more commonly furnishes an ever-growing number of podiums, memorials, and museums.

When one examines various T-34s closely, it becomes obvious that many changes were implemented into the design of the tank over time. However, sources on both sides of the Iron Curtain have failed to understand how complex it was to design, manufacture, and repair the T-34. Perhaps the greatest factor feeding this production change intrigue is the flood of private German photographs from the Second World War that, without which, almost nothing about the technical features of wartime T-34s would be known. Many photographs can now be obtained from long-forgotten photo albums from which a wealth of information about the T-34 and its production changes can be gained. That said, to fully understand the T-34, one must start at the beginning and move forwards through time.

This book will begin with an explanation of the methodology used to identify different T-34 production batches. After this, we begin with a history of pre-Second World War Soviet tank production leading up to the T-34's prototypes so that the reader understands the context in which the T-34 design appeared. This will take the reader through the fledgeling development of Soviet tank industry in the late 1920s and early 1930s, focusing especially on the development of the BT series and the impact of the Spanish Civil War (1936–1939) on Soviet tank designs. Next, the history of the T-34's prototypes will be explored in detail, drawing out the perpetual conflict between Soviet high command, engineers, and factory managers. Following this, there is an exterior and interior technical description of a common T-34 from 1940, which is written in parallel with two other technical descriptions later in the book—the T-34/76 in 1944 and the T-34-85 in 1945. To end this section, there is some insight into the T-34's contemporary tanks, from which the reader will discover that the tank was not intended to be a 'war-winning tank' and may not have even been fit for service in the first place.

Following the first section, the main bulk of the book begins. This is chiefly made up of sections discussing the production changes to the T-34, factory by factory, and in given timeframes. This goes from T-34s with L-11 guns, T-34s with F-34 guns, the introduction of the hexagonal turret, specialised T-34/76s, the T-34-85, and post-Second World War upgrades to the T-34. Interludes in this narrative are made to explore the T-34's changing contexts, such as the shift from peacetime to wartime, the appearance of new German tanks, the need for a new turret, the need for a new gun, and some contemporary T-34 upgrade prototypes.

After the main bulk, the next sections comprise brief explorations of the T-34's major variants—the SU-122, SU-85, and SU-100—as well as the use of T-34 turrets on armoured trains and boats. The wartime history is completed by a brief overview of *Beutepanzer* T-34s.

The last section focuses on the post-war era, which begins with an exploration of the T-34's replacements: the T-34-85M (an ultimately rejected wartime project), T-44, and T-54. The T-34's whole factory production story is complete with an exploration of the T-34's biggest post-war producers and modifiers—Poland, Czechoslovakia, and the People's Republic of China. To complement all this, colour plates and technical drawings are provided.

Also integrated throughout the book are four battle stories. The first battle is the Battle of Seseña (29 October 1936), which is given to explain how the Spanish Civil War influenced Soviet tank design ultimately leading to the T-34. The second battle is the 21st Tank Brigade's assault on Kalinin (17–20 October 1941), which is included not just to give the history of the famous T-34 with ZiS-4 57-mm gun, but to give a typical example of early war combat use of the T-34. The next battle, much later in the book, is the Battle of Ogledow (13 August 1944), which is intended to show how the T-34 (now the T-34-85), Soviet tactics, and Soviet crews had improved since the start of the war. Finally, the story of Major General William F. Dean's (United States Army) North Korean T-34 'tank hunting' at the Battle of Taejon (20 July 1950) is given to demonstrate that even though the T-34 was outdated by that time, 'tactics were the ultimate decider for the T-34's combat use rather than technical specifications'.

1

HOW TO USE THIS BOOK:
OUR METHODOLOGY

The main bulk of the book consists of an exploration of even the smallest production changes done to T-34s. However, most of the wartime changes are not specified in factory documents, and official photographs from Soviet archives are simply not numerous enough to capture all the details. Therefore, to understand the production changes and get a grasp of their chronology, one must compare private photographs of T-34s from several sources.

The first source of private photographs comes from *Wehrmacht* soldiers during the Second World War. When the Germans went to the front, many of them carried with them a personal camera. With this, they would usually chronicle their lives throughout their service—with some even including photographs of their initial training, their frontline living quarters, and comrades during sightseeing—but many photos show knocked-out enemy vehicles, including aircraft, tanks, and armoured cars. Of course, there were strict regulations that had to be followed, such as the prohibition of photographs of dead German soldiers.

For our purposes, these photographs are useful because of the T-34s they show. Sometimes, these simply show the T-34 on its own, but often, they are photos of Germans inspecting or even posing on the tanks. One must keep in mind that most of the latter are just 'tourist photos', meaning that the people in the photo had nothing to do with the tanks and instead just came across them while on duty (typically when travelling to the front). Perhaps most wartime photos in this publication were taken by German lorry drivers on supply runs; combat photos are incredibly rare, although some photos in this book were taken mere hours after fighting.

One must also consider that most *Wehrmacht* photographs come from 1941 and 1942. As the war progressed, private photographs became increasingly rare. Put simply, most German photographs were taken when they were advancing, as there were interesting things to see and chronicle, but as they began their long retreat, the Germans had more important jobs to do than take photographs (to put it mildly).

The second source of private photographs is post-war photographs from Soviet, Bulgarian, East German, Polish, Lithuanian, Egyptian, Yugoslav, and Chinese tank crews or soldiers. These follow the same format as German Second World War photograph albums and are (almost) never combat photographs, although some war-games photos are available. Fortunately, most of these photographs do not show tank wrecks, too, so their technical features are intact.

The third source of photographs are tourist photographs in the true sense, for example, Syrian T-34s abandoned in the Golan Heights, tanks on memorial plinths, or museum pieces. One must consider that these photos typically show tanks that have been modified or restored inaccurately by museums, and so their technical features are sometimes wrong. For example, the Czechoslovakian T-34-85 in the Imperial War Museum, London, has incorrect road wheels and a headlight fastened in what is actually a buzzer for infantrymen to get the attention of the tank crew, just to name a few inaccuracies.

One limitation of using private photographs from soldiers is that they are not always the best quality. Soldiers are soldiers and not photographers, so therefore one must not expect every single photograph to be a work of art. Sometimes, they are overexposed, out of focus, or taken at a poor angle. One must also consider that soldiers are typically not 'rivet-counters', so they are not to know that if they took a step to the right when taking a photo, they would capture an incredibly rare production detail on a T-34, such as a vent for a command tank's radio exhaust.

However, perhaps the biggest limitation of using private photographs is that they are taken out of context by their modern-day sellers. Typically, sellers will divide a full album up and sell the photographs individually with very limited information given (sometimes titles of the sales are as uninformative as '*Zerstörter russischer* Panzer, Ostfront'). Therefore, unless a whole album is put up for sale (which is more common with post-war albums), one will have to carefully research each individual tank by cross-referencing the photographs with other known images of it. Private photographs from soldiers sometimes have locations and dates written on the back, although this is not only rare but sometimes inaccurate. Sometimes, for example, a German will take a photograph of a BT-5 and suggest that it is a 'T34'.

Despite these limitations, from all the private photographs of T-34s, one will quickly be able to see that there were many design changes done to the T-34, from the jarringly obvious (such as new turrets) to the very minor (such as a change in fuel tank placement). With rough dates, locations, and sometimes Red Army units established, one can cross-reference (to some degree) with Soviet factory photos and documents of T-34s to work out which factory produced a given tank, and roughly when. However, as mentioned, Soviet factory photos and documents are insufficient to help work out what details came from which factory and in what timeframe, so a large amount of detective work is needed.

Such detective work takes place in esoteric 'rivet-counting' circles (such as on 'The T-34 Interest Group' on Facebook), where countless photographs are compared and debated before a conclusion can be reached. From these debates, agreements can be made on which factories issued tanks with which technical features, and roughly when. However, as more and more photographs become available, previous conclusions sometimes need reconsideration in light of new evidence.

From this methodology, one can (tentatively) give these specific tanks made-up designations to distinguish them. It should be stated at this point that the term 'T-34/76' is not one that was used in contemporary Soviet documentation. T-34/76s were simply called 'T-34', and when the 85-mm gun was introduced, these new tanks were known as 'T-34-85' in the documentation. However, the post-war terms 'T-34/76' and 'T-34/85' have become commonplace due to their quick differentiation. In this book, T-34/76 will only be used when it is necessary to distinguish between the two; otherwise, official Soviet terms will be used.

Dates have been used to identify various versions of the T-34 in post-war literature; for example, all T-34s with an L-11 gun are known as 'T-34/76 Model 1940', even though tanks were issued with an L-11 gun up until February 1941. Other attempts have rightly referred to the factory the tank came from, but this, too, is also insufficient (e.g. T-34-85 174) because there were various subtypes of T-34-85s made at Omsk 174.

Instead, this book (again, tentatively) proposes many made-up designations to refer to certain production batches from certain factories. Usually, our names are in three parts. First, the type of tank is specified (this can be T-34, T-34-85, OT-34, or OT-34-85, and so on). Secondly, the factory name is specified (this being KhPZ 183, STZ, UTZ 183, Krasnoye Sormovo 112, ChKZ 100, UTZM, or Omsk 174 for Soviet-made vehicles). Finally, a distinguishing feature is used to refer to a certain production batch (post-war non-Soviet production vehicles follow a similar pattern).

For example, T-34 (KhPZ 183 8-Bolt Turret) refers to a T-34/76 made at KhPZ 183 (Kharkov Locomotive and Tractor Factory) that has the turret type with eight bolts on the gun inspection hatch at the rear of the turret (the turret type commonly being known as an eight-bolt turret).

However, there are some complications with this system.

First, there was a phenomenon in Soviet wartime factories of 'first in, last out'. This means that as new production features were introduced (such as a new exhaust shroud type or an engine access hatch type), old stocks of these features would be used up first or used in conjunction with the newer stocks seemingly arbitrarily.

Secondly, one has to keep in mind that many T-34s were rebuilt. When tanks suffered combat damage, if they were salvageable, they would be salvaged and taken back to a factory for repairs. Often, this was long after the tank was produced, meaning that new features were in production at the time of its repair. Therefore, it is common to see rebuilds that are older types of T-34s that have been given newer features.

As a result, one must be cautious not to rigidly stick to the designations system that this book employs, but instead one should use it as a rule of thumb (and one still much more accurate than previous categorisation attempts).

Another way to refer to a specific T-34 would be by its chassis number, but such details exist only for very few individual T-34s, and without a full list of T-34 chassis numbers (something that simply does not exist, and almost certainly can never be pieced together), this task is impossible. Even if possible, there is a serious problem with this system—it tells us nothing about a tank's technical features. For example, according to a factory photograph, the chassis number of a T-34 (A-34 Turret) is 811-65, but the chassis number 811-78 can be seen on another factory photograph of a T-34 (L-11 Gun and Turret Radio). This indicates that the chassis numbers bear little correlation with actual technical features of the tanks, as one might reasonably expect '811' chassis numbers to look the same. This is a telling example of the 'first in, last out' phenomenon.

Another designations method would be to simply refer to a rough production time frame and factory. However, this methodology is complicated by insufficient evidence to work out when certain production features were implemented, and also the additional problem of rebuilds having two (or possibly more) production batch dates, a phenomenon that may have slightly inflated estimates on the total number of T-34s produced. Moreover, this method would never be totally accurate due to the aforementioned problem of 'first in, last out'. Thus, we arrive back at the designations system that this book will employ—a description based on the factory and technical features. Despite its limitations, this is the most useful (as it references technical features) and accurate system that can be devised using current evidence.

With the strengths and limitations of the identification methodology outlined, one should be able to replicate this system for themselves when looking at any given T-34.

Finally, it is our duty in writing this book to remind the reader that tanks were a weapon of war used to kill countless numbers of people, but they likewise were also a weapon inside of which countless people were killed.

Many photographs in this book will show war dead, and due to the nature of the photographs (mostly being taken by German soldiers), the identities of these men can perhaps never be traced. Even when human remains cannot be seen, one expects that many, if not most, knocked-out tanks contained the remains of their crews. For that reason, one should be careful not to fetishise the tank or to use the tank as a soulless and distanced or even sanitised representation of war. All wars that this book refers to were brutal, bloody, and inconceivable numbers of human beings were killed during them as either soldiers, civilians, or otherwise.

2

ANTECEDENTS: THE BT SERIES

By the mid-1920s, many prominent Bolsheviks dashed their hopes of a world revolution, following the failure of a socialist seizure of power in countries such as Germany, Great Britain, and Hungary. As such, after Lenin's death in 1924 and Stalin's rise to power, the policy of 'Socialism in One Country' was adopted. This policy advocated for the USSR to build socialism (chiefly) within its own borders, seeing as though apparently only they had both the will and means to do so. Part of this included defending the state from external threats such as 'western counter-revolutionaries' who wanted to 'strangle Communism at its birth', to borrow Bolshevik phraseology. Therefore, in the late 1920s and early 1930s, the USSR began investing heavily in modernising its army to defend its borders, and one crucial feature of this was the building of a modern tank corps.

At first, work began on domestic designs. However, the earliest projects, such as the T-18 light tank, T-19 medium tank (both effectively copies and modernisations of the Renault FT), and many other more obscure designs were falling flat, either being too complex to manufacture, outdated upon their very conception, or both. Only the T-12 and T-24 medium-tank projects, beginning in 1927, looked promising. However, these tanks were not even in the prototype stage until 1931 and were terminated shortly after anyway due to the introduction of superior medium tanks, namely the T-28. It was obvious to Soviet leadership that indigenous designs were simply not able to make the grade, and this was clear only by 1930. Therefore, it was decided that the best course of action was to acquire foreign tank designs to build on if the USSR was going to modernise its tank corps.

This process began by purchasing a small number (unknown, but under ten) of Medium Mark II* tanks from Great Britain in 1930, but this was a technological dead end. Later in 1930, Semyon Alexandrovich Ginzburg, one of the USSR's most important tank designers, oversaw the purchasing of a Vickers Mark E Type B and the licence to manufacture them, which ultimately led to the highly successful T-26 light tank. At the same time, the new Medium Mark III was observed and measured illegally by Ginzburg, which would partially inspire the relatively successful T-28 medium tank.

This group of T-24s abandoned in 1941 was waiting for conversion to BOTs (armoured firing points). The T-24 had a long career training Soviet tank crews before being assigned this fate. These tanks were abandoned in the Leningrad Military District; a total of twelve T-24s were abandoned here.

However, apart from the eventual development of the T-26, none of these other projects led to any highly successful design. While, indeed, the T-26 was an unprecedented success, arguably being the most influential and potent tank of the so-called inter-war era, the Soviet Union was keen on experimenting with new tank tactics, and therefore, there were still gaps in the tank corps that needed to be filled with new tank types.

Cavalry was still considered by many to be a necessary feature of an army, but one of the many lessons learned from the First World War was that it needed mechanisation if it were to remain relevant on the battlefield. In fact, this theory was not unique to the Soviets, so the USSR needed to look abroad again to find a design that would fit this role of a 'cavalry' or 'fast' tank.

THE CHRISTIE M1940

The Soviets found a glimmer of hope in the American inventor Walter J. Christie, with his 'Christie fast convertible tanks'. However, the USSR's acquisition of a Christie tank was quite troubled.

On 28 April 1930, the USSR eventually agreed with Christie a sum of $60,000 (almost $1,000,000 in today's money) for two Model 1940 fast convertible tanks (not to be confused with the Model 1931), $4,000 for spare parts, and $100,000 for a set of patents with a production licence for ten years. The contract also required for a Soviet engineer to be based in the

Rahway Factory in New Jersey where Christie worked, whose role was to inform the Soviet Union on new tank designs from the US Wheel Track Layer Corporation.

The first 127 pages of the blueprints were safely sent to Moscow in August 1930, but the shipping of the Christie tanks to the USSR was more troublesome. The United States of America did not have any diplomatic relations with the USSR until 1933, which would make arms deals problematic for legal reasons. Therefore, while the Soviet–Christie documentation stated that they were sending tanks, in a phone conversation to the US State Department, Christie stated that he was only sending tractors. Nothing could be checked by American authorities, however, as the shipment had already been dispatched from the USA.

When the vehicles arrived in the USSR on 24 December 1930 (four months late), it was found that Christie had sent the hulls of the tanks, but not the turrets. Worse still, the tanks' full documentation was also lacking. As a result, the USSR withheld $25,000.

One possible reason for the missing turrets and documentation is that Christie was likely afraid of being discovered selling arms to the USSR by the US government, which could land Christie in serious legal trouble. It is also possible that the turrets and paperwork would have been shipped later, but there appears to have been little communication between Christie and the USSR after this time, and therefore further details are lacking. Perhaps Christie's dislike of communism was also a factor.

To make up for the missing money, Christie organised a contract with the US Army for ten tanks and passed on the military secrets of the USSR that he had access to. In response to this, the USSR bribed engineers working for Christie to deliver the complete documents, thus giving the USSR a complete design to work with.

Now with a chassis both modern enough and suitable for their production lines, the Soviet Union developed the design of the Christie M1940 with an indigenous turret and modified the hull. This new tank was rushed into production, with 100 vehicles ordered to be manufactured starting on 1 May 1931, before 'Original I and II' (the names given to the two Christie M1940s), had even been fully tested. The Soviet series production tank was to be named 'BT-2'.

THE BT SERIES

The BT series was a desirable mix of speed and manoeuvrability, but it sacrificed armour protection as a trade-off. The design's defining feature was the Christie-type suspension, which consisted of vertical spring suspension with large-diameter road wheels. The hull also included a 'double skin' for protecting the spring suspension. The nose of all standard production BT tanks came to a flattened point, allowing for external steering mounts on either side of this nose.

The BT-2 was armed with either a 37-mm B-3 gun or a twin 7.62-mm machine gun mount.

The next tank in the series, the BT-5, was a stopgap upgrade made in 1933, which concerned the introduction of a newer and larger turret housing a 20-K 45-mm anti-tank gun. This new turret was originally designed for the T-26 (which prior to this was a dual-turret design), but the design specified that it should also be interchangeable with the BT tank. This same turret was also lightened in weight and issued to BA-3 and BA-6 armoured cars, which were also staples of the Soviet tank corps. Other than the turret, some BT-5s has moderately

The BT-2 tank was the Soviet-produced version of the Christie Model 1940. It featured a Soviet-designed turret but was powered by a copy of the Liberty Engine, designated 'M-5'. Behind is a BT-7, the last major variant of BT manufactured. The BT-2 has a camouflage pattern on it, likely of a lighter green or a very worn winter whitewash.

A BT-5 that suffered an ammunition detonation in the rear of the turret.

strengthened hulls, but the base BT-5 hull was near-identical to that of a BT-2. Additionally, the BT-5 had pressed road wheels, whereas the BT-2 had cast road wheels. However, being only a mere stopgap, the BT-5 was only in production for less than a year before a replacement was designed to mitigate the inherent problems with the BT hull.

The BT series had a unique feature that initially attracted the Soviet Union, which was the wheel-track convertible drive. This was both a useful feature and a design flaw of the tank. When travelling long distances, the tracks were stowed, and the tank ran on its road wheels, with one of the road wheels being connected to the drive sprocket by a chain and steering with the front road wheels. This meant that the tank could travel faster than it could on its tracks.

The BT was an integral part of the Soviet tank corps, with 620 BT-2s, 1,946 BT-5s, and 5,556 BT-7s (to be discussed later) of all types being manufactured by 1940. More importantly, much had been learned by engineers from trials of, and experiments on, the vehicles.

However, while the design was acceptable and great speed could be attained, the suspension proved to be very weak, especially around the front idler wheel, and tended to snap off. This was due to the stress of running the vehicles on the tracks, and the tracks themselves were too thin and difficult to stow when the vehicles operated in the 'wheel mode' of driving. The wheel-track convertible drive also meant that the nose of the tank had to be tapered to allow the front two wheels to turn. This limited the internal space due to the equipment necessary for the wheel-track convertible drive, which was very fragile and prone to breakdowns. These problems, especially the weak suspension, led to calls for the series to be replaced as soon as the vehicle entered service, but with no real alternative, production began anyway.

The Spanish Civil War (1936–1939) provided the first opportunity for the Soviet Union to test their tanks and tactics in combat, and it was in Spain that many flaws of Soviet tanks were highlighted. While a deep modernisation of the BT-5 (the BT-7) was already in production in 1934, the already well-known flaws of both the BT and T-26 designs were magnified by the experience, and worse still, whole new ones were pointed out.

3

SOVIET COMBAT EXPERIENCE IN SPAIN

CONTEXT: THE SPANISH CIVIL WAR

The Spanish Civil War began on 17 July 1936 when a military uprising organised by a group of generals (led by Emilio Mola and José Sanjurjo) sympathetic to a wide range of ideas, such as pro-monarchism, conservatism, Catholicism, anti-communism, fascism, and various other ideologies associated with the right wing. The Second Republic, which had been established in 1931 following the abdication of Alfonso XIII, had from 1931 until 1934 introduced progressive legislation including land reforms and taking power away from the church, which for the traditionalist elements of Spain tore down the fabric of what the country was supposed to be. When the left wing Popular Front got elected in 1936, it was a step too far for the right wing opposition who felt that something had to be done.

Following the success of the uprising in Spanish Morocco (where the largest part of the Spanish army was) and various failed ones in the big cities, Spain was ostensibly divided between the Republicans (a very loose alliance of social democrats, communists, socialists, anarchists, Basque Nationalists, Catalan Nationalists, and others) and the Nationalists (monarchists, fascists, most Catholics, and other right-wing elements, and were also supported by Italy and Germany). It cannot be overstated that these were loose alliances, and often of sheer necessity as opposed to conviction.

Throughout July, the Nationalists, with German and Italian aid, began airlifting their forces from Spanish Morocco onto the mainland nearly unimpeded due to the elements of the army still loyal to the Republican government usually refusing to act. In fact, the most active Republican combat units were local militia, who were even more poorly armed and organised than the official army. By September, the Nationalists had captured areas across the south-west, west, and north-west of Spain.[1]

SOVIET INTERVENTION

Despite signing the Non-Intervention Agreement with the League of Nations (not to mention the policy of 'Socialism in One Country'), the Stavka decided to intervene in Spain, albeit as covertly as possible, although Germany and Italy preferred a more direct approach. The USSR had agents working in Spain since 1920 (who organised the Spanish Communist Party), but when a 'genuine revolutionary struggle' emerged in 1936, it was one chiefly headed by Social Democrats, anarchists, and socialists—not communists in the Soviet sense. It may be concluded that Stalin's decision to intervene was part of a broader security strategy against Germany, but this historical debate rages on.[2]

On 29 September 1936, a meeting was held regarding the possibility of sales of tanks to the Spanish Republican forces, with the BT-2, BT-5, T-26, T-28, and T-35A being proposed. People's Conmmisar for Defence Kliment Voroshilov reported to Stalin that the Military Council were prepared to send 100 tanks, 387 specialists, and thirty aircraft to Spain. On 9 October, at the proposal of the People's Commissar of Defence of Spain, sixty armoured cars also entered the agreement, namely three BA-3s, thirty-seven BA-6s, and twenty FAIs. These vehicles made up the initial order, with additional vehicles sent later. In total, an estimated 281 T-26s (not including fifty which were lost at sea when their transport ship was sunk) were shipped to Spain, along with fifty BT-5s. These tanks consisted mainly of the elliptical turreted type, but some cylindrical turreted tanks were also sent. These were all paid for using Spanish gold reserves, the majority of which were shipped directly to the USSR.

The first ship carrying Soviet supplies to reach Spain was the *Campeche*, which arrived at Cartagena on 4 October 1936. This was followed shortly by the *Komsomol*, disguised as a tourist ship, which arrived on 12 October and brought the first shipment of fifty T-26s.

BATTLE: T-26 ASSAULT ON SESEÑA

The first T-26s in Spain were fielded at the Battle of Seseña on 29 October 1936. The Nationalists had taken the town of Seseña, around 27 miles south of Madrid on 27 October along with other areas, leading to a major Republican counteroffensive being announced by Prime Minister Francisco Largo Caballero. The plan was to hammer Nationalist positions with artillery and tank fire at dawn. Then, the air force was meant to begin their assault, followed by infantry of the *1a Brigada Mixta* under Enrique Líster.

Fifteen T-26s were dispatched for the counterattack under the command of Red Army Captain Pavel Arman. The crews of the T-26s consisted of thirty-four Soviet instructors as commanders and drivers, and eleven Spanish trainee gunners recruited from lorry and bus drivers in south-east Spain. Originally, it was intended that the Soviets would only be instructors, but the situation in Spain was so dire (with fears that Madrid could be taken imminently) that Soviets also had to form part of Spanish units.

However, things did not go to plan. At 6.30 a.m., the assault began with three T-26s commanded by Lieutenant Ivan Lobach scouting the foggy road towards Seseña. However, Nationalist troops guarding the entrance to the town did not see that the tanks came from Republican lines due to the fog, and because they were told to expect new Italian tanks to arrive soon, they did not open fire. The tanks passed unimpeded, and during breakfast, an officer in charge of an artillery unit ordered his soldiers to stand to attention facing the tanks, which were passing through the town square towards the exit of the town leading to Esquivias. At this time, some Nationalist soldiers shouted that the enemy was attacking at nearby Torrejón de Velasco with artillery and aeroplanes, so a general alert was raised.

Four Schneider de 105/11 Modelo 1919 mountain guns of the Nationalist *2a* and the *6a Batería de la Agrupación de Artillería de Melilla* were deployed under the command of Captain Andrés Sánchez Pérez. Two guns were placed at one exit of the town, and a third was placed at an exit leading to nearby Esquivias. The fourth gun was placed looking out to the road to Cuesta de la Reina, from where twelve more T-26s began to appear. The guns were ordered to hold their fire as the identity of the tanks could not be ascertained. Confusingly, it did not quite seem like an attack because the crews were hanging out of the hatches of the tanks and therefore exposed.

As a result, six or seven men were sent out onto the road to check the identity of the tanks, but shortly after, the tanks opened fire, scattering the men into the road. The shots completely missed, indicating the poor and limited training of Spanish Republican gunners, but a 105-mm howitzer returned fire on the tanks and also missed. Following this, the tanks made it into the town square, firing on everything that moved, especially lorries and cars to prevent soldiers from escaping or deploying more weapons.

At this point, it was clear that the T-26s were not supported by any infantry. Líster later suggested that after advancing 1,500 m, the infantry lost sight of the rapidly advancing tanks, got tired, and stopped together in small groups in some hills around the town. Artillery fire and the Republican air force were nowhere to be seen here, either.

Just after the tanks entered the square, Lieutenant Angel Suanzes ordered the Nationalist soldiers to reorganise their field guns. This was a tricky affair because of all the confusion about the attack and all the chaos being caused by the destruction of motor vehicles from the twelve tanks in the square. Nevertheless, one gun stayed put to cover the exit to Esquivias, but one was brought into the town square. However, a lorry transporting this field gun was rammed by the leading T-26, which caused the tank to throw a track and become immobilised outside a tavern. This tank continued firing on the square despite the damage sustained.

The fourth field gun, at that point loaded onto a lorry, was unable to leave the town square to redeploy to a more suitable position due to the roads being blocked by damaged vehicles and was instead deployed on a side street. From this position, under the command of Suanzes, it began to open fire on the immobilised T-26, but missed, hitting various buildings. The crew was unable to fire accurately at such a short range because the gun was a howitzer, not an anti-tank gun. The T-26 returned fire on the howitzer, causing its crew to flee, with Suanzes and another crew member being wounded in the crossfire.

While this was happening, the field gun covering the exit to Esquivias began to engage the three T-26s, which had been passing through the town earlier. The commander of the gun, Lieutenant Candamo, ordered his men to take cover while he fired at point-blank range. Unfortunately for him, like the crew in the town square, he also missed his shot. A T-26 then rolled over the field gun, disabling it and trapping Candamo, but when a second tank rolled over it, he was freed with only minor wounds and bruises.

Meanwhile, back in the town square, Nationalist soldiers began siphoning petrol from lorries and gathering bottles and jars to make petrol bombs to destroy the immobilised T-26 that was still hammering the area. Once they had enough materials, soldiers then ran into a nearby building and began pouring petrol onto the tank from above. Once the tank was soaked, a lit rag was dropped onto the tank, causing one crew member to be burned alive, and two others to be gunned down when bailing out. However, Camps, the soldier who dropped the rag, fell off the building and was seriously injured.

While this was happening, the T-26s began to leave Seseña and headed towards Esquivias, at which time the remaining three field guns were reorganised and began firing on the tanks at a distance, but seemingly to no avail.

During this phase of the assault, the Nationalists suffered sixteen dead, sixty wounded, and lost a howitzer, sixteen cars, ten lorries, and eight transport wagons, whereas the Republicans lost a single T-26 and suffered three dead.

The T-26s then advanced towards Esquivias where the Nationalist *Columna Monasterio* was aiming to use the town as a staging ground for a broader assault on Valedomoro, which was under attack from the Republican air force. Here, various Nationalist units began to rally. The last two units to enter the town consisted of Italian-operated CV-33 tankettes and the *5a Batería* commanded by Captain Arjona fielding *Cannone da 65/17 modello* 13 guns.

The T-26s engaged a CV-33 tankette, destroying the track with their 45-mm cannon fire, after which the tankette was rammed into a ditch where its crew escaped, somehow unharmed. At this point, the 65-mm guns began to open fire on a T-26, with one penetration being made. The tank reversed behind a wall but was immobilised due to a hit to the front right wheel. Other tanks returned fire, wounding some soldiers of the battery, and forcing them to abandon their guns.

From this point, Nationalist reinforcements under Colonel Cebollino reached the road east of Yeles, a town just under 3 miles away, and saw the intense fighting taking place in Esquivias. Various units were dispatched to aid the 5a *Batería* from the road leading to Yeles.

Seeing that by midday the tanks did not intend to advance further, the 5a *Batería* began to move closer to the town to fire on the tanks, with one gun covering the north-east exit from the town. It was decided that the guns needed to be covered before they could advance close enough to engage the tanks, though, so a single CV-33 armed with a flamethrower charged into Esquivias.

The tankette rushed over open ground to engage the T-26s, which were hidden behind walls and buildings, so the CV-33 suffered a fatal hit that killed the crew before it was in range. Witnessing this failure, it was decided that a 65-mm gun commanded by Lieutenant Ramos-Izquierdo would enter the town using a tractor while being covered by the other guns. However, by this point, the tanks began to leave via the south-east, heading towards nearby Borox, and in doing so abandoned the damaged T-26.

After deploying from 500 m, Ramos-Izquierdo began to open fire on the wall the abandoned T-26 was stuck behind. This created a break in the wall that both Ramos-Izquierdo and the T-26 used to exchange fire through for half an hour. Ramos-Izquierdo fired an estimated 150 shots before he noticed that he had hit the turret ring of the T-26 and killed the crew. Upon inspection, it was found that there were four dead crew members inside instead of the usual three, and a set of battle plans was also found.

After passing through Borox, the T-26s tried to head to Valedomoro by heading north, but they were accidentally fired upon by Republican artillery, who mistook them for Italian tanks. As a result, the tanks withdrew and headed towards Seseña again. They most likely entered the town in single file, where one T-26 was knocked out by another Molotov cocktail, although the crew was rescued by other tanks. After passing through the town, the tanks returned to Republican lines where they were congratulated and fed, but the crews kept asking where Líster's infantry were.

Julián Muñoz Lizcano, Commissar delegate for the war in Aranjuez, asked for volunteers from Líster's infantry to try to recover the tanks lost in Seseña, but only receiving two volunteers, the plan was abandoned. Instead, these tanks were recovered by the Nationalists and sent to the Condor Legion ground forces training grounds at Cubas, where they were repaired and pressed back into service.

Arman suffered a loss of three tanks, with eleven or twelve dead (six Soviets consisting of three drivers and three commanders, and five or six Spaniards) and six wounded from various tanks. Soviet documents suggest the Nationalists lost thirteen guns, two CV-33s, two lorries, and six cars. Arman suggested Nationalist losses included two infantry battalions, two cavalry squadrons, ten 75-mm field guns, two tankettes, twenty–thirty trucks, five–eight cars, some tank transporters, and that they had captured two field guns. However, in reality, the Nationalists lost two CV-33s, one 105-mm gun, one 65-mm gun, ten lorries, sixteen cars, and other vehicles in Esquivias.[3]

While the assault seemed successful in terms of losses, Seseña had not been taken because Republican infantry did not occupy the area. This battle was typical of the more successful Republican assaults throughout the Spanish Civil War, with great losses being inflicted, but no tactical advantage being gained for fair friendly losses; in this case, one-fifth of the tanks and crew members were lost. However, later assaults were often much costlier than this, such as the ill-fated offensive in Guadalajara in March–April 1938, during which the Republicans lost up to half of the armoured vehicles they committed for no gain whatsoever.

This Republican FAI was destroyed while retreating by the guns of Nationalist warships near Málaga, although the damage indicates it was toppled by the force of an explosion, not a direct hit. Having been abandoned, it was captured by Nationalists in the morning of 8 February 1937 by the column of Colonel Barbón.

T-26 'IX' was knocked out at Torrejón del Velasco on 3 November 1936, just five days after the Battle of Seseña. This tank was later towed by the Nationalists to their lines and salvaged. The tank has combat damage, which shows it was engaged from both the left and right. A shell went straight through the turret, leaving the antenna broken on the opposite side. It is possible that after the Republican attack on Seseña, the Nationalists moved AT artillery pieces into the area to defend against further attacks.

T-26 'IX' from the opposite side as to the other photo. Here, it is clear that the tank took a hit to the small idler wheel second from the front, dislodging it, and as a result, the track was thrown. Part of the mudguard was also blown off, which has landed near the rear idler wheel. This was most likely caused by infantry attacking the tank with explosives. One can also see the exit hole of the shell that hit the turret and damaged the antenna.

Furthermore, two things could be learned just from looking at the Battle of Seseña—the T-26 needed infantry support (especially in urban areas) and its armour was simply too thin (with pre-First World War field guns of a mere 65 mm in calibre being able to knock them out).

LESSONS FROM SPAIN

Throughout the war, Soviet and Spanish (both Republican and Nationalist) crews alike were impressed with the 45-mm 20-K gun used on the T-26, BT-5, BA-3, and BA-6. In fact, it was deemed so impressive that Nationalist soldiers were even paid 500 pesetas for every T-26 that they captured.[4]

Furthermore, there is evidence that even total wrecks of these vehicles were salvaged by both Republicans and Nationalists for any and all parts. Turrets especially were salvaged by the Republicans, who placed these onto an indigenous 6 × 4 heavy armoured car series known as the 'Chevrolet BC' (also known as the 'AAC-1937'), which was heavily based on the BA-6. This is even though the Republicans had their own indigenously produced turret for the vehicle.[5]

Perhaps, most tellingly of all, was the fact that Nationalist forces used their captured T-26s as their main tank and had more of them than any other tank by the end of the war, despite vast sales of Panzer Is from Germany.[6]

An abandoned Spanish Nationalist BT-5, believed to be in Aragón (possibly Fuentes de Ebro), being posed on by Italian soldiers, *c.* 1938. This one was captured from the Republicans during the Zaragoza Offensive (24 August–7 September 1937) along with other tanks. The tracks are missing, indicating it was driven in wheel mode before being abandoned.

In short, the 45-mm 20-K gun proved to be far superior to anything the German or Italian tanks fielded in Spain (and this was arguably still the case in 1941). That said, the gun was not flawless. One problem was that the gun was not able to engage soft-skin targets effectively due to the small size of the projectile fired by a 45-mm gun, which meant that limited explosives could be carried in the warhead. Therefore, in the pre-war years, the Soviets employed tanks with 45-mm guns to primarily engage tanks, and tanks with a larger gun of 76.2-mm to engage soft targets. This was the primary thinking behind the Soviet behemoth that was the T-35A tank, which fitted both 45-mm 20-K guns for engaging tanks, and a 76.2-mm KT-28 gun for engaging soft targets. In the Battle of Seseña, only around twenty-six motor vehicles were destroyed by fifteen tanks in what was quite a close-range engagement, with some being rolled over or crushed under tank tracks.

Furthermore, returning Soviet crews reported that the performance of their tanks as a whole was not as impressive as expected. The BT-5's and the T-26's armour was found to be inadequate as its thickness did not exceed that of the tanks from the First World War (as little as 10–12 mm thick) and could be knocked out by most field guns fielded in Spain. This caused great concern in and of itself.

There were also other issues—the BT-5 especially was too fast for the infantry to keep up with, meaning that many entered enemy lines unsupported, and the same problem is noted with the T-26 to a lesser degree. This is one of the reasons why many Republican tanks were lost in urban fighting, an arena that has proven to be highly disadvantageous for tanks especially operating without supporting infantry even to this day.

Additionally, to convert the BT-5 from tracks to wheels or *vice versa*, the crew had to exit the vehicle, remove the tracks, split the tracks into halves to then lift them onto the fenders, and use leather straps to fasten them down. Next, adjustments then needed to be made to the front road wheels to allow them to traverse via a steering column. The steering wheel had to be stowed while operating with tracks, then taken out of stowage and fitted to the steering column while operating on wheels. This was obviously a long, laborious, and impractical system that certainly could not be done while under fire in combat. Due to these drive system problems, BT-5s in Spain were often abandoned after major breakdowns by both Republican and Nationalist forces alike.

In summation, the BT-5's wheel-track convertible drive was impractical, the 45-mm gun was not fit for multiple roles (although still highly praised in Spain), and the tank's armour was inadequate.

All this was sour news to the Stavka (Soviet High Command), who began to investigate the possibility of an unprecedented modernisation or total replacement of both the T-26 series and the BT series for the 'cavalry tank' role, which was still considered an important part of Soviet tactical doctrine.[7]

A heavily damaged T-26 (most likely Republican, based on the white '8' marking) being salvaged by Nationalist and Condor Legion soldiers using a ZiS recovery lorry. The soldiers are removing the transmission from the tank, but other photos of this scene show this to be a poorly thought-out operation as the ZiS lorry's front two wheels were lifted off the ground due to the weight. Despite the extensive damage to the tank, the T-26 was such a coveted vehicle that as many parts as possible would have been salvaged. (*Will Kerrs Collection*)

T-26 'C 1' in Nationalist service, believed to be of *3a Sección de la 5a Compañia*, likely at the Ebro Offensive in late 1938 (but probably before December based on the markings). This T-26 had the P-40 AA mount for the DT machine gun. Another photo of this particular tank shows it to be fitted with a Polish Wz.30 machine gun in this mount. (*Will Kerrs Collection*)

4

BT SERIES MODERNISATION

Even before Spain, it was as early as 1933 that the BT-2 was thought to need imminent replacement. The biggest concerns were a weak engine, weak suspension, exposed turning gears at the front, and above all, a need for greater firepower (again, only twin 7.62-mm guns or a 37-mm gun were mounted on the BT-2). While the BT-5 had partially addressed the latter problem, serious design work was needed to rectify all of the flaws in the hull.

Two design teams, therefore, started work on a deep modernisation, which would still include a convertible-drive system (seeing as though the impractical nature of the design was not exposed until the Spanish Civil War three years later, and not considered a technological dead-end until 1937). The first design team was KB-T2K, headed by Afanasiy O. Firsov (an experienced naval engineer with a specialisation in diesel engines), and the second was a smaller team headed by Nikolai Fedorovich Tsyganov (a tanker in the 4th Armoured Regiment and self-taught engineer).

THE KB-T2K DESIGN TEAM

Firsov and his KB-T2K team began BT modernisation work in 1933, which included the BT-3, a conversion of the BT-2 design using metric measurements instead of imperial. This was essentially a paper exercise but was likely done as a first step in modernising the archaic Soviet design bureau system. This was technically implemented into production, but it was known as the BT-2 in manoeuvre units because the BT-2 and BT-3 were outwardly identical. The team also came up with the BT-4, a fully welded (instead of riveted) BT-2, which never entered production, but was another step towards making the BT design sturdier and therefore combat viable.

Most importantly of all, the team designed the BT-7 which entered production in 1934. This was a deep modernisation of the BT-5, for which they were awarded the Order of the Red Banner. The BT-7 had a completely redesigned hull to be totally manufactured, where

Two BT-7 tanks from the 67th Tank Regiment of the 34th Tank Division, 8th Mechanised Corps, on 30 June 1941, lost in the village of Verba. The T-34 was designed as a direct replacement for the BT-7 tank.

possible, from welded construction. The turret remained the same, but the nose of the chassis was redesigned to be round rather than coming to a point. The driver no longer had a blister, but they had a compartment built within the nose of the tank. The vehicle was also issued the M-17T aero engine, which generated 500 hp, replacing the weaker M-5 435-hp engine (a copy of the American Liberty engine). The exhaust system was greatly improved, and the rear of the tank was better protected, not needing a recess for an exterior muffler.

Despite the BT-7's apparently promising design, the transmission was unable to cope with the stress from the higher power of the new M-17T engine. Ironically, as opposed to solving the mechanical issues of the BT series, Firsov and his team had created a new one. Worse still, the Kharkov Locomotive and Tractor Factory (KhPZ) refused to continue production of the vehicle until the transmission design flaw was resolved. This catastrophically halted BT-7 production, something the Stavka was deeply concerned about. Therefore, in August 1936, Firsov was demoted and Mikhail Koshkin was installed as the new head of design in December 1937.

TSYGANOV'S DESIGN TEAM

Tsyganov, the other major name in BT tank modernisation, first gained attention in 1934 by developing an automatic towing device for the T-26, T-27, and BT series, for which he was reportedly awarded a gold watch by Kliment Voroshilov. Following this, Tsyganov wrote a letter to Voroshilov in which he suggested improvements to the BT-5, which had only recently entered production. Voroshilov agreed with the proposals, leading to Tsyganov being assigned to Kharkov Tank Repair Plant No. 48 to begin design work.

Tsyganov and his team of engineers were working on improvements to the basic BT-2 design, but the original BT-IS was simply meant as a proof of concept as the BT-5 had already entered production in 1933. As seen here, a complex series of gears was tested on the tank. This powered the three rearmost road wheels. (*Maxim Kolomiets*)

Tsyganov and another engineer sit atop the BT-IS prototype. The tank has had the front two road wheels removed to test the gears that drove the six remaining road wheels. As can be seen by the ground, the tank has been performing manoeuvres to demonstrate its new abilities. (*Maxim Kolomiets*)

Here, Tsyganov began work with a small team on a project known as the 'BT-IS' ('IS' standing for 'Iosif Stalin'), which used a BT-2 chassis. However, the project progressed slowly, and several poor designs were ultimately rejected. As a result, the team was assigned some experienced engineers, leading to the 'BT-5IS' prototype. The new BT-5IS differed by powering three sets of wheels instead of just the rear set like standard BT-5s. Additionally, armour was reconsidered, and thus sloped armour was implemented on the hull sides. This seemingly marginal change actually greatly improved the ricochet chances of incoming rounds and thus theoretically improved the survivability of the tank on the battlefield. However, this project, while it sounds promising, did not progress past the prototype stage, but a much more ambitious project commenced shortly after.

Tsyganov's new design was called the 'BT-SV-2', 'SV' standing for 'Stalin-Voroshilov'. Overall, the project was a radically redesigned BT-7, but it was chiefly concerned with improving armour protection. As such, the hull armoured plates totally encompassed the running gear and nose of the tank. A new turret was also designed. The BT-SV-2 was presented to the Red Army (RKKA) in late 1937, and while it did impress observers, Tsyganov complained that all his designs were being derailed by his rival design bureau, KB-T2K.

Far from the truth, this was more likely a cunning move by Tsyganov to remove his competitors. During this time, the Great Purge (1936–1938) was underway. At the direction of Stalin, the NKVD (People's Commissariat for Internal Affairs) arbitrarily arrested countless innocent citizens who were then sent to forced labour camps or executed on the grounds that they were 'enemies of the people'. In total, an estimated 1 million people died as a result. However, one of the most nefarious features of this period is that many professionals in all areas of Soviet industry were able to use this context against their rivals. Essentially, various vague and often baseless accusations of anti-Bolshevism could be made against a rival individual or group, leading to them being arrested, internally exiled, sent to labour camps, or executed.

Furthermore, many people who were accused became 'plague-bearers', with almost any of their associates becoming targets for the NKVD, too. In this context, following Tsyganov's complaints, Firsov was arrested in 1937 and sentenced to three years of hard labour by the NKVD, having been deemed a 'counter-revolutionary agent', probably with the weak transmission issues of the BT-7 in 1936 and its disastrous impact on production looming over him. However, Koshkin, the head of KB-T2K, was apparently unaffected. In an ironic turn of events (and typical of the Great Purges) Tsyganov, too, was later internally exiled and sent to work at the Academy of Mechanization and Motorization of the Red Army (as an aside, Tsyganov would later unsuccessfully experiment with concrete armour on T-34s in 1942).[1]

Due in part to Tsyganov's forced career move, the BT-SV-2 project never began production. In short, some of the most prominent men involved in the replacement of the BT series had been arrested and internally exiled, and their design work was politically tainted and therefore unusable in its totality. However, the technical requirements of the BT-SV-2 still needed fulfilling.

The BT-5-IS during trials in 1936. The tank's hull sides have been completely redesigned and are now angled. The fenders of the tank can fold upwards but can also stow track when operating in truck mode. (*Maxim Kolomiets*)

The BT-5-IS from the front right. The new angled plates can be clearly seen. These plates were not the only differences, as internally, the drive wheel powered three road wheels, and a complex system of gears was hidden under the uppermost armour plate. The combat lights on the 45-mm gun were very common on standard tanks. (*Maxim Kolomiets*)

The BT-SV-2 during winter trials in 1937. This was the ultimate BT tank designed by Tsyganov, who is one of the engineers in this photograph. (*Maxim Kolomiets*)

The BT-SV-2 undergoing trials in autumn 1937. Unfortunately, it was not long after the trials that Tsyganov was arrested and the BT-SV-2 project scrapped. (*Maxim Kolomiets*)

5

BT SERIES REPLACEMENT

After all the turmoil surrounding the BT modernisation and the damning reports received from tanks crews in Spain (especially regarding poor armour performance), on 28 September 1937, the director of KhPZ 183 (the factory having now been given the '183' serial code), I. P. Bondarenko, was ordered to implement Resolution 94ss. This resolution formed a committee tasked to investigate a totally new design of a wheel/track convertible tank to replace the BT-7 altogether.

Following Resolution 94ss, on 13 October 1937, the ABTU RKKA (Armour and Automobile Management Bureau of the Red Army) issued a technical requirement decree to KhPZ 183 stating that designs needed drawing for a new BT tank capable of withstanding 12.7-mm rounds (an estimated armour of 25 mm), as well as other requirements including Christie-type suspension, armaments of either a 45-mm or 76.2-mm gun, and the transmission developed for Tsyganov's prototype BT series.

Technical drawings for this design were to be delivered by 1 December. It was also decreed in this letter that the vehicle's name should be 'BT-20'. While the name 'BT-20' was specified in the documentation, the factory gave the vehicle the name 'A-20' as this followed the naming conventions for all prototype tanks.

KhPZ 183 set up a new design team named 'KB-24' to design the new tank, with Mikhail Koshkin as the head. Koshkin had previously worked on the T-29 medium tank project which was started in 1934 and saw prototypes manufactured in 1936. The T-29 was a moderate attempt to improve the T-28 multi-turreted medium tank, which was the primary medium tank in the Red Army from 1933 to 1940. However, the T-29 was very expensive to produce and had no major advantages over the T-28, so it was therefore cancelled. However, when designing the A-20, Koshkin incorporated many features present on the T-29, such as the steering and braking mechanisms. So, in many respects, the A-20 combined the best features of the BT-SV-2 and the T-29, but with the addition of shell-proof armour.

On paper, the A-20 boasted some cutting-edge advancements. The armour thickness of the glacis plate was 25 mm, sloped at a 60-degree angle that increased the effective thickness of

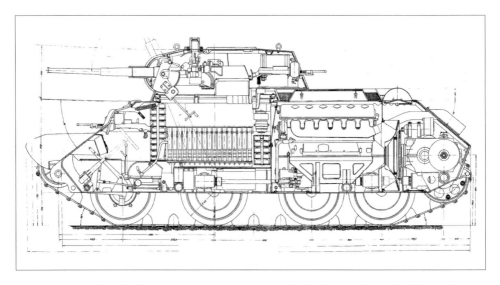

A factory drawing of the A-20. The tank shares more features with the BT-7 that it does with the T-34. (*Maxim Kolomiets*)

the armour and increased the chances of shot deflection. This tank was driven by a rear pair of drive wheels while in tracked mode and two rear road wheels while operating without tracks. Unlike earlier BT tanks, the hull did not come to a point with the steering gear externally, but rather it was kept under the armour of the tank. The A-20 had a 45-mm Model 1934 gun (the replacement of the 45-mm 20-K gun) and a crew of four. Weighing in at 18 tons, it was 5.7 m long, 2.6 m wide, and 2.4 m high.

It took until 25 March 1938 before the drawings were finally approved and submitted to the AAD (Armoured Automotive Directorate), but however successful the A-20 design was shaping out to be, there were still some serious questions over the likely battlefield performance of the A-20 owing to some of its features, with both the convertible drive and gun in question.

On 28 March 1938, the commander of the Soviet forces in Spain, Dmitry Grigoryevich Pavlov, met with the ABTU to discuss the A-20. In this meeting, he outlined his improvements that the tank required. These included a slight weight increase to 15 tons (although 14 tons had been specified in Resolution 94ss), the removal of the wheel-track convertible drive, thicker armour, a new V-2 diesel engine, and a 76.2-mm L-10 gun. The report from this meeting was copied and forwarded to KhPZ 183, and KB-24 immediately began work on the newly desired design, although it had no name at this stage.

On 20 April 1938, Joseph Stalin, Kliment Voroshilov, and other members of the Stavka met with the AAD to discuss future Soviet tank development outlined in Resolution 94ss. A report on Red Army tank development was presented by Pavlov, in which he suggested an overhaul of all tank types, including (but not limited to) a heavy breakthrough tank to replace the T-28 and T-35, new amphibious tanks to replace the T-38, and crucially, a light tank to replace the BT and T-26, of which two types of tanks should be developed and tested, with one ultimately being accepted for production. Pavlov's report acknowledged the latter point, as explained in the following paragraphs.

The first design should be a wheel-track convertible drive tank with six driving road wheels (six per side), armed with a 45-mm gun paired with a machine gun and two additional machine guns, with armour resistant to 12.7-mm rounds, a speed of 50–60 km/h on wheels and tracks, and a weight of no more than 15 tons. This undoubtedly describes the A-20, seeing as though the plans had been submitted earlier, and the A-20 was conveniently presented later in the meeting. The second was a purely tracked tank with the same specifications but weighing no more than 14 tonnes.

This suggestion was accepted, so the new A-20 was presented as the tank to fulfil the role of a convertible drive tank in the first category and was accepted for trials, but a new tank fitting the requirements of the second category was required by June 1939 for testing against the A-20 tank. It should be noted that Pavlov had already organised the design of the second, non-convertible tank a few weeks earlier.

It should be noted the weights of the tanks specified in the documents for the meeting with the ABTU on 28 March, the meeting with the AAD on 20 April, and the eventual prototype weights do not match up. It is quite normal for the prototype tanks to not be the exact weight desired in design protocols, but it is unusual that the weights specified in the two meetings do not match.

On 7 August 1938, Resolution 198ss was passed by the ABTU and was the official protocol on what should be done next. This document formally requested Factory KhPZ 183 to begin work on the A-20 and the new tank (now known as the 'A-20 Gus' (Russian: 'A-20 гус'), although in western literature known as the 'A-20G'). However, KB-24 had already started work unofficially on 28 March 1938 on the 'track-only' tank.

On 6 September 1938, another meeting was conducted with the ABTU, at KhPZ 183. This was done to lay out clearly what the A-20G's characteristics should be. The notes of the meeting concluded that the new tank should be equipped with a 76.2-mm L-10 gun and should weigh no more than 16.5 tons. Being heavier than 16 tons pushed the A-20G into the 'medium' tank category, as defined by the Red Army. Importantly, 30 mm of frontal armour was also requested, along with a few other minor changes. From this, the design for the A-20G was finalised.

6

A-20 AND A-32 TRIALS

In November 1938, final plans were submitted to the AAD for the A-20 and the much heavier A-20G. These plans and mock-ups were then sent to the Supreme Military Council on 9 December 1938 and approved the production of prototypes on 27 February 1939. The A-20 prototype was built in May 1939. KB-24 was renamed 'SKB-520' and the A-20G was renamed 'A-32' in May 1939. The A-32 prototype was built in mid-June 1939.

The A-32 prototype was a very different tank from the A-20 as it had five road wheels rather than four and the track was much wider. It also had 30-mm frontal armour, compared to the A-20's 25 mm. The armament was also the 76.2-mm L-10 gun instead of the 45-mm Model 1934 of the A-20. This new vehicle weighed 19 tons, more than the desired weight of 16.5 tons, and had similar dimensions to the A-20, being 5.7 m long, 2.7 m wide, and 2.4 m high.

From mid-June 1939, both prototypes were tested, but the A-32 was far from a finished product. Six of the road wheels were taken from a BT-7 tank and no tools or deep wading equipment were supplied, yet tests were conducted regardless.

During factory tests conducted from 17 to 23 July 1939, the A-20 and A-32 were put through their paces. The A-20 was tested for longer than the A-32, and both performed well. On 23 September, the A-20 and A-32 were taken to the Kubinka proving grounds to be tested alongside the KV, T-100, and SMK prototypes.

The A-32 impressed the delegation throughout these tests, and it was suggested that due to its power to weight ratio, it was practical to mount 45 mm of frontal armour on the tank instead of the original 30 mm.

A side profile of the A-20 during trials against the A-32. The A-20 was a very potent vehicle, but it was outclassed by the superior design of the A-32. The A-20 in many respects looks like a heavily modified BT-7, which is in essence what it was. (*Maxim Kolomiets*)

A front view of the A-20. Interesting points are the tie-down points for track stowage. (*Maxim Kolomiets*)

The underdog at the trials with the A-20 was the A-32. Designed in a very short space of time under the suggestion that the A-20 could field heavier armour and a 76.2-mm gun, testing would prove that the A-32 was superior to the A-20. (*Maxim Kolomiets*)

A rear view of the A-32. A striking resemblance between the A-32 rear and the rear of A-34 No. 1 can be seen. A-34 No. 2 differed heavily from this angled rear, having a rear plate pressed to form a rounded gear plate. (*Maxim Kolomiets*)

7

A-34 PROTOTYPE

On 19 December 1939, the DCCPC (Defence Council of the Committee of People's Commissars) passed Resolution 433ss. This, in conjunction with Resolutions 198ss and 118ss, authorised preparations for full-scale production of the A-32 at KhPZ 183 and Stalingrad Tractor Factory (STZ), albeit with modifications to begin as soon as possible. Regarding the A-32, the document stated:

II. The Tank T-32 [A-32]—tracked tank, with a diesel engine V-2, [is ordered to be] manufactured by Plant No. 183, with the following changes:

a) increase the thickness of the main armour plates to 45 mm;

b) improve visibility from the tank;

c) install the following weapons on the T-32 tank:

   1) F-32 76-mm gun, paired with a 7.62mm machine gun;

   2) a separate 7.62mm machine gun from the radio operator;

   3) a separate machine gun of 7.62mm calibre;

   4) anti-aircraft machine gun of 7.62mm calibre.

Assign the name to the specified tank 'T-34'.

Actions for Plant No. 183.

a) to organise the production of T-34 tanks at the Kharkov Plant No. 183.

b) to make two prototype T-34 tanks by 15 January 1940 and manufacture ten tanks by 15th September 1940;

c) produce in 1940 at least 200 T-34 tanks;

d) prepare T-34 production lines at Plant No. 183 for the production of T-34 tanks and make 1,600 tanks by 1 January 1941;

e) until the full development of the serial production of the T-34 tanks, continue production of the BT tank, with the installation of the V-2 diesel engine on 1st December 1939;

f) to produce at the plant No. 183 in 1940 at least 1000 BT tanks with a V-2 diesel engine;

g) in 1942, remove the BT tank from production, replacing it completely with the T-34;

Actions for plant STZ.

a) to organise at STZ during 1940 the production of tanks for a capacity of 2,000 tanks per year;

b) release in 1940 twenty T-34s;

It was also agreed that KhPZ 183 would finalise and make working drawings and restore the tanks to a factory-fresh standard after testing.

Immediately after the order was received at KhPZ 183, work began on the new A-34 prototypes. The A-32 was not intended for production; as mentioned, it was merely a rushed testbed to see if that general design could feature thicker armour and a 76.2-mm gun. Therefore, the design of the A-32 required a major overhaul to become the A-34. SKB-520, therefore, had additional tasks, such as organising and preparing material for subsidiary plants to supply KhPZ 183 for the redesign and production of the new models.

One such subsidiary plant was the Mariupol Metallurgy Plant, which was organised to produce turrets and hulls of the new A-34. This was an important task, and because one could not simply increase the A-32's armour thickness, a total redesign was necessary. Even fundamental things, such as the way that the turret would be manufactured, had to be reconsidered and redesigned. The A-32, for example, had a turret manufactured from four pieces of rolled plate, either side of which a vertical reinforcing bar was placed down the turret exterior side. This was to protect the seam between two armour plates from incoming fire, capable of withstanding 12.7-mm machine gun bullet hits. While this was standard on all other Soviet tanks, the A-34 was required to be even more thickly armoured, thus making it shell-proof. As such, this reinforcing bar was inadequate, as anything larger than a heavy machine gun bullet (12.7 mm) would cause the seam to break.

Mariupol Metallurgy Plant was primarily a ship-building plant, and up to this point had little experience in the manufacturing of tank armour. Nonetheless, throughout the last quarter of 1939, the plant set about manufacturing two armoured hulls and turrets for KhPZ 183.

The biggest issue the plant had was manufacturing the glacis and nose plate. The nose of the A-34 was designed to be manufactured from a single piece of armour that had to be bent meaning a special press had to be designed for this job, but this was both costly and time-consuming.

Furthermore, there was a myriad of other items that needed to be redesigned for the A-34, so delivery of the two prototypes by KhPZ 183 was late and the 15 January deadline was missed.

One major problem was the armament. The armament specified in Resolution 433ss was the 76.2-mm F-32 gun, but this gun was not yet in full production and therefore not available. As a result, the 76.2-mm L-11 gun (which was widely available) was instead implemented onto the first prototype, which had the chassis number '311-11-3'. By the 15 January deadline, the first prototype was still being fitted with the 76.2-mm L-11 gun, and it was also decided that the second prototype, with the chassis number '311-18-3', was to be armed with the 76.2-mm L-10 gun taken from the A-32 to speed up delivery. The A-32 in turn had its gun replaced with a 45-mm Model 1934, and this can be seen in photographs taken during some additional tests that the A-32 later underwent.

Due to all these problems, it was not until 10 February 1940 that 311-11-3, was presented to the Red Army, with 311-18-3 finally delivered for testing on 12 February 1940. These two prototype A-34s were very different in design, with 311-11-3 resembling the A-32 more than 311-18-3, even though the latter had the A-32's 76.2-mm L-10 gun.

A front-on view of A-34 No. 1. Notice the driver's blister position, which has a hatch on the top of the position. There is a headlight on the hull's right upper side. The turret face has a separate cut out for the coaxial DT-29 machine gun. (*Maxim Kolomiets*)

A rear view of A-34 No. 1. The rear of this tank is more akin to the A-32 tank, with an angled rear plate. Notice the cover for the mesh radiator cover.

The front of A-34 No. 2. Notice the driver's hatch that is flush with the glacis plate. Production tanks would have a square spacer around the hatch door to stop spalls from entering the tank. Notice the front of the turret, with the protected coaxial DT-29 machine gun. (*Maxim Kolomiets*)

The rear of A-34 No. 2. Contrast this to the rear of A-34 No. 1 on page 41. It was A-34 No. 2 that was chosen for production, albeit with modifications. (*Maxim Kolomiets*)

No. 311-11-3 was issued with a distinctive bulged driver's compartment, not unlike that of the BT-5, but with an escape hatch in the top of the protrusion, and three vision ports around the driver. The rear of the tank retained many features of the A-32, such as an early pattern of screened transmission cover that bolted onto the exhaust plate, and an angled joint between the exhaust plate and the gear plate. No. 311-11-3's turret also was like that of the A-32, with the main armament having a small gun shield, with the coaxial DT-29 not being protected by the gun-shield.

No. 311-18-3 was different. The driver's hatch was flush with the glacis plate of the hull, with a single large vision port forward, and two angled vision ports on either side of the driver. The screened transmission cover was attached to the hull via four leather buckles, and the gear plate had a distinctive curve to meet the exhaust plate. The exhaust plate could also now be unbolted and, with the aid of two hinges at the base of this plate, could also be removed and swung downwards from the tank without completely removing the plate from the tank.

These A-34s were very impressive tanks, with 45 mm armour on the nose, a 76.2-mm L-11 gun (or, for testing purposes, 311-18-3 had a 76.2-mm L-10), the V-2-34 diesel engine, and Christie-type suspension. The tank had a crew of four: driver, engineer, gunner/commander, and loader. These prototypes included a 71-TK-3 radio set in the turret as well. The interior layout of the A-34s was the same as that of the A-32, that being fighting compartment, turret, engine, and transmission.

On 23 January 1940, Directive No.135669 was signed that stated: 'to carry out, during the period from 25th January to 25th March 1940, the army tests of the A-34 tanks in the Kharkov Military District, Factory No. 183.'

A-34 No. 2 photographed at KhPZ 183 before being sent to Moscow in March 1940. The tank has very sleek lines but lacks most of the stowage seen on standard T-34s. (*Maxim Kolomiets*)

A side view of A-34 No. 2. This tank would differ little from the first ten production T-34 tanks because they were manufactured from A-34 parts. (*Maxim Kolomiets*)

The Red Army, at this stage, required that any prototype tanks had to cover no less than 3,000 km before being accepted for production. However, by 26 February, the first prototype had only run 650 km and the second a mere 350 km. This was mostly due to the delayed completion date of the two tanks. Both vehicles were therefore required to at least travel 500 km during factory tests, and then the tanks had to travel at least 300 km over highways, 1,000 km over roads, and 1,200 km over 'virgin and rugged terrain', giving a total of 3,650 km and 3,350 km respectively.

It was decided that a march to Moscow would be the only solution. Therefore, on 12 March 1940, the two tanks set off from Kharkov to Moscow on a road that was 756 km long, travelling north via Kursk, Orel, and Belgorod. During the march, the tanks were renamed—311-11-3 was now known as 'Tank No. 1' and 311-18-3 as 'Tank No. 2'.

The march was conducted in great secrecy, with the tanks only being allowed to travel at night, and with minimal support. Due to the secrecy, highways were out of the question, so the tanks had to travel across small, often dirt, roads.

The march, in general, was uneventful. However, both tanks required major repairs through-out the journey. It is often quoted that one of A-34's gearbox failed, and therefore it had to be returned to Kharkov. However, this is not the case, and instead, major onsite repairs were conducted to allow both tanks to make the journey. Tank No. 1 suffered the worst breakdowns (but nothing so major that it would stop the testing) and was also marginally less fuel-efficient.

Eventually, both A-34s made the journey and were delivered to Factory 37 in Moscow on 17 March (which was making T-38 amphibious tanks at the time) and here they received many repairs from the journey. Both tanks were inspected by high-ranking Communist party members, including but not limited to, Stalin, Molotov, Kalinin, and Voroshilov. Tank No. 1 was then taken away for ballistics testing at Kubinka. While this was not a requirement of official tests, it was decided that it was necessary. Between 18 and 22 March, Tank No. 2 was shown off to visitors at Factory 37, performing many manoeuvres, which greatly impressed bystanders.

A-34 No. 1 during snow trials. Overall, No. 1 would be tested more thoroughly than No. 2 as the latter was visiting factories and officials in Moscow. (*Maxim Kolomiets*)

A-34 No. 2 during snow trials at Kharkov. Note the wire connecting the combat light to the gun mantlet. (*Maxim Kolomiets*)

A-34 No. 1 conducting burning liquid tests. The tests were a failure, and burning liquid made its way into the engine and fighting compartments. (*Maxim Kolomiets*)

A-34 No. 1 conducting forest tests. (*Maxim Kolomiets*)

During ballistics testing, Tank No. 1 was fired upon by a Bofors 37-mm gun of a captured Finnish Vickers Mark E Type B, and the standard Model 1934 45-mm anti-tank gun. The shelling of the tank was conducted from a range of 100 metres, with two shots being made from each gun, aiming for the turret below the left turret vision port. It was concluded that the tank was indeed impervious to such projectiles, but the security of the internals of the tank was lacking. Even though the shots failed to penetrate, items such as glass shattered, and there was a 190-mm crack observed in the weld seam for the vision port.

After shelling tests, the A-34 conducted deep snow trials, which it also excelled in. From almost every report given to the Stavka, the A-34 was undoubtedly a superior tank to the BT and other medium tanks currently in service with the Red Army.[1]

A-34 ACCEPTANCE

On 29 March 1940, the two A-34s returned to Factory 37 to receive minor repairs before being presented to the Kremlin. On 30 March, the two A-34s drove 11 km to the Kremlin where Stalin, Kalinin, Voroshilov, and the rest of the Stavka were waiting.

The two tanks performed manoeuvres in Ivanovskaya Square which impressed the delegation, who also approached the tanks and inspected them after the displays were concluded. With the delegates pleased, the two tanks then returned to Factory 37.

On 31 March, Protocol 848 was passed. This was the authorisation to begin full-scale production of the A-34 at KhPZ 183 and STZ, and following this, the A-34 was officially accepted into the Red Army and re-designated 'T-34'.

Voroshilov visited Factory 37 and conducted a meeting regarding the future of the T-34. The meeting concluded:

1. The Tank—T-34, manufactured in full accordance with the resolution of the Defence Committee under the Council of People's Commissars of the USSR No. 443ss from 19th December 1939, passed the state tests and the Kharkov-Moscow run without any breakages and significant defects, immediate preparations for the production at factories No. 183 and STZ.
2. To increase the volume inside the turret to improve operations for the crew, increase the space inside the tank turret, preventing changes in the inclination of the turret sides or the turret face. The radio should be placed outside the turret [meaning not on the exterior of the tank, but in the hull].
3. Instruct the State Commission for testing a tank within five days to approve the drawings of the T-34 tank for production in 1940.

The design of 'Tank No. 2' was, at this stage, chosen for production.

Now that the trials in Moscow had ended, the two prototypes began the return journey back to Kharkov. This began on 2 April 1940 and took the exact same route on the return journey. On 8 April, Tank No. 1 broke down. The issue was the gear oil pump, so it was therefore towed for most of the rest of the journey by a Voroshilovets tractor. This led to Tank No. 1 falling behind Tank No. 2, but by 10 April, it caught up. For the last 50 km back to Kharkov, Tank No. 2 towed Tank No. 1 to test the tank's towing capability.

Now back at KhPZ 183, it was decided to conduct more trials, and between 16 and 27 April, many trials were conducted from tree crushing to having burning liquid testing. Burning liquid testing involved the vehicle being attacked with flamethrowers and 'Molotov cocktails'. The two A-34 prototypes later became testbeds for other vehicle types on the T-34 chassis, such as flamethrower tanks (to be discussed later).

After the testing, the final report from KhPZ 183 concluded the following five improvements for the tank:

1. The experimental samples of the T-34s, presented by Factory No. 183, basically correspond to the tactical and technical requirements. In terms of armour protection, armament capacity, and cross-country ability in winter conditions, the T-34 tanks far exceed existing tanks.
2. The main shortcomings of the T-34 tank are the following:
    a) The turret is insufficient in terms of ease of use of weapons, surveillance, guidance devices, and ammunition stowage, all of which do not allow full use of the main armaments.
    b) Radio communication with the T-34 is poor due to it being located in the turret.
    c) The observation instruments delivered on the T-34 tank do not provide reliable and sufficient visibility.
    d) The tank's is insufficiently protected from burning liquids such as petrol.
    e) The T-34 tank is reliable in operation and when the shortcomings noted in the conclusions on the military tests have been eliminated, it will be suitable for operation in the troops. Without eliminating the noted shortcomings, the T-34 tank cannot be put into serial production.
3. The serial diesel V-2 installed in the T-34 tank does not fulfil its warranty, and also has an inadequate in operation lifespan with less than 100 hours before failure.
4. In view of the fact that the T-34 tank was tested in winter conditions, the following issues remained unproven:
    a) The thermal regime of the engine in summer conditions.
    b) Overcoming natural and artificial obstacles in summer conditions.
    c) Dynamics of the tank.
    d) The reliability of the operation of the mechanisms of the tank in the summer road conditions over long distances.
5) For all these points, one T-34 tank must be subjected to an additional test range test, followed by shooting and shelling.

In April 1940, a long list of improvements was drafted for the tank and presented to the engineers at KhPZ 183. The list contained improvements for nearly every aspect of the new T-34 (which will be referred to as 'the April Report' from hereon):

The Engine
Eliminate escaping gases from under the gaskets of the cylinder heads.
Strengthen the design of the oil pump drive, ensuring reliability in operation.
Increase the warranty period for the V-2 engine to 250 hours, with a minimum loss of power by the end of the warranty period.
Allow for the removal of the exhaust pipes without removing the exhaust shrouds.

Power and Lubrication System
The construction of fuel and oil tanks to be made more rigid—eliminate leaks.
Air Cleaner
Provide for the possibility of installing and removing the air cleaner without removing the motor roof.
Main Clutch
The clutch is not reliable, because of the warping of the disks.
Engine cooling fans installed on T-34 tanks are unreliable. Cracks appeared repeatedly on the shoulder blades and rim, which led to accidents. It is necessary to develop a new fan.
Drive Wheel
Strengthen the wheel design by thickening the disks.
Strengthen the fastening of the drive wheel to the axle by increasing the diameter and number of bolts from four to six.
Side Gear
Ensure the interchangeability of the covers of the on-board transmission (clutch).
Suspension
Ensure the reliable operation of the suspension by a suitable reinforcement of the axle rods.
Ensure sufficient access to the outer bearing of the swing arm for lubrication.
Driver's Seat
Increase seat adjustment travel by 50 mm.
Add seat cushions.
Tools
Provide tools for track tensioning.
Develop a set of tools, pullers, and accessories needed to make repairs in the field.
Install two thermos bottles for drinking water.
Prepare brackets for four spare fuel tanks, each with the capacity of fifty litres.
Provide external tie down points for stowing previsions and other items on the exterior of the tank.
Hull
Develop a driver's hatch which provides the possibility of entering and exiting the tank with the turret turned in any direction. [This is referring to the first prototype, as the driver's position had an escape hatch at the top of a blister. The driver's hatch for the second prototype did not have this problem.]
Inner welding of the hull, turret and welding of the hammers is performed by austenitic electrodes. From the outside, the hull and the turret are welded with MD electrodes.
Replace the towing tugs with hooks to ensure speed and convenience while taking the machine under tow.
Turret
To ensure the convenience and free work of the crew, the turret needs to be expanded. Expand the turret, but do not change the thickness or angle of the armour.
Mount grips to the turret to strengthen it.
Reinforce the turret seams as to allow for stronger turret integrity.
Lower the turret bustle by 20 mm.
Armament
Consider the broadening of the turret, move the PT-1 periscope to the left, providing access to the installation of the TOD gunner's sight.
PT-1 and TOD eyepieces should be installed in the same plane (horizon and vertical).

Put a chain to protect the PT-1 periscope from falling out.

Eliminate the possibility of grazing hands whilst working with elevation and turning mechanisms (the elevation mechanism should be moved to the right).

Radio

Move the 71-TK-3 from the turret bustle and transfer it to the bow of the tank.

Viewing Instruments

T-34 tank sight devices do not provide observation and driving of the tank (with closed hatches).

The viewing instruments have a large dead space, were viewing from certain angled from the tank is impossible.

In winter conditions they do not provide visibility.

The device is loaded with snow and mud (both in the driver and in the turret).

When firing a gun, protective glasses burst in all devices.

On the basis of the aforementioned shortcomings, it is not appropriate to consider the construction of inspection instruments. To develop new observation devices taking into account elimination of all the listed deficiencies.

Tracks

Develop and manufacture the construction of spurs and winter tracks.

This is a greatly reduced list; the original document lists nearly 140 changes.

8

PRE-PRODUCTION OF THE T-34

Again, back in December 1939, it was decided KhPZ 183 and STZ would begin production of the A-34 (the designation 'T-34' was not used until 31 March 1940), which was before the prototypes were even made and tested. While A-34 production began at KhPZ 183 immediately (by assembling the prototypes), T-34 production (to be clear, this is the A-34 with some changes outlined in the April Report added) began in May 1940.

While the two A-34 prototypes were being manufactured, KhPZ 183 spent most of the time setting up subsidiaries for A-34 production. It had been agreed that ten A-34 tanks were expected to be delivered by May 1940, and production was to continue after this date.

Along with Mariupol Metallurgy Plant, Factory Number 75 was another major supplier, sending V-2 engines to both STZ and KhPZ 183. This supply chain took a long time to establish, and Vyacheslav Molotov was directly involved in the setup of these subsidiaries.

By late February, subsidiary production and shipment had been finalised by I. A. Likhachev, the People's Commissar of Medium Machine Construction (for clarity, this title is not a reference to tank classifications). While A-34 production was to begin, it was expected that other tanks KhPZ 183 had produced should still be adequately supplied with spare parts, and facilities for their capital repairs maintained, including the T-35A and all the BT series.

By 29 March 1940, the successful testing of the two A-34 tanks on the Moscow–Kharkov March led to Pavlov, now the chief director of ABTU RKKA, to order immediate full-scale production of the T-34. A deadline of 7 April 1940 was given for technical drawings of some of the major plate changes to the turret to be submitted.

Even though up to this point things had gone somewhat smoothly for Soviet bureaucracy, KhPZ 183 was facing delays due to two issues.

The first cause of delays came from a backlog of delayed parts. This was due to a major dispute between KhPZ 183 and Mariupol Metallurgy Plant over the design and production of the armoured parts for the hull and turret. KhPZ 183 wanted to make the glacis and nose single-piece, but Mariupol Metallurgy Plant wanted to change the design to make the nose from three separate pieces because the single-piece pressing process could produce cracks in the plates, thus making them unusable. The turret bustle's attachment was also in dispute.

A second cause of the delays was that KhPZ 183 was waiting for the April Report (the aforementioned testing reports from the Kharkov–Moscow road marches) to arrive, which contained a list of 140 necessary design changes.

Delays were getting so serious that a letter was written to Pavlov asking for an official opinion on how to undertake production, especially given these issues. The letter read as follows:

> In order to launch T-34 production in 1940, it is urgent to receive an opinion of the military commission on the results of the testing of the prototypes. The delay in the release of drawings for the development of technology and the launch of tank production [means that] the deadlines for the State Commission for testing a tank are overdue. We ask you to instruct the commission to immediately give an opinion on the vehicle.

Upon reading the letter, Pavlov scrawled over the letter in red pencil: 'The tank should immediately be put into mass production and in 1940 no less than 450 tanks should be delivered'. The message was simple—the Stavka did not care about these disputes and production was to begin immediately. Therefore, Mariupol Metallurgy Plant won the debate over construction methods as they were the ones making the turret and they therefore had the right to decide how it was made. With regards to the April Report, production began without it, and a total of ten unchanged A-34 hulls were made in April, with thirty-seven A-34 turrets made by

An Initial Production T-34 (A-34)—one of the first ten T-34s but manufactured with A-34 parts. This vehicle was issued to the 8th Mechanised Corps and lost in the Ukrainian SSR in June 1941, north of Lvov. Notice the angle of the vision ports on the turret, the lack of turret cheek supports, and the one-piece glacis plate, which are key identification features. The tank blew up, and many items of the tank are scattered about, including what appears to be an ammunition box and a 76.2-mm warhead.

The interior of the tank on page 52. This is an exclusive look inside an Initial Production T-34 (A-34)—something which has never previously been published. The wall between the engine compartment and the fighting compartment is missing. One can also see the original V-2-34 engine, lacking an air filter on the top. Notice, too, the bent and burned spanner next to the fuel cap cover next to the turret ring.

Mariupol Metallurgy Plant. However, the list of improvements arrived shortly after, along with the two prototypes which had just returned from Moscow, and in this consolidation period, many of the April Report's suggested changes were implemented.

Production of the improved T-34 at KhPZ 183 was due to commence on 18 May 1940. However, parts that had been made before the April Report was delivered were used until stocks ran out, whereupon the newly designed parts were used.

Therefore, ten T-34s were produced using the ten A-34 hulls manufactured before the April Report was submitted, and ten of the thirty-seven A-34 turrets were issued to these tanks. This, therefore, made these tanks identical to A-34 Tank No. 2. These ten tanks can be referred to as 'Initial Production T-34 (A-34)' for our categorisation. Despite outwardly being A-34s, they should not be called A-34s because period Soviet documents referred to the design as 'T-34'. Four of these Initial Production T-34 (A-34)s were produced in June 1940, with the other six being made in July, whereupon the new hull was introduced. The first six tanks manufactured had the chassis numbers 311-05-3, 311-09-3, 311-21-3, 311-16-3, 311-01-3, and 0618-4, but the other four are not known.

Following this, the first twenty-seven T-34s with the newly improved hulls were issued the remaining twenty-seven A-34 turrets. These were produced in July and early August 1940. While also called T-34 officially, these can be referred to as 'T-34 (A-34 turret)' for our categorisation purposes. The exact details of the new hull are discussed on pages 73–82.

Another Initial Production T-34 (A-34). This vehicle was also likely a part of the 12th Tank Division, 8th Mechanised Corps, and was lost in the town of Zholkva, north of Lvov. Notice the single piece glacis plate, the often-overlooked straight edge turret hatch, and the lack of cheek armour placed over the seams of the turret. Notice also the two hull headlamps, which are often destroyed or missing on other tanks.

An Initial Production T-34 (A-34) that was knocked out on 27 June 1941. The tank has suffered an internal explosion that tore the turret from the hull. Notice that the driver's hatch has been retrofitted with bars to stop spalling entering the tank. This is a retrofit, as it was introduced in September 1940. The vehicle likely belonged to the 9th or 12th Mechanised Corps and was knocked out during the advance north of Lvov. (*Maxim Kolomiets*)

The same Initial Production T-34 (A-34) as on page 54. Despite being such an early T-34, the tank is still equipped with the appropriate stowage needed for deployment.

A rather unusual Initial Production T-34 (A-34) that is one of at most two of the initial tanks that survived into the winter of 1941. This T-34 was likely given to the Leningrad Tank School. The vehicle was retrofitted with spalling guards around the driver's hatch, though retains the bracket for the combat light.

STZ had more organisational problems than KhPZ 183 and did not begin production until late 1940, most likely sometime between October and November. One setback was that technical documents had to be delivered from KhPZ 183. These were delayed because KhPZ 183 was waiting for the April Report to be delivered to them so that the documents could be updated with the design changes. Even after the correct documents arrived at STZ, production lines took time to organise at its subsidiaries, as was typical of Soviet industry. Furthermore, Mariupol Metallurgy Plant's production levels were not high enough to send parts to KhPZ 183 as well as STZ until later in 1940.

As the T-34's post-April Report plans were sent to STZ, its subsidiary, Factory 264, never produced any A-34 hulls. By this time, Mariupol Metallurgy Plant had also switched to T-34 production, too, meaning that no A-34 turrets were issued to STZ.

Despite these delays, it is thought that as many as ninety hulls were prepared at STZ before the end of 1940 but were not assembled as complete tanks until 1941. Ten complete tanks are referenced as to have been made by the end of 1940, but this is not confirmed.

9

TECHNICAL DESCRIPTION
OF THE T-34 IN 1940

The initial production run of the T-34 had a combat weight of 26.8 tons. Suspension consisted of five pairs of road wheels per side attached to Christie-type suspension of swing arms and internally mounted angled springs. The drive wheels were at the rear of the tank pulling 550-mm-wide tracks. Each set of tracks consisted of thirty-seven pairs of toothed and flat links. Rollers in the drive wheel engaged the toothed links. Both road wheels and idlers were fitted with rubber tyres.

The vehicle was powered by a V-2 12-cylinder diesel engine that generated a nominal 500 hp at 1,800 rpm. Power was transferred to the final drives through a combination clutch and engine cooling fan, to a four-speed gearbox, steering clutches, then to the final drive gears and drive wheels.

Six internal fuel tanks held a total of 460 litres of fuel. Production vehicles were fitted with brackets to hold an additional four externally stored fuel boxes like those in use on the BT-5/7 fast tanks. Each of these boxes held 50 litres.

Initially, the front of the tank was made from a single 45-mm plate, machined and then rolled to create both upper and lower glacis. This was an extremely time-consuming and difficult process and was soon dropped for a more conventional arrangement of separate upper and lower plates, still 45 mm thick, joined by riveting and welding to a bow 'fillet', often referred to as the 'bow girder' or 'bow beam' in Soviet literature. It maintained the same general layout and profile as the single piece glacis with both upper and lower sections angled at 60 degrees.

Lower hull sides were 40mm at 90 degrees. The upper hull sides were also 40 mm and angled at 40 degrees. The upper and lower rear plates, also 40 mm thick, were angled at approximately 42 degrees and 45 degrees respectively. Hull, roof, and floor plates were 20 mm thick.

The hull interior was divided into four compartments—the driver's and machine gunner's compartment, fighting compartment, engine compartment, and transmission compartment. The forward section of the tank housed the driver and machine gunner. The driver sat on the left. In front of him was the large hatch with a wide episcope. Opening and closing the hatch was assisted by a cylindrical spring-loaded counterbalance which was attached to the hull roof and connected to the hatch via an operating rod and welded bracket. To either

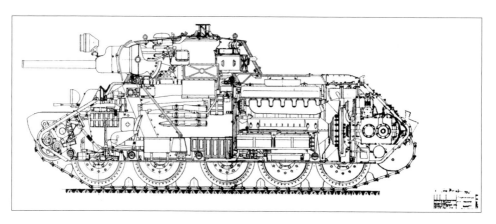

Factory drawings of the interior of A-34 No. 2 from the side. (*Maxim Kolomiets*)

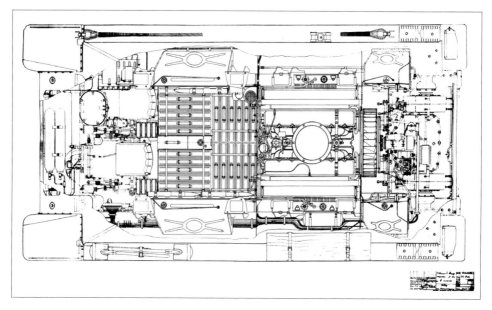

Factory drawings of the interior of A-34 No. 2 from above. (*Maxim Kolomiets*)

side of the hatch was an additional smaller episcope whose mounts were built into a formed bulge in the glacis plate (initially, this bulge was a separate piece welded into the glacis). They were angled to give the widest possible view forward for the driver when the tank was 'buttoned up'. Immediately under the opening for the hatch was an instrument panel holding various engine management gauges—engine oil and coolant temperature gauges, manometer, tachometer, clock, etc.

On the floor in front of the driver were pedals for the transmission clutch, brake, and accelerator. To his right was the gear shift for the four-speed transmission and on either side of his seat levers, which worked on the steering clutches attached to the transmission.

Between the foot pedals was a hand-operated air pump used to pressurise the fuel tanks. This forced fuel into the lines and primed the fuel distribution pump.

Behind and to the left of the pedals was a sheet metal enclosure that was attached to the lower hull side plate. This covered the front road wheel suspension spring—essentially, a spring inside a spring and cam. Due to the restricted space created by the upper and lower plate angles, the first suspension assembly was of a notably different design than that of the other four. Also, to the left and attached to the lower hull side plate was the main wiring hub for the tank. The upper section held a printed plate with a wiring schematic. Below this were two gauges, an ammeter, and a voltmeter, and below that were the engine start button and various switches.

Again, to the left and attached to the second suspension spring tower was an actuating lever working on a rod that ran the length of the fighting and engine compartments to linkages for the engine cooling air exhaust louvres above the transmission.

The machine gunner/engineer's station consisted of a padded seat identical to that of the driver but located slightly further to the rear. In front was the cast 'blister' and ball mount for the 7.62-mm DT-29 machine gun. An oval escape hatch was in the floor in front of the seat. To the right and front was another sheet metal enclosure for the first wheel suspension spring, like the one on the driver's left. Spare magazines were stored in racks on the right and in front of the seat with four additional magazines on the floor to the left of the engineer and four more to the left of the driver. On later T-34s, the magazines on right were relocated to make way for 71-TK-3 radio set previously mounted in the turret. At that point, the machine gunner/engineer became the machine gunner/radio operator.

Between the driver and machine gunner and mounted to the lower glacis plate were two compressed air bottles. These were used to start the engine in cold weather or if the electrical starting motor failed.

The 71-TK-3 radio set was an older piece of radio equipment, which had a range of 18 km on the move, and 25 km at the halt and in telegraph mode. In normal operations, the radio could only manage reliable two-way telephone communications up to 4 km. The radio also took up around 100 litres of space inside the tank and was therefore quite bulky.

Immediately behind the driver and machine gunner's seats was the fighting compartment and turret ring. On either side were the suspension towers for second and third road wheels. The third suspension tower was at a notably steeper angle to clear the turret ring. To these towers were bolted sheet metal partitions. Behind the partitions and between the suspension towers were two fuel tanks per side.

On the commander/gunner's side, racks for six main gun rounds were bolted to the partition and racks for three more rounds were to the loader's right.

The floor of the fighting compartment was made up of twenty-four 'suitcase' style ammunition boxes. Twenty of these boxes contained three 76.2-mm main gun rounds and four held two rounds each (the reduced capacity was to allow for clearance of the floor-mounted suspension axle tubes). The boxes held a total of sixty-eight main gun rounds and the complete load out of 76.2-mm ammunition, including ready racks, was seventy-seven rounds.

With the introduction of the F-34 gun, the ammunition storage changed. Now the floor was made up of eight steel boxes, six of which contained nine rounds and two holding seven rounds (again, the reduced number was to allow clearance of the suspension tubes/stubs). Racks for the ready rounds were unchanged, and the total number of rounds remained seventy-seven.

Bolted to the floor and centred on the turret ring was a large bracket that held a rotating electrical union through which power was supplied to the turret, and in front of that was a metal box that held various spares and tools.

At the rear of the fighting compartment was a firewall separating it from the engine compartment. The firewall had four, later five, sheet metal covers allowing access to the engine, fuel distribution, water and oil pumps, and the tank's four batteries. Also attached to the firewall on the loader's side was the fighting compartment and turret's fume evacuation fan, a fuel tank selection valve, and grease fitting for lubricating the engine's main bearing before start-ups. Actuating levers for the louvres above the radiators were on either side and on the commander's side was a fuse box access cover.

The turret shell was an extremely complicated assembly made up of rolled, formed, and intricately machined 45-mm-thick plates. The face of the turret was a semi-cylinder, and the side and rear plates were angled inward 30 degrees. The rear plate, held on by four bolts, could be detached for removal of the main gun. On the centre line of this plate was a conical steel plug. It has very often been misidentified as a 'pistol port'. It was instead an access port for equipment used in the maintenance of the L-11.

On either side of the turret were cast mounts for another set of episcopes, and below these were pistol ports closed with conical plugs. On the earliest examples, the mounts and ports were at 90 degrees to the turret's centre line. However, when the turret was widened, they followed the change in the side plates and angled forward slightly.

The roof was made of 15-mm plating and held a single large crew access hatch. The hatch itself held the mount for the commander's POP episcope on early tanks, later deleted due to it being vulnerable to enemy fire and being of little practical use. On the loader's side was a small signal flag hatch. Opening and closing the hatch was assisted by a spring-loaded counterbalance.

The forward portion of the turret roof held a mount for the PT-1 periscope, part of the gun sighting arrangement, and offset to the loader's side was an armoured vent. The turret dome was indeed simply an open vent, with no fan installed. Fresh air would be drawn through this vent, into the turret, and out via the firewall-mounted exhaust fan into the engine compartment. Interestingly, the dome was hinged internally and could be opened forward.

The commander and loader were provided seats to the left and right of the L-11 gun, attached to the turret ring. The commander sat on the right side in the very tight space between the main gun and turret ring. On his left the side vision port, pistol port, and slightly in front, mounted to the turret ring, the turret traversing gear. This was driven by an electric motor for fast rotation or by hand wheel for fine adjustment.

In front was the PT-1 periscope. This provided the commander with a wider field of view and its head could be rotated for battlefield observation. It was linked to the gun cradle and was used for rough laying of the gun on a target.

To its right and attached to the gun was the TOD 2.5 power telescopic sight used for precise aiming of the L-11.

A bracket connected to the gun's trunnion bearing held the elevation mechanism and hand wheel. This was located on the commander's right. Also connected to the bracket was a steel extension that held the foot-operated trigger for the main gun.

The loader's position was essentially a mirror of the commander's, with the exception of the optics and trigger. Instead, the coaxial DT machine gun was mounted on the gun cradle to his front.

Behind the fighting compartment's firewall was the engine compartment. This held the V-2 diesel on either side of which was a large radiator. The floor between the radiators and engine held the tank's four batteries. Two engine oil tanks were bolted into the sponsons, one per side (the V-2 engine used a significant amount of lubricating oil during normal operation).

Another sheet metal partition defined the transmission compartment. Here were housed the engine fan/clutch assembly, transmission, steering clutches, and final drives as well as two fuel tanks.

External stowage consisted of two shovels on the front left fender, snow cleats (these were to be bolted to every third set of links when used) held in place by leather straps, a box for spare track pins, a large tarp, and at the very back two spare track links were bolted. Slightly later production tanks would add a longer ZIP box for track maintenance tools just to the rear of the track pin box.

The right fender held a towing cable, more ice cleats, a pair of towing shackles, and a second set of track links. Later production T-34s would have a pair of screw-type bottle jacks mounted to the fender.

The rear mudguards held brackets for wooden wheel chocks/jack blocks. These jacks were used for lifting the turret out of the turret ring. A jack was placed on either side of the turret bustle and slowly elevated the turret out. It should be noted that some very early, perhaps pre-production, tanks appear to have been fitted with none of these exterior accessories.

10

T-34: FLAWED DESIGN?

Even though most of the documents regarding the T-34 made positive comments, and the tank had been ordered for full production, there were some major concerns that the T-34 was not fit for service. Most issues were discovered and reported during the April trials of the A-34 and the early Red Army use of the T-34, when the T-34s were first given to Red Army crews in the Western Military Districts who trained with them. Crew issues with the tanks were wide-ranging, including such things as frequent breakdowns and crew discomfort. Both breakdowns of the drivetrain and crew discomfort were discussed in the April Report from KhPZ 183, and they were the most commonly reported issues of the T-34.

Due to the number of changes needed, it was in 1940 that the T-34 was in discussion for cancellation and that a new tank should be developed. Thankfully, the Red Army ultimately decided to continue production until the T-34's intended replacement, the T-34M (to be discussed later), would be available. This meant that when Operation Barbarossa started, T-34 production lines were still going, and an estimated 1,225 T-34s had been manufactured by 1 July 1941.

Perhaps the biggest issue of all with the T-34 was the hugely limited internal space, which was limited by a number of inherent design flaws.

The suspension imposed significant limitations to the interior space available in the tank. The suspension arms were connected to vertical springs mounted on the lower side of the tank and angled forward. Much of the interior of the tank, therefore, had to be designed around these springs. For comparison, with a torsion bar suspension, the arms were placed under the floor of the tank, thus imposing fewer limitations on the interior size. It should be stressed that the suspension was not poor in design and was more than adequate for the job at hand. It was the vertical springs that were the limiting factor in this case. One serious issue with suspensions is that the USSR had trouble producing suspension springs due to a lack of spring steel between March 1942 and May 1943. The lack was only partly satisfied by Lend-Lease deliveries, and this was rationed as much as possible, leading to poor-quality production of suspension springs until the shortage ended.

Another limitation of the T-34 was the location of the fuel tanks, which had to be placed between the vertical springs, meaning this also placed them next to the hull sides. Four fuel tanks were placed between the second and third spring casing, and another two were between the fifth spring casing and the final drives. This limited the amount of fuel that could be carried, but it also meant a rear upper hull penetration would undoubtedly cause the fuel to ignite and explode. However, this was an issue not exclusive to the T-34, as many German tanks, including the famed and feared Tiger and Panther, had their fuel tanks placed against the hull sides.

Another issue caused by the large springs and their location was ammunition placement, which was an additional complaint brought against the T-34 from various sources. Ammunition was carried on the interior walls of the tank and under the turret in boxes attached to the floor of the tank. This further limited the space inside the T-34 and made accessing the floor-mounted ammunition boxes difficult. The only advantage of the floor-mounted ammunition boxes was that they created a second floor for the turret crew to stand on if necessary and protected the driving rods from being touched by the crew.

The hull sides of the tank were essentially double-skinned as a sheet of metal was placed between the first and second spring casing on the inside portion of the tank. On the very rear of the second spring casing, a wall was placed between the fighting compartment and the engine compartment. This not only narrowed the already cramped interior, but it also meant that only a maximum of nine shells were stored on the hull sides, and the other seventy-eight shells were stored under the loader's feet in ammunition boxes.

The V-2 engine, while quite meritorious, never reached its guaranteed factory mileage. Testing of a KV-1 and T-34 by the USA in 1943 at Aberdeen Proving Grounds led to the T-34 breaking down beyond repair due to an engine fault after travelling 343 km. This was due to a huge build-up of dirt because of the poor engine air filter, which had caused the pistons and cylinders to become damaged beyond repair. The report 'Assessment of the T-34 and KV Tanks by Workers from the US Aberdeen Proving Ground, Business Representatives, Officers, and Members of the Military Committees Who Conducted Tests of the Tanks' ('Aberdeen Assessment' from hereon) reported that '[t]he diesel [engine] is good and light' but the air filter was 'criminally poor', so poor in fact that the report remarks that 'only a saboteur could design something like this'. It was reported that sufficient air did not reach the engine, even when idling, so it never developed full power.

Of course, when mentioning the Aberdeen Assessment, the reader must keep in mind that this is a single T-34 produced at a time when the USSR was suffering from some of its greatest production disruptions and when it had significantly simplified the design and production of the tank to meet wartime needs.[1]

Soviet engineers were also aware of the problem with the air filter early on in production. At a meeting in January 1941, V. A. Malyshev, the head of Soviet tank industry, ordered 'by 1st June 1941, a new design for an engine air cleaner has to be developed and installed.' At the end of 1942, the new centrifugal-type Cyclone air cleaners were developed, providing 99.4 per cent air purification, but these were only issued to some of tanks produced at ChKZ 100. Furthermore, they still required cleaning and lubrication after every three to four hours of use in dusty environments. This issue was finally resolved when a new air filter developed for the IS heavy tank, the Multicyclone air cleaner (which provided nearly 100 per cent air purification for up to eight hours without maintenance), was fitted to T-34-85s as standard from 1944.

The transmission of the tank was also described in the Aberdeen Assessment as 'very poor' because during testing, the teeth on all the gears crumbled. Chemical testing revealed that their heat treatment was very poor and did not meet American standards. This was an issue that the T-34 grappled with from its earliest days, and it is unsurprising that at least one T-34 is known to have carried a spare gearbox (see page 107).

To compound the internal space issues, the turret of the tank was especially cramped. Even after the A-34's turret had been widened in the new T-34 turret design, it was still too narrow. To fix this issue, and to relieve the commander of the job of being a radioman as well as gunner and commander, the radio was moved from the turret rear to the hull right side next to the engineer, who would now take on this role. This turret, however, was still unsuitable for fighting effectively as there was barely enough room for the crew to move. The Aberdeen Assessment remarked that the American assessment team could not understand how it was possible to fit all the crew inside during winter conditions when they were wearing sheepskin outerwear.

Adding to the list of issues with the turret was that the turret hatch was too large and heavy. Also, once opened, the hatch left both crew members in the turret exposed to enemy fire. In addition, all T-34s until (but not including) the last batch of 76.2-mm L-11 gunned tanks were issued the POP episcope, which was placed into the turret hatch.[2] Not only was it hard to use because the bottom of the episcope got in the gunner's way, but it also meant that the turret hatch was ungainly and heavy.

Furthermore, the Aberdeen Assessment reported that the turret's electrical traversing gear was poor due to a weak motor that was overloaded and sparked terrible, thus meaning that the rotational speed resistors burned out and the gear teeth crumbled.

Further problems were caused by water damage. The Aberdeen Assessment reported that the lower part of the hull was permeable when crossing water obstacles (such as fording a river), and the rest of the hull was permeable to rain. In fact, the assessment reported that heavy rain would damage electrical equipment and ruin stowed ammunition because it could seep in through gaps in the tank's armour.

The assessment additionally reported that the radio set was of decent quality and quite compact but suffered from improper shielding and a lack of protective devices. Interference from the running engine meant that it was impossible to maintain normal communications at a distance of more than 10 miles. The tests were conducted on a 9-R radio set, a copy of a British design introduced in 1943. The 9-R radio set was later made standard on all T-34-85s.

As production continued, some of these flaws were rectified. However, many were inherent to the design of the tank, such as the suspension issues. Certainly, by June 1941, the T-34s leaving the factory were superior to the tanks of 1940, though. That said, the issue of limited internal space was never resolved on the T-34 design. The Aberdeen Assessment concluded that in addition to the aforementioned problems, the Soviets paid little attention to accurate tooling of small parts and components, leading to 'the loss of advantages that result from the generally well-thought-out design of the [T-34].' In other words, the design of the tank was, for the most part, quite meritorious, but its production was rushed and therefore poor. This was, no doubt, the result of both the stress of the war and the normal stresses of a command economy—production quotas were always higher than factories could manage, thus leading to quality being discarded to make up for the demanded quantity. Such production stress had plagued the Soviet economy from its inception and would do so until its demise.

Indeed, had Soviet factories not been under such pressure to mass produce as many T-34s as possible, it is not unreasonable to expect that the tanks would have been of a much higher quality. Smaller but still important issues, such as water permeability, were not a design flaw, but instead a production flaw. Pre-war T-34s did not suffer as badly as their mid-war counterparts, and T-34-85s (in particular) were of a much higher quality finish, especially post-war production Soviet, Czechoslovak, and Polish vehicles.

With all of these problems noted, it is important perhaps to dispel two myths that still continue to be echoed in military history circles. Both of the following assertions have been made for many years, but they hold no merit and often come back to German or Western propaganda.

Firstly, it is common to hear that 'The T-34 had no or limited optics for its gun, and there were no optics for the crew'. The reality is that the TOD gunsight was issued to T-34s from the start back in 1940, and at no time during T-34 production did the main gun not have a gunsight; there would be little point fielding a tank gun without the proper optics to successfully engage the enemy. Soviet gunsights were issued with protective caps, too, so the chance of damage was lessened. Furthermore, the gunsight was roughly comparable, but still inferior in terms of quality, to contemporary German optics. That said, German sights were more complex than Soviet ones, making them costly and inappropriate for the scale of mass production that the T-34 saw, especially during disruption to the supply of raw materials.

Regarding the quality of Soviet gunsights, on the one hand, Boris Kavalerchik ('Once Again About the T-34', *The Journal of Slavic Military Studies* 28 (2015), 186–214) reports that early war T-34 sights often became 'clouded and bubbled', and that from August 1941 to October 1943, sights worsened in quality because raw materials needed for their production became increasingly scarce, or were lost altogether, and as optics factories were evacuated to the east, qualified production personnel became unavailable. As a result, new equipment and materials for their production were ordered through the Lend-Lease programme. On the other hand, the Aberdeen Assessment reported that it 'is the best in the world. There is no comparison with any existing (as far as is known here) one or anything being developed in America.' From these conflicting reports, one might reasonably conclude that the T-34's gunsights were of decent quality but were certainly not 'the best in the world'.

Later in the war, having captured many German examples, the Soviets developed a new set of optics, the TSh-16 articulated sight, which was first fitted to the T-34-85. Needless to say, this was a vast improvement.

As for more general optics, the T-34 in 1941 had vision ports to the left and right of the turret with bulletproof glass for protection and the commander was given a PT-1 (late PT-4 and PT-4-7) periscopes. Admittedly, the fields of view from these devices were lacking, but this is a problem inherent with all tanks. This perennial issue could be partly solved by the use of a cupola, a feature that gave German tanks in 1941 an advantage over Soviet ones.

The second common claim is that 'The F-34 was copied from a German design'. The reality is that the 76.2-mm F-34 was designed by Soviet designer, V. Grabin, as a lighter-weight version of the F-32, itself the evolution of other native Soviet guns, like the F-22 and L-10. This claim likely came from the capture of Tsarist Russian 76.2-mm field guns in the First World War and their use by German forces. These Tsarist Russian guns were 76.2-mm Model 1910 field guns—the predecessor to the Model 1927 regimental gun, which was designed for tanks as the KT-28. What appears to have happened is that multiple distortions have led to the Model 1910 being interpreted as German, and the KT-28 has been conflated with the F-34 (likely because they are the same calibre weapon), resulting in the absurd myth that the F-34 was a German design.

11

CONTEMPORARY SOVIET DESIGNS

While the T-34 was advanced by Soviet tank standards, it was still a primitive design. It did have two noteworthy features—the sloped glacis and the main armaments—but other tanks being fielded at the same time as the T-34 were inherently superior designs, such as the KV-1. The T-34's greatest flaws included the poor suspension layout and small turret. These flaws were so great that the question was raised as to whether the tank was even fit for service.

KV-1

The KV-1 was a heavy tank project started about the same time as the T-34, but it was intended to replace the T-35A heavy tank. The KV-1 was perhaps the most modern Soviet tank when it was released in 1940; it boasted 90 mm of frontal and turret armour, torsion bar suspension, a 76.2-mm L-11 gun, and most importantly, a three-man turret. It is interesting to note that many of the desirable features of the KV-1, such as the three-man turret and torsion bar suspension, would be incorporated not only in the T-34M (the intended replacement of the T-34) in 1940, but also in the eventual post-war replacements for the T-34, namely the T-44 and T-54.

Compared to the T-34, the KV-1 was superior in crew layout, armour thickness, suspension layout and vision (having a superior layout of optics for the crew). The T-34 was superior only in manoeuvrability (the T-34 weighed less at 26.8 tons, compared to 42 tons of the KV-1) and was also cheaper to produce.

Upon the outbreak of war, KV tanks were fewer in number than T-34s, but their impact was, perhaps, even more greatly felt by German forces. However, the inability to manufacture enough KV-1s in a short space of time, plus its heavy weight that only increased as production continued and the vehicle's tendency to get stuck in one gear, ultimately led to it losing favour within the Red Army.

Due to these factors, while the KV-1 was ultimately the superior tank on paper, the T-34 was the tank that was favoured by the Red Army.

At the same time that the T-34 was being designed, the next generation of heavy tanks was being worked on. This is the prototype KV tank, 'KV-U0'. This was the first KV manufactured and was the KV sent to Finland in 1940. KV-U0 served in the Second World War, photographed here after capture by German forces in July 1941.

T-50

One cannot discuss the T-34 and its role during Operation Barbarossa without talking about the T-50 tank, which was intended to replace the T-26 as both the main and most numerous tank in the Red Army. It is strange to think with hindsight that tanks in the war would get heavier and more powerful, but the Red Army held the T-50 in higher regard than the T-34 at that time. However, at the time, it made perfect sense.

One major influence of the T-50's design was the Spanish Civil War, which had proved that the T-26 needed replacing because its armour was simply too thin on modern battlefields. As a result, the T-126 SP was developed by Plant 185 in 1938. The T-126 SP (Infantry Support) was a hexagonal-hulled tank with six torsion bar suspension arms and a two-man turret with a 45-mm gun. However, during the development cycle, many flaws were discovered, and high maintenance was an issue.

However, Soviet engineers spent most of the last months of 1939 crawling over two Panzer IIIs purchased from Germany under the Molotov-Ribbentrop Pact. From this, it was found that the Panzer III was a perfect balance of manoeuvrability, weight, speed, and layout. It was no heavier than the later models of T-26, but in all respects, other than armaments, the Panzer III was superior to the T-26.

Possibly the most important factor of why German tanks had the advantage in 1941 when invading the USSR was the fact that their main tanks, the Panzer III and Panzer IV, had three-man turrets. While not the most numerous tanks on the battlefield, these tanks posed a serious threat to most of the tanks that the USSR could field. The huge advantage with a

Six Panzer IIIs of the 16th Panzer Division, photographed during an advance in June 1941. The Panzer III had an innovative three-man turret with a cupola for the commander. The vehicle also had a favourable power to weight ratio and was highly manoeuvrable, hence why the USSR was eager to copy the success of this vehicle.

three-man turret, and one that Soviet engineers were all too aware of, was that it gave the commander of the tank more time to make decisions as he did not have to also be the gunner of the tank. This was an issue with most pre-war tanks regardless of their origin.

Shortly after the Panzer IIIs were trialled in 1939, it was decided to improve the T-126 SP project and to design a superior version of the tank. It was also decided that the new tank should differ from the Panzer III's design as a direct copy of it would sit unfavourably with the Stavka because Soviet–German relations were tenuous at best, and it would look poor if the Soviet Union copied a German design.

The new Object 135 (T-135) was Plant 185's improvement and was accepted for production as the T-50. This tank differed slightly from the T-126 SP's design by having reduced armour on the hull (45 mm reduced to 37 mm), a three-man turret (although it was very cramped), and only one crewman in the hull—namely, the driver. The angles of the hull stayed relatively the same, but its weight was reduced from 16 tons to 14 tons.

The documentation was taken to the SKB-2 design bureau for finalisation. It, therefore, credited SKB-2 as the developer. Plant 174 was selected for production of the tank, which officially ended production of the T-26 Model 1940 in the last quarter of 1940, with the last units being manufactured in January 1941.

The T-50 was meant to be the most-produced tank of the third and fourth five-year plan, in which it was planned that 14,000 T-50s would be produced. Again, it must be stressed that as a replacement of the T-26, the T-50 was intended to be the Red Army's main tank, which the huge production order suggests. Soviet tank tactics had little changed since the 1930s, and the idea of many light tanks being able to exploit breakthroughs in front lines created by heavy and medium tanks were still in mind when the tank was accepted. Therefore, the KV-1 tank was intended to be the breakthrough tank, with the KV-2 being a close support variant. The T-34 and T-34M were to be tank-on-tank fighters, and the T-50 was to be the backbone of the tank corps.

Despite these promising features, the T-50 only began production in May 1941, just a month before the outbreak of war with Germany on 22 June 1941. At this time, the T-50 proved to be a very complex tank to manufacture, and production was very poor. This was mainly due to the complexity of the T-50 compared to that of the much simpler T-26 and the inability for Factory 174 to therefore produce the tank as quickly. Worse still, Factory 75 could not manufacture enough V-4 engines for Factory 174's chassis output.

Between June and December 1941, only fifty T-50s were manufactured, and after the evacuation of Plant 174 from Leningrad to Omsk, a further fifteen tanks were manufactured. Additionally, the first T-50s did not reach front line units until August 1941, and this was at nothing more than a trickle.[1] It was discussed that Plant No. 37 in Moscow should also attempt to produce the T-50, but the proposal was so illogical that it led to the plant requesting to build its own light tank, namely the T-60. The T-50 did not have the desired effect on the battlefield that the designers thought it would have, but in such small numbers, it is difficult to evaluate its performance. Perhaps if it were produced in larger numbers, its sophisticated design would have made it one of the most formidable Soviet tanks of the early war. After two separate evacuations, Omsk 174 stopped manufacturing the T-50 tank and began production of the T-34.

This T-50 was shot to pieces. One theory for all this damage is that the gunner who shot at this tank thought it was a dreaded T-34 and that 37-mm rounds would have mostly bounced off, hence so many shots were fired. The tank was lost in early October 1941.

Two T-50s lost in March 1943. Notice the wooden crosses placed onto the turrets to indicate that the tanks were already destroyed.

As a result of all the problems of the KV-1 and the disastrous nature of the T-50 project, in 1941, the only capable tank available and in production for the role of the Red Army's main tank was the T-34 (the KV-1 remaining in the role of heavy breakthrough tank). Thus, in a very real sense, the T-34 was only made the Red Army's main tank out of the circumstances of the war. Perhaps if the Germans had invaded later on in 1941, the T-34 would never have become the legendary tank it was, especially considering that the T-34 was little more than a stopgap, with its intended replacement, the T-34M, being very nearly put into production.

T-34M

While tests against a Panzer III purchased from Germany through the Molotov-Ribbentrop Pact showed the T-34 to be superior with regards to armour and armament, the Panzer III was still superior in other respects, such as crew comfort, manoeuvrability, and crew communication. Due to the already stated flaws, along with other factors such as the difficulty of manufacture and poor reliability of the drivetrain, the Red Army saw fit to explore the possibility of replacing the T-34 before a single unit had even been manufactured.

The two main influences for the need to update the new tank were the Panzer III and the T-50 light tank. Both tanks shared very similar features as the T-50 was significantly influenced by the German design. Both the Panzer III and T-50 tanks were similar in specification as the T-50 was somewhat based on the Panzer III. These tanks had torsion bar suspension, good manoeuvrability, and a three-man turret.

The wooden mock-up of the T-34M. There are many differences between this vehicle and the T-34. Notice the return rollers for the running gear; along with torsion bar suspension, the running gear was a total redesign. The hull was more akin to the T-50's hull, having strange angles on the hull sides. The driver is on the right, rather than the left. The turret was designed to have a crew of three men. (*Maxim Kolomiets*)

The new tank to replace the T-34, under the designation 'T-34M', began its development cycle amid doubts that the T-34 could attain the factory's guaranteed mileage of 3,000 km before needing an engine replacement.

The requirements for the T-34M were a turret that could comfortably fit three crewmen; the suspension was to be of the torsion bar type with return rollers; and a five-speed gearbox. There had been another previous attempt to upgrade the T-34 with the A-41 project. This, however, never left the paper project stage as the designer Mikhail Koshkin passed away due to pneumonia, contracted during the winter trials of the A-34.

The T-34M design was approved for production in May 1941, and construction began with the assembly of five turrets. In addition to this, track links were also made. Despite the development of a replacement, it was decided to keep T-34 production up in the meantime while the T-34M was being designed. At this time, the guaranteed mileage of the T-34 was reduced to 1,000 km, which was still an unattainable number.

However, Operation Barbarossa would get in the way of the T-34M project as the desperate need for tanks on the front lines surpassed the need for designing a superior tank to the T-34. The initially promising project was therefore cancelled on 25 June 1941, within the first days of the war. As it was, only a 1/10th scale model, five cast turrets, and track links were manufactured before KhPZ 183 had to evacuate to Uralmash at the end of 1941. The track links were fitted to an estimated thirty T-34s in mid-1941, but the cast turrets were never used despite being shipped to UTZ 183. That said, the project was revisited in 1943 as the T-43, as part of the process of investigating possible upgrades to the T-34 before the ultimately successful T-34-85 was made. The story of the T-43 can be found in Chapter 39.

Speculating on what would have happened if the T-34M had begun production and replaced the T-34 instead of being shelved, it is fair to say Red Army would have been in far worse condition due to the disruption to production this change would have caused.

T-34 PRODUCTION ON THE EVE OF WAR

As it was, before the war, T-34 production was to be continued until the T-34M was introduced, but this did not stop the basic T-34 from being improved upon. Pre-war changes were usually done to fulfil the requirements of the April Report and were generally improvements that made the design more complex, whereas wartime changes were done to simplify production or to improve battlefield survivability.

Also, seeing as though the T-34 was such an imperfect product, it went through multiple major redesigns throughout its service career to bash into shape what was in some respects a stop-gap tank into the Red Army's main tank.

Many factors influenced or necessitated these modifications, but most were done to speed up production. These alterations were very important in the story of the T-34 and a key in identifying the origins of each of these tanks. Many changes were not documented, and therefore the level of detail will not be as high as with the story of the A-34. However, with thanks to *Wehrmacht* photographers, the story of the T-34 has been relatively well mapped out. We begin the story of post-prototype production changes with tanks made before Operation Barbarossa.

12

L-11 GUNS: JUNE 1940–FEBRUARY 1941

Factory Number 183, also known as the Kharkov Locomotive and Tractor Works (KhPZ), was the first factory to begin production of the T-34 tank. The factory and the chief designer I. P. Bondarenko from KhPZ 183 were both directly involved in the design and development of the T-34 tank.

Before the T-34 had been approved by the Red Army, KhPZ 183 had been ordered to begin production of 150 A-34s as stated in Order 433ss. After the two prototype tanks, production continued until the order came with the improvements of the tank. Therefore, ten Initial Production T-34 (A-34)s were made, along with twenty-seven T-34 (A-34 turret)s until new parts began to arrive at KhPZ 183 to be fitted to tanks from June 1940.

Initial Production T-34 (A-34)s were manufactured and distributed throughout the Red Army; they can be identified by the solid nose piece, along with turrets lacking cheek armour and mounting a turret radio.

Resolution 848 was passed on 31 March 1940 and was the order to begin T-34 production at KhPZ 183 and STZ but with the list of improvements. This April Report to KhPZ 183 engineers was taken very seriously and was implemented as soon as possible. Serious redesigns also followed, with the most important concerning the main turret, the hull nose, and the engine deck. Some of the early improvements were also there to help maintain a high production rate of the new tank.

T-34 (L-11 GUN AND TURRET RADIO)

Mariupol Metallurgy Plant began production of the new nose plate and glacis plate in May 1940. This was now made of three parts. The original A-34 prototypes had a one-piece nose and glacis, with the armour having to be bent with a 10,000-ton press. The original method was chosen to strengthen the glacis plate, but failures during manufacture were very common. Therefore, this nose was simplified after the debate between KhPZ 183 and Mariupol Metallurgy Plant came to an end. The glacis plate, the nose, and the under-nose plate were now made separately on the T-34. This was more time-consuming, but it did not require the press, which was not a very common piece of equipment. These three items were bolted together, and distinctive bolts were placed onto the nose.

Next, the engine deck was redesigned. The original engine deck had a single plate that contained cut-outs for radiator air intakes, fuel tank plugs, and a central raised engine access port, that was covered by a large hatch. However, it was found that for maintenance, it was too difficult to remove the whole plate. Therefore, the redesigned engine deck was now in three parts. The central raised engine access port was now separate from the left and right radiator access ports. These two were bolted onto the central portion.

Hulls like this were delivered to KhPZ 183 in June 1940 to be fitted with the A-34 turrets as previously discussed. T-34s in this configuration can be called 'T-34 (A-34 turret)'. Only twenty-seven were produced as a new turret was designed and released that attempted to address the issues discussed in the April Report.

A redesigned turret was used that kept the same armour thickness and plate angles as the A-34 turret but was wider. The turrets of the A-34 prototype and production T-34s were almost identical in shape, but minor changes were made regarding where bends were placed on the turret sides to maximise space inside the turret. Both turrets were manufactured from four rolled plates, excluding the turret roof, the rear turret bustle floor, and the rear access door. These plates were the turret ring, the left and right turret sides, and the turret face, with cut-outs for the gun.

A T-34 (A-34 turret) lost in June 1941. The turret is clearly an A-34-style turret as it is lacking turret fillet armour; notice the distinctive shape of the turret hatch. The white triangle on the turret roof is a distinctive feature of many Soviet tanks in June 1941 and was intended for friendly air identification.

The same T-34 (A-34 turret) as on page 74. An often-overlooked feature on these tanks is the turret hatches with straight sides. This was fitted due to the narrower shape of the A-34 turret. When the turret was redesigned and marginally widened, the hatch was also redesigned to match this redesign. One can also see the seam for the new nose fillet.

One of the twenty-seven T-34s manufactured with A-34 turrets, known as 'T-34 (A-34 turret)'. This tank was lost in Minsk in June 1941. The glacis plate is manufactured from three separate pieces and bolted into position. The turret displays all of the A-34 features, including the lack of support armour around the turret seams. Notice the bracket for a combat light—something only the A-34 turrets had.

This T-34 (A-34 Turret) was knocked out in July 1941 somewhere in Ukraine. Notice the lack of protective armour plate over the forward turret seams, indicative of the A-34. Additionally, this vehicle has three tie-downs at the rear left of the hull.

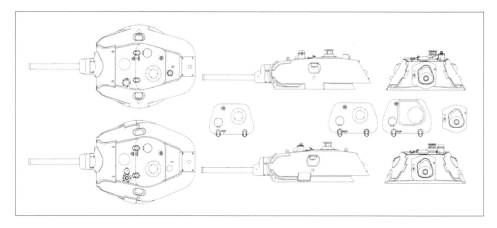

A comparison of the A-34 turret (top) and the redesigned T-34 turret (bottom). The turret was widened by moving the bend in the turret side plates from the centre of the turret ring, backwards. This required no new tooling other than the shape of the turret hatch.

The A-34's turret side plates were bent twice. A bend was made at the 90-degree mark of the turret ring, while a second bend was placed at the rear of the turret that then would attach to the removable rear access door.

To redesign the turret while keeping the same angles of the plates, the bend in the turret side next to the turret ring was moved rearwards, no longer in line with the turret ring. This bend in the turret plate was now roughly central on the turret, whereas before, the bend in the turret's plate was roughly one-third down the turret.

Due to this subtle redesign of the turret, many items were re-engineered. Most obviously, the change widened the rear of the turret, which meant the turret hatch also had to be redesigned. The A-34's hatch had straight sides, but the new hatch was more bulbous, giving it a slightly more rounded shape. The hatch lacked any pressings on it, which was a feature of later hatches, as to marginally raise the POP episcope.

The side vision ports had originally been placed in the centre of the bend, facing outward at a 90-degree angle. On the new turrets, the vision ports were still placed in the same position on the plate; this now meant that they were not centred on the curve of the turret and were now forward of the bend in the rolled plate. Therefore, the new position of the side vision ports was at an angle of 83 degrees. This was a by-product of the change in turret shape, rather than a specified change.

During testing at the Polygon (outside Moscow), it was found that the joint between the turret ring, the side plate, and the nose plate was weak. Therefore, a small rectangle of supporting cheek armour was placed over the seams to stop a direct hit from damaging all the joints of the turret plates.

The radio was supposed to be removed from the turret and placed on the right side of the tank's front hull, next to the engineer, but this was not initially done, and it is believed that no more than fifty to 100 tanks had this feature. However, only one in five of these tanks had the radio at all, and those without the radio had either a simple plug welded over the hole or retained the distinctive radio antenna collar (a hollow cylinder roughly ten or so inches high that was intended to protect the aerial base) with a small plug fitted inside this. Hence, these tanks with the radio mount still in the turret can be referred to as 'T-34 (L-11 Gun and Turret Radio)'.

Lastly, a lip was placed around the driver's hatch edges to stop spalling from entering the tank through tiny gaps between the glacis armour and the hatch. This was issued in September 1940, but it was also retrofitted to most of these early tanks. According to a factory photograph, the chassis number of a T-34 (A-34 Turret) is 811-65, but the chassis number 811-78 can be seen on another factory photograph of a T-34 (L-11 Gun and Turret Radio). This indicates that the chassis numbers bear little correlation with actual changes to the tanks, as one might reasonably expect '811' chassis numbers to look the same. This is the most telling example of the 'first in, last out' phenomenon.

These tanks were generally of a very high finish quality but were lacking spare parts. Part failures were a common reason for breakdowns, with the transmission being a major weak point. In summation, they were outwardly very fine tanks, but mechanically lacking.

The future of the T-34 at KhPZ 183 was already subject to further change, however. The plant was expected to produce 450 T-34s in the first year, but this was an impossible task, especially with the implementation of further improvements listed in the April Report. That said, production was supposed to continue only until the T-34M was to enter production.

A T-34 (L-ll Gun and Turret Radio). Notice the radio antenna port in the turret, that the turret's vision ports are angled forward slightly, that the turret hatch has rounded edges, and that the hatch is lacking any pressed shaped on the hatch, thus indicating the turret to be an initial production T-34 type, not an A-34 turret.

Another T-34 (L-ll Gun and Turret Radio) that was destroyed in combat. The antenna port in the rear of the turret and the cheek armour over the turret seams are clearly visible. Take note of the early initial production track. The rubber has come off a road wheel where a dead crewman can also be seen. Note that the jack block on the left has fallen off, but the one on the right remains in place. The turret hatch is also missing.

The same T-34 (L-11 Gun and Turret Radio) as seen below. The strange colour of this tank is due to the dust that has clung to it while on the move.

This T-34 likely broke down rather than being knocked out in combat and has thrown a track. The antenna port in the turret gives its identity away as being a T-34 (L-11 Gun and Turret Radio). The strange light colour of this tank is not camouflage but instead comes from dust that has clung to the tank while travelling, likely at a high speed, hence why the tank may have broken down. The tank was also likely pushed to the side of the road by German forces.

This T-34 (L-11 Gun and Turret Radio) was disabled in combat. The antenna port is clearly visible. This vehicle was likely serving in the 15th Mechanised Corps and was lost on the Ukrainian SSR–Polish border, 5 km north of Lvov. This tank was likely one of the first T-34s encountered by German forces.

An example of a T-34 (L-11 Gun and Turret Radio) as this tank has a plug over the hole that the antenna would have been placed in. The hatch, once again, is lacking pressings to allow for greater gun clearance. The hits on the turret are likely 50-mm gun hits. Note the DT magazine next to the rear lifting hook.

The same T-34 (L-11 Gun and Turret Radio) as on page 80, but instead shortly after it was initially abandoned. This tank has an unditching beam on the hull side that could be deployed to allow the vehicle to advance over soft ground. The numbers on the rear were written on by the Germans. The top four numbers are '16/99', referring to the 16th Company of 99th *Gebirgsjaeger*-Regiment (1st Gebirgs-Division). The bottom number is the date '28/6/41', indicating the tank was lost six days after Operation Barbarossa began.

Another T-34 (L-11 Gun and Turret Radio). The fenders of this machine do not have the extensions that most tanks were given. Note the missing headlamp next to the hull MG blister. The tank was clearly lost due to a huge fire, as discerned by the burned paintwork, burned rubber, and the immolated crew member beneath the tank.

This T-34 (L-11 Gun and Turret Radio) burned after combat. The tank ran over a Pak 38 anti-tank gun (as seen on page 111). The tank is lacking a radio, but it likely has a plug over the hole. Some of the track links at the front of the tank are the 550-mm reinforced type.

These tanks were first deployed in August 1940 in the 8th Tank Division, 4th Mechanised Corps. This unit was based in the Kiev Special Military District, specifically Lvov (modern-day Lviv). The first deliveries would have consisted of the first ten Initial Production T-34 (A-34), the twenty-seven T-34 (A-34 turret)s, and a few of the T-34 (L-11 Gun and Turret Radio)s. However, between the first deployment of the T-34 and the beginning of Operation Barbarossa, evidence suggests that many of these early tanks were transferred to the 12th Tank Division, 8th Mechanised Corps, which was based around Lvov.

Many of the early T-34s described were lost on the opening day of Operation Barbarossa. At that time, the 8th and 12th Tank Divisions was deployed around Lvov and bore the brunt of the opening thrusts by German forces. Many of these tanks were lost due to combat or broke down. Some of these early T-34s were involved in Lieutenant-General Nikolai Popel's counterattack at Dubno in June 1941. Some of the early T-34s from the 8th Tank Division, 4th Mechanised Corps, are thought to have been encircled in Belostok. There is also some tenuous photographic evidence to suggest that some of these tanks broke out towards Minsk.

T-34 (L-11 GUN)

The next major change to the T-34 was the relocation of the radio. After the aforementioned batch of tanks, the radio was relocated to the right hull side. Interestingly, in August 1940, several meetings were conducted with regards to the location of the radio. Every meeting concluded with the decision to not only relocate the radio, but also upgrade it. Despite this, the relocation took a long time, and letters from the commander of the 8th Mechanised Corps attest to his dismay at the cramped nature of the turret and also his desire for KhPZ 183 to relocate the radio to the hull.

Eventually, the move did happen, and from late 1940, the radio was moved to the hull. Tanks were issued the external mount on the hulls forward right side regardless of whether the tank had a radio or not. Tanks with the new turret type but the radio moved to the hull can be referred to as 'T-34 (L-11 Gun)' because this was the new standard T-34 design.

As recommended in the long list of changes to the T-34, four 50-litre external fuel tanks were adopted for the tanks. The boxes were rectangular, with a width to length ratio of 1:6. Each box required four leather straps to attach it to the hull side and, therefore, small hardpoints were welded to the hull sides. These fuel tanks were first used on the BT-7. These were not symmetrical to either side of the tank, as the radio interfered with the placement of the right fuel tanks, the right-hand boxes were placed further rearwards. These fuel tanks were originally were simple unmarked rectangles with a small cap at one end, but later, these would be marked with two indents running the length of the box, intended to strengthen the box, as they tended to warp while containing liquid.

Changes to the tracks of the T-34 were also made. The original track was found to be weak and did not have enough grip. To remedy this, the track was slightly redesigned to have strengthening bars across the track and triangular 'teeth' on the outside of the track. This track can be known as 'reinforced 550-mm type'. These were very minor changes, and this track would be used until 1942.

The same collection point as on page 84, this T-34 (L-11 Gun and Turret Radio) has no radio port but does have a plug to cover the hole. A keen eye will be able to spot a mixture of armoured vehicles, including BT-7s, BA-10s, a T-28, a BA-27, a BA-20, and perhaps even a T-18.

The same collection yard as on page 83, but this time facing the other way to the other pictures. A cast-turreted T-34 (L-11 gun) tank can be seen; that is the tank as seen below.

Another collection point for captured Soviet armour. The tank in the foreground is a cast-turreted T-34 (L-11 Gun), but the T-34s in the background are T-34 (L-11 Gun and Turret Radio), although all these vehicles do not have the distinctive port in the turret but instead have a cap covering the hole for the port. (*Maxim Kolomiets*)

All T-34 tracks from this early period were generally poor, with little grip, and created too much noise, being heard from up to 500 metres away. This would later be rectified, with different patterns of track being trialled.

Additionally, new patterns of turret hatch were fielded. The newer hatch had a pressing on the inside of the hatch to allow for greater POP episcope clearance of the gunner. T-34s were still issued the older, pressing-less type of turret hatch until stocks ran out.

It was tanks of the T-34 (L-11 Gun) configuration that STZ would have begun production of in the last quarter of 1940. There is some dispute over whether STZ issued any T-34s with L-11 guns at all, but if they did, then tanks of this type from both STZ and KhPZ 183 would have been identical, so information on the tanks from both factories will be discussed up until the point noticeable changes appear.

From as early as the testing of the A-34 prototypes, Mariupol Metallurgy Plant was interested in casting turrets for the new T-34. Tests for casting turrets were done between March and May 1940, with one fully-cast turret prototype being manufactured. The turret was 45 mm thick and cast in two separate parts. In April, this turret was put through ballistics tests which it passed. Therefore, it was decided to manufacture two T-34 turret types, one from cast metal and one from rolled plates. These turrets had the same armour thickness as the welded turrets but were stronger due to the nature of casting. The implementation of the two turret types also gave birth to the unofficial post-war terms 'T-34/76 cast' and 'T-34/76 welded'.

Cast turrets had a different casting pattern than the prototype, and additionally, the casting pattern of these early production turrets additionally differed marginally with the cast turrets of T-34s issued with F-34 guns. Initially, the vision ports were cast as a part of the turret, but this made the process complicated, and therefore turrets had the hole that the vision port was going to fit in cut out of the tank, and a vision port welded into position instead. This gave the early cast turrets a distinctive look.

After the early cast turrets were made, it was found to be easier to gas cut out the vision port, like that on the T-34s manufactured with rolled turrets. Therefore, this was quickly integrated onto the T-34's cast turrets.

Due to this separation in turret production, about one-third of T-34s with L-11 guns were issued with a cast turret. The turret kept the same basic shape, with minor variations in turret cheek dimensions due to the cast turret cheeks being fatter.

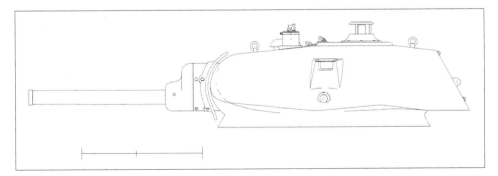

A cast turret with an L-11 from the first production batch. The vision ports on the turret side were cast as a part of the turret side, rather than being welded into place.

A T-34 (L-11 Gun Cast Early) knocked out in fighting. A surprising number of T-34s were knocked out in June and July 1941 as opposed to being abandoned, which one might expect of such mechanically lacking tanks. Notice the casting pattern on the turret vision port, a clear indicator that the turret is an initial production cast turret.

One of the initial production cast turrets. This T-34 (L-11 Gun Cast Early) was lost in the village of Hranivka on 19 June 1941. The tank served in the 8th Mechanised Corps and was lost with another T-34, a BT-7, and a T-40.

A T-34 (L-11 Gun Cast Early), lost in the village of Hranivka in the eastern Ukrainian SSR. This road is looking north towards the village of Verba, where on 30 June 1941, four T-35A heavy tanks attempted a counterattack towards Hranivka. The attack was totally halted, with all Soviet tanks involved being lost.

This cast-turreted T-34 (L-11 Gun) was abandoned after taking a shot that broke some of the track links over the rear road wheel. Notice the hardpoints for the exterior fuel tanks. Empty brackets for the jacks can be seen on the fender. The gun has also come out of its cradle.

A cast-turreted T-34 (L-11 Gun) lost in the Ukrainian SSR. The track is the reinforced 550-mm type. While the fenders are lacking the extensions, the bracket for them is still on the front left fender. The exterior fuel tanks are the later type as they have pressed strengthening indents to help the fuel tank keep its shape. Three dead crewmen can be seen around the tank. Slight residue from burning rubber on the road wheels indicates the tank was set alight.

T-34 (L-11 GUN LAST PRODUCTION)

The last major change to the production of T-34s with the L-11 gun was the removal of the POP periscope in the turret hatch. This was officially ordered in January 1941 as it was clear that there were more disadvantages to using the episcope than removing it from the design. This periscope was heavy and not only made it difficult to open the hatch, but it also took up valuable room inside the turret, something that was already a major issue. Hatches were given a simple circular cap to cover the hole where the POP periscope was situated. These T-34s can be referred to as 'T-34 (L-11 Gun Last Production)'.

As production continued, the T-34's toolset also changed. Initial production tanks had no tools whatsoever, but subsequent tanks were issued an ever-growing set of tools. Standard L-11-gunned tanks (including those with the turret radio) were issued with two spades that attached to the front left fender, along with a small box on the rear left fender. Snow cleats for the track were also stowed on both sides of the tank about halfway down the fender.

Two wooden blocks were stored on the rear fenders, and two jacks were placed on the rear right of the hull side fender. The wooden blocks were used in conjunction with the jack.

Later additions to the stowage included two metal-braided tow ropes. All T-34s with L-11 guns (both standard L-11 T-34s and the earlier turret-radio type) were supplied with a small box that contained only track and split pins. The later box was several times longer though not as tall. It contained tools for track repairs as well as spares.

One of the many German collecting points for abandoned Soviet armour. This T-34 (L-11 Gun) is from the last production batch. This can be identified by the lack of a POP episcope in the turret hatch. There are four BT-7s in the photo and a BT-7A (right) among the wrecks. Just in shot on the left is another T-34.

A T-34 (L-11 Gun Last Production) lost in the Ukrainian SSR in June 1941. The barrel to the gun took a hit that disabled the gun. Notice the turret hatch lacking a POP episcope. (*Will Kerrs Collection*)

Three L-11-gunned T-34s that drove into a bog in the Byelorussian SSR. The tank in the foreground is a T-34 (L-11 Gun Last Production). Notice the tarpaulin stowage, which often burned when tanks were hit but is intact on the tank in the foreground. The tank in the middle is another T-34 (L-11 Gun and Turret Radio), but lacking a radio port, and has four tie-down points on the hull rear left side. It also has a three-tone camouflage scheme. The last T-34 is a cast-turreted T-34 (L-11 Gun).

Another three-tone painted T-34 (L-11 Gun) lost in soft ground in the Byelorussian SSR. Notice the turret hatch pressing that allowed for greater clearance of the POP periscope in the turret. The 76-mm shell in front of the tank indicates that German soldiers have typically been rifling through the tank. In the background is a T-26 with a conical turret and P-40 anti-aircraft. There is also the hull of another T-34 at the bottom left.

The same three-toned T-34 on page 90. Notice the colour changes at the rear of the turret. There is much debate on if this pattern is three- or two-tone. This photograph clearly displays three tones.

In all, 117 T-34s were produced in 1940, and 2,996 in 1941. Of these tanks, 746 tanks were issued with the 76.2-mm gun L-11, whereas the other tanks were issued with the more powerful F-34 76.2-mm gun. Interestingly, therefore 629 T-34s were issued with the L-11 gun in 1941. In some sources, the T-34s with L-11 guns are known as 'Model 1940s', but considering that over five times as many T-34s with L-11 guns were issued in 1940 compared to 1941, it is easy to see why categorising T-34s by year is an ineffective method of categorisation.

The L-11 gun was not a flawless weapon, however, as it had inferior recoil control leading to many shots going off target. Therefore, it was decided to consider manufacturing a new gun for the T-34M and, by extension, the T-34. Almost at no point in T-34 production with L-11 guns was the F-32 considered to be reintroduced. This was mostly due to the slow production of the F-32, and all of them going to KV-1s. It is interesting to note that the L-11 gun in 1940 was far superior to any other gun issued to German tanks, with greater penetrating power than the 75-mm KwK 37 L/24 of the Panzer IV, albeit with the previously stated design flaw.

This T-34 (L-11 Gun Last Production) was lost in the Ukrainian SSR in June 1941. More of what are considered 'standard' T-34 features are visible, such as the two jacks for the tanks are on the rear right fender, along with ice cleats. An STZ-5 tractor is lying upside down in the ditch behind this tank on the left. In the background right is another T-34 (L-11 Gun), upside-down.

The same T-34 (L-11 Gun Last Production) as seen above. Notice the external fuel tanks and ice cleats laying in the ditch next to the tank.

A T-34 (L-11 Gun Last Production) that got stuck in soft ground. This tank displays many features of the last production L-11 tanks, such as a plugged POP periscope port and the standard stowage layout. The tank also shows signs of burning across the hull.

The same T-34 as seen above. This tank was likely bogged down and overheated, leading to a large fire at the rear, as can be discerned by burn marks on the engine deck. Note also that the DT is still in the turret, indicating it to have been destroyed, hence why it has not been removed by German forces.

13

F-34 GUNS: JANUARY–JUNE 1941

In June 1940, the main armament of the T-34 was in even more serious contention. The prototype tanks had been equipped with the 76.2-mm L-11 and L-10 guns. However, those guns had been decommissioned in January 1939, and it was decided that the 76.2-mm F-32 gun would instead be issued.

This turned out to be a sticking point, however. The Kirov Works was assigned to produce the gun but did not want to produce a weapon not native to the factory, whereas the L-11 was. There was much debate over what gun should be installed into the tank, and the Kirov Works only produced fifty guns, all of which were sent to KV-1s being produced in Leningrad. Some sources incorrectly claim they were issued to T-34s.

In the end, only the L-11 gun was available, and even this gun was not produced quickly or efficiently enough to supply the trickle of tanks being produced. It was in mid-August 1940 that the new 76.2-mm F-34 gun was being tested for the T-34M, and the prototype gun was very similar to what was envisaged for the final product.

Live firing tests were conducted on a BT-7A, with the 76.2-mm KT-28 replaced with an F-34. The weapon was finally commissioned on 21 October 1940, and almost straight away, talks began about fitting the T-34 with it. It was easy to install into the pre-existing turret of the tank, although the gun did have to be shortened to 40 calibres from 42.5 calibres. This was still superior to the 31.5-calibre F-32 and 30.5-calibre L-11.[1]

PRE-WAR T-34 (F-34 GUN)

It is interesting to note that, at this point, the gun had not officially been adopted by the Red Army. It was in February 1941 that the F-34 gun began reaching the factories, with eighty-two guns being shipped to Kharkov, but the gun was officially adopted only in July 1941.

The early F-34 gunned tanks, which we will call 'Pre-War T-34 (F-34 Gun)', up until June 1941, differed little from the L-11-gunned tanks, except the changes to the internal ammunition

The BT-7A with prototype F-34 76.2-mm gun. Notice that the tank still has the gun mantlet of a KT-28 with the barrel and recoil mechanisms forward of the gun shield. Other than the F-34 gun, this is a standard BT-7A. The only other item of interest is the track, which is the earlier type most commonly used on the BT-2 and BT-5, although early BT-7s used this track, too. (*Maxim Kolomiets*)

A very early Pre-War T-34 (F-34 Gun). The only major exterior changes compared to L-11-gunned tanks were the obvious new gun, along with a stowage box on the front left fender for the gun's cleaning equipment and some minor alterations here and there. Note the signs of a fire, such as burned rubber road wheels.

A Pre-War T-34 (F-34 Gun). Just before the war, tanks started being issued with rear turret access doors with six bolts, whereas this T-34 only has four bolts.

stowage. Externally, two guides were added on either side of the gun mantlet to stop spalls from entering the turret from either side of the gun.

The only other major change then implemented in this stage of T-34 production was the change from a four-bolt access door in the rear of the turret to a six-bolt access door. Crucially, only F-34-gunned tanks had the six-bolt door. This door in the rear of the turret was intended for gun inspection and removal. The six bolts were implemented to stop the access door in the rear turret from shaking loose. It has been suggested that even firing the coaxial MG could cause this door to come loose.

Smaller changes were also made. A new pattern of turret hatch was manufactured without the hole for the POP periscope. This was only implemented on new hatches being manufactured, but these were fielded alongside the original hatch until stocks of the old hatch ran out. The hole on the old hatch was also now covered with a cap.

Two patterns of turret hatch were issued from hereon. Firstly, a hatch was issued with the same pressing on the hatch that was put onto the hatches with the POP periscope. However, a second type was also manufactured. This hatch had a long square pressing on the hatch, which matched the F-34 gun internally. It is thought that this was intended to give the maximum gun depression possible. This type of turret hatch can be known as the 'parallel pressing' hatch.

It is sometimes incorrectly claimed that the 'parallel pressing' hatch was only issued to STZ and later Krasnoye Sormovo 112. This is not true, as the turret hatches were manufactured originally at Mariupol Metallurgy Plant and shipped to both STZ and KhPZ 183. When Mariupol Metallurgy Plant stopped shipments of turret hatches to STZ after the factory was captured, STZ manufactured their own turret hatches. The pressing on these hatches was noticeably wider. After February 1942, Krasnoye Sormovo 112 only issued the 'parallel pressing' type hatch and stopped issuing the earlier pressing type.

This F-34-gunned T-34 was lost in soft ground in the Byelorussian SSR. Notice that the turret has two periscopes indicating this to be a command tank. This is the same group of tanks as on page 92.

This Pre-War T-34 (F-34 Gun) became stuck trying to evade approaching Germans. It likely crashed into the bus and then attempted to climb the hill. Curiously, the engine hatch is missing just below the gun mantlet.

The T-34 in the foreground is the same as on page 97. It can be clearly seen that these tanks, along with the BA-10 in the background, were engaged in combat from the left of frame because all vehicles have some signs of damage.

This Pre-War T-34 (F-34 Gun) suffered a large-calibre penetration at the rear of the tank, along with multiple shots to the barrel. It is likely that this tank was lost in an uncoordinated attack that broke through the frontlines but met stiff resistance from 88-mm anti-aircraft guns or 110-mm field guns. The turret markings are believed to have been painted on by the Germans after the tank was knocked out.

A knocked out Pre-War T-34 (F-34 Gun) tank. The front left idler wheel has been dislodged from its proper position. Strangely, an ice cleat is stuck in the driver's hatch.

This Pre-War T-34 (F-34 Gun) was lost in the opening days of war with Germany. The white air identification triangles were a common feature of Soviet tanks but were usually restricted to the turret roof. Only a few examples of Soviet tanks were covered in more triangles. T-35 tanks of the 34th Tank Division was covered in up to fifteen white triangles. A blown-up T-34 sits behind this example, which itself has two turret periscopes, indicating it to be a command tank.

Along with the new F-34 gun, a new gun-cleaning kit had to be issued to the tanks. This was stowed on the front left fender in a large metal container. This had wooden racks for a two-piece wooden gun-cleaning rod, among other items such as track pins.

Even smaller changes were also done to the tanks, such as the exhausts being slightly shortened on tanks manufactured at KhPZ 183. Minor variation can be found with stowage and other minor items. Additionally, both KhPZ 183 and STZ added a second periscope into the turret of command tanks.

T-34s did not dispense with the two shovels; these were instead moved to the rear left hull. A bracket for the shovels was placed here as they had previously been stowed onto the front left fender, a space now taken up by the gun-cleaning kit.

The vast majority of the listed changes were conducted in February and March 1941, and many were done as soon as the F-34 was introduced. While pre-war production of the F-34-gunned tanks was relatively short, this was perhaps the longest period of stable T-34 production until much later in the war. Due to the circumstances of war, the T-34 was redesigned for efficiency, and many of the items introduced from May 1940 were revised or removed altogether to suit needs.

Up until the outbreak of war, both T-34s manufactured at STZ and KhPZ 183 were practically identical. It was only after the war that serious changes were made to the design separately at each factory to best suit their own production problems. However, the baptism of fire for the T-34 was done with pre-war tanks.

Attempting to cross rivers was another common way that T-34s and other tanks were lost. Here, two T-34s (both the Pre-War T-34 (F-34 Gun) type) and a camouflaged BT-7 (with a P-40 anti-aircraft mount) were abandoned in the soft mud of this riverbank. Notice the wooden boards used by people to access the tanks.

This T-34 was likely manufactured at KhPZ 183 and is a command tank, as indicated by the two turret periscopes. Notice that the turret hatch has a new pressing pattern in the centre to maximise the interior space of the tank and allow for the greatest gun depression possible.

A very rare photograph of a Pre-War T-34 (F-34 Gun) that is painted in camouflage. There is much debate on whether the paint scheme is two- or three-toned. Evidence suggests that at least one vehicle was painted in three tones. Due to the trees and the German soldiers, it is impossible to tell what this vehicle has.

A Pre-War T-34 (F-34 Gun) and a KV-2 heavy tank sit in a repair centre in June 1941. The T-34 was in the process of having the transmission replaced but appears that the contents of the tank were hastily put back in, likely intended for transport away from the front for repair. Notice the wood saw bracket hiding under the mesh cover.

Lost in July 1941, this Pre-War T-34 (F-34 Gun) displays the interesting turret roof markings often seen in the early war period. The white stripe was intended for friendly aircraft recognition.

This Pre-War T-34 (F-34 Gun) has lost the right-hand track set and suffered a great explosion. Notice that the DT-29 machine gun is still in the blister, which likely indicates it has been destroyed, hence why it has not been removed by German forces. Notice also the ice cleats and 76.2-mm shells strewn around the ground.

Here, a Pre-War T-34 (F-34 Gun) cast-turreted tank was knocked out and heavily damaged. The F-34 gun is completely missing, as is the driver's hatch. There are multiple penetrations to the front and clear signs of a fire having scorched the tank. Even the DT-29 in the hull blister was hit and bent.

The same tank as on page 103 and below. This is a command tank, as indicated by the turret periscopes.

A close up of the tank as seen above and on page 103. Notice the damage to the hull DT-29, as well as the details of the F-34 gun shield. Note that the turret DT-29 remains but has been hit by small arms fire.

14

T-34 DEPLOYMENT IN JUNE 1941

T-34s of the aforementioned types are the ones that would have been fielded in the earliest days of Operation Barbarossa. Therefore, it is worth debunking some myths about the T-34 at this stage in the war and exploring the earliest deployment. Indeed, while the T-34 has gained much acclaim and fame in the post-war era, the same assessment could not be made at the start of the war. In fact, the performance of the tank pre-war and during the first months of the war were evidently quite the mixed bag.

While most are aware that the T-34 was something of a shock to German soldiers, the T-34 was not a total enigma, nor was it a shock for very long—something that can be seen in period documents. For example, perhaps as early as July 1941, German anti-tank gunners learned to exploit weak areas of the T-34, namely the turret ring and the armour between the wheels and the tracks. Even the 37-mm rounds often quoted as being 'door knockers' could in fact disable a T-34 at close range of around 50 m.

Additionally, as in France a year previously, and in North Africa, the formidable Flak 88 anti-aircraft gun was increasingly used to engage ground targets. Although their anti-tank use was not common, a round from a Flak 88 could knock out a T-34 at ranges exceeding 1,000 m.

Perhaps the most disappointing feature of the early T-34 was its mechanical unreliability. It is not unheard of that T-34s, especially the earliest versions, would carry a spare transmission on the rear of the hull because these often broke. Whether this breakage was due to poor driver training, poor maintenance, or poor construction, the tanks nonetheless were riddled with flaws.

Furthermore, one only has to look at the opening days of the war to see the poor deployment and tactics used with the T-34, meaning that a flawed but still fairly impressive vehicle was effectively squandered due to the incompetence of crews and generals.

There were 832 T-34 tanks deployed in the Western Military Districts in June 1941, with 250 T-34 and KV tanks (both KV-1 and KV-2s) deployed in the Kiev Special Military District. It was in this sector of fighting that the T-34 was first encountered by the Germans.

This tank suffered an internal explosion that blew off the turret. The L-11 gun has also been 'banana peeled'. Reinforced 550-mm type track and hull hardpoints for fuel tanks indicate this to be a T-34 (L-11 Gun).

This T-34 (L-11 Gun and Turret Radio) was victim to a major flaw with the early T-34s—mechanical reliability. It is likely that the track snapped, causing the tank to be irrecoverable. Notice the pattern of the underside of the gun shield, which was redesigned in later L-11 gun shields.

The same T-34 (L-11 Gun) as seen below. One can clearly see the transmission being carried on the rear of this tank. Transmission failure was a common reason for breakdowns in the pre-war and early war tanks.

A T-34 (L-11 Gun), abandoned in the streets of Lvov in June 1941. This tank has a spare transmission on the rear engine deck. It is likely that the tank was being towed as there is a tow rope draped over the gun.

While 250 T-34s and KVs is an impressive number, the available T-34s did not have fully trained crews. Most T-34s that had been produced were waiting for crews and were in storage because of this. In fact, only 10 per cent of the T-34s had even partially trained crews, which was reflected in their poor combat performance in June 1941.

Germany invaded the USSR on 22 June 1941, and by 24 June, *Panzergruppe* 1 had discovered and began to exploit a gap between the Soviet 5th and 6th Armies, deployed in western Ukraine. The Red Army quickly moved to counter this advance, and four mechanised corps were used in this counterattack. The 8th and 15th Mechanised Corps fielded the largest number of T-34s and moved in from the south.

Some 181 T-34s and KV-1s were committed to this battle, but only half were available as the other half were in a non-combatant state. The Soviet counterattack began on 24 June, but it was a muddled and mishandled affair. Many tanks and units marched in gruelling 200-km columns to the front. The fragility of the early T-34's engine and gearbox meant that many tanks were simply abandoned because they could not be recovered. However, the tanks that did make it to the front proved to be quite effective in dealing with German tanks. The 76.2-mm L-11 and F-34 guns of these tanks could destroy any German tank they faced, and indeed successes were made.

Local successes, however, were never enough, and as the T-34s often found themselves attacking in small groups of tanks, they were easily divided and picked off one by one. However, several accounts of T-34s breaking though the German front lines and causing havoc prove that these tanks could take a beating.

Even though the Germans' 37-mm guns could disable a T-34 at close ranges, in the earliest days of the conflict, German gun crews had no experience of fighting against them. As such, the 37-mm gun quickly gained the nickname 'door knocker', as their gunners found their shells simply bouncing off T-34s and KV-1 tanks.

In T-34 attacks that were initially successful, it was often found that the T-34s would easily penetrate the first line of defences, but once they encountered 88-mm anti-aircraft guns, or even 110 mm artillery guns, they could easily be knocked out or disabled. To be sure, it was

Two T-34s burn after an attempted counterattack in June 1941. These two tanks broke through the German front lines, only to be engaged by heavy guns, perhaps 110 mm in calibre.

A close up of the burning T-34 lost during the failed attack on page 108. Multiple large penetrations can be observed, which might be from 88-mm or 110-mm guns.

only a matter of months (or even weeks) before German anti-tank gunners adjusted their tactics, but it took the Red Army perhaps over a year to begin to adjust theirs.

Only in very rare cases did Soviet tactics improve in 1941. It was not until later in the war, by November 1942, that new tactics and improved communications arose. However, even with poor tactics, in the winter of 1941, the Soviets managed to push back German forces from Moscow. This was achieved mostly due to the German forces being exhausted and fatigued by months of hard fighting and harsh winter and their overly extended supply lines. However, even by this stage, the Red Army was on the brink of defeat. It is in this context that the first production changes to the T-34 were made to speed up production and improve battlefield survivability.

Even the heaviest of German guns might have been overcome in the devastating early months of the war with superior tactics. The real issue was the incompetence of Soviet crews and lack of effective communication methods, meaning that attacks were often led by a single tank leading the rest of the tanks, and using semaphore (flag signals) to communicate with the rest of a company. Only one in five T-34s had radios, and these were often only used to communicate with the division commander, not individual tanks.

From 24 to 30 June, the Germans successfully fought off the Soviet counterattack, but in doing so lost 408 out of 585 tanks, whereas the Soviets lost every single tank they committed to the offensive—a total of 3,046 tanks, including the 181 T-34s and KV-1 tanks.

From June 1941 onwards, German forces began to learn how to tackle the T-34. Isolation was key, as many of the T-34s attributes could be simply overwhelmed. Additionally, more often, 88-mm guns and the new 50-mm Pak 38 guns were fielded at the front lines. Furthermore, German tanks and assault guns were converted into anti-tank weapons, but these only started to be fielded in 1942. Perhaps most telling of how badly the Germans perceived the T-34 threat were the crash courses implemented to create superior tanks, such as the Panther. Even though the T-34 in June 1941 made up less than 5 per cent of tanks in the Red Army, and as it was poorly fielded, its impact was sorely felt throughout the *Wehrmacht*.

A Pre-War T-34 (F-34 Gun) and HT-133 flame-throwing tank. These tanks are still burning and smouldering, being lost in July 1941.

Two Pre-War T-34 (F-34 Gun) tanks—one cast turret in the foreground and one welded turret in the background. Both tanks have the newly designed turret hatch. The tanks were bogged down and abandoned. This picture was taken after parts of the tanks were removed such as the exhaust covers, something that strangely seems to have been done by the Germans to all types of abandoned vehicles, but exactly why is a mystery—most likely for scrap purposes.

What would at first glance appear to be a T-34 lost in combat is actually a tank used for infantry anti-tank training. The vehicle was set on fire with flame units by attacking infantry.

The same T-34 (L-ll Gun and Turret Radio) as on page 82. The T-34 ran over a Pak 38 anti-tank gun. The track is initial production, but as seen from the front, a few links are the newer 550-mm reinforced type.

15

PREFACE TO WARTIME PRODUCTION CHANGES

With the counterattacks beaten off and the majority of the Red Army's tank force made up largely of the small and obsolete T-26, which was being utterly decimated across the outer Soviet Republics, production of vital war materials had to be frantically increased, including the T-34. As such, the People's Military Council met to discuss the war situation.

On 2 June 1941, Resolution 1ss was passed. This resolution gave permission for KhPZ 183 and STZ to increase the production of the T-34 and focus all efforts on production. In addition, Factory No. 112 (also known as 'Krasnoye Sormovo' or 'Gorky') was ordered to cease production of ships and begin production of T-34s. This resolution was passed three days after the German invasion of the Soviet Union.

As KhPZ 183 was the home of the T-34, all changes had to officially be approved from this factory. In reality, this was not the case. KhPZ 183 tanks were supposed to be the baseline that all T-34s from other factories had to follow. However, each factory made changes to the basic T-34 design to best suit the needs and capabilities of the plant. Initially, all changes to the T-34 were officially frozen, but as the war progressed, changes began to be implemented to either speed up production or improve the battlefield performance of the T-34. Many of the early war changes were those requested on the June 1940 change list for the T-34 but were postponed due to the T-34M's expected release. Additionally, some of the changes made were initially intended for the T-34M.

It should be noted again that almost all the documents for the changes made are missing or unpublished. Therefore, the majority of the changes have been dated with help of the photographic record. In addition to this, stocks of older items in factories were always used up in conjunction with new items, meaning tanks could be fielded with a confusing mixture of items. Furthermore, factory rebuilds were not uncommon, which sometimes complicates matters further.

However, with the context of the early months of Operation Barbarossa now established, we resume the narrative of T-34 production changes at KhPZ 183.

16

KhPZ 183: JUNE–SEPTEMBER 1941

From 22 June 1941, KhPZ 183 began to increase the output of the T-34. Initially, in late June, these tanks would be identical to their pre-war counterparts. Quickly, however, changes began to be made from a mixture of new and improved parts designs left from the now-cancelled T-34M and new requirements from the front lines.

Two T-34s lost in late July 1941. Notice that the T-34 on the left has a turret hatch lacking the hole for the POP periscope.

A Pre-War T-34 (F-34 Gun) lost in late July 1941. This T-34 has the new turret hatch. The number '503' was likely drawn on by German forces. The turret air extractor fan in front of the periscopes is on a hinge and is open in this photograph.

T-34 (KhPZ 183 REDESIGNED STOWAGE)

In late July, KhPZ 183 began to issue a new double chevron V-type track. This track was initially designed for the T-34M, and it was produced in small numbers for the upcoming prototype T-34M. However, it was never used on the T-34M because this prototype tank never entered production, but it was almost perfect for the T-34.

This track had more grip than the old track, the reinforced 550-mm type, was noticeably thicker, but also 50 mm narrower at 500 mm. Every link of double chevron V-type track had a 'V' pattern on the exterior of the link. Toothed links had a small gap under this 'V', which was a casting sink for where the track tooth was, and toothless links had a single hole in the centre of the link. Only a small number of these tracks were manufactured as new patterns of V-type track were issued later in 1941.

In 1941, the double chevron V-type track was incredibly rare; far more common was the old track type, of which stocks were still plentiful. It slowly became more common until it became totally standard issue in 1942. Therefore, it is common to see new tanks with the old reinforced 550-mm type tracks at this stage of production.

At the same time as the introduction of the double chevron V-type track, the size and volume of the gun-cleaning toolbox were also reduced. It was reduced from 290 mm tall to 195 mm, and now only contained the gun-cleaning kit.

In June 1940, it was requested that the old pin-type towing clevises were to be replaced by a hook, and this was implemented in July 1941. Instead of the pin-type tow hooks (two triangular protrusions with a bolt to feed through the eye of the tow hook), a hook-type tow hook was implemented. This was a curved single hardpoint that the eye of the tow rope would be placed onto. A spring lock, originally absent, was placed above the hook to allow for a more secure attachment. This simplified the tow system greatly as these tow hooks were cast and required no moving parts (other than the small spring latch on later hinges).

This T-34 (KhPZ 183 Redesigned Stowage) has the early double chevron V-type track. This very early example has the 'V' pattern on every track link. This track was designed for the T-34M and used on T-34s shortly after the project was cancelled. The turret is the early type, with a six-bolt access door in the turret.

Another example of a T-34 with the double chevron V-type track. This tank ran over a German truck, tipped over, caught fire, and is still smouldering. The turret is facing the rear.

This T-34 was lost in August 1941 and is photographed here in the winter of 1941. The tank is equipped with the T-34M double chevron V-type tracks.

The same T-34 as seen above. The snow has brought out some of the highlights of the tank. Notice the track pattern and the bolts on the glacis plate.

Two T-34 (KhPZ 183 Redesigned Stowage), with the early type turret, but both have the new tow hooks, as seen on the rear of the tanks. The tank in the foreground has one jack, but no hull-mounted jack block, indicating that this tank had two jacks, but one has gone missing.

This T-34 (KhPZ 183 Redesigned Stowage) has two new hooks but has two jacks, with the jack blocks being stowed on the rear fenders, implying it is an earlier example of a redesigned stowage vehicle. The white hexagons are a Soviet marking, but the numbers on the hull side are German.

This T-34 is equipped with the new tow hooks, indicating that is a T-34 (KhPZ 183 Redesigned Stowage). Notice the jack block on the hull side. The tank is being inspected by various officers and what appears to be soldiers of their motorcade.

Another early example of the new two hooks implemented by KhPZ 183. This tank has the early driver's hatch, the turret is not yet the eight-bolt type, and a rubber-rimmed idler wheel—clear indicators that this is a T-34 (KhPZ 183 Redesigned Stowage). Notice the faded Soviet divisional marking on the turret.

A T-34 (KhPZ 183 Redesigned Stowage) lost in September 1941. A spent 76.2-mm casing sits on the turret roof of the tank. Multiple small penetrations can be seen on the turret hatch, likely 37-mm hits. The tank has two periscopes, indicating this was a command tank.

In late August 1941, the toolset was simplified and rearranged. KhPZ 183-made tanks were issued with only one jack and jack block. The block was placed on a new bracket on the hull right side just behind the jack. The track toolbox was moved from the left side to the right side. This placed the jack above the track toolbox.

T-34s manufactured at KhPZ 183 from this time until the introduction of the eight-bolt turret can be known as 'T-34 (KhPZ 183 Redesigned Stowage)', seeing as though these stowage changes are a key identification feature of the type.

T-34 (KhPZ 183 8-BOLT TURRET)

In general, as the production of the tank increased, new methods at all the plants were explored to simplify and speed up production. After items from the T-34M were implemented and the stowage was changed to be simpler, more major changes began to be made to the actual design of the tank.

A new turret for the T-34 began to roll out of KhPZ 183 that was later used by STZ. This new turret was welded with a separate turret face with interlocking plates like earlier turrets, and from the front, it looked identical to a standard T-34 turret. The main difference was to the rear of the turret.

The same T-34 (KhPZ 183 Redesigned Stowage) as seen below. This tank has many features that are of interest. Noteworthy are the gear covers, tow hooks, jack block, and the location of the track tool kit. All of these items, with a lack of an eight-bolt turret, indicate that the tank is of the July 1941 production batch.

The same T-34 (KhPZ 183 Redesigned Stowage) as seen above, with a Maxim machine gun's ammunition belt hanging from the gun. Snow has begun to blanket the area. Notice the redesigned rear gear covers, introduced as early as August 1941. The tank was dismantled partially by the Germans. Notice also the white aerial identification stripe on the turret.

An early example of a T-34 (KhPZ 183 8-Bolt Turret). The turret was redesigned for simplicity, as this new turret did not require any machining at the rear to bend the turret plates. Notice the jack block on the hull side and the track tool kit, too. The '5' on the turret is presumably German.

A T-34 (KhPZ 183 8-Bolt Turret) stuck in some trenches, near an oil field. The turret number is likely of Soviet origin and was done hastily. The person inspecting the tank on the right is a Ukrainian volunteer working for the Germans.

The turret rear was designed to omit the two bends needed on the rear of the turret plate, so therefore the gun removal hatch was much wider and was now attached to the turret with eight bolts. This meant that the turret was slightly longer towards the rear, and it was far easier to manufacture. This turret is often called the 'simplified', 'wide back', or 'eight-bolt' turret, but for our purposes, tanks of this type will be known as 'T-34 (KhPZ 183 8-Bolt Turret)'.

This change was implemented in late July 1941 at Mariupol Metallurgy Plant, first fielded in August on KhPZ 183 tanks. It should be noted that cast turrets were still being produced and were mixed in among the new turrets on these hulls. It should also be noted that cast-turreted tanks issued at the same time as the new eight-bolt turrets would have looked like T-34 (KhPZ Redesigned Stowage). Additionally, stocks of older turrets were also used in conjunction with the eight-bolt turret, and the earliest known eight-bolt turreted tanks might not have had redesigned stowage. These vehicles would have been incredibly rare, however.

This new turret construction method took out two bends of the rolled turret armour while retaining the ability to remove the turret rear for gun removal. Even though this change was small, it impacted production. The turret was first issued at KhPZ, but STZ began to also receive the turret. After Mariupol Metallurgy Plant stopped distributing parts due to the proximity of German forces to the factory, STZ had to manufacture their own version of the turret (which will be discussed later). Interestingly, many sources claim the eight-bolt turret to be an exclusive STZ feature, but this is false as is clearly shown by photographic evidence.

Next, the machine gun blister's face was redesigned for simplicity. Originally, to attach the ball jig for the machine gun, a horseshoe faceplate was placed onto the front of the MG position. This was replaced with a round-type face. This used the same number of bolts to attach it to the MG position but was simpler to produce.

This T-34 has fallen into a small ditch. Notice the subtly different air filter cover on the turret roof that is welded on. This tank is a T-34 (KhPZ 183 Redesigned Stowage), as proven by the jack on the hull side, in conjunction with the hardpoints for fuel tanks.

A T-34 (KhPZ 183 Redesigned Stowage). Notice the placing of fuel tank hardpoints on the fender of the tank. This tank also has newly designed front fenders.

The electrics of the tanks were also rethought, and the hull-mounted headlights were redesigned. Still retaining the left-hand light on the glacis plate, the right-hand light was removed entirely. This was also done in August 1941. Later in production, after the move to UTZ 183, but before the implementation of the hexagonal turret, headlights were removed entirely, then re-introduced.

When the new eight-bolt turret was implemented, a new V-type track was also issued. Rather than every link having a cast 'V' onto the face, only toothed links now had a cast 'V'. The toothless links had a single vertical ridge cast instead. This became more common as 1941 progressed, eventually becoming standard by April 1942. This type of V-type track can be called 'V-type 1941' track.

The more famous waffle track was not introduced on the T-34 until late 1941, and not introduced on KhPZ 183 T-34s until after the evacuation to the Urals in October 1941.

One thing that never changed at KhPZ 183 (at least, not until after the plant's evacuation) was the pressed-type rubber-rimmed road wheels.

Another small yet important change was those done to the air intakes for the radiator. The old slats were replaced with a much simpler design. This was implemented between late August and early September, like most aforementioned changes.

As the war continued, the number of external fuel tank hardpoints for T-34s made at KhPZ 183 increased, with various changes taking place in a similar timeframe. From December 1940 to August 1941, hardpoints for four fuel tanks were provided. This increased to five in late August 1941. This was achieved by moving the hardpoints for the existing four fuel tanks forward to allow for an extra fuel tank at the rear. This was not done to all tanks, though. Furthermore, the number of fuel tanks on KhPZ 183 T-34s did not exceed the number being issued to STZ manufactured tanks.

A close-up of a cast turret of a T-34 (KhPZ 183 Redesigned Stowage). Notice that the mantlet above the gun sight has been shot at with rounds that did not penetrate. One penetration can be seen on the mantlet nose just to the bottom right of the gun.

Another T-34 (KhPZ 183 Redesigned Stowage) lost just before the first major snows fell for the winter of 1941–1942. Notice the redesigned tow hooks. The rear of the hull has been painted with a German road sign. Something may have originally been painted on the turret by the Soviets, but it is difficult to tell from this photograph.

A T-34 (KhPZ 183 8-Bolt Turret). Notice the radio antenna in the port, along with standard features of the redesigned stowage—most noticeably, one jack, the hull jack block, the moved track tool kit, and the eight-bolt turret. A *Stalhelm* is also sitting on top of a fuel tank, likely placed there by the German inspecting the turret. The hatch appears to have a German road sign painted on it.

A T-34 (KhPZ 183 Redesigned Stowage). This cast-turreted tank was likely manufactured in conjunction with the eight-bolt turrets, but no new name has been made for this as there were no changes yet done to the cast turrets. Just visible are hardpoints for exterior fuel tanks. Notice also the jack block. This tank appears to have suffered a fire and may have also suffered some road wheel damage.

This T-34 suffered an internal explosion that blew off the entire upper hull, dislodging the turret and engine. Notice the unusual fuel tank stowage. Several patterns were experimented with before fuel tanks were removed entirely. There is a dead crew member at the rear of the tank.

This T-34 (KhPZ 183 Redesigned Stowage) has a rare type of extra fuel tank loadout. Notice that the second fuel tank is placed higher on the hull side to allow for another fuel tank to be stowed on its side below it. This was not done often, and normally, only the four fuel tanks were carried.

While much rarer than the four external fuel tanks, some tanks were issued with hardpoints for an additional four fuel tanks on each side, increasing the exterior fuel tank count to eight. This was achieved by moving the current brackets up the hull side and placing the four additional fuel tanks (two per side) on their sides. This was like how STZ added so many fuel tanks onto the tanks, but STZ only placed the rear four fuel tanks on their sides.

The rarest type of fuel tank layout was issued about the same time as the previous type. Six fuel tanks could be stowed on the hull sides of the tanks, and an additional four tanks could be placed flat on the tank's hull side fenders. Not many tanks were issued fuel tanks in this configuration as they were prone to damage due to being placed on the hull fenders; this placed them close to the track and debris kicked up while driving.

It should be noted that often brackets for only five fuel tanks were issued from August, and the other methods of fuel tank attachment were far rarer. By the end of September, KhPZ 183 had reduced the number of fuel tanks on the exterior of the tanks back to the original four. In late September 1941, the exterior fuel tanks issued to KhPZ 183 T-34s were removed altogether.

A final small but noteworthy change was the introduction of simplified fenders at the front of the tank. These fenders retained the same shape and angle as the previous type, but they were much simpler, without the ability to remove the front portion. Interestingly, the simplest type of fender, without a curve, but a simple angle, was not implemented until the T-34-85 entered production.

17

KhPZ 183: SEPTEMBER–OCTOBER 1941

T-34 (KhPZ 183 LAST PRODUCTION)

The period from September to October 1941 saw the production of tanks that were ever more simplified. This simplification was justified as the *Wehrmacht* was not only close to Kharkov, but getting ever closer to Moscow, and the need for tanks was therefore great. As a result, more simplifications and improvements were made to the T-34, thus resulting in what can be termed 'T-34 (KhPZ 183 Last Production)'.

During the final month of T-34 production at KhPZ 183, the tanks were fielded with no hardpoints for external fuel tanks. These T-34s retained all the discussed stowage changes, such as a single jack and jack block, and the replacement of the track took kit from the left to the right hull side.

Perhaps the most important change to the KhPZ 183 T-34 design was the driver's access hatch. In late September, a new 'intermediate' driver's hatch was introduced onto the tank. The hatch was now cast, rather than cut from rolled plate. The periscopes were removed from the top of the hull, which was replaced with two periscopes in the hatch itself, which were protected by two armoured lids. This driver's hatch had been designed for the T-34M, but as the project was cancelled, many of the superior items designed for that tank could be salvaged and given to the T-34. The hatch was not identical to the T-34M's and had to be somewhat adapted to fit the T-34.

This 'intermediate' driver's hatch was attached to the glacis plate of the tank via the pressed bulge on the upper portion of the glacis plate. This meant that the hinges were still vertical rather than flat against the hull. This 'intermediate' hatch was designed to be placed directly over the glacis plates designed for the previous type of driver's hatch and therefore had to be placed over the pressed bulge in the upper portion of the cut out for the driver's hatch.

This 'intermediate' hatch would be replaced with the standardised hatch after a handful of examples were manufactured as the glacis plate was now not pressed with the bulge for the periscopes on either side of the hatch. This time, the top hinged portion was flush against the glacis plate.

The same T-34 as seen below. This picture was taken in 1942. Faint chicken-wire type winter paint can be seen on the turret just on the right of the vision port. It appears as though the tank was bogged down before being lost. The tank likely suffered an internal explosion.

This KhPZ 183-manufactured T-34 displays a number of new features, including the simplified turret, the redesigned V-type 41 tracks (which lack a 'V' on the toothless links), the new round MG blister face, the newly-designed grates for the air intakes on the hull sides, new idler wheels that lack rubber, and a jack block bracket on the hull rear right side. This tank is therefore a T-34 (KhPZ 183 Last Production).

This T-34 (KhPZ 183 Last Production) was deployed with the 11th Tank Battalion of the 1st Guards Special Rifle Corps. The tank was lost on 10 October 1941 in the town of Mtsensk. The tank suffered an internal explosion that has removed the turret from the turret ring. Notice the eight-bolt turret and the new driver's hatch, but with the pressing on the glacis plate as for the original driver's hatch.

This T-34 (KhPZ 183 Last Production) is equipped with the 'Intermediate' type driver's hatch. The hinge that the driver's hatch is attached to is placed above the pressed bulge that was intended for the earlier pattern of the driver's hatch. The tank has had most of the front road wheels blown off. Notice the lack of fuel tanks on the hull sides and the new driver's hatch. The turret has the number '113' painted on the turret.

A T-34 (KhPZ 183 Last Production). What makes this a KhPZ 183 tank is the lack of fuel tank hardpoints in conjunction with the late driver's hatch and the jack block. Notice that the rear three wheels have been replaced with STZ wheels. The turret has also been graffitied by an SS division, with the date '6.7.1942' indicating when it was knocked out.

The machine gun blister's face was again changed. However, this time, a simple reduction of the round face bottom portion was implemented. These tanks retained the tie-down points on the hull for snow cleats and tarpaulin stowage. Tanks would be issued in this configuration until KhPZ 183 was evacuated to the Urals from October 1941. Tanks were issued in relatively the same configuration after the move, but more changes were made shortly thereafter.

A redesigned pattern of cast turrets was issued for the first time in late September 1941. These turrets were meant to be 52 mm thick. This turret can be called the 'cast heavyweight' turret. However, the British Army was sent a single example of a T-34 in spring 1942 equipped with this pattern of cast turret but when they evaluated them, they noted a thickness of 60 mm, thus indicating the lack of quality control. Distinctive fillets can be found around the turret cheeks and under the bustle of these turrets, which were implemented to stop a void from forming during the turret casting process. When KhPZ 183 supplied the first kits to Krasnoye Sormovo 112, it would be this type of turret that was sent to them.

New radios were introduced from mid-1941 onwards. This was the 9-P radio. It used quartz stabilisation to achieve greater performance. The radio set did not have an integrated microphone system and rather relied on a laryngophone.

T-34 No. 6 (see page 144) after the tank finished burning. Technical features include a new driver's vision hatch, a round MG blister face, lack of any exterior fuel tanks, a single jack and jack block, a V-type 1941 track, and a subtly redesigned cast turret. Notice the casting number on the turret cheek which referred to which mould was used to cast the turret. The fence in the background is the fence that runs around the perimeter of the airfield.

After suffering a major internal explosion, this T-34 (KhPZ 183 8-Bolt Turret) is being used as an observation post as can be discerned from the pair of periscope binoculars poking above the debris in the rear of the tank.

18

T-34s WITH ZiS-4 57-MM GUNS

In 1940, the standard 45-mm 20-K and Model 1934 guns were deemed inadequate for modern anti-tank duties. Therefore, Factory 92 was ordered to begin work on a new gun with a calibre between 55 and 60 mm. It was meant for use as the latest standard anti-tank gun.

On 19 May 1941, testing began on the new 57-mm ZiS-4 anti-tank gun. This gun was designed by V. G. Grabin and was based on the 57-mm ZiS-2 field gun. It could fire a 3.14-kg warhead, and at a range of 1,000 m, the 57-mm ZiS-4 could penetrate 70 mm of armour at a 30-degree angle, whereas the 76.2-mm F-34 could penetrate 60 mm of armour at 1,000 m, although this figure is based on the plate being flat and not angled at all. Due to these excellent results, the 57-mm ZiS-4 gun was also to be modified for mounting on the T-34.

The only outward difference between the F-34 76.2-mm gun and the ZiS-4 57-mm gun was the barrel, with the latter's barrel being thinner, longer, and given a circular patch placed on the nose of the gun mantlet so that it could be properly fitted in place of the original 76-mm barrel. The breech, mount, and most of the internals were identical.

A prototype T-34 was tested with this new gun installed in April 1941. It was almost identical to a T-34 (L-11 Gun and Turret Radio), without the radio, shielding around the driver's hatch, and with the aforementioned longer barrel and a flat gun mantlet nose. Unsurprisingly, its trial results were highly impressive, but not without some problems.

Noticeable wear was spotted on the gun after only 100 rounds had been fired. In addition, the gun had very poor accuracy due to improper rifling on the barrel. This was rectified when the barrel rifling was re-bored. The T-34 with ZiS-4 was tested again later and accepted for production in July 1941. These production tanks are called 'T-34 with ZiS-4' in Soviet records, but they are sometimes incorrectly called 'Exterminators' or 'Fighters' (Russian: истребитель—'Istriebitiel'). This name has stuck as a post-war nickname, a common feature of Soviet Second World War tanks. Sometimes, these tanks are also called 'T-34/57', which is not an original name either.

The T-34 with ZiS-4 started production in September at KhPZ 183, and only ten were built before the project was cancelled. The chassis for these full production tanks would have been

'White 20' of the 21st Tank Brigade, commanded by Major Mikhail Alekseevich Lukin. His tank is a T-34 (KhPZ 183 Last Production) tank with a 57-mm ZiS-4 gun. The tank was damaged and abandoned in the village of Troyanovo, on the Volokolamansk Highway, on 17 October 1941.

T-34 (KhPZ 183 Last Production) tanks. These ten tanks were issued with the following chassis numbers: 895-20, 875-17, 0859-6, 469-07, 553-06, 609-20, 609-96, 875-14, 609-15, and 609-95.

Of the ten tanks manufactured, only two have been found in a mere eight currently known photographs as of writing this book. Their technical features are interesting but typical of the last production KhPZ 183 tanks. Both vehicles were issued to the 21st Tank Brigade, and therefore both were painted with white numbers on their hull sides. T-34 No. 2 was issued a ZiS-4 gun. The tank was issued the 'intermediate' driver's hatch, which used the glacis plate with a pressed bulge as for the earlier pattern of driver's hatch, but the newer, cast driver's hatch with two periscopes. The machine gun blister face was rounded. This tank was issued with a radio. The track issued to this vehicle was the V-type 41 track, with a 'V' only on toothed links and a simple vertical line on toothless links. Finally, the turret was the eight-bolt type.

T-34 numbered 20 also had a ZiS-4 gun. No. 20 shared many features with No. 2, but with some noticeable differences. The driver's hatch was the standard later type, with a hinge that was flush with the glacis plate. The tank had a radio as this was the commander of the 21st Tank Brigade's tank, and finally, this T-34 was issued a heavyweight cast turret. This demonstrates the variety that T-34s of the same production batch can come in.

The cancellation of the production run was due to many factors, including inadequate resources to manufacture the guns and the lack of AP shells for the 57-mm ZiS-4. Most importantly, the Red Army did not want to disrupt the production of a vital tank such as the T-34. After all, between June 1941 and September 1941, the USSR had lost 20,000 tanks. In October 1941, the number of Soviet tanks fell (for the first and only time during the war) below that of the *Wehrmacht*.

The ten T-34s with ZiS-4 were most notably fielded during the Battle of Moscow, by the 21st Tank Brigade on the Kalinin front (situated around the modern city of Tver). On 17 October 1941, the 21st Tank Brigade, unsupported by other units, air power or even artillery, succeeded in advancing, with haste, to the city of Kalinin, and nearly captured the city, suffering a tremendous loss of life, including two Heroes of the Soviet Union (Soviet citizens officially awarded this title). The story is so typical of early war Soviet assaults, and so well-documented, that it is worth reproducing here so that the reader can get a grasp of the sort of combat that the T-34 was engaged in during the early war, and hence why the tank needed so many changes.

19

BATTLE: THE 21ST TANK BRIGADE'S ASSAULT ON KALININ

THE GREATER BATTLE FOR MOSCOW

On 2 October 1941, after the destruction of the Smolensk pocket, the order was given by Hitler to begin Operation Typhoon. This was the order to advance to Moscow. Early German victories included the encirclement at Vyazma and the capture of Orel and Bryansk. These victories were swift and left open the road to Moscow.

The next major city the Germans had to take was Kalinin (modern-day Tver). This lay to the north-west of Moscow and was only 170 kilometres away from the capital. The city was taken with little resistance on 13–14 October 1941.

The capture of the city left the highway to Moscow dangerously exposed and open. It was therefore decided by the Stavka that the city should be retaken.

The city had two airfields. One aerodrome (an airfield without a runway allowing planes to take off from any direction) lay on the south-eastern corner of the city. The second airfield with a concrete runway was situated to the north-west of the city.

PRELUDE TO BATTLE

On 12 October 1941, the 21st Tank Brigade was ordered to assault the city of Kalinin.

The commander of the brigade was Colonel Nikolai Stepanovich Skvortsov, and the deputy commander was Alexander Sergeevich Sergeyev. The brigade was formed from the military school at Vladimir, situated to the east of Moscow.

The brigade received tanks on 5 October and was issued fresh T-34 tanks delivered from KhPZ 183, some sources state that some tanks were received from Krasnoye Sormovo 112. The brigade was listed as fielding ten T-34 tanks equipped with 76-mm guns (delivered from KhPZ 183), seven T-34s with 76-mm guns (delivered from Krasnoye Sormovo 112), ten T-34s with ZiS-4, two additional OT-34s with 76-mm guns but equipped with hull flamethrowers

A Ju-52 3M g4e German transport plane flies into the aerodrome at Kalinin. Ominously, the plane flies over a Soviet 76.2-mm F-22 gun. The 'boots' on the Ju-52s wheels are an attractive feature of the early aircraft.

(also from KhPZ 183), two HT-26s, five BT-2s, fifteen BT-5s and BT-7s, ten T-60s, and four ZiS-30 tank destroyers. This was the first time both ZiS-30 and T-60 tanks were deployed.

The 21st Tank Brigade was organised into three fighting groups. Group One was commanded by Mikhail Pavlovich Agibalov, Group Two by Mikhail Alekseevich Lukin, and Group Three by Iosif Isaakovich Makovsky.

The unit was unique among the Red Army at that time by being mostly made up of veterans. Due to the unit being put together from the tank school in Vladimir, experienced tank men were therefore available. Unfortunately, due to the severe losses earlier in the war, many more veterans had been killed. The commanders of the tanks had often fought in theatres such as the 1939 Khalkin Gol battles, the Winter War, and the early stages of the 'Great Patriotic War' (Second World War).

PLANNING

The order to attack was given to the 21st Tank Brigade from Lieutenant General Rokossovsky. His order read:

> Immediately move to the offensive in the direction of Pushkino, Ivantsevo, Kalinin with the aim of blowing the flank and rear of the enemy to assist our troops in the destruction of the Kalinin group of troops.

This was reinforced by orders from General G. K. Zhukov:

> To take possession of Turginovo, in the future the combined detachment to advance in the direction of Ilinskoe, Tsvetkovo, Negotino with the task of destroying the enemy grouping in the Kalinin region.

This assault on Kalinin was unsupported by other units or aircraft, and the entire task of liberating the city was put onto the shoulders of the 21st Tank Brigade. This was an impossible task, and the order was given because the Stavka had little actual knowledge of the full strength of the German forces at Kalinin and thought that the bulk of German forces in the area were further north.

SOVIET ORDER OF BATTLE

Group One was commanded by Captain Mikhail Pavlovich Agibalov, an experienced soldier who had risen through the ranks of the Red Army after joining in 1932. His combat experience included the war with Japan and the Winter War with Finland, both in 1939. For his service in the Khalkin Gol battles, he was awarded the Order of Lenin (the USSR's highest award) and was also awarded the title Hero of the Soviet Union.

The assault of Kalinin was devised as a two-pronged assault. From the staging area at Turginovo, Group One would move west to capture Pushkino, then move north along the Volokolamansk highway to enter Kalinin on the eastern side of the city and attack the airfield and the main station.

This would also involve the destruction of the forward command post of German forces in the area stationed at Pushkino. Once at Kalinin, the Groups would split, with the first attacking the airfield, then moving into the city to help with its liberation. Group Two was to move into the city centre and capture the station, then move into the central city up to the River Tver.

The tanks of Group One were painted with white numbers on their hulls to help with friendly tank identification. Numbers 1, 3, 4, and 6 have been found, with M. P. Agibalov's tank being number 1.

Group Two was commanded by Major Mikhail Alekseevich Lukin, who, like Agibalov, was a veteran soldier. During the Khalkin Gol battles, he successfully led a raid that resulted in a large Japanese supply dump and many trucks and other vehicles being destroyed. He was also awarded Hero of the Soviet Union and the Order of Lenin.

Lukin was made commander of the 21st Tank Regiment of the 21st Tank Brigade and therefore was in overall control of the battle. Group Two was to also advance for the Volokolamansk highway, but to enter the highway south of Pushkino at Panigino. Here it would advance north at speed, linking with Group One, and attack Kalinin.

Lukin commanded a T-34 with ZiS-4. This tank was painted with a white '20' on the hull sides of his tank. His second-in-command of Group Two was Starshina Shpak, he was equipped with a T-34/76 with a white '21' painted onto the right hull side, right turret side, and on the rear of the turret. It is thought that there might have been tanks numbered 20 to 25 in this group, with the highest found number being '24'.

Group Three was commanded by Senior Lieutenant Iosif Isaakovich Makovsky, who was as well-decorated as his comrades. He had received the title Hero of the Soviet Union and an Order of Lenin for his actions during the Winter War.

Group Three was to move directly north along the Turginovskoye highway north and enter the city at a similar location to Groups One and Two as the two main roads almost linked up at Kalinin.

The Turginovskoye highway entered Kalinin to the north-east of the airfield, and Group Three could either go south of the field into the micro-district of Yuzhny or move further north to enter the city north of the station. Here they would link up with Groups One and Two to capture more key objectives in the city itself. The plan was made flexible to allow for different tanks to attack different areas if one group suffered heavy losses.

Group Three appears to have not adopted the numbering system on their tanks. However, no definitive pictures have surfaced of their tanks, therefore it is possible that tanks numbering from '31' exist. Group Three is also known as the 'Makovsky Shock Group'.

While the main attack was happening, this third group was to advance up the Turginovskoye highway and assist in occupying the villages to the south of Kalinin. It is thought that they were originally going to enter the city after it was recaptured, but the course of events meant that this never happened.

In total, twenty-seven T-34s and eight T-60 tanks were available for the battle. These tanks were divided into their respective groups and prepared for the attack. In theory, this was nine T-34s per group and two groups equipping three T-60s with a third with only two T-60s. It is unknown at present exactly how many tanks were in each group, however.

GERMAN ORDER OF BATTLE

Facing the Soviets were elements of the 1st Panzer Division (which had been ordered to move north to help in the Leningrad sector) and the 36th Motorised Division, plus a mixture of other German units.

In Kalinin itself was the German 660th Assault Gun Battery, who were resting there. Roughly 10,000 troops were stationed in the newly captured city. It is known that a day prior on 16 October, two Panzer battalions were stationed in the city, but the exact battalions are unknown.

The 36th Motorised Division is known to have deployed heavy guns of 105 mm in calibre in the village of Troyanovo, and the trucks carrying personnel engaged by the Soviets are also likely from this division.

This force of Germans was not prepared for or expecting a Soviet counterattack so shortly after taking Kalinin. That said, fortifications had been made to the train station, and the airfield at Kalinin was already requisitioned by the Luftwaffe. At the Kalinin aerodrome, *Stukageschwader* 2 was deployed. In this unit was Hans Urich Rudel, the renowned Stuka ace. Interestingly, his account of the battle was told in his autobiography. Additionally, at the Kalinin aerodrome, Ju-52 transport aircraft parked about the field, along with the older and outdated Hs 123 dive bombers.

Unfortunately, the German records on the official account of the Soviet counterattack are lacking greatly, with only a small combat report from the 36th Motorised Division mentioning the attack; therefore, the only documentation to refer to is that of Soviet origin. The Soviet documentation seems to be largely accurate, albeit with some typical wartime embellishment.

A StuG III Ausf. C or D of the 660th Assault Gun Battalion in Kalinin.

THE ADVANCE NORTH BY GROUPS ONE AND TWO

On the morning of 17 October 1941, the attack began. One tank had been lost during the move towards the city the day before due to an accident on crossing a pontoon bridge. The commander of this tank was Issac Okrane; his crew were killed in the accident.

From the village of Turginovo, Groups One and Two advanced north then west. Group One moved to capture the village of Panigino. Here, the main highway from Volokolamansk to Kalinin lay ahead.

The attack was signalled by three red flares fired into the air. Immediately after beginning the assault, the Soviet tank crews of Group Two struck upon luck. A large column of German trucks and personnel carriers was advancing north towards Kalinin; it had not noticed the Soviet tanks joining the rear of the column. Lukin ordered his unit to not open fire until they were discovered or until the time was right.

The same luck could not be said for Group One. The column of tanks advanced towards Pushkino and were due to break through to the highway at the village of Emelyantsevo. At this village, however, they were spotted, and German anti-tank guns opened fire.

The lead tank of the advanced guard was commanded by Lieutenant Kireev (thought to be Sergey Mikhailovich Kireev, although this is not clear), but his tank was hit and exploded, killing the crew. It is thought his tank was number '2'.

The second tank in the forward column was tank 3, commanded by S. Kh. Gorobets. It engaged and dealt with the German guns, leading Group One to the Volokolamansk highway and linking with Group Two.

The next major village north was the village of Pushkino. This was being temporarily used as a headquarters for local German forces. As the column passed through the village, the order to attack was given, and the Soviet tanks swiftly gained the advantage, destroying many German vehicles and routing many men. The village was taken, and the headquarters was destroyed. The groups advanced north, taking Kvakshino before hitting the village of Troyanovo.

No. 2 was commanded by Sergeant Sergey M. Kireev. This tank is equipped with a 57-mm ZiS-4 gun. Other features include a reinforced 550-mm type track, the eight-bolt turret, a lack of fuel tank hardpoints, the new driver's hatch, and the round MG blister face. T-34s with ZiS-4s were manufactured on the hulls of T-34 (KhPZ 183 Last Production).

No. 2 of the 21st Tank Brigade likely the day after the engagement. Take note of the details on the turret; the barrel length can be clearly seen in conjunction with the ring around the barrel, thus indicating the ZiS-4 gun. Notice that this T-34 with ZiS-4 has the redesigned gear covers as well.

By this time, the news had spread that the Soviets were advancing up the highway, and Ju-87 dive bombers were dispatched to engage the tanks. The column was attacked from the air, but reports conflict as to whether any tanks were lost due to bombing. Hans Urich Rudel was one of the pilots engaged in the bombing of the 21st Tank Brigade. He reported that he and his crew flew many sorties against the T-34s, taking off, attacking the tanks, then returning to the Kalinin aerodrome to quickly re-arm and take off again to engage the tanks once more.

Troyanovo was more heavily defended by the German forces, and the two groups faced a heavy wall of German anti-tank fire. It is known that 105-mm guns of the 611 Heavy Artillery Platoon engaged the Soviet force here. In this village, the tank of Major M. Lukin became disabled. The reports are unclear whether his vehicle simply broke down or was shot at. Whatever the case, the left track broke and the vehicle ended up in a ditch to the left of the road, stuck in the River Kamenka.

It was later claimed by his crew that Lukin single-handedly covered the escape of his crew, operating the 57-mm gun of his tank alone. He was killed in his tank, but no damage is known on the tank in photographic evidence other than the broken track.

The groups moved on towards Kalinin, now under the command of the leader of Group One, Captain Mikhail Pavlovich Agibalov. The column broke through to the village of Naprudnoe, 16 km from Kalinin. It was here that Agibalov was also killed.

The combat report tells a similar story to Lukin's: Agibalov's tank drove off the highway to the right. Here, he disabled a German fuel truck that blew up. His tank, now off the road and isolated, took heavy fire. The main gun of his tank was seen to have stopped firing, but the machine guns were still active. It is claimed that his crew bailed out, and to cover them, Agibalov stayed in the tank. The accounts of Major Y. A. Maistrovsky claim that after the machine gun fell silent, he was found in his tank with his pistol drawn, apparently having taken his own life.

'White 20', once again. The tank is stuck in the Kamenka River. Notice the distinctive ring around the 57-mm gun's barrel. Apart from the obvious gun change, very little is different on the 57-mm-gunned tanks compared to the last production KhPZ 183 tanks. Internal ammunition stowage was different, however.

No. 1, which belonged Captain Mikhail Pavlovich Agibalov. He led Group One that attacked Kalinin on 17 October 1941. His T-34 is a T-34 (KhPZ 183 Last Production), lacking external hardpoints for fuel tanks. Notice the white '1' in the middle of the tank's hull. Combat damage includes the snapped idler wheel and the damaged main gun.

GROUPS ONE AND TWO IN KALININ

Upon reaching Kalinin, Groups One and Two attacked the Kalinin airfield and the train station, which was also being engaged by Group Three. The group that attacked the Kalinin station was commanded by Senior Lieutenant Iosif Isaakovich Makovsky (deputy commander of the 21st TB), who was in command of Group Three, and received help from the remnants of Group Two.

The airfield is thought to have been attacked mainly by Group One. This group had a bit more success than the ones attacking the station. One tank commanded by Senior Political Instructor G. M. Gnyry drove up the Volokamansk highway with the main group of tanks where he destroyed some vehicles.

He then broke into the Kalinin aerodrome on the right of the Volokolamansk highway inside the city limits. Here, supported externally by other tanks, he successfully engaged enemy aircraft in the field where approximately fifty aircraft were parked. Gnyry's tank was likely tank number 6 due to the photographic evidence of the T-34s at Kalinin.

One of the tanks supporting him was commanded by Sergeant S. E. Rybakov. His tank drove into the micro-district of Yuzhny (the modern name for this location) and supported Gnyry. This is the southern road that connects the two highways south of the aerodrome. He was, however, surrounded and captured by enemy forces, but he later escaped. It is unknown what tank number he commanded.

Gnyry was not as lucky. Photographic evidence, along with the combat reports tell how the German dive bombers targeted his tank. A bomb fell in front of his tank, and it fell into the crater. When it fell, it took damage from the bomb, the driver's escape hatch was blown

No. 6 of the 21st Tank Brigade, commanded by Gnyry, who famously attacked the Kalinin aerodrome, destroying many aircraft. The tank is likely lost on the southern side of the airfield, facing east, a bomb landing in front of the tank, causing the tank to be damaged, and fall into the crater. This machine is a perfect example of what the last T-34s to leave KhPZ 183 would have looked like. Although the tank has been heavily burned (and still burns), the '6' can be seen on the hull side.

off, and the tank began to burn. His tank was disabled, and he was forced to abandon his tank. The crew in the hull was killed, but he and his loader escaped. Interestingly, Rudel tells of attacking tanks at the aerodrome too; perhaps it was even his bomb that disabled Gnyry's tank, but it will likely never be known.

This airfield at Kalinin was attacked by tanks of Groups One and Three. The airfield was situated to the east of the city, but the second airfield to the west of the city was not attacked. At the eastern airfield, at least sixteen aircraft are to be known to have been shot at or ran over by Gnyry.

While the T-34s of Group One were attacking the airfield at Kalinin, the unit was unexpectedly engaged by assault guns of the 660th Assault Gun Battery. During this engagement, Tank number 4 engaged a *Sturmgeschütz* III Ausf. A. The StuG III was commanded by Lieutenant Tachinsky, and the T-34 was commanded by Lieutenant D. G. Lutsenko, who, after sustaining damage to the gun barrel, rammed the StuG. This caused the StuG to ride up and sit on top of the T-34.

The ramming took place on the Volokamansk highway itself, and this allowed for the withdrawal of the remaining T-34s. After the T-34 rammed the StuG, the Soviet tanks apparently made their escape, but no. 4 stayed in its position with the crew refusing to escape the tank. The crew were forcibly removed from the tank by Germans using crowbars. Some sources claim the commander was shot, but there are no contemporary sources for this; indeed photographic evidence suggests the crew of no. 4 was treated well, despite the ramming.

One of the aircraft attacked by Gnyry during the assault on Kalinin. The engines have been removed, likely as the machine was to be cannibalised after the damage it sustained.

This T-34 (KhPZ 183 Last Production) is No. 4, which rammed a *Sturmgeschütz* III Ausf. A of the 660th *Sturmgeschütz-Batterie* outside of the Kalinin aerodrome. The commander of the T-34, Lutsenko, is being dragged out of the turret.

No. 4 about two or three hours after the ramming incident. The '4' is just visible behind a German soldier.

Lieutenant D. G. Lutsenko, commander of No. 4, after he had been forcibly removed from his tank. He is currently being searched by his German captors, including one of the crew members of the rammed StuG III. It is unknown what happened to Lutsenko and his crew, but evidence suggests that he survived the war as a POW.

Elements of Group One are known to have assisted in the attack on the central position of Kalinin. This was commanded by Staff Sergeant Stepan Khristoforovich Gorobets, who commanded the third tank in Group One. According to the Soviet report, his tank was painted with a white '3', but because his tank was not knocked out and therefore not later photographed by the Germans, it is unknown if his tank was a 57-mm or a 76-mm gunned tank (alternate sources claim it either way).

A combined number of eight tanks entered the city past the airfield into the suburbs. As some of the tanks headed towards the station, '3' of Group One drove with haste west past the station. It then took the tank north, crossing the railway lines far to the west of the action, then turned north, almost making it to the River Tver. The tank then turned east, and with speed, he drove the entire length of Kalinin. Along the way, it disabled guns and tanks, and successfully rammed a German half-track. Interestingly, it was reported that it rammed a 'light tracked vehicle', which in some post-war sources is claimed to be a Panzer III. This seems to be a typical Soviet embellishment. Here, it exited the city on the eastern side unscathed.

Other tanks were less successful, with seven tanks being lost with their crews fighting in Kalinin itself. Most of the crews that made it into the city were lost fighting at the station. T-34 21 was commanded by Starshina Shpak. His tank broke through towards Kalinin station. The tank likely entered the Kalinin aerodrome, but there are two entrances to this aerodrome.

No. 21 of the 21st Tank Brigade, commanded by Starshina Shpak, lost near Kalinin station. This tank had the old reinforced 550-mm type track and was lacking a '21' on the left hull side. This tank was issued with the old driver's escape hatch, as is known from other photographs. This is also a T-34 (KhPZ 183 Last Production).

Since Shpak was heading for the station, it is likely that he entered the aerodrome at the second, more northerly entrance, as this has a road that leads almost to the station.

After briefly entering the aerodrome, Shpak headed north and exited the aerodrome to cross two sets of railway tracks to approach the station. Here, the tank approached 'School Number 25', which backs onto the main railway lines at the station. The tank drove past the eastern side of the building, to then turn towards the north back side. This placed Shpak between the building and the railway lines. This is where Shpak's tank met its end.

Driving forwards, the tank fell nose-first into a drainage ditch. The nose of the tank balanced the chassis over the ditch, meaning that the tank was immobile. The crew had to bail out, and in the confusion, the crew was killed by infantry. Evidence suggests that the crew were not killed near their tank; they were likely trying to make it back to their comrades. Other T-34 crews killed in Kalinin were those of 'Vorobyov' and 'Maleev' (the only names that were given).

The attack eventually was broken off, and the tanks of Groups One and Two were forced to make their escape back down the Volokolamansk highway, and even back down the Turginovskoye highway, the road that Group Three advanced up. It is unknown during what time frame the escape was made.

No. 24, serving in the 21st Tank Brigade, is an example of a T-34 (KhPZ 183 Last Production), with the early driver's vision hatch, but lacking hull-mounted fuel tanks. This tank would have looked identical to No. 21 lost at Kalinin station. It is not known where No. 24 was lost. The tank is now a German field post as noted by the 'FP' (which stands for *Feldpost*) and the accompanying number, which appears to be '25108'.

ATTACK BY GROUP THREE

While Groups One and Two advanced up the Volokolamansk highway, Group Three advanced with haste up the Turginovskoye highway. Commanded by Iosif Isaakovich Makovsky, the group seems to have met little resistance until the village of Pokrovskoe. Here there was heavy resistance, but the group defeated the Germans and continued north to enter Kalinin.

Once in Kalinin, Group Three attempted to attack the main train station. It is known that some tanks assisted in the destruction of the airfield between the Volokolamansk and Turginovskoe highways. It is unknown from what direction Group Three attacked the station, but it was likely from the north-east as the Turginovskoe highway crosses the east–west railway lines.

The train station, however, was never successfully recaptured, as the location had been heavily fortified by the Germans. Group Three is assumed to have received help from the remnants of Groups One and Two as some of their vehicles are known to have been lost near the station. Here, Group Three advanced no further.

Many tanks were lost, and the remnants of Group Three were forced to withdraw back down the Turginovskoye highway.

WITHDRAWAL

When it became clear that the battle was swinging in favour of the German units, Regimental Commander G. I. Zakalyukin organised and conducted the withdrawal of Soviet forces from the Kalinin area down the Turginovskoye highway. Here, they set up positions at the village of Grishkino and the 21st TB's Motorised Rifle Battalion with light tank support was available to assist.

Over the next two days, major fighting broke out between advancing German units and the Soviets who had survived the assault on Kalinin. Makovsky himself was seriously injured on 19 October. At this time, he had taken command of the motorised unit.

The entire area was recaptured by the Germans and fighting involving the 21st Tank Brigade in this sector ended on 19 October 1941. Troyanovo, where Major General Lukin's body was, was likely recaptured on 17 October, but fighting continued around to the east. Lukin's body remained in the tank, and German soldiers looted the Order of Lenin that he had received for service at Khalkin Gol in 1939. His body was recovered by four boys from the village of Troyanovo and buried in a small wooded area. His body was later reburied in Kalinin in 1942.

AFTERMATH

In total, the brigade lost twenty-one T-34 tanks, three BT tanks, and a T-60 tank. The combat records of the 21st TB list enemy casualties as thirty-eight tanks, 200 motor vehicles, eighty-two motorcycles, seventy guns and mortars, twelve fuel trucks, and many soldiers.

The 21st Tank Brigade continued to fight over the winter months, but it was later brought into reserve on 5 January 1942.

The Traveling Palace, which was a palace for the Tsar when travelling between Moscow and St Petersburg, in Kalinin was used by the Germans as the gravesite for their fallen comrades. All of these graves belong to the men the 21st Tank Brigade killed.

Kalinin was recaptured during the massive Soviet counterattack in December 1941. During the German occupation, war graves were erected outside of the Travelling Palace in Kalinin. The two airfields had been requisitioned from the Soviets. Much of the city was destroyed, and Kalinin was the first major city liberated from the Germans.

Kalinin gave the name to the Soviet 'Kalinin Front', which was active from 17 October 1941 until mid-1943, when the German forces were pushed far away from Moscow.

From the outset, the cards were stacked against the men of the 21st Tank Brigade, and many people can make the case that the Soviet Union needlessly lost two experienced tank commanders and Heroes of the Soviet Union.

The attack, however, did tie down units that otherwise could have been used further afield. It is also true that the units attacked were severely shaken by the incident. It is quite possible that by sheer numbers, this was one of the most successful Soviet counterattacks conducted to date at that point of the war.

For the first time in the Great Patriotic War, a coherent brigade assault had been conducted where experienced tank crews assaulted German positions, not only destroying more vehicles than were lost, but also exploiting weak areas and using teamwork to take out the enemy.

It should not be forgotten, however, that the primary objective was never completed. The Stavka had not correctly briefed the crews on the size of the force at Kalinin and underestimated the numbers of troops here. Also, the attack was conducted with minimal infantry support.

Some sources claim that tank riders were present on a handful of vehicles at Pushkino; however, there is no contemporary evidence for this.

It can also be stated that the T-34s with ZiS-4 were not used in an effective role. The 57-mm gun was specially designed for tank hunting, and during this battle, the Soviet crews mostly fought guns and trucks—far more suited to a low-calibre heavy round. It is also interesting to consider some of the similarities of this battle to the Battle of Seseña—tanks totally unsupported by other units wreaked havoc on enemy forces occupying small suburban areas but made no strategic or tactical gains and also suffered some losses in the process. Perhaps the Red Army had not learned all of the lessons from Spain that it should have.

While the assault was ultimately a failure with regards to its original objective, schools have been named after members of the 21st Tank Brigade, and statues erected in their honour. It was not so much a physical victory, but it was certainly a victory for morale and of legends.

During the Battle for Kalinin, it is speculated that only two T-34s with ZiS-4 guns were knocked out—Lukin's and Kireev's tanks. This is perhaps confirmed by reports that in early 1942, the 18th Tank Division reportedly listed eight ammunitionless T-34s with ZiS-4 deployed with them.

While this was the last time the T-34 with ZiS-4 was fielded, the 57-mm gun project was not entirely dropped, with one tank being fielded with a modified ZiS-4M gun at Kursk in 1943. This tank did not see service, and the project was entirely dropped after the T-34-85 project began.

20

UTZ 183: OCTOBER 1941–FEBRUARY 1942

Resolution No. 667 was passed on 12 September 1941, which was permission for the KhPZ 183 to relocate to Nizhny Tagil in the Ural Mountains. The first train left Kharkov on 19 September. KhPZ 183 merged with Krasny Proletary Plant from Moscow, and a factory from Stankolt, to become Uralmash Tank Plant No. 183, also known as UTZ.

A Plated T-34 (UTZ 183 Initial Production) with the chicken-wire winter camouflage. The additional armour plate can just be seen on the front of the hull. The rear of the turret has blown out, and one can see the four brackets for the bolts.

The same T-34 as on page 152. The chicken-wire camouflage is obvious here. The tank is a T-34 (UTZ 183 Initial Production) with an eight-bolt turret and a glacis plate up armour.

The following day, on 13 September 1941, Resolution 4ss was passed. This was direct from People's Commissar of the Tank Industry of the USSR V. Malyshev:

In pursuance of the decree of the State Defence Committee of 12th June 1941 for No. 667ss on the evacuation of Plant No. 183 and Mariupol Plant, I order:

1. Director of the Plant No. 183, Comrade Maksarev to start evacuation of equipment and personnel of the plant No. 183 to the Uralvagonzavod square in the city of Gorbachev. Nizhny Tagil.

2. Establish the following procedure and terms for evacuation of plant No. 183:

    a) first stage—50% of the operating equipment used in the production of T-34 tanks together with personnel of workers and engineers.

    Evacuation finish by October 10, 1941;

    b) the second stage—the remaining 50% of the existing equipment used in the production of T-34 tanks and all other equipment of the plant engaged in the production of aerial ordinance.

    The second evacuation is to start after installation and commissioning of the items evacuated in the first stage.

3. To oblige the director of the plant No. 183 Comrade Maksarev:

    a) to ensure during the evacuation of the plant the production of T-34 tanks of seven pieces per day and two months after the complete evacuation of the plant, the release of fifteen T-34 tanks a day at Uralvagonzavod;

    b) to ensure the release of 50 engines per month one month after installation of the equipment and two months later—75 pieces per month;

c) immediately to send to the Uralvagonzavod brigade of engineering and technical workers, headed by the chief engineer of the factory Comrade Krivich for carrying out preparatory work for the placement, reception and installation of equipment and personnel of the plant No. 183;

d) inform me daily by telegraph about the progress of equipment shipment, route numbers, and their progress.

4. Director of Mariupol Plant, Comrade Ilyich Garmashov, to proceed with the evacuation of the equipment and personnel of the plant to the Uralvagonzavod in the mountains, Nizhny Tagil.

5. To establish the following procedure and terms of evacuation of the Mariupol plant:

a) the first stage—50% of the existing equipment of the plant, engaged in the production of parts for tanks T-34, together with the personnel of workers and engineers.

Evacuation to finish by 10th October this year;

b) the second stage—the remaining 50% of the existing equipment engaged in the production of parts for T-34 tanks, as well as all equipment involved in the production of air bombs.

Evacuation begins after installation and commissioning of the items evacuated in the first stage;

c) the equipment and personnel of the workers and engineers of the Mariupol plant, engaged in the production of armored plates, are to be evacuated to the Nizhny Tagil plant of the People's Commissar Committee, to the Uralvagonzavod and StroySem in the order according to Appendix No. 1.

The evacuation should begin immediately.

The transfer from Kharkov to the Urals was not a smooth one, with some machinery being lost along the way, presumably falling off the train. Regardless, most of the manufacturing equipment and tank parts were delivered to the new location, including some prototype parts. However, upon arrival in the Urals, there was not a factory waiting for the workers. As such, workers' accounts describe having to build their factory and their accommodation, all while making fresh tanks.

The factory was named Uralsky Tankovij *Zavod*, with the serial code '183', so therefore the factory's post-war nickname is UTZ 183. However, there were two Ural-based factories that produced the T-34: UTZ and UTZM, with UTZM beginning life as a subsidiary of UTZ 183, before producing their own tanks in 1942.

T-34 (UTZ 183 INITIAL PRODUCTION)

As predicted, the turnover of tanks was slow, with the first twelve tanks being manufactured from parts brought from Kharkov in late December 1941. From here, production slowly crept up in the first quarter of 1942, and it was not until May–June that the production levels of the plant reached that of the pre-move KhPZ 183.

Like previously at KhPZ 183, UTZ 183 did not manufacture every piece, so the construction process included many subsidiary factories. As hulls and turrets could not be delivered to UTZ 183 or STZ from Mariupol Metallurgy Plant, new, smaller factories had to be set up for such work. One such plant was UTZM, which would later manufacture T-34s wholesale.

During the move, one item that was lost was the tooling machine for the rolled armour

This T-34 (UTZ 183 Initial Production) suffered an internal explosion that blew away the turret, which is now on the right of the tank. The 'xxx' painted onto the rear of the tank just above the engine access hatch is actually leftover paint from the winter chicken-wire paint scheme as seen on T-34s in December 1941. The turret, now on the ground to the right of the hull, also shows some evidence of this pattern, too. V-type 41 track can be clearly seen on the tank.

type turrets. Therefore, shortly after the move to the Urals, the only T-34s being manufactured were ones with cast turrets. These can be referred to as 'T-34 (UTZ 183 Initial Production)' but can only potentially be distinguished from T-34 (KhPZ 183 Last Production) tanks based on the date of their photographs because these tanks were identical.

The welded-type turrets were briefly introduced in early 1942 after the tooling machine was presumably recovered, but few were made due to the implementation of the new hexagonal-type turret.

While production was slow, the plant tried to keep up with resolutions passed on the T-34, including the introduction of 15-mm plates onto the glacis of the tanks. These plates are very rare as production was terribly slow for the first few months of production at Uralmash (which will be discussed later).

It was ordered that twenty tanks were to be manufactured per month throughout October, November, and December, but even this small number was not attained; in November and December, ten and fifteen tanks were manufactured respectively. It was only after this period that production once again increased.

One item that changed during the move from KhPZ 183 to UTZ 183 was the drive wheel, which was simplified. The face of the drive wheel did not have elaborate rims around the cut-outs for strengthening and instead had six ribs extending from the hub to the rim.

A well-hidden T-34 (UTZ 183 Initial Production).

A rear view of the T-34 (UTZ 183 Initial Production) as seen above and on page 157. Notice the V-type 1941 track and the angled gear bulges.

The same T-34 as on page 156. Notice the simplified drive wheel—a clear indicator that the tank is from UTZ 183.

This T-34 (UTZ 183 Initial Production) was lost during the winter fighting around Moscow in early 1942 in an attempt to destroy the many salients created during the Soviet counterattack. The tank's turret, engine cover, and mesh radiator cover have been blown off. The distinctive chicken-wire camouflage can be seen painted onto the tank's side. The new pattern of drive wheel can be seen on the left of the frame.

Rare on the battlefield due to poor turnover, this T-34 (UTZ 183 Initial Production) was lost after a fire. The tank looks almost identical to the last production KhPZ 183 tanks, but notice here the simpler pattern of the drive wheel which a clear indicator that this tank was made after the move to UTZ 183. Notice the 76.2-mm shell casings discarded around the tank.

A T-34 (UTZ Final Early Turret) lost at the train station of Sakhnovshchyna. This is roughly halfway between Kharkov and Pultova to the south. This machine has a good example of V-type 1941 track. Notice the new blister face, but with an old 'horseshoe' mounting. This was fairly common. A collapsed water tower can be seen in the background left.

The same tank as on page 158. Notice the redesigned turret, with small fillets as to stop the armour from misshaping during the casting process. Notice the damage to the fender side.

A burning T-34 (UTZ Final Early Turret) that was at one point repaired with STZ road wheels. It is likely that the tank is a partial rebuild or at least had an in-field repair. Notice the rubber that has come loose from a road wheel.

T-34 (UTZ FINAL EARLY TURRET)

The chassis of the T-34 did not change dramatically; however, the turrets did. From December 1941, a new, larger turret had been approved for production and began to roll out of UTZ 183 from December. These tanks were very rare to begin with, but as production of the turrets increased, and stocks of older turrets were used up, they became the standard turret issued from UTZ 183 by June 1942.

The chassis changes will be discussed on pages 234–259, but it is important to note that the older turrets were still issued until stocks ran out. While rare, T-34s from UTZ can be found with much later features, such as a ball guard for the MG blister, an angled rear plate, and a mixture of road wheels.

An example of old parts still being used; the turret of this T-34 is clearly the early type on the hull of a T-34 (UTZ 183 Early Production Composite), as seen by the armoured cover for the MG blister. This tank is known as a T-34 (UTZ Final Early Turret). Notice that this tank does not have a headlight. The road wheels are either all pressed type or a mixture of pressed and cast spider type.

21

UTZ 183 PLATED T-34s

Increasing a tank's armour with additional armour plates was not a new thing. During the Winter War, 10-mm thick plates were added to the hulls and turrets of T-26s to make them capable of stopping Finnish 37-mm rounds. Some of these tanks were still available in June 1941 and can be found during Operation Barbarossa. Before the Second World War began for the Soviets on 22 June 1941, some of their modern tanks were also being considered for additional armour.

The formidable KV-1 had been issued additional armour plates for their tanks from May 1941, and it was not long before the same sort of sets were considered for the T-34. As such, KhPZ 183 drew up plans for a fully plated T-34 in July 1941. This consisted of 15mm thick plated that was bolted to the tank's body, like the plates issued to KV-1s. Two full sets were manufactured—one with no armour around the nose fillet and one with a fully plated nose.

The two T-34s chosen were standard pre-war F-34-gunned T-34s, and they were demonstrated in July 1941. The project was not continued, however, as it was found to be too time-consuming to produce. Additionally, the Soviets had not faced serious opposition regarding German tank or anti-tank guns, meaning that there was thought to be little need for the armour sets anyway.

Both fully plated T-34s were sent to the front, and similar plated projects were conducted on BT-7s (which were paraded on 7 November 1941). It is known that one fully plated T-34 survived until the Battle of Moscow in January 1942.

RESOLUTION 1062

Although the fully plated T-34 project was dropped, there was still a fear that the T-34's armour was not thick enough. After German 50-mm guns started fielding APDS (armour-piercing disposing sabot) rounds in late 1941, a desperate order was issued to the manufacturers of the T-34 to produce tanks with thicker glacis and turrets.

A front view of the fully plated T-34 from KhPZ 183 in a courtyard in Kharkov, July 1941. Notice the thickness of the plates. The apparent thickness is deceptive as there was a gap between the plate and the hull. Two full sets were manufactured and issued to two tanks. It is unknown what happened to them. (*Maxim Kolomiets*)

On 25 December 1941, Resolution 1062 was passed. This was the demand that T-34s should begin being manufactured with 60-mm-thick frontal amour. It was decided that the easiest way of doing this was to manufacture plates to cover the hull glacis plate and even include turret coverage. Changing the thickness of the armour during the manufacturing process would be too complicated and would inevitably disrupt production.

The decision to increase armour thickness was taken due to the fear that German tanks and artillery corps were fielding heavier guns and equipping their medium tanks with ammunition designed to specifically defeat the armour of the T-34. The ammunition that particularly scared the Stavka was the APDS. This is because the standard 50-mm anti-tank gun fitted to a Panzer III or used as a field gun could now quite effectively defeat the sloping armour of the T-34 at acceptable combat ranges.

The term 'Ehkranami' (экранированный) is the post-war name for the armour plates attached to the hulls and turrets of Soviet tanks to increase their thickness. The translation is literally 'screened', or 'shielded'. In Soviet documents, these updates are simply known as 'plates'. To call these tanks 'T-34/76E' as a blanket term is very incorrect. Reference should, instead, be done by the factory of origin, and then the plates type. Other tanks, such as the T-28 have, over the years, been named as such so often that they fall under the false term 'T-28E' or 'T-28Eh'. Therefore, to use the example of the following tanks, the tanks to be discussed here is best referred to as 'Plated T-34 (UTZ 183 Early)'—long-winded, but more descriptive and accurate.

This Plated T-34 (UTZ 183 Early) is painted in the distinctive winter camouflage seen during the Battle of Moscow, the so-called chicken-wire paint scheme. Evidence of this can best be seen from close inspection of the left side of the turret and the left fender. Notice the barrel that has been broken at the end, possibly by a misfire, or perhaps a German demolition charge down the barrel.

This Plated T-34 (UTZ 183 Early) displays additional armour on the glacis and under the nose plate. Notice the cut-outs for the bolts. A German anti-tank rifle lays against the tank. Notice the winterised German soldiers, some lacking helmet covers.

PLATED T-34 (UTZ 183 EARLY)

UTZ 183's plate programme was short-lived, and only a few tanks were equipped with it, though even these were only on the glacis plate. These were T-34 (UTZ 183 Initial Production) tanks, with the new driver's hatch, improved tow hooks, redesigned fenders, and lacked exterior fuel tanks. The plates applied by UTZ 183 were identical to the first type used by STZ. There were five separate plates covering the entire glacis plate. The lower plate on the nose was also updated. The lower glacis plate was manufactured with U-shaped cut-outs for the bolts on the front of the tank.

Resolution 1062 was rescinded shortly after its implementation as it was noted that German guns did not field APDS rounds very often, and many German guns still struggled to damage T-34s.

UTZ 183 was the only factory to manufacture hexagonal-turreted tanks and equip them with plates. Several photos exist showing two examples. These can be referred to as 'Plated' followed by the type of T-34 that it is, but this will be expanded on later.

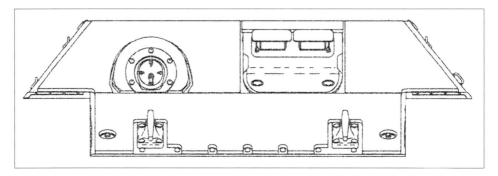

The glacis plate pattern used by UTZ 183. This plate was simple to produce and was widely used during early UTZ 183 production. This still meant, however, that not many tanks were given this type of glacis plate. This main distinguishing feature is the bolts on the glacis plate with cutouts on the additional armour plate.

This Plated T-34 (UTZ 183 Early) suffered an internal explosion that demolished the tank. Notice the plates on the glacis and nose, with distinctive cut-outs for the bolts. The tank was lost in the early spring of 1942.

A close-up of a Plated T-34 (UTZ 183 Early Production Composite), that can also be found on page 244. This hexagonal-turreted tank is from the earliest production batches, but the vehicle has the new angled rear. This is not uncommon as stocks of the old hulls were used up until entirely new parts were standard. The DT is clearly damaged, hence why it has not been removed by German forces.

OTHER UP-ARMOURED UTZ 183 T-34s

After the official plating programme was dropped, some UTZ 183 T-34s still received moderate to extensive hull plates. These were done purely for faulty glacis plates and was done both on factory fresh T-34s and rebuilt T-34s.

Furthermore, many UTZ 183 T-34-85s were equipped with so-called bedspring armour during the Battle of Berlin. This was an attempt to mitigate the threat of German anti-tank rockets, especially the ubiquitous and stealthy *Panzerfaust*. This armour consisted of a metal rectangular frame, with wire (like chicken wire) threaded throughout. The most famous example shows that three pieces were placed on the turret (two on one side, and one on the other), a single piece above the mantlet, and three pieces were also placed on the hull sides and the engine deck.

It is unknown how effective these armour add-ons were, but the 2nd Guards Tank Army fighting in Berlin reported that 22.8 per cent of the T-34s lost in Berlin were lost due to anti-tank rockets, compared to 88-mm guns at 29 per cent. It is fair to say that if one compares these to similar modern-day attempts (such as in the Syrian Civil War) to mitigate shaped charges, the so-called bedspring armour packages were less effective than desired, and likely helped only with crew morale.

22

STZ: JUNE 1940–OCTOBER 1941

The city of Tsaritsyn had been one of the first major cities in the USSR to industrialise after the Bolshevik victory in the Russian Civil War in 1922. The city's defence in the Russian Civil War was organised by Stalin, and therefore after the victory, the city was named in his honour—Stalingrad.

STZ was one factory within Stalingrad, but T-34 production took place across the city, with many factories within the plant. One such factory was Factory 264, the Stalingrad Ship Works. Once the order to begin T-34 production was given, it began construction of armoured hulls. Other factories that supplied STZ were the Barrikady Gun Factory, the Red October Factory, and the Mariupol Metallurgy Plant.

STZ was ordered to begin manufacture of the A-34 in December 1939, before the A-34 prototypes had even been made and tested. The organisation of the production of the tank was slow, with the first complete tanks being manufactured only in January 1941, although it is thought ninety hulls were manufactured before this date. Additionally, these tanks could have been unarmed, as it has been suggested that no STZ T-34 was equipped with the L-11 gun. No evidence has been found either way, but as the F-34 gun was adopted in February 1941, it is likely that only a few dozen STZ T-34s were equipped with the L-11 gun if STZ ever did issue the L-11 gun.

Initially, production was kept along the same lines as KhPZ 183, and therefore it implemented the same changes that KhPZ 183 did.

From January to June 1941, no more than fifty to 100 tanks were manufactured at the plant per month. However, it was after the invasion of the USSR on 22 June 1941 that led to a gearing up of T-34 production at STZ. In June and July, ninety-three and ninety-seven tanks were manufactured respectively. Then in August, 115 vehicles were manufactured. For at least the first couple of months after the war broke out, the T-34s produced at STZ would have looked identical to T-34s produced at KhPZ 183. Only with an inspection of the pressed chassis number on the nose of the tanks would one truly know the tank's origin. However, it is thought that KhPZ 183 was the first factory to issue a second PT-4 periscope in the turret.

What could be an STZ-manufactured T-34, lost in early September 1941. STZ did not make any major changes to the design of the T-34 until August 1941. Notice the number '8' painted onto the turret side, which is Soviet in origin. Shortly after this tank was manufactured, production changes began.

It should be noted that a memo dated 10 January 1941 outlined STZ's poor output and quality control of cast items. One problem was the poor design of the 'Reinforced 550-mm Type' tracks that were made worse by STZ's poor manufacturing process. These were suggested to be a major reason for the limited production at STZ (and KhPZ 183, for that matter).

T-34 (STZ REDESIGNED STOWAGE)

In August 1941, as with KhPZ 183 tanks, the stowage box was redesigned to be reduced in size, but from late August 1941, the first changes began to appear onto STZ T-34s that make it possible to identify these tanks. The earliest change to the design was the exterior fuel tanks on the sides of the chassis. Initially, only four tanks were carried on the exterior of T-34s, two on each side, but now STZ made tanks began to be issued with ten such fuel tanks.

There was some variation with the fuel tank placement, but they were usually placed towards the front of the tank, and a single fuel tank was placed properly onto the hull side. Then rearwards, four fuel tanks were placed in pairs on their sides to allow room for these tanks.

It is unknown how many T-34s rolled out in this configuration, which can be referred to as 'T-34 (STZ Redesigned Stowage)', before the new simplified KhPZ 183 turrets were used on the tanks.

A T-34 (STZ Redesigned Stowage) abandoned after suffering a drive wheel malfunction. Notice the bracket at the rear of the tank, above the exhaust shrouds, which is for the shovels. The gun-cleaning tool kit is the earlier pattern. The brackets for the extra fuel tanks in conjunction with the new shovel locations is the key feature of these STZ tanks. The turret is painted with a white circle, and a white stripe has been painted on the rear plate of the tank.

A STZ-manufactured T-34, as indicated clearly by the extra fuel tanks. These tanks can be called T-34 (STZ Redesigned Stowage). This tank suffered a huge explosion that dislodged the turret and engine. Notice that this T-34 is a part of the same regiment as the tank above, with the same three-digit turret number scheme.

A T-34 (STZ Redesigned Stowage). Notice that the front idler wheel is missing, so the track was attached around the front road wheel. Notice the fuel tank brackets on the hull side. The tank was likely lost in October 1941.

T-34 (STZ 8-BOLT TURRET)

Many T-34s get misidentified as STZ tanks simply for having the eight-bolt rear, but both KhPZ 183 and STZ used this turret because they were manufactured at the Mariupol Metallurgy Plant and sent to both factories. Identification at this time should instead be made via the fuel tanks on the hull sides, and if possible, the following changes—two shovels stowed on the rear of the tank and two metal brackets above the exhausts on the rear plate. These changes were likely made in early September 1941.

T-34s manufactured at STZ up until October 1941 can still be very hard to distinguish apart from T-34s manufactured at KhPZ 183. Some items, however, such as tow ropes with cast eyes, are also indicators that the tank's origin was in fact STZ. Very shortly after this, major changes were made to T-34s from STZ. These tanks can be called 'T-34 (STZ 8-Bolt Turret)'.

T-34s in the described configuration were seen in Moscow on the 7 November 1941 parade and can be distinguished most easily by their side fuel tanks configuration and the rear shovel stowage.

Lost in October 1941, this T-34 (STZ 8-Bolt Turret) was one of the first STZ T-34s equipped with the simplified eight-bolt turret. It still retains the early tow hooks, a 'horseshoe' blister face for the DT position, and the early driver's hatch. The tank was likely lost due to a fire, as discerned from the burned-out wheels.

This T-34 (STZ Redesigned Stowage) was knocked out in combat and one crewman died at the side of the tank after bailing out. There is a bracket at the rear of the tank, above the exhaust shrouds, that is for shovels. Notice that the gear bulges are the KhPZ 183 angled-type, and the tow hooks are the new hook type.

23

STZ: OCTOBER–DECEMBER 1941

While all changes to the design of the T-34 had to be run by KhPZ 183, in October, STZ began making changes to simplify the production process of the tanks without the permission of KhPZ 183. Due to the lack of rubber in Stalingrad, the first noticeable change to T-34 production was the removal of the pressed-type road wheels and their replacement with STZ cast-type road wheels with internal shock absorbers.

An interesting example of an early T-34 (STZ Cast Wheels) with the turret slogan 'Chapayev' ('Чапаев') has the new steel cast road wheels and 550-mm waffle-pattern track, but still retains the pin-type tow hooks.

T-34 (STZ CAST WHEELS)

Stalingrad had some of the USSR's best casting plants, and therefore as much of the tank that could be cast was cast. Initially, only road wheels were cast without rubber, but shortly thereafter, the drive wheel and idler wheel were also cast. Tow rope eyes were cast along with other smaller items.

The new cast road wheels lacked any external rubber but had internal shock absorbers. The wheels had ten circular cut-outs each, with ten strengthening ribs that flanked these cut-outs. The wheels used the same hub cap as the previous wheels.

While this did help the shortage of rubber, the harmonics created while running on steel alone caused the inside of the tack to be very unpleasant and even caused damage to the internals of the tank. Cast road wheels began to be issued from 29 October 1941.

As the war began and production increased, STZ still began to follow the same design changes to KhPZ 183. The tow hooks were changed to the hook-type tow hook from the pin-type hook. The STZ hooks were simpler still than those of KhPZ 183, however. Rather than having a spring lock above this hook to allow for the tow rope eye to lock in place, a simple metal spacer was welded vertically directly onto the glacis.

The STZ T-34's air intake grilles on the hull rear side was still the early type, along with the early type of driver's hatch.

Very shortly, if not at the same time as the implementation of steel road wheels, new 550-mm waffle-pattern tracks were developed. All STZ T-34s after this time were equipped with them. STZ never moved onto using the 500-mm waffle-pattern track, but the 550-mm and 500-mm track were interchangeable.

A T-34 (STZ Cast Wheels). This tank is one of the earliest examples, with rubber idler wheels, and the early pattern of blister face. Notice the STZ exclusive tow hooks. The eight-bolt turret is also clearly visible.

The same T-34 (STZ Cast Wheels) as on page 172. Notice the two new hooks, coupled with the reinforced 550-mm type track. There is a shovel still in place on the rear of the exhaust plate. It is likely that the tank broke down, so the crew removed the engine deck while attempting to fix the problem but ultimately abandoned the vehicle altogether.

A cast turreted T-34 (STZ Cast Wheels). Notice the plugged radio port, along with the pattern of the fenders.

This T-34 (STZ Cast Wheels) is one of the tanks that was still manufactured with rubber parts such as the rubber idler wheel. This tank also has the new STZ-type tow hooks with no spring lock, but a simple welded piece of metal to act as a lock. (*Sergey Lotarev Collection*)

From early November 1941, the new pattern of air intake grilles over the radiator area was introduced like those at KhPZ 183, which had moved to UTZ 183 in October 1941. Interestingly, KhPZ 183 had been issuing these new grilles since September 1941.

It is in this phase of production that the changes at KhPZ 183 began to affect STZ less and less. In late September, KhPZ 183 decreased the number of exterior fuel tank hardpoints to none, whereas STZ was still issuing T-34s with ten hardpoint attachments.

Tanks with all these changes can be known as 'T-34 (STZ Cast Wheels)', with the wheels being a particularly useful identification feature.

T-34 (STZ INTERLOCKING HULL)

One of the biggest and most noticeable changes made to STZ hulls was the new method of construction. On normal T-34s, the glacis and rear plates were simply bolted, then welded onto the side plates of the hull, but this was not the case at STZ. This was done in part due to the fact that hulls had stopped being shipped from the Mariupol Metallurgy Plant.

Tanks originally began to roll out with interlocking front plates in October 1941. This was swiftly followed by interlocking rear plates. This method of construction was also done at Krasnoye Sormovo 112, but only onto the front plate. The interlocking plates construction was adopted due to the appearance of new methods of welding the parts together and because it helped with structural integrity. These tanks can be referred to as 'T-34 (STZ Interlocking Hull)'.

A whitewashed T-34 (STZ Cast Wheels) lost in the winter months of 1941. Notice the idler wheel is lacking rubber, and the tank has 550-mm waffle-pattern track. The tank still has the early driver's hatch. The DT machine gun is still in the tank, indicating that the photo was probably taken not long after the tank was knocked out, as most had their armaments removed by the Germans if they were still intact.

This T-34 (STZ Interlocking Hull) was lost in the winter of 1941 and photographed in the spring of 1942. Notice the whitewash paint that clearly shows where the fuel tanks were once situated. The interlocking plates can just be seen on the front hull, too. Notice the early pattern of radiator intake covers.

This T-34 (STZ Cast Wheels) exploded, revealing the interior. Notice the vertical springs and the fuel tanks between them. The fuel tank between the second and third spring is missing, likely being the one that exploded. The tow hooks are the newer pattern, being thicker than both the type with the fillet and the type without the fillet.

The new type of driver's hatch (with the two periscopes protected by armoured covers) was implemented at the same time as the interlocking plate construction. A second periscope was also installed onto the turret. Additionally, a new forward-facing driver's periscope was placed to the right of the driver's hatch. This 360-degree rotating periscope was added due to the lack of suitable vision for the driver. It sat on a small blister welded onto the hull.

STZ from October to December 1941 was the only plant producing T-34s in significant numbers because of the evacuation of KhPZ 183. While Krasnoye Sormovo 112 was operational, their turnover was poor (to be discussed later), as was UTZ 183's. Therefore, it fell to STZ to bear the burden of T-34 supply to the front. As another side-effect of the evacuation of the Mariupol Metallurgy Plant, parts that had been shipped to STZ no longer came. Therefore, STZ had to manufacture more of its own parts and subsequently ended up simplifying or removing them altogether. Only from the beginning of 1942 did production levels of T-34s from other plants begin to increase greatly.

As an interesting detail, due to the lack of the V-2-34 engines being manufactured, 209 T-34s manufactured by STZ between September and December 1941 were powered by the M-17F engine. The M-17 was a copy of the BMW VI series engine that was initially intended for airships. In October 1927, a contract was signed with BMW to licence build it. It was also the same basic engine that powered the T-28, T-35 (M-17L), BT-5, and BT-7 tanks (M-17F). While less powerful than the V2, it could still power the tanks, even if the power to weight ratio was inferior. This feature is unnoticeable in photographic evidence, except if the engine is exposed, which is a rare sight. This engine was issued to various types of STZ T-34 but first appeared on T-34 (STZ Interlocking Hulls).

This T-34 (STZ Interlocking Hull) was lost in the fighting for Kharkov in the spring of 1942. Notice the interlocking glacis plate with the side plates. The tow hooks are the heavier type and now have spring locks. Notice the '<' mark on the turret. Just below the turret on the upper glacis plate, the driver's 360-degree periscope can be seen.

Another T-34 (STZ Interlocking Hull) from the same unit as the T-34 as seen above. Notice the '>' mark on the turret. The tank is stuck in heavy mud near Kharkov.

In all, as with the other T-34s of this era, quality control was abysmal, and STZ had the poorest quality tanks. Put simply, with every change made to simplify production came less and less quality. As production continued, many issues with the turret were found, and often plates cracked while they were being made.

A T-34 (STZ interlocking Hull) of the 83rd Independent Tank Battalion of the 47th Tank Brigade from the 4th Tank Corps. The battalion was heavily photographed for propaganda purposes in April 1942, before going into action around Kharkov. All of the vehicles were given the tactical number 'L2-KS' on the front turret sides, the transmission hatch and the glacis plate, next to the driver's hatch on the left-hand side. Additionally, all were given a slogan on the turret, this one being '*За Родину, Вперёд!*' ('For the motherland, Forward!').

A T-34 (STZ Interlocking Hull) of the 83rd Independent Tank Battalion of the 47th Tank Brigade from the 4th Tank Corps. The tank has the expected markings for this unit, 'L2-KS', along with the slogan 'За Родину, Вперёд!' ('For the motherland, Forward!'). The tanks internal's have been removed partially, including a radiator for the engine. Forward of the tank one can just see the turret traverse and elevation gears.

The same (STZ Interlocking Hull) of the 83rd Independent Tank Battalion of the 47th Tank Brigade from the 4th Tank Corps as seen above. A front view of the tank reveals STZ plates on the glacis, along with 'L2-KS' markings. This turret side says 'щорс' ('Shshors'), which is referring to Nikolay Shchors, a Red Army commander during the early civil war period.

24

STZ PLATED T-34s

On 25 December 1941, Resolution 1062 was passed. This was the demand that T-34 tanks should began being made with 60-mm-thick frontal amour, and the easiest method of fulfilling this order was the addition of extra armour plates.

PLATED T-34 (STZ EARLY TURRET)

STZ's T-34s began rolling out with plates from roughly early January to March 1942. The additional glacis plate armour was made up of three separate pieces arranged on the top glacis plate, with a fourth on the nose underside. Due to STZ ending production of hulls with the bolted nose in December, the lower glacis plate was without the arches over the bolts, and instead, the additional armour was slightly shorter than the comparable plate at UTZ 183.

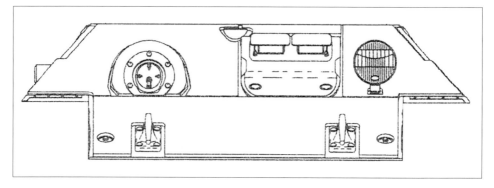

The glacis plate used by STZ. This glacis was very similar to the one used by UTZ 183. This plate does not have cut-outs for bolts on the glacis and has cut-outs around the interlocking plates on the glacis sides.

This Plated T-34 (STZ Early Turret) displays the three-part glacis plate. Without plates, this T-34 would be identical to a T-34 (STZ Interlocking Hull).

Late into glacis plate production, a similar design was implemented. Four plates instead of three were now on the glacis plate, which was done by adding a small plate above the driver's vision hatch and is basically identical to the other types.

Some photographic evidence suggests that some STZ T-34s were issued with a solid applique glacis plate that covered the entire glacis, which had holes cut out for the driver's hatch, machine gun position, and tow hook hardpoints.

PLATED T-34 (STZ SIMPLIFIED TURRET)

By far the rarest T-34 plates on STZ tanks were those attached to the turret. There were only 200 pieces made for the turret and only a handful of photographs are confirmed to show examples of such plates on STZ T-34s. These were a very similar plate structure to turret plates manufactured at Krasnoye Sormovo 112.

However, STZ's plate layout for T-34s was subtly different, being made from two plates around the vision port on the turret with the seam between the plates running vertically. A single plate forward and aft is evident in some photographs, but not others. Unfortunately, as this type is so rare, it is very difficult to speculate what the other plates next to the vision port plates were used for. It has been suggested that turret plates were merely a repair done to the tank in manufacture to not waste broken parts.

This Plated T-34 (STZ Early Turret) has suffered a fire that killed the crew member on the front of the hull. The track is the 550-mm waffle pattern but it has been filled with mud, hence it looks as though it were cast smooth. Some sources claim this to be a distinct type of track, but this is not the case. Note also that a shell has pierced the main gun. Notice the 360-degree driver's periscope.

The same Plated T-34 (STZ Early Turret) as seen above and on page 183. Notice that the tank has been issued the hardpoints for exterior fuel tanks, but these tanks have not been issued. The turret hatch is the parallel-pressing type.

The same T-34 as on page 182. From this angle, the glacis plates can be harder to spot. Notice the penetrations to the turret. The tank clearly suffered a major fire that the driver was unable to escape.

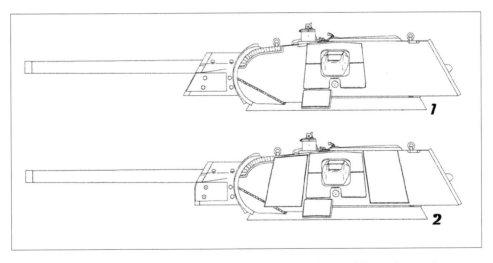

Very little is actually known about the turret plating programme at STZ, but two different plating techniques are known. First, the most basic plating used on STZ was two small plates around the vision port. It is likely that this was a repair plate as it was not very extensive. Secondly, the far more extensive plating seen here has only been found on two tanks on page 184. An additional plate was placed forward and behind the two around the vision port. The plate of armour over the cheek had some overhang. One example of the plating was with the older style of recuperator armour (as depicted) and another with the Barrikady chiselled recuperator.

This very rare Plated T-34 (STZ Simplified Turret) was lost somewhere in the city of Voronezh. The tank is issued with turret armour with a total of four plates: Two vertically above and below the vision port, and one plate forward and rearward of these two plates. Only 200 examples were made. The tank does not have the chiselled gun mantlet.

This Plated T-34 (STZ Simplified Turret) also had the rare turret armour. Notice, too, that the hull was repaired with a partial glacis plate around the hull MG blister.

Plated T-34 (STZ Simplified Turret) with the turret inscription 'Bagration' (Багратион), with the distinctive turret plates. It is thought that only 200 pieces were made, and it has been suggested that this was simply to fix broken turrets at the factory.

'Bagration' as seen above. One can see that the turret's left side is lacking the slogan but does in fact have the additional plating.

Only the later simplified turret was used with this type of turret plate, which somewhat supports the theory that the turret plates were there to cover cracks in the turret rather than being designed to thicken the turret armour. No evidence has yet been found with the turret plates on a cast turret.

In February, Resolution 1062 was rescinded. It was decided that as the Germans were not using APDS rounds as often as they had originally thought, and therefore, it was acceptable to keep on producing tanks without plates. The Soviets, however, had no idea of what was to be produced by the Germans in the upcoming years, and perhaps reintegration of the plates later in the war would have helped battlefield survivability when encountering mid–late war tanks such as the Panther and Tiger, as well as high-calibre field guns.

STZ REPAIR PLATES

One last group of glacis plates were used by STZ; these were repair plates. If a glacis plate was damaged during any of the manufacturing processes, a patch or even a full glacis plate could be placed on the offending glacis. The plates were between 10 and 45 mm thick, depending on the damage done to the plate. These plates were also used by UTZ 183 and Krasnoye Sormovo 112. While sometimes this did not line up with Red Army guidelines on plate quality, due to the dramatic need for tanks, it was often overlooked.

This T-34 (STZ Chiselled Mantlet) has been subject to a repair on the glacis plate through the addition of a 45-mm-thick repair plate onto the defective plate. This has subsequently increased the glacis thickness to a massive 90 mm thick, though the original glacis would not have been as strong. This was a simple and effective way of fixing factory faults. It is thought that the turret plates on STZ tanks, which were still relatively rare, might have also been repair plates.

A close-up of the repair armour plate on page 186. The thickness of the plate is evident in this picture. Notice that the tow hooks have been placed on top of the repair plate, lacking cut-outs for tow hooks. Notice the cut-out around the periscope above the driver's hatch.

A very rare type of one-piece glacis plate used by STZ. Almost nothing is known about this type of glacis plate due to its rarity. Notice the Barrikady chiselled gun mantlet, just barely in shot.

25

STZ: DECEMBER 1941–OCTOBER 1942

T-34 (STZ SIMPLIFIED TURRET)

At this critical stage in the war, STZ took drastic steps to simplify production. The toolset of the tanks was gradually simplified, and by the end of STZ's 1941 production, stowage had been reduced to hardpoints for just four exterior fuel tanks, two jacks, spare track, and tie downs for ice cleats, along with the gun-cleaning tool kit and the track tool kit. Furthermore, some STZ tanks were equipped with the M-17F engine in 1942 to get production figures up.

It was in December 1941 that STZ T-34s began to be equipped with a second turret periscope. This was vastly different from the PT-4 periscope being used at STZ and KhPZ 183, being a squat flat structure with a square magnifying lens. These became standard on all STZ T-34s from December 1941.

As UTZ 183 and Krasnoye Sormovo 112 began to churn out hundreds of T-34s per month, STZ was no longer the main producer of T-34s. However, as production at STZ was so important, other production changes like the implementation of the new hexagonal turrets did not occur because they would disrupt production. Similarly, from both UTZ 183 and Krasnoye Sormovo 112, newly designed turrets and hulls, specifically designed to increase output per factory, were being made. These changes also did not get implemented at STZ for production line disruption reasons, but some other changes continued in parallel.

In December 1941, the first major and defining step in T-34s at STZ was made. The turret was completely redesigned for simplicity but was also designed due to the capture of the Mariupol Metallurgy Plant by the Germans, which had previously supplied turrets to both KhPZ 183 and STZ.

These turrets had a reduced turret cheek to save on materials, but this compromised the turret's structural integrity. Furthermore, they were notorious for being poorly made and often had gaps between the turret cheek plate and the turret side plates.

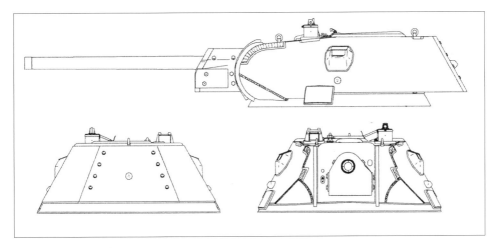

The STZ Simplified Turret was created to be as easy to make as possible. While requiring more parts, it was simpler to manufacture. The turret cheek underside was notoriously poor, often leaking. Elements of the turret were made interlocking, much like the hull of the tank.

Here, a T-34 (STZ Simplified Turret) is abandoned after combat in spring 1942. The turret is the new simplified type, but the gun mantlet is still the older type, therefore suggesting that this tank was manufactured between December 1941 and March 1942. The exhaust shrouds are the newer type, and the rear plate is lacking bolts.

While UTZ 183 was increasing the T-34's turret volume with the implementation of the hexagonal turret, STZ had actually reduced the area inside their turrets. The reduction in volume inside the tank by the reduction of the turret cheeks was not made to cast-turreted T-34s. This is an excellent example of how the T-34's desired improvements and circumstances of the war pulled the tank's design in separate and contradictory directions. These simplified turrets additionally had a turret roof with interlocking plates to attach it to the turret.

Another view of the Voronezh T-34s on page 196. A cast turret T-34 lies in pieces. This tank does not have the chiselled gun mantlet.

The simplification of the T-34 at STZ was not limited to the turrets as the hulls of STZ tanks were also changed. After the interlocking plates for the hull were introduced, the number of bolts for the rear exhaust plate attaching it to the gear plate was reduced from eleven to six.

The exhaust shrouds were also of a slightly redesigned pattern, being attached to the exhaust plate via eight bolts each that grew closer together in their placement the further to the top of the shroud they were. It has been suggested that this pattern of exhaust cover was originally designed for the T-34M, but only wooden mock-ups of the T-34M are available, so this cannot be confirmed.

Interestingly, the two shovels were moved from the exhaust plate back to the position it held before it was moved—the bottom left rear corner of the hull.

T-34 (STZ CHISELLED MANTLET)

In early March 1942, the Barrikady Gun Factory redesigned the gun recuperator armour for the F-34 gun. To make production as easy and simple as possible, the gun recuperator armour was no longer bent below the gun barrel and was left 'chiselled', which left it at a straight angle from the top to bottom. This was fitted to tanks as early as April 1942 and was unique to STZ tanks.

The turret hatches also began to be manufactured in vastly different styles to simplify it. The 'chiselled' gun recuperator armour was equipped after the simplified turret was introduced, so some turrets were issued with the reduced chin and the original mantlet.

A common use of STZ T-34s was as dug-in 'bunkers', which was favourable because it reduced their silhouette. This was done on the vast steppe before Stalingrad as a means to attempt to slow the relentless German advance. This is a T-34 (STZ Chiselled Mantlet).

A train carrying T-34 and T-70s. The T-34s all have a white stripe that is painted along the entire length of the tank, from nose to tail. The T-70 is a very rare cast turret T-70. Only ten such turrets were manufactured, and only this one has been photographed.

Two T-34 (STZ Welded Turret Back) that fell down a ditch. The rear of the left tank's turret has '57' painted in white, as well as with a triangular unit marking on the turret cheek. This tank still has hardpoints for the fuel tanks on the hull side. A German is inside the turret of the left T-34, and one can see the lower escape hatch on the tank on the right.

Two cast-turreted T-34 (STZ Chiselled Mantlet). The turret has been blown off the front tank, and it landed back onto the hull. The wheels are the STZ reinforced cast type, and the hull lacks hardpoints for fuel tanks.

This T-34 (STZ Chiselled Mantlet) was being shipped on a train with an American Lend-Lease-supplied M3 Lee when it was attacked, likely from the air. Notice the hull details with the wheels removed.

The same train as seen above. The turret of the exploded T-34 can just be seen behind the hull, and the chiselled gun mantlet can be seen.

It was in April 1942, too, that the cast turrets of STZ tanks were also changed following developments made at Krasnoye Sormovo 112, where the rear inspection door in the turret was completely removed. Gun removal was now done by lifting the turret out of the ring and then resting the turret's forward cheeks on the turret ring. This system meant that the gun had to be removed from the gap between the hull and the turret. This system was proposed by Krasnoye Sormovo 112 as a way of improving the integrity of the turrets.

The same STZ T-34 as on pages 186–187. The damage to this vehicle is quite evident from this side also. Notice that the turret's entire left side has been torn away. This vehicle likely was attacked by an aircraft.

The same STZ T-34 as seen above. The Russian steppe was not good terrain for tanks, being very open and barren. Many STZ T-34s were dug in along the steppe as pillboxes.

T-34 (STZ WELDED TURRET BACK)

The last major change was made to the eight-bolt turrets. As the Germans approached Stalingrad, it was decided that, due to the tank's life span being less than ten combat hours, it would be satisfactory for the factory to remove features that were necessary for tanks to operate over large distances and for many weeks at a time. Therefore, gun removal and inspection features were considered superfluous. The rear of the turrets that had been attached by eight bolts was now simply welded onto the turrets. This was first done between late May and early June 1942.

The tank's stowage at the beginning of 1942 was a single stowage box on the front left and rear right fender, with a single jack and jack-block and hardpoints for the ice cleats. The two shovels were now on the hull rear left side, like they had been in June 1941.

Stowage was also reduced to the simplest point when the Germans were approaching the city of Stalingrad in the early summer of 1942. As the T-34s no longer had to travel long distances, the hardpoints for the additional fuel tanks were no longer added onto the tanks as they were not needed in the intense fighting for Stalingrad. The jack is also thought to have been dispensed with.

In early June, STZ tanks were equipped with the UTZ cast steel-rimmed wheels, with reinforcement rings around the cut-outs in the wheel. These were marginally stronger and became standard at STZ from June. These wheels had been designed at UTZ 183 in May 1942.

As the Battle of Stalingrad raged on, STZ continued to manufacture and repair tanks. It was on 5 October 1942 that the plant finally was evacuated. STZ did not manufacture any tanks in 1940, but in 1941, it manufactured 1,250, and in 1942, 2,520 tanks rolled out of the plant.

A T-34 (STZ Chiselled Mantlet) that has had the road wheels replaced with two pressed-type road wheels. The middle three wheels are STZ reinforced cast type.

Three STZ T-34s in Voronezh. This is the modern E38 highway, and during the war, it was the main road through Voronezh.

A T-34 (STZ Welded Turret Back). Notice the new pattern of road wheels. These were stronger than the older STZ cast type. The turret number '367' is likely Soviet in origin.

The turret of this T-34 (STZ Welded Turret Back) sits on its side in the hull of the tank after being blown off. The interior of the turret is of interest, as it differs greatly from UTZ turrets. The seats for the gunner and loader are round, and the design of both the F-34 and turret traverse controls are different.

The streets of Stalingrad near the Stalingrad Grain Elevator. The T-34 (STZ Cast Late Production) is lacking any fuel tank hardpoints and is flanked by two T-60 light tanks.

This achievement was outstanding, but due to the poor conditions at STZ, especially during the Battle of Stalingrad, the quality of STZ tanks was always less than that of other factories.

These tanks were less smooth to drive, often lacking components, and were perhaps over-simplified. The STZ T-34s are some of the oddest-looking T-34s ever made, relatively speaking. After Stalingrad was recaptured in February 1943, the factory was rebuilt but did not return to T-34 manufacture, and instead continued to manufacture agricultural machines.

Finally, it should be noted that a couple more myths about STZ T-34s need to be dispelled—first, STZ never issued T-34s without primer paint or green 4BO, and secondly, tanks without turrets were never sent into battle. Both of these assertions are unfounded and ludicrous to suggest.

A ChTZ 100 cast turret KV-1 and a T-34 (STZ Chiselled Mantlet). The T-34 is equipped with 550-mm waffle-pattern track which has been filled with mud. '631' is a Soviet marking. (*Will Kerrs Collection*)

A T-34 (STZ Welded Turret Back), with a good look at the rear interlocking plate. Notice the redesigned exhaust shrouds and the fewer bolts on the lower exhaust plate. The hull sides also lack fuel tank hardpoints, and the shovels have been moved back to the hull side.

26

KRASNOYE SORMOVO 112:
JULY 1941–APRIL 1942

On 1 July 1941, a rectification of Resolution 1ss authorised the People's Commissariat of the Shipbuilding Industry at Krasnoye Sormovo (sometimes referred to as Gorky) to begin production of the T-34 tank. The factory was not equipped or ready for such a task as it was originally a shipbuilding plant. As such, production of the tank was therefore very slow in 1941. Krasnoye Sormovo, however, had produced tanks before, namely the 'KS' in 1919, otherwise known as the Russian Renault. The tank was a copy of the French FT tank, a small number of which had been captured during the Russian Civil War.

A string of orders and resolutions were passed in July 1941 to help set up production. One such problem that was addressed early on was the production of V-2-34 engines. Production of V-2 engines was already slow in June 1941, so when Krasnoye Sormovo 112 set up shop, it was ordered to work on M-17 aero engines for use in T-34s.

Resolution 280ss was issued to Krasnoye Sormovo on 2 July 1941, which partially read as:

In pursuance of the decision of the State Defense Committee of 1st July this year 'on the organisation of production of medium-sized T-34 tanks' I ORDER:

1. Director of the Gorky Automobile Plant, Comrade Loskutov:

   a) immediately proceed to the production of M-17 aircraft engines in the aircraft engine shop;

   b) within a three-day period expect to receive from plant No. 26 NCAP all technical documentation, devices and tools for equipping the M-17 motor;

   c) start production of parts and components of the M-17 engine from 15th July;

   d) the launch of M-17 aircraft engines starting on 1st September 1941;

   e) in all calculations for the manufacture of aircraft engines, proceed [and match projected figures] from the T-34 tank production program [meaning that you should produce] in 1941—700–750 pieces and in 1941—3000 units;

   f) in a four-day period, submit to me for consideration and submission for approval to the State Defence Committee, a monthly schedule for the issue of M-17 aircraft engines and, within ten days, submit to me for approval a timetable for organising the preparation of production and production of M-17 aircraft engines;

g) in a week's time to establish the amount of cooperation on the plants involved in helping the
Gorky Automobile Plant them. Molotov for the production of M-17 engines.

On 11 July 1941, Order Number 319cc was passed by S. Akopov:

In pursuance of the decree of the State Defence Committee of 9th July 1941, 'On ensuring the
production of T-34 tanks at the Krasnoye Sormovo plant,' I ORDER:
1. Oblige the director of the Gorky Automobile Plant. Comrade Loskutov to ensure the supply of
the Krasnoye Sormovo plant of M-17 engines for the assembly of T-34 tanks in 1941:
in August 1941—15 pieces
in September 1941—80 pieces
in October 1941—160 pieces
in November 1941—230 pieces
in December 1941—260 pieces
delivering them evenly for a month.
2. To oblige the director of the plant No. 183 Comrade Maksareva to ship [them to] the Krasnoye
Sormovo plant in July 1941.

T-34 (112 EARLY PRODUCTION)

The first tanks manufactured by Krasnoye Sormovo 112 were kits supplied from KhPZ 183, and
therefore, they are indistinguishable from a T-34 (KhPZ 183 Redesigned Stowage). These tanks
can be known as 'T-34 (112 Initial Production)'. As suggested by the relatively small number
of T-34s outlined in Order No. 319cc, Krasnoye Sormovo 112 did not make a large impact
on T-34 production until September and October 1941. Very shortly after these initial tanks,
Krasnoye Sormovo 112 began indigenous production, and almost straight away the factory
began to make a change in September 1941 to best suit their production lines.

As Krasnoye Sormovo 112 was originally a shipyard with a casting facility, all its turrets
were cast. Early tanks did not differ hugely from KhPZ 183 tanks, but one early change was the
relocation of the jack block, which was moved rearwards on the right hull, to be as rearward
on the hull side as possible. The jack block would stay here until the exterior fuel tanks were
removed in early 1942, therefore giving an easy identification feature for these Krasnoye
Sormovo 112 tanks. These tanks can be known as 'T-34 (112 Early Production)'.

The turret casting was redesigned very quickly into production. The reasoning for this was
very much the same as the 'heavyweight' turret at KhPZ 183. The turret seam was much heavier
and more defined than at KhPZ 183, with the line of the cast that was at a much shallower
angle on the cheek. Heavy casting nubs can be found, along with often rough appearances on
the cheeks. These turrets were also thicker, being 52 mm thick rather than the 45 mm thick
that previous turrets had been. This change was done at the same time as KhPZ 183 began to
issue their cast-heavyweight turret.

When KhPZ 183 implemented the new driver's vision hatch with two periscopes under
armoured lids, so did Krasnoye Sormovo 112. This change was done after KhPZ 183 but before
STZ, roughly in mid-October 1941.

This T-34 (112 Simplified Rear) is highly unusual as it has the KhPZ 183 intermediate driver's hatch. This hatch was attached to the glacis plate by a small bulge that the original driver's hatch attached to. Notice the subtle differences between the KhPZ 183 turret and this Krasnoye Sormovo 112 turret, and the placement of the jack block on the rear right hull side. The track has the ice cleats attached. Note the whitewash, which indicates where stowage was kept.

A T-34 (112 Early Production) lost in spring 1942. This tank has been used as a target as the earliest known photographs of this tank show that it was intact. Notice the nose of the tank is lacking bolts, therefore the glacis is welded to the nose fillet. Notice, too, the placement of the jack block on the rear hull right side. The rounded rear plate can just be seen above the drive wheel.

Two T-34 (112 Simplified Rear) lost in the winter battles of 1941. Notice the '9', presumably painted in red on the turret side of one tank, and the square of unpainted green on the turret cheek.

Unlike KhPZ 183, the tow hooks used on Krasnoye Sormovo 112 tanks when the 'pin' type were removed from the design did not have a spring latch and sat high on the glacis plate. Glacis plates were issued until early December 1941 with the typical bolts to attach them to the nose fillet, but this was redesigned to remove the bolts, so the glacis and nose plates were just welded together.

During this period, four exterior fuel tanks were carried in the same position that pre-war KhPZ 183 T-34s had. Towards the end of December, the fuel tanks were increased to five by adding another fuel tank and bracket on the hull left side.

T-34 (112 SIMPLIFIED REAR)

Due to the difficulty that Krasnoye Sormovo 112 had in manufacturing certain items of the T-34, ever more avenues were explored in simplifying the tank. As such, the entire hull rear was redesigned to improve the efficiency of production.

The original rounded rear was redesigned - this was done in part to speed up the production of the tanks, and due to the difficulty that Krasnoye Sormovo 112 had in shaping the gear plate. Instead of a rounded rear, a sharp right angle was created by simply placing one plate onto another. The hinges were redesigned to fit over this new angle, and photographic evidence suggests that Krasnoye Sormovo 112 experimented with different designs before settling with distinctive large hinges with two teeth on the bottom hinge and a single tooth on the top hinge.

One small change made to the construction of Krasnoye Sormovo 112 T-34s was that the brackets that the upper hull plates rested on were given an additional bracket at the rear of the tank. This was attached to the rear exhaust plate, which meant that when the exhaust plate was unscrewed from the hull, the rear roof plate, which the variable pitch radiator intake slats were attached to, also had to be removed. This was likely done for structural integrity reasons.

At the same time that STZ introduced the driver's 360-degree periscope on the top of the glacis plate, 112 also implemented the periscope. This small periscope was added as the driver's field of view was limited, and it was viewed that he needed a wider arch of view. This periscope was placed on a blister above and to the right of the driver's hatch.

These hulls were still issued with the original square transmission plate and are very rare tanks. Tanks were issued with these rear plates from December 1941 and were produced with rounded rears as stocks were used up. Many of the tanks during the Battle of Moscow manufactured by Krasnoye Sormovo 112 had either the original rounded rear or this new rear plate.

Only a small number of tanks were manufactured in this configuration before the design was once again changed. A new circular transmission hatch was designed, with a single hinge at the bottom of the hatch which only had three teeth. When closed, the transmission hatch was attached to the tank with four bolts. Due to this configuration, the type is referred to as the 'four-bolt transmission hatch'. It is thought that this was done in December 1941.

A T-34 (112 Simplified Rear). Notice the highly non-standard hinges at the rear of the tank. It is clear that this tank was manufactured after the initial twelve KhPZ 183 T-34 kits sent to Krasnoye Sormovo 112 were manufactured. Notice also the placement of the jack block on the rear right hull side.

A close-up view of a T-34 (112 Simplified Rear), which is a clear illustrator of the features to expect from these tanks. Notice the bracket for the jack block that is very close to the rear of the tank. This is a clear indicator that the tank is a Krasnoye Sormovo 112 vehicle. Additionally, notice the bracket on the exhaust plate that the rear upper hull roof would rest on. This also has the electronics for the brake light. These two features are also clear indicators that the tank is a Krasnoye Sormovo 112 vehicle. Additionally, notice that the transmission hatch is square. This means that either the rear hull is rounded off like earlier T-34s from KhPZ 183, or that the vehicle has the new squared-off rear plate, with the new Krasnoye Sormovo 112 style hinges, being an intermediate type of rear plate.

Between December and March 1942, Krasnoye Sormovo 112 began to issue plates on their tanks to increase their armour thickness. This was not the only change made, as additionally, the side-mounted fuel tanks were moved rearwards. There were still four fuel tanks, but now the rear-most fuel tanks were placed against the joint with the exhaust plate.

T-34 (112 SIMPLIFIED STOWAGE)

The four exterior-mounted fuel tanks that like at KhPZ 183 and STZ, were attached in pairs on the hull sides. This was moved backwards on the hull sides as for the four fuel tanks to be as rearward as possible. This configuration was initiated in January 1942. This was then changed again in mid-February 1942. The fuel tanks carried were reduced to a single unit that was placed at the left rear of the tank. These would be removed entirely when the Krasnoye Sormovo 112 T-34s began to be equipped with handrails in April 1942.

Two T-34 (112 Early Production). Notice the redesigned two hooks that lack a spring lock. Krasnoye Sormovo 112 issued these throughout the winter of 1941. Also, this tank has external fuel tanks, a feature that would be removed in later Krasnoye Sormovo 112 tanks. This tank would later be operated as a *Beutepanzer* T-34, according to other photographic evidence.

A T-34 (112 Simplified Rear) abandoned in the winter of 1941–42. Notice that the rear plate and gear plate meet at a right angle, but pay close attention to the square transmission hatch. Also notice the jack block placement and the 550-mm waffle tracks.

A T-34 (112 Simplified Rear) lost in a wooded area, likely around the ring of Leningrad. Wooded areas are highly unsuited to tank warfare, as the tank can get stuck on trees and were generally restricted to using paths through woods.

A close view of the tank as seen above. Notice the driver's hatch that was completely blown away from the hull of the tank. The 360-degree periscope can be seen on the upper centre of the glacis plate. The protective ring has been blown away, but the weld seams can be seen.

The same tank as seen on page 206. Notice the 550-mm waffle-pattern track, as well as the distinctive angle of the rear plate.

Another T-34 (112 Simplified Stowage) from the same unit as on page 208. Notice the lack of external fuel tanks, and that the jack block was moved back to where it was placed on UTZ 183 made tanks. Notice the dead soldier on the ground.

This T-34 (112 Simplified Stowage) belongs to the same unit as on page 207. Notice that the rear left of the tank has external fuel tank brackets which can be seen to the right of the soldier holding the MP 40. This feature is unique to Krasnoye Sormovo 112.

This T-34 (112 Simplified Stowage) tank was lost due to being bogged down in soft ground. A triangle was painted into the turret by whitewashing the tank, leaving a triangle of green on the roof blank. This was for air identification.

It should be noted that in 1941, Krasnoye Sormovo 112 only manufactured 173 tanks in total. All, except for vehicles made by kits provided by KhPZ 183, were powered by the obsolete M-17F aero engine (a total of 163 tanks).

T-34 (112 TURRET FILLET)

From March 1942, by learning from combat, Krasnoye Sormovo 112 added fillets onto the upper glacis plate and the upper hull plate around the turret to stop spalls from entering the tank. A useful side effect was that it helped with the removal of the main gun for maintenance.

These tanks are often mistaken as KhPZ 183 tanks, but close inspection of the turret shape and the rear of the tank gives away the identity of the tank. Stress should be made on the subtle shape of the turret, which, once understood, makes identification far easier. The Krasnoye Sormovo 112 turret had a straight seam that did not dip like that at UTZ 183. Once the seam got to the turret cheek, it then curved sharply to meet the turret cheek halfway up the turret face. In conjunction with this, fuel tank placement and the transmission are clear giveaways of the tank's origin.

Two T-34 (112 Simplified Stowage) tanks that were abandoned on a riverbank. The rear plate can be clearly seen with the new Krasnoye Sormovo 112 hinges. Notice that the rear plate and the gear plate meet at a right angle, and the rear plate sits over the gear plate. New hinges and a round transmission hatch were also used. Notice the external fuel tank brackets for a single fuel tank, which was dispensed with in the spring of 1942.

During this time, a new hardpoint for towing field guns was added into the T-34s being manufactured at 112. This was a simple small vertical piece of armour with a hole to allow for guns and limbers to be attached to the tank. This feature was only used at Krasnoye Sormovo 112 and was used until the end of production.

The stowage on Krasnoye Sormovo 112 manufactured tanks was very similar to that of KhPZ 183. For example, Krasnoye Sormovo 112 only issued one jack and hull-mounted jack block at the same time as KhPZ 183. The track tool kit was moved to the right rear side with KhPZ 183, and Krasnoye Sormovo 112 only issued the smaller type gun-cleaning toolbox.

A T-34 (112 Turret Fillet) with a white '8' on the turret in the spring of 1942. Some new features are visible. For example, notice the round MG blister face with a cut-off at the bottom. Also notice that the upper glacis has fillets that run along the top. This was to stop shots from entering the turret ring. The rear left has the brackets for one fuel tank.

27

KRASNOYE SORMOVO 112: APRIL 1942–AUGUST 1943

After the teething problems with the slow production of the T-34s from Krasnoye Sormovo 112, production began to pick up the pace. The tanks rolling out of Krasnoye Sormovo 112 had cast turrets and round transmission hatches connected to the hull with four bolts. At this time, additional armour plates were being added to the tanks (to be discussed later).

T-34 (112 WITH HANDRAILS)

In early spring 1942, the defining feature of Krasnoye Sormovo 112 tanks was implemented—handrails for embarked infantry. Both the hulls and turrets of the tanks were given handrails, but some early examples exist with the handles only on the turrets. When the handrails were introduced, not all tanks were initially given them, but within a month of implementation, all T-34s being released at Krasnoye Sormovo 112 were given handrails.

The handrails were made from one piece of metal bar, with a small bend on either side of the bar that attached it to the hull. Each side of the hull had four such handrails, with two very small ones attached to the front glacis plate. It is commonly agreed that this was first implemented between late March and early April 1942. In 1942, only Krasnoye Sormovo 112 issued the bent-type handrails, but Omsk 174 later also issued this type of handrail from June 1943, and only on hexagonal-turreted tanks. Therefore, any tank with an early turret type with the bent-type handrails is a Krasnoye Sormovo 112 tank.

The turret had two handrails on each side of the turret, one forward and one behind the vision port. The engine deck of the tanks was also given handrails—two were on either side of the engine access hatch, two more were placed on the grated cover for the radiator intake, and a final two were over the exhaust pipes (these would later be removed). This allowed for not only maximum infantry embarkation but also allowed for stowed goods to be strapped to them.

This T-34 (112 with Handrails) is one of the very early examples of this type of tank. The tank's hull has sixteen brackets for the attachment of four external hull-mounted fuel tanks. These were very rare, but evidence suggests that they were briefly re-introduced in early 1942 at Krasnoye Sormovo 112. Notice the green air identification triangle on the turret hatch. Notice also the rare pattern of fender, which was used by STZ in the winter of 1941 and by Krasnoye Sormovo 112 in the first half of 1942.

The same T-34 (112 with Handrails) as seen above. One can clearly see the hardpoints for the four fuel tank brackets, which were very rare when this tank was manufactured.

This T-34 (112 with Handrails) was issued with handrails on the turret only. This is unusual as hull handrails were introduced first. The German soldier riding the horse was likely a message runner.

This T-34 (112 with Handrails) is a typical example of the early fully-handrailed tanks. The handrails on the turret and glacis have been damaged, but one can still see details of the original placement.

Interestingly, the photographic evidence suggests that four external fuel tanks brackets were provided for the tanks, in their 1940 position. This is highly strange as shortly after they were reintroduced, the hull side-mounted fuel tanks were propped all together. Some very late Plated T-34s were given handrails, and at least one example also has brackets for four fuel tanks.

The T-34's turret was again redesigned by Krasnoye Sormovo 112 as it was found that firing the coaxial machine gun in the main turret caused vibrations that damaged the rear gun inspection port. Therefore, it was decided to make changes to the design to stop the damage being done. However, the Red Army still wanted the tanks to have the ability to remove the guns for maintenance.

It was decided that in order to allow this, two metal stoppers were welded onto the bottom of the turret bustle. This was done so when the turret was tipped and lifted from the rear, the cheeks would rest on the turret ring, allowing the gun to be removed through the gap between the turret ring and the hull ring. This was introduced in late spring 1942 and was quickly adopted at STZ.

At this stage in production, the hull glacis was also given interlocking plates like at STZ. Additionally, the tracks primarily used by Krasnoye Sormovo 112 were either the reinforced 550-mm type track or the 550-mm waffle-pattern track. After November 1942, the reinforced 550-mm type track had stopped being issued.

All the changes listed so far were conducted between April 1942 and July 1942. For a very long time in Krasnoye Sormovo 112 production, the tanks did not change that drastically, other than fitting V-2 engines once they became available in greater numbers.

A knocked-out T-70 and T-34 (112 with Handrails) in the winter of 1942. Notice that the T-70 is equipped with a radio, which is a very rare feature for a T-70.

This T-34 (112 with Handrails) was manufactured in June of 1942 and is still issued with the old reinforced 550-mm type track. The tank was lost in the winter of 1942–1943. Notice the handrails on the rear of the tank, but the new PT-4-7 periscope is in the turret.

A T-34 burns after combat. T-34s commonly caught fire because there was little protection of the fuel tanks and ammunition.

This T-34 (112 with Handrails) was manufactured in the summer of 1942. Take note of the tie-downs and the lack of fuel tanks.

In October 1942, new UTZ box-type external fuel tanks were fitted. These were cubic boxes that sat on the rear fenders of the tank. They were originally manufactured at UTZ 183, before being manufactured and equipped to Krasnoye Sormovo 112 tanks. These were introduced in October 1942 as a part of a decree from the GKO (National Defence Commission).

Around ten months later, a new fuel tank type was implemented at Krasnoye Sormovo 112 in the summer of 1943. These new drum-type fuel tanks originated from ChKZ 100 and were also adopted by other factories in mid-1943. No T-34 was issued with both types simultaneously.

From June 1942, the turret periscope was replaced with the PT-4-7 scope. This had a distinctive cast protective cover that rotated with the periscope. These were first issued by UTZ 183 in June 1942 before being issued to Krasnoye Sormovo 112 manufactured tanks.

This T-34 (112 with Handrails) was lost in the winter of 1942–1943. Notice the interlocking glacis plate and the glacis plate handrails. The tank has likely suffered a major internal explosion which has ripped right through the tank and dislodged the turret, engine, and the floor of the tank.

Likely lost in the Third Battle of Kharkov (19 February–15 March 1943), this T-34 (112 with Handrails) is lacking rear handrails, which were removed towards the end of 1942.

T-34 (112 7-BOLT TRANSMISSION)

From January 1943, Krasnoye Sormovo 112 began to distribute new transmission plates that used the same seven-bolt round transmission hatch that UTZ 183, ChKZ 100, Omsk 174, and UTZM tanks were being issued with. This was due to the much easier access to the transmission that it provided, but also to standardise the tanks as it was felt that there was beginning to be too much variation between factories.

Variation can be found between Krasnoye Sormovo 112 tanks on the reinforced ball mount for the hull machine gun. Some T-34s were issued this from early 1943 onwards, but some other later examples seem to lack this feature.

In early 1943, the headlight, which had remained on the glacis plate since production began, was moved to the hull side. In addition, a new 500-mm waffle-pattern track was introduced, and almost exclusively issued after the first quarter of 1943.

A T-34 (112 with Handrails) that blew up during the winter of 1942. Notice the box-type fuel tanks on the rear of the tank, which were introduced in October 1942. The entire engine deck has been lifted from the tank due to an internal explosion.

The swampy forest of the Volkhov Front was not a good environment for tanks. This T-34 (112 with Handrails) was lost in 1943 and is being used for some training by the Germans. The vehicle likely had box-type fuel tanks and a seven-bolt transmission hatch.

A T-34 that was knocked out on the advance to Orel in August 1943. This perfect example of the mid-war 112 tank has an interesting mixture of features. Evidence suggests that some 112 T-34s were not given MG blister armour, as seen on this tank. Notice the turret marking '39-Л'. The tank would have had box type rear fuel tanks, though they are absent here.

T-34 (112 DRUM-TYPE FUEL TANKS)

Krasnoye Sormovo 112 began to issue the drum-type external fuel tanks from June 1943. This was standard throughout the T-34 production lines, as it was found that the ChKZ 100 drum-type fuel tanks were the strongest, largest, and most efficient way to increase in volume on the tanks.

The type of hardpoint used by Krasnoye Sormovo 112 was a solid-bracket type that cradled the tank, with a strap across the top to secure it in place. This matched ChKZ 100's pattern but differed from UTZ 183's pattern.

The basic shape of Krasnoye Sormovo 112 manufactured T-34 tanks changed little from the implementation of the handrails, and Krasnoye Sormovo 112 was the longest producer of the early small turret. After the Battle of Kursk, Krasnoye Sormovo 112 introduced the hexagonal turret with command cupola and was the first plant to do this.

A rare *Beutepanzer*, this T-34 (112 Drum-type Fuel Tanks) represents the last of the earlier pattern of T-34 turret to be produced before Krasnoye Sormovo 112 would move onto the hexagonal turrets. Notice that the tank now no longer has the box-type fuel tanks, and now is equipped with the drum-type fuel tanks. These tanks are attached to the hull via crescent moon 'solid bracket type' brackets. Unlike ChKZ 100 and UTZM, who also used these brackets, the bracket did not attach to a handrail and were simply welded to the hull.

28

KRASNOYE SORMOVO 112 PLATED T-34s

Krasnoye Sormovo 112 was the plant that experimented the most with additional armour plates, and therefore, it had the greatest variation and oddities. From late December 1941 to as late as May 1942, the factory fitted a large variety of plates to their tanks. Interestingly, Krasnoye Sormovo 112 also provided a small number of additional armour plates to the glacis of tanks as late as summer 1943. There were as many as four different glacis plate types and as many as three turret types.

PLATED T-34 (112 EARLY)

The turrets were given a full wrap-around of armour. Each turret side was given at first five plates: one behind the vision port, one partly over the port, and three in front of the port. The last plate covered the turret cheek and had three smaller plates at the front of the turret to follow the contours of the turret.

The first plate over the cheek was not flush with the cheek but was in fact parallel with the gun barrel. This left a small gap on the bottom of the plate between the lower turret cheek and the additional plate. The front cheek plate was made of three pieces of metal that were shaped around the front of the turret cheek, with a fourth making the new turret side. This gave the turret cheek a bulged look and has been compared to a squirrel storing food in its cheek pouches.

The second type of plates around the turret only differed slightly, having two pieces to the rear of the vision port. The third type only differed slightly by having a shaped plate covering the turret vision port, but with a cut-out for said port. The plate around the vision port was sometimes one piece, but was also sometimes cut down the middle, with the seam of this plate running vertically, unlike those of STZ tanks, which ran horizontally.

The glacis plates of Krasnoye Sormovo 112 were the most complex plates developed for the T-34 during the war. The first hull plate was developed from seven separate plates that covered the entire glacis plate. There were cut-outs in this plate for the tow hooks, the headlight hardpoint, and other items. There were two four plates on the lower glacis with octagonal cut-outs around the tow hooks, another two plates around the MG position, and the seventh was left of the driver's hatch.

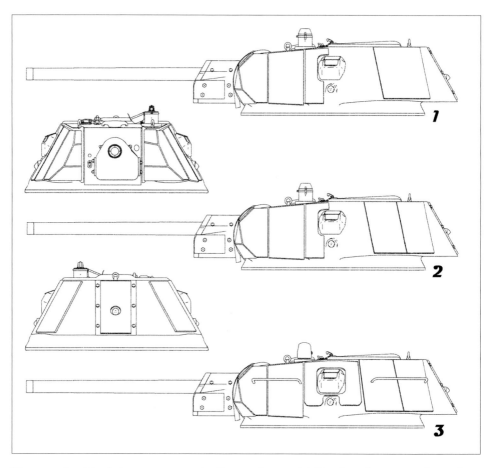

Three examples of the plating programme used at Krasnoye Sormovo 112. First, the earliest pattern of turret plates. This type has a single plate at the rear of the turret. Secondly, the second and more common type of turret plate, the rear plate was increased to two smaller plates that covered a larger surface area. Thirdly, the last type of turret plating was the most extensive. Interestingly, the known example of this type of turret armour does not have glacis plate armour. A plate was placed around the vision port. The known example of this type of turret plate also has handrails on the hull and turret. Notice the PT-4-7 periscope as well.

OPPOSITE PAGE:

Above: The two main types of glacis plate produced during Resolution 1062. First, by far the most common of the two glacis plates. This seven-part glacis was used from the inspection of the plated programme. Secondly, only known from one example, this plate could have been an attempt at a repair plate. The only known example was equipped with handrails. Very late examples of plated T-34s were only given turret armour, not glacis armour.

Below: A factory photograph from Krasnoye Sormovo 112 showing the glacis plate additional armour. Notice the cut-outs around the tow hooks, and other cut-outs for other items, such as for the driver's hatch, machine gun blister, and track tensioning ports.

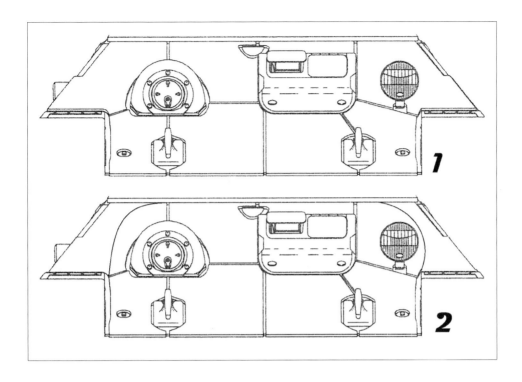

A Plated T-34 (112 Early) with a five-part glacis plate and a full turret wrap around. This is the earliest type of glacis plate, and the seven-part plate was introduced soon after the five-part plate. Notice the hull-mounted jack block.

A T-34 with the full turret armour set. Notice the gap under the plates between the turret and these new plates. The glacis plate would also have been updated. These tanks can be called Plated T-34 (112 Early).

In an attempt to improve the armour protection of the T-34, plates were added to the turret and hull. This T-34, a Plated T-34 (112 Early), was given the full turret wrap-around plate. This tank was lost on the Volkhov Front in spring 1942.

A smouldering Plated T-34 (112 Early). Take note of the plate over the rear access door, with the pistol port unplugged.

The same T-34 as seen below. The tank was totally obliterated by German forces, leaving nothing much left of the tank. The vehicle was lost on the Volkhov Front, an area totally unsuited to tank warfare.

This Plated T-34 (112 Early) was demolished after combat by German engineers. Notice the 'B' and '4' painted onto the turret side (with possibly another marking, too), which are Soviet in origin. This tank had a seven-part glacis plate before being destroyed.

A very late example of turret armour. A single piece was placed over the vision port, with two pieces before and after this. The piece of armour that sits over the turret cheek has been blown away and is still present on the tank. This is still referred to as Plated T-34 (112 Early). Notice that this example is additionally rare, for having hardpoints for exterior fuel tank stowage in the '1940' locations.

The same T-34 as seen above. Notice the lack of armour on the glacis plate and the turret armour. Also notice the handrails on the tank, both turret and hull. The triangle marking on the turret is the original tank scheme, and the whitewash was merely painted around it to make the triangle.

By far the rarest type of plate was the second type. The seven-piece simplified plate system was introduced very late into plate production and did not cover the entire glacis. The top left and right corners of the original plate were removed and cut in a distinctive curved shape.

When the plate programme was concluded, some tanks were issued with only very small plates to cover vital areas. Again, it has been suggested that this was done to repair faulty glacis plates. Two additional plates can be found around the MG position on some tanks. While these MG blister plates are repairs done to faulty glacis plates, they were originally from the 'seven-piece simplified' glacis.

The last plated T-34s from 112 were issued with handrails and are incredibly rare. The plated programme was phased out as the handrails were phased in.

PLATED T-34 (112 FULL COVER)

By June 1942, Soviet forces had begun to encounter newer and heavier German guns. Of note was the 75-mm KwK 40 anti-tank gun, first fielded in the early months of 1942, which could easily take on T-34s and KVs from ranges greater than 1,000 m. The appearance of this new gun, among others, put the T-34's battlefield survivability into serious question.

As a result, and as a development of the earlier plated T-34 projects from Resolution 1062, in Autumn 1942, Krasnoye Sormovo 112 experimented with a full turret and hull armour plate program. This was not the first attempt at a full plate system for the T-34 (the other taking place as a one-off at KhPZ 183) but was perhaps the most extensive. The turrets were given bolted frames, and angled 10-mm plates were attached to the turrets, hull, and the running gear as side skirts, very similar to that of the later Panther.

A 1/10th scale model of the fully plated T-34 from Krasnoye Sormovo 112. The turret plates were very similar to this on the real vehicle. Notice the placement of the track toolbox under the main turret. (*Maxim Kolomiets*)

Twelve sets were manufactured (some sources claim up to sixty-four sets) and fitted to T-34s, but on their combat debut in the spring of 1943, the tanks encountered a battery of Pak 40 75-mm anti-tank guns. All twelve of the fully armoured T-34s were destroyed easily, and the project was dropped because of their ineffectiveness.

A top view of the model of the fully plated T-34. Small details on the model are rather curious, such as accurate Krasnoye Sormovo 112 rear hinges and plate configuration. The gun-cleaning toolbox is on the front left hull side. (*Maxim Kolomiets*)

A fully plated T-34 from Krasnoye Sormovo 112, which has been abandoned. This tank does not have turret plates, but most tanks of the type did. Notice the side hull plates and the way that they attached to each other and the hull. This attachment differs from the scale model made in late 1942. Fuel has also spilt out of the rear fuel tanks. (*Maxim Kolomiets*)

112 T-34 WITH REPAIR PLATES

Repair plates were somewhat common on T-34s and were added during the production of
the tank rather than in the field. If a finishing process failed, such as a glacis plate cracking,
a patch could be placed over the offending glacis or a small patch over the crack. This was
done over many MG blisters at Krasnoye Sormovo 112 as it would appear that many tanks
had finishing issues with the blister cut out.

Finally, in mid-1943, some Krasnoye Sormovo 112 tanks were given full hull plates once
more. This was actually done to repair defective glacis plates. Interestingly, the plate was 20
mm thick rather than 10 mm. The repair plate was made of one piece and placed over the
entire glacis plate. It had cut-outs for the driver's hatch, MG blister, tow hooks, and track
tension access ports.

The plate programme was short-lived but was a true sign of how the Stavka panicked
about the survivability of their tanks. The irony was that, at least in the winter and spring
of 1942, the T-34 and KV tanks were by far the superior tanks on the battlefield in terms of
armour protection.

The same T-34 as on page 209. Notice the plates around the MG position. This can be called a Plated T-34 (112 Repair
Plate). Notice that the engine access hatch is on the ground left of the tank.

On the right is the same T-34 as on page 230. From this angle, the plates can be more easily seen, and the unit is revealed to be the same on page 209 based on the turret marking.

One of the very rare full glacis plates issued on Krasnoye Sormovo 112 T-34s in 1943. These were simply a general repair to fix broken glacis plates at the factory. The plate is perhaps as thick as 20 mm, which would mean that the glacis plate would be 65 mm thick in total. These tanks have likely had the UTZ 183 box-type fuel tanks. This *ad hoc* track stowage is very rare to see.

29

HEXAGONAL TURRETS

From its inception, the T-34's turret had always been a concern, with huge complaints about the limited internal space being made as early as the April 1940 trials reports for the A-34 prototypes. After the cancellation of the T-34M in June 1941, KhPZ 183 began drawing up designs to improve the T-34's turret. While it is true that a Red Army decree was issued that strictly forbade any disruption to T-34 production, the need for a new turret was felt to be necessary.

The new turret had to work within limitations, chiefly turret ring size, but also clearance of the engine deck. Design work took place at KhPZ 183 in the closing stages of September 1941, but prototyping had to halt so that the factory could evacuate to the Urals. However, a design was drawn up, so the paperwork and machine tools were moved to UTZ 183 where prototyping resumed. The move gave engineers time to complete prototyping, especially as they were out of range of German bomber aircraft.

UTZ 183 had experimented with several designs before settling on the eventual winner. Some designs had a cupola to allow a third crewman, but these were all rejected due to the cramped space inside the tank with the third man in the turret. As a result, the cupola concept was (temporarily) shelved. Eventually, a turret without a cupola emerged as the victor. Production began in late December 1941 and the first new turrets were fielded in March 1942.

The new turret was hexagonal in shape, hence the unofficial name hexagonal turret, with turret walls that gently sloped upward. It was built by two separately cast parts. The lower cast part consisted of the turret ring and lower turret bustle. The upper cast part consisted of the six sides of the turret. The casting moulds for the upper part was made from twenty interlocking pieces, which left an interlocking cross pattern on the turret's surface.

The air filter was moved to the rear of the turret, and the lifting hardpoints were increased from three to four. The first turrets had six intakes cut into the air filter dome at the rear of the turret roof, compared to the previous four cut-outs. The turret had two escape hatches at the top that were round. The gun was mounted in an external housing that allowed the turret to be shorter.

Interestingly, like many other items on the T-34 that had been changed during the war, the turret resembled the turret that would have equipped the T-34M. Indeed, KhPZ 183 had cast five such turrets before the war broke out, even shipping them to UTZ 183.

Like many Soviet items in the Second World War, there was no official name given to the new turret. The Russian crews who operated these new tanks called these new turrets 'Gayka' (Russian: 'гайка', English: 'nuts') as they looked like the top of a hexagonal hardware nut. It should also be noted that the turrets from as early as 1940 were also hexagonal, but these were much longer as the housing for the gun was inside the turret walls rather than an external mount.

Post-war enthusiasts and historians have also come up with names to easily define the hexagonal turret. One such name presented is 'Laminate Turret', due to the texturing on the turret resembling that of laminated materials. This, however, does not adequately describe the turret and can plant false ideas on the turret's construction into one's mind. The authors settled on the name of hexagonal as a generic term and 'composite' to refer to this specific initial subtype of turret, seeing as though the method of producing the cast's mould was with blocks that formed the mould. Therefore, the mould was of composite construction. Other subtypes of hexagonal turrets will be discussed later.

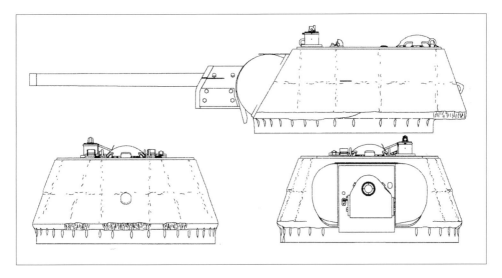

The turret that UTZ 183 eventually would design and produce was this composite type of turret. The turret has gained this post-war name due to the composite nature of the mould for the turret casting, which left distinctive patterning on the turret walls.

30

UTZ 183: HEXAGONAL COMPOSITE TURRETS, DECEMBER 1941–SEPTEMBER 1942

T-34 (UTZ 183 INITIAL PRODUCTION COMPOSITE)

The new hexagonal turrets would have been issued to the hulls being manufactured at the beginning of 1942. T-34 (UTZ 183 Initial Production Composite)s would therefore have pressed 'all rubber' road wheels, reinforced 550-mm type or V-type 1941 track, and the rounded rear transmission plate with a square transmission hatch. The first hexagonal-turreted T-34s rolled out of UTZ in December 1941.

While the turret had been accepted for production in December 1941, the earliest recorded sighting of the hexagonal-turreted T-34s was on the Karelian Isthmus on 19 April 1942, though undoubtedly hexagonal-turreted tanks were used before this date. Photographic evidence (with dates provided by the Finnish Ministry of Defence, SA-kuva) shows two such initial production hexagonal tanks lost on this date near the River Syvärin, the Russian name being 'Svir'. These tanks were also painted with the distinctive dazzle-patterned white with patches of green, with a white mesh painted over this. This paint scheme is commonly called the 'chicken wire' pattern due to the nature of the white mesh painted over the 4BO green.

A small number of these hexagonal-turreted tanks were equipped with the additional armour plates that were implemented to try to thicken the glacis armour of the tanks. Photographic evidence suggests that they had bolts on the lower glacis, therefore the 'U' cut-outs of the original hull in the lower plate were visible. One such vehicle survived until at least the battles at Voronezh in June 1942.

While the earliest hexagonal-turreted T-34s were issued with unchanged hulls, from December 1941 until June 1942, the T-34 design at UTZ 183 was simplified. This was both done to speed up the production of the tank and to make the tank as simple to produce as possible.

The first item changed on the hull was that done to the rear. The original gear plate was redesigned as to not require a bend in the plate. This then required the rear plate to be extended to meet the gear plate. The transmission access hatch was also redesigned with a rounded hatch being implemented, with seven bolts to attach it to the hull. This was like how Krasnoye

Sormovo 112 designed their access hatches, except the UTZ 183 type was larger, with seven bolts rather than four. This met at a 90-degree angle and matched that of the rear of Krasnoye Sormovo 112 tanks, but the gear plate sat above the exhaust plate, with the retention of the diamond hinges. A third hinge was added onto the plate for integrity when opening the rear. While this was done shortly after the hexagonal turret was introduced, older rear plates were used until stocks were used up, so both types of rear plates can be found until June 1942.

The first fielding of the T-34 (UTZ 183 Initial Production Composite) was on the Karelian Isthmus. This tank was lost on 19 April 1942. This tank has the chicken-wire-type camouflage. This machine is equipped with the pressed-type road wheels, reinforced 550-mm-type track, and the round cut-off type machine gun position. (*SA-Kuva Collection*)

This T-34 (UTZ 183 Initial Production Composite) is one of the very rare tanks to be painted in a two- or three-tone camouflage. The tank has an unusual pattern of green and whitewash, and potentially a darker green or even brown. The tank was lost in the early spring of 1942.

This T-34 (UTZ 183 Initial Production Composite) displays all the major features of the early tanks that make these vehicles stand out. Notice the early rounded rear gull with square transmission hatch, in conjunction with all pressed road wheels. Turret markings consist of a white line painted around the top of the turret, a white '52' on the turret side, and a white air-identification triangle painted onto the turret roof. It is likely that a patriotic slogan is painted onto the rear sides of the turret but obscured by the curious German soldiers.

A T-34 (UTZ 183 Initial Production Composite) tank, with an additional armour glacis plate. The tank is named *Bolshevik* (большевик), and it had a white '77' in a circle, next to another white divisional marking which has been hit by a shot. Notice the six cut-outs for the air extractor and a bracket for a 200-litre fuel drum on the rear plate.

This T-34 (UTZ 183 Initial Production Composite) is being used for infantry anti-tank training. Notice the multiple penetrations on the hull side from magnetic mines. The rear two road wheels are not standard for Initial Production Composite tanks.

This T-34 (UTZ 183 Initial Production Composite) survived in Soviet ranks until the winter of 1942. The tank has not lasted the entire time without damage as a clear repair patch can be seen on the hull side just below the dislodged turret ring.

T-34 (UTZ 183 EARLY PRODUCTION COMPOSITE)

Shortly after the implementation of the hexagonal turret at UTZ 183, avenues for simplifying production were explored. Between April and June 1942, 770 items on the tank were simplified and 5,641 items were completely removed, with a further 206 items being manufactured indigenously at the plant rather than being manufactured by subsidiaries.

The first major external item that changed during this simplification process was the road wheels. It is thought that this change occurred in mid-April 1942. Tanks were issued initially with the pressed-type road wheels that had stayed relatively unchanged from 1940. This was changed to cast spider-type road wheels (so named as they looked like spiders' webs), with spoked ribs with circular holes in between the ribs. These wheels had ribs that alternated between one long rib from the rim to the axle to a half rib from the rim that ended halfway between the rim and the axle. The front road wheel was still issued as the pressed type.

These tanks were produced in small numbers, and each batch was slightly different to the next, always adding or retracting items, examples being the implementation of the MG position gun shield and the switch to and from pressed-type and cast spider-type wheels as supplies were used up.

Special note should be made that tanks were issued with pressed-type road wheels while cast spider-type wheels were being issued to other tanks; however, all pressed wheels were phased out towards the end of the simplification process.

This exceptional example of a T-34 (UTZ 183 Early Production Composite) displays many rare and unique features of the transitional period of the T-34 at UTZ. First, the glacis plate is equipped with additional armour, indicating this to be one of the earliest examples of composite turrets. Interestingly, the glacis plate is also the earlier type with a pressed bulge above the driver's hatch, intended for the early styles of periscopes on the earlier driver's hatch. The wheel configuration is standard of this period—four cast spider type and one pressed type. The engine deck has been simplified, as can be seen by the angle of the engine deck covers that are less refined and more angular. Notice that there is no jack or jack block. The turret took damage, and the loader's hatch has been torn off, as has the smoke extractor dome. Lastly, the markings are likely from the 1st Guards Tank Brigade. The photograph was taken during the Second Battle of Kharkov (12–28 May 1942).

Here is an excellent example of the T-34 (UTZ 183 Early Production Composite). The changelog is large, but what is visible is the new cast spider type and thin cast spider type wheels with one pressed-type road wheel in the first position. The rear of the hull is curved, and the rear of the turret has an air intake with six cut-outs. This tank has no radio.

This T-34 (UTZ 183 Early Production Composite) is equipped with the reinforced 550-mm-type track. Notice the turret markings, thought to be '38 3a ....' '3a' in Russian means 'For ... !'. It is possible that the full slogan reads 'For Russia!' or 'For the Motherland!'. This tank is lacking a headlight and radio. It was likely lost during the Second Battle of Kharkov in spring 1942, as many tanks lost there were early hexagonal-turreted tanks.

T-34 (UTZ 183 Early Production Composite) *For the Homeland 113* is another intermediate type T-34. The PT-4 periscope cap can be seen on the gun cheeks. There are no radio or headlights on this tank.

This interesting example of a T-34 (UTZ 183 Early Production Composite) is rather strange, for instead of having a single pressed road wheel in the first position, all of the road wheels are the cast spider type. The markings, too, are strange. The number '241' is stencilled in red inside a red box on the rear left of the turret, and 'For Stalin' ('За Сталина') is written on the front lower turret, also likely in red. The upper half of the turret is painted white, whereas the lower turret appears to be green. The turret roof is possibly also green, as indicated by the air extractor dome. The drive wheel is the type lacking return rollers.

The same T-34 as seen above. The relatively bizarre colour scheme on the turret can be clearly seen.

This T-34 (UTZ 183 Early Production Composite) is equipped with the V-type 1941 track. Once again, notice the markings on the turret. The spring and summer of 1942 was the period during which almost every tank was painted with a slogan. This tank has no headlight but has a radio.

The drive wheel was simplified, and many different variants of drive wheel can be found, most common of which are the 1942 plain-type drive wheels that lack any reinforcing ribs or rings.

Cast hull blisters were also made during the simplification process. These blisters were slightly more bulbous than the earlier type of blister, and sometimes, a casting nub can be seen. It is thought that this change was done while the armoured cover was placed onto the machine gun.

The electrics of the tanks were greatly simplified, with no headlight and radio on the early pressed-type wheeled tanks. However, these items were slowly re-introduced during the consolidation period, when the tanks were evaluated on their performance. The radio was reintroduced while the cast spider-type wheels were still being fielded.

Fielded still was the 71-TK-3 radio set. This was becoming outdated and had been issued from 1939. From late 1942, a new set was introduced that was more compact and easier to use. This was the R-9 transmitter/receiver. The type fielded on T-34s was the 9-RM.

This rear plate was also attached to the hull sides via four bolts per side instead of five. A notable gap can be found on UTZ 183 tanks where there was a bolt missing. The angled rear plates with a round transmission became ever more common at this time as the stocks of older rounded rears were used up. By June 1942, only the angled rear plate was used.

The headlight that had been placed on the glacis plate since 1940 was reintroduced and moved to the left hull side, above the toolbox, and a horn was placed below this in later models. It is thought that the headlight was reintroduced after the hull was redesigned, and the standard configuration of road wheels road was introduced.

T-34 (UTZ 183 Early Production Composite) *Commissar Pozharsky* (Комиссар Пожарский) belonged to the 51st Tank Brigade of either the 194th or 155th Armoured Battalion. The unit was engaged in fierce fighting in the Voronezh sector of fighting, and this tank was lost with another six tanks on 9 July 1942, near the village of Bloznovsky. Notice the blister armoured cover to protect this position. Ivan Pozharsky was a posthumous Hero of the Soviet Union who died at the Battle of Lake Khasan (29 July–11 August 1938) against the Japanese.

Commissar Pozharsky, again. More of the strange technical features of the T-34 (UTZ 183 Early Production Composite) can now be seen. The tank still has a rounded gear plate but has UTZ angled gear covers. The middle road wheel is the cast spider thin type. A large bracket can be seen on the rear of the tank; this was thought to be for a 200-l fuel tank.

T-34 (UTZ 183 Early Production Composite) *Dmitry Donskoy* (Дмитрий Донской) of the 51st Tank Brigade. The tank was lost in combat on 9 June 1942, along with the T-34s on page 243. Notice the road wheel set up, along with the blister protective mount.

Two T-34s that belonged to the 51st Tank Brigade. The tank in the foreground, upside down, is a late example of a T-34 (UTZ 183 Early Production Composite). The tank has been issued with three cast steel-rimmed type wheels in the central positions, but the first road wheel is a pressed-type wheel. In standard production tanks, the pressed road wheel was replaced with a cast spider-type wheel. The second vehicle has had its turret blown off but is a Plated T-34 (UTZ 183 Early Production Composite) from the initial production batch.

This T-34 (UTZ 183 Early Production Composite) tank drove into soft ground and was an easy target for a German gunner. The turret markings are common in style for June 1942. It is hard to tell if the road wheels are pressed or cast spider type. However, due to the PT-4-7 periscope in the turret (which was introduced in May 1942), it is more likely to have cast spider type road wheels, with a single pressed wheel on the first position, which was introduced in April 1942.

One weak point on the tank was strengthened. Now, the hull MG position was given an armoured cap that finally gave some protection to the engineer's position. It is thought that this was implemented before the hull was simplified, with some photographic evidence supporting this.

With all this said, it should be noted that there was likely during this time that a 'first in, last out' phenomenon was being experienced because old items were still being issued alongside new items.

T-34 (UTZ 183 STANDARD PRODUCTION COMPOSITE)

The road wheels were further simplified, introducing new UTZ cast steel-rimmed road wheels like those at STZ on the second, third, and fourth road wheels. These wheels differed slightly from STZ-cast type, with strengthening rings to the inner holes on the wheels. This change was implemented in mid–late May 1942, first appearing on the battlefield in early June 1942. This became the standard wheel configuration from May 1942 to early 1943.

The first T-34s issued with the three cast wheels were given a cast spider-type rear road wheel, but a pressed-type rubber wheel was still placed on the forward most road wheel position. Two rubber-rimmed cast spider-type road wheels were then positioned in the first and fifth position, with the three steel-rimmed road wheels situated in the inner three positions.

This OT-34 (UTZ 183 Early Production Composite) is being used as a temporary shelter for German soldiers, as discerned by the piling up of logs on the right. The turret's slogan is '46' with a double underscore followed by 'For the Homeland!' ('За Родину!'). Notice the single pressed-type wheel, then the three cast steel-rimmed type wheels in the middle.

A T-34 (UTZ 183 Early Production Composite). The vehicle has three cast steel-rimmed road wheels in the central positions but retains a single pressed-type road wheel in the first position. Note that the vehicle appears to be heavily damaged, with the hull jerked forwards indicating both front springs wheels have snapped.

One of the earliest examples of the T-34 (UTZ 183 Standard Production Composite), which was the somewhat standardised hexagonal-turreted T-34. No. 211 was lost on 4 June 1942, but this photograph was taken likely on the 5th or 6th. Notice the hull machine gun position and the cable for the hull side-mounted headlight. The track is the 550-mm waffle-pattern type.

No. 211 on 4 June 1942. The tank is equipped with a cast spider-type rubber wheel on the first and fifth position, with cast steel-rimmed road wheels on the second, third, and fourth positions. The rear hull would have been angled with a round transmission hatch attached with seven bolts.

No. 206 on the Volkhov Front. Here the rear plate can be seen with only four bolts attaching it to the side plates. It is thought that this tank reversed into the wooden bunker as opposed to the bunker being made specifically for the T-34. The track is also the 550-mm waffle-pattern type.

A new track was also implemented. The old reinforced 550-mm type track was dispensed with and a new 550-mm waffle-pattern track was used alongside V-type 41 and the later V-type 42 and V-type waffle tracks. This track was quite rare at UTZ 183, and the standard T-34 track at UTZ 183 throughout the rest of 1942 was a V-type track and its variations.

The V-type track that was being used was redesigned slightly, as to now have a waffle pattern on the toothless links. This track can be called 'V-type 42'. The previous pattern was simple lengthways strips, of which there was three. After the hexagonal-turreted tanks had become standardised, V-type track became the only track issued to the tanks. This track type was mainly issued between September 1941 and January 1943, before other patterns of track became far more common.

The first turrets had six intakes cut into the air filter, but this was reduced to four when the hull simplification occurred. In addition, the periscope was changed from the old PT-4 to the new PT-4-7. Outwardly, the PT-4 was a long cylinder with an armoured cap at the top, whereas the PT-4-7 was an upside-down cone shape, with no cap, but a hole roughly halfway down the periscope revealing the lens. These turrets with the new air-filter intakes and periscopes seem to be the last outward changes made to the tanks during the simplification process.

Additionally, it was during this time that the distinctive buffer for track pins was first implemented. Initially, this was a curved piece of metal that was placed above the drive wheel, attached to the bolts on the exterior of the gear bulges. This was designed to hit track pins back into position as the track moved. Later in 1943, this would be changed to a single square piece of metal attached to the hull side, with a triangular raised portion in the centre as to knock track pins back into position.

Many items, including the road wheels, were redesigned to be cast rather than pressed or rolled. Two types of 'spider' wheels were manufactured; these were the UTZ cast steel-rimmed type and the UTZ cast steel-rimmed thin type. The UTZ cast steel-rimmed type was the same diameter and thickness as the steel road wheels. The UTZ cast steel-rimmed thin type wheels

The T-34 (UTZ 183 Standard Production Composite) is the final product of the major simplification process. This tank was lost on 1 July 1942 near Voronezh. The wheel set is now standardised and consists of two cast spider-type road wheels on the first and fifth positions and three cast steel-rimmed type road wheels.

Another T-34 lost on 1 July. Notice the counterweight of the F-34 at the rear of the gun inside the turret. This tank is another T-34 (UTZ 183 Standard Production Composite).

A T-34 (UTZ 183 Standard Production Composite), named *Spartak* (Спартак) after the Moscow football club. This name was painted onto the gun mantlet and the hull side, but the soldier obscures this detail in this photo. Notice the PT-4-7 cap on the turret, apparently being unscrewed from the rest of the scope.

were also the same diameter but were much thinner than the regular road wheels. This was done to save on rubber by having to use less of it on the tank's wheels. A very rare item used was a new pressed drive wheel that had no return rollers for the track's teeth. These lacked any form of strengthening points on the drive wheel and were very simple. The standard types with return rollers were far more common.

Despite all that has been stated, it must again be stressed that items were introduced gradually, and some tanks were issued with newer items before other items, even if these parts were made at the same time. Examples exist of T-34s with pressed-type wheels, reinforced 550-mm type track, and the PT-4 periscopes, but have the new angled rear. Such examples have been found in photographs with the additional armour plates on the glacis, implying that these tanks, despite the angled rear, were likely some of the first hexagonal-turreted tanks manufactured. One must remember that T-34s were recovered from battlefields and repaired or rebuilt, often with parts from other factories—road wheels especially. However, rebuilds only make up 15 per cent of all tanks at any given time and are therefore unusual.

Generally, it is thought that the angled rear hull was introduced at a similar time to the new turrets, which was in December 1941, but stocks of the older, rounded rear hull were still being used up at this time.

Some vehicles from this production run were additionally equipped with a large bracket on the rear of the tank which is thought to have been a holder for a large 200-litre fuel tank. Between October 1941 and October 1942, UTZ 183 tanks were not issued with exterior fuel tanks.

Two standardised T-34 (UTZ 183 Standard Production Composite)s lost on 5 July 1942, during the Battle of Voronezh (23 June–6 July 1942).

The eventual finalisation of the simplification process is perfectly shown in the next four pictures, taken on 5 July 1942. Notice the new redesigned hull with three hinges. Two features on show are from a UTZ 183 subcontractor; first, notice the redesigned exhaust covers, which was an attempt to simplify production. Second, the gear covers on the rear are angled. This feature is unique to UTZ tanks, and not all tanks at that. This tank is equipped with a V-type 1942 track.

The same tank as on page 251. Notice, too, new features. For example, the road wheels are all cast, with the three UTZ cast steel-rimmed wheels. Furthermore, the headlight is now on the hull side, the periscope is the PT-4-7 type, and the rear air filter has only four intakes. The angle of this photograph also reveals that the tank still retained the rear light and the cut-out in the open mesh cover. This feature would be removed from production shortly after this tank was produced. The driver's hatch has also been blown out and lies on the ground.

The last tank photographed on 5 July. The final item added can now be seen—namely, the hull MG blister has been up-armoured to protect the gunner. Notice how both tanks photographed have lost their driver's hatch. All these features can be called T-34 (UTZ 183 Standard Production Composite). An immolated crew member is on the right of the tank.

The same tank as on page 252. The damage here is extensive. Notice the simplified drive wheel, which is very plain. The writing on the hull of the tank is German graffiti.

A small variation can be found with the rear of T-34s being manufactured at UTZ 183 between April 1942 and the end of production. For example, the rear transmission plate had two rounded bulges that protected the gears for the drive wheels, and some tanks were issued with redesigned gear covers. These were angled rather than being manufactured with a distinctive round edge.

This is a feature found on UTZ 183 and Omsk 174 T-34s. Not every tank from UTZ 183 was given this gear plate either, with some tanks being manufactured with the typical round style. This was due to subsidiaries manufacturing slightly different pieces.

A similar situation can be found with the rear exhaust covers. One of the subcontractors who issued rear exhaust covers to UTZ 183 (and other plants) issued ones that had a distinctive zigzag pattern on the edges of the exhaust. Each peak of this exhaust cover was there for the three bolts that attached the cover on each side. This, once again, was not universal, but appeared on other tanks from different plants and was in use up until T-34 production ended.

In September 1942, the question of the quality of the T-34 was revisited, and after a two-day conference at UTZ 183, it was decided that the tanks should be more carefully made. As a result, items removed from the tank were then reintroduced back into the tank, such as certain lubricating devices. In addition, it was decided that tanks would be issued with five-speed gearboxes taken from the T-34S project.

Composite turrets were manufactured at all the plants except for Krasnoye Sormovo 112 and STZ. The turrets were manufactured between March 1942 and August/September 1942, before UTZ 183 moved into hard-edge production. The composite-turreted tanks were in service throughout the harsh fighting during the Battle of Stalingrad (from August 1942–February 1943),

This T-34 is typical of the June–September production of T-34 (UTZ 183 Standard Production Composite). Notice the three-hinged rear plate. The redesigned exhaust shroud is clearly visible, which were also delivered to factories other than UTZ. The gear covers too are the redesigned angled type, a feature only of UTZ tanks. Notice the V-type waffle track. Interestingly, this tank has turret markings painted in Georgian. This tank is lacking a rear light, and the rear cover has a very small cut out still retained.

The same T-34 as seen above. From this angle, it is clear that the turret was blown from the hull and handed back onto the tank. Russian script is written on the turret's right side, with Georgian on the left.

Early to mid-1942 was a period when turret markings became very popular, so slogans were common. This tank has 'Kotovsky 176' painted on it. Grigory Kotovsky was a general of the Bolshevik forces during the Russian Civil War. Notice the PT-4-7 periscope. (*Will Kerrs Collection*)

Two T-34 (UTZ 183 Standard Production Composite) tanks knocked out likely during the Battle of Voronezh, 1942. Notice both tanks have V-type 1942 tracks, and both tanks have their radio antennas plugged. It is easy to see why Germans soldiers called these tanks 'Mickey Mouse' due to the two circular hatches on the turret.

This tank was lost on 11 July 1942 during the opening engagements of Case Blue, the German advance south towards Stalingrad. Most of these T-34 (UTZ 183 Standard Production Composite) tanks were lost in the fierce fighting for Voronezh and the Don.

A T-34 (UTZ 183 Standard Production Composite) knocked out in fighting around Voronezh in July 1942. The turret numbers are Soviet in origin, but the inscription on the hull side is German. The last road wheel on the hull sight side is a cast spider thin road wheel. This was introduced in April 1942 but was phased out by August 1942.

A T-34 (L-ll Gun Last Production) in three-tone camouflage, lost in the Byelorussian SSR, June 1941. This paint scheme was quite rare, but at least two examples are known. Photographs of these T-34s can be found on pages 90 and 91.

A Pre-War T-34 (F-34 Gun), lost in September 1941. This example survived for a few months after the invasion of the USSR on 22 June 1941. A photograph of this T-34 can be found on page 117.

A T-34 (KhPZ 183 Last Production) commanded by Captain Mikhail Pavlovich Agibalov, 21st Tank Brigade, 17 October 1941. Agibalov's T-34 was knocked out in fighting on the Volokolamansk highway. Agibalov is claimed to have covered the retreat of his crew before taking his own life to not be captured by German forces. A photograph of this tank can be found on page 143.

A T-34 (KhPZ 183 Last Production) commanded by Senior Political Instructor G. M. Gnyry, 21st Tank Brigade, 17th October 1941. Gnyry's T-34 is credited with destroying upwards of sixteen Ju-52 transport aircraft stationed at the Kalinin Aerodrome. A bomb was dropped in front of his tank, and his tank fell into the crater. In the ensuing fire, two of his crew were killed, but Gnyry survived. A photograph of this tank can be found on pages 132 and 144.

A T-34 with ZiS-4 57-mm gun, commanded by Major Mikhail Alekseevich Lukin, 21st Tank Brigade, 17 October 1941. Being one of ten T-34s issued with the ZiS-4, the 57-mm gun was a rare sight. Lukin's T-34 was knocked out in fighting on the Volokolamansk highway, in the village of Troyanovo. A photograph of this tank can be found on pages 134 and 142.

Opposite page: A T-34 (STZ interlocking Hull) of the 83rd Independent Tank Battalion of the 47th Tank Brigade from the 4th Tank Corps (pages 178 and 179). The battalion was heavily photographed for propaganda purposes in April 1942, before going into action around Kharkov. The turret markings for the unit included a red star, with the tactical number 'L2-KS'.

Bagration, a Plated T-34 (STZ Chiseled Mantlet). This T-34 was lost in the late spring of 1942, likely in the delaying actions after the partial capture of Voronezh. The tank can be seen photographed on page 185, and the inscription could be either yellow with red or white with red. The inscription is only on the turret's right side.

T-34 No. 419 is a T-34 (STZ Welded Turret Back), photographed in Stalingrad itself, sometime in August 1942.

An early Krasnoye Sormovo 112 T-34, as seen in the spring of 1942. A lot of 112 T-34s were painted in this scheme; it was either the camouflage ordered for the front or they were part of a specific, well-photographed battalion.

T-34 No. 162 is a Plated T-34 (112 Early), equipped with a full turret and hull plate. This T-34 was extensively photographed for Soviet propaganda in March 1942. The turret roof had a white air-identification triangle painted onto the hatch. The tank was knocked out and was, interestingly, photographed for German propaganda. Notice the placements of the fuel tank brackets, typical of plated T-34s from Krasnoye Sormovo 112.

This T-34 (112 with Handrails) was present at the Battle of Kursk. Here, it is depicted before battle.

The same T-34 (112 with Handrails), but after combat. The tank sustained a hit to the turret side above the vision port, but miraculously, it was not knocked out, continued fighting, and was even filmed for propaganda purposes by the Soviets.

This T-34 (UTZ 183 Initial Production) is equipped with the eight-bolt turret and is painted in the distinctive chicken-wire paint scheme. This was very common throughout the winter months of late 1941 and early 1942.

This T-34 (UTZ 183 Initial Production Composite) was lost in combat on the Karelian Isthmus on 19 April 1942 and is the earliest known hexagonal-turreted T-34. This T-34 was photographed by SA-Kuva (page 235), and portions of the tank are still on display at the Palora Tank Museum in Finland. It should be noted that the hexagonal turret was in production from December 1941.

46 For the Motherland! is an OT-34 (UTZ 183 Early Production Composite). Still issued the pressed road wheel in the first position, the middle three wheels are the cast steel-rimmed type. The tank was photographed in June 1942 (page 246), abandoned and being used as a shelter by German forces.

Spartak is a T-34 (UTZ 183 Composite Turret) that was lost in July 1942. *Spartak* could either refer to the 'Moscow Spartak' football club or with a more direct translation, simply mean 'Spartan'. Photographic evidence (page 250) suggests that the hull sides and nose of the gun had the name on it, and some artistic renditions of the tank have a white circle on the rear of the turret.

This T-34 (UTZ 183 Hard-Edge Mid) belonged to the 30th Guards Tank Brigade, and the unit was issued the Order of the Red Banner, as painted on the turret's side. The unit's T-34s were originally green with white slogans before the winter came.

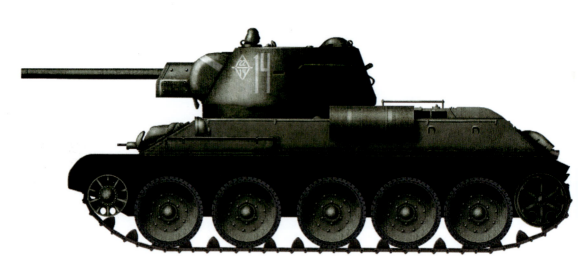

A UTZM T-34 from the 22nd Tank Brigade, heavily photographed for propaganda purposes in June 1943. A white line was painted on the gun cheeks, and the tank's number was also painted on the rear of the turret.

A UTZM manufactured T-34 at the Battle of Kursk (1943) as seen on page 250. The markings are only present on the turret's left side. A white square is painted on the turret roof over the dome air extractor.

This 'Moscow Collective Farm' was a T-34 (174 Early Production). This tank belonged to either the 59th or 60th Tank Regiment and was active throughout the winter of 1942 and early 1943. Tanks of this unit can be found on pages 268, 286, 287, and 326.

Opposite page: This OT-34 (174 Last Production) was lost in early 1944. The tank is numbered 'D-44' and was photographed for propaganda purposes with the skull of a dead soldier balanced onto the front fender. The tank, and indeed all Omsk 174 T-34s from this period, only carried two exterior drum-type fuel tanks.

T-34-85 (112 Initial Production) of the 38th Separate Tank Regiment, 53rd Army, 'Dmitri Donskoi', March 1944. The quite well-known T-34s of this unit were donated by the Russian Orthodox Church, and the vehicles were named after a fourteenth-century Russian monk.

T-34-85 (UTZ 183 Late) of the 56th Guards Tank Brigade, 7th Tank Corps, 3rd Guards Tank Army, on the Seelow Heights, April 1945. This unit was photographed in detail by Soviet propaganda in the closing days of the war.

T-34-85 (UTZ 183 Early) of the 62nd Guards Tank Brigade, 10th Guards Tank Corps. This Brigade was the first Soviet tank unit to reach Prague in Czechoslovakia (see page 393). The vehicle was knocked out during the fighting and was loaded onto a recovery flatbed.

A North Korean People's Army (NKPA) T-34-85 (UTZ 183 Late). The vehicle is typical of North Korean T-34s, with no major turret markings other than a white three-digit number on the turret side.

Opposite page: A Chinese Type 58. This was essentially an upgrade package to the T-34-85 which concerned giving the vehicle a second cupola and turret stowage hardpoints for a 12.7-mm Type 54 machine gun, as well as a new hinge system for engine access. This illustration is based on a Type 58 in the Beijing Tank Museum and has the '8-1 star' painted on. The earliest photos of Chinese T-34-85s (and other Chinese tanks in the late 1940s and early 1950s) appear to show that decals were used for '8-1' stars, but later photos show that '8-1 stars' were later painted on. No evidence for camouflage schemes on T-34-85s or Type 58s exists outside of inaccurate museum restorations, although an abandoned three-tone SU-100 is noted.

A Syrian-operated T-34-85 (Martin 1952–56). A slogan is painted onto the turret side that reads 'Suleman Ahmad'. Vehicles like this were lost on the Golan Heights in 1967, and many were photographed by Israeli tourists. Many still sit where, or near to, they were knocked out to this day.

The world-famous Mandela Way T-34 *Stompie Garden*, as seen in the mid-2010s. This paint scheme was designed and painted by the artist 'Tee'. Two artists painted this tank: Tee, who was the first artist to paint the tank, and Spizzenergi frontman 'Spizz'. The 'Love Tank' is perhaps the most famous scheme that it has ever been painted in. Other well-known schemes are 'Tank Taxi', 'UFO', and 'Remembrance', painted in poppies for the 100th anniversary of the beginning of the First World War.

mostly in the winter fighting during Operation Uranus (19 November 1942–3 February 1943), and the advance to Kharkov (3 February–15 March 1943); most were lost in the latter two periods. As such, the type was scarce by the Battle of Kursk in July 1943. These tanks formed the backbone of the tank units and were integrated with hard-edge and soft-edge turrets (to be discussed later).

The advantage over the early type turrets was that they were easier to manufacture and maintain. One misconception with hexagonal turrets was that they had a greater internal volume than the early type turret. While it is true that they are taller, allowing for greater headroom, the turrets were actually not as long as the early turrets as the gun mantlet was not integrated into the turret design.

Internal stowage for these turrets was somewhat increased, with improved placement for the machine gun magazine racks at the rear of the turret. That said, there were still some issues with ammunition layout and crew coordination that were not resolved until the introduction of the T-34-85, which only partially resolved them.

As much of an improvement to the T-34 that these new composite hexagonal turrets were, they were not being produced at a rate to keep up with the production of hulls. Therefore, new casting methods were explored. This led to the development of soft-edge and hard-edge turrets, along with pressed turrets.

A burned-out T-34 (UTZ 183 Standard Production Composite), with the turret inscription '14.8 Woronesch', indicating the tank was lost on 14 August (1942) somewhere near Voronezh. It is likely that the turret side has some Soviet inscription painted onto it, but this has been painted over as to make way for the German inscription.

Another T-34 (UTZ 183 Standard Production Composite) lost near the T-34 on page 257. The tank has two wooden logs for unditching stowed on the hull sides. The damage to the fender is strange, with the top of the left hull fender having been removed, but the sidewall for the glacis is still intact.

This T-34 (UTZ 183 Hard-Edge Early) got stuck in a marsh. Just visible on the turret is '43' with a double underscore. It is likely that, like the tank from the same regiment on page 246, a patriotic slogan is written on the rear of the turret side.

Two T-34s knocked out in fighting during the summer of 1942. The T-34 on the left is a T-34 (STZ Cast Late Production), with the STZ reinforced cast-type road wheels. The other tank, however, is an interesting rebuild. The turret is a composite type from UTZ 183, but it has a Krasnoye Sormovo 112 hull with handrails. Furthermore, the wheels are either STZ late or UTZ cast road wheels. Rebuilds made up less than 15 per cent of all T-34s on later battlefields. Note what appears to be evidence of a burned slogan on the turret on the tank on the right.

EARLY WAR ALTERNATIVES TO THE HEXAGONAL TURRET

It should be noted that due to the dire need for tanks, some extreme avenues were explored to simplify and speed up production at this time. For example, in November 1941, UTZ 183 drew up plans for a new T-34 turret that was manufactured from crude rolled plates that were welded together. The design also featured a 45-mm Model 1934 gun, instead of the 76.2-mm F-34 of standard T-34s. The design was rejected as the turret's integrity was in serious question, and the 45-mm gun was less desirable than the 76.2-mm gun as had been decided long ago during the A-20's presentation to Pavlov on 28 March 1938.

Simplification of the T-34 was always on the mind of engineers at UTZ 183, and another project was drawn up in spring 1942 even after the introduction of the hexagonal turret. At the same time the KV-1 was being simplified to produce the KV-1S (Russian: 'С'—'Скорый'; English: 'S'—'Speedy'), UTZ 183 began work on a design along similar lines for the T-34 in April-May 1942, with a single T-34S prototype being manufactured in September 1942. This tank had a three-man turret with a command cupola, which was one of the rejected designs for the hexagonal turret earlier that year. Yet the turret was too small for three men, so the project was cancelled. The only thing retained from this project for standard T-34s was a newly developed five-speed gearbox.

On the subject of a three-man turret, a T-34 with a 122-mm gun was drawn up in mid-1942 which was similar to the KV-2. This never left the drawing board, but several designs were proposed on a large turret that allowed for three crewmen to work with either a single 122-mm gun or a 76.2-mm with two coaxial 45-mm guns. These were all rejected, as it was decided to not complicate T-34 production at such an important time.

The T-34S prototype. The turret was expected to hold a third crewman, but it simply could not - this being the main reason the project was dropped. Other minor changes are the handrails on the hull side lacking a central bracket. Other than this, the chassis externally is almost identical to a standard T-34/76. Internally, the T-34S had a five-speed gearbox, which was the only feature salvaged from the design. (*Maxim Kolomiets*)

A side view of the T-34S. Notice the simplified drive wheel, which was used on some T-34s. The cupola in the turret does not have a hatch to escape from but does have a small hatch for signal flags. (*Maxim Kolomiets*)

31

UTZ 183: SOFT-EDGE AND
HARD-EDGE TURRETS, 1942–1943

The composite turrets were a step in the right direction in making the T-34 more comfortable to operate in. However, these new turrets were manufactured using a time-consuming composite casting mould that required a lengthy assembly before casting could occur. Therefore, new turret designs were experimented with to increase the production rates of the T-34 turrets.

T-34 (UTZ 183 HARD-EDGE EARLY)

From September 1942, two distinct turret types were created. First was what is known as the hard-edge turret. Rather than being cast from a mould with twenty individual parts, the new turret mould was simply two pieces for the upper turret and two pieces for the lower turret to form the walls of the turret.

The lower turret consisted of the turret ring and the bustle, and the upper turret consisted of all the turret walls. This does not include the turret roof. The rear of the turret had distinctive casting nubs around the rear bustle. A single seam ran around the turret, which was obscured by the forward portion of the turret on the hard-edge variants.

During the process of making these turrets, an entire turret's upper portion would be cast, and then gas cut. Areas that were cut out include the hole for the gun mantlet, vision ports, and the rear pistol port, not to mention the casting nubs. This process was the same for both soft-edge and hard-edge turrets.

This turret began production in early September 1942. Hard-edge turrets get their name from the noticeable sharp edge at the front portion of the turret cheek underside. Hard-edge turrets lacked pistol ports, and very early examples lacked handrails. Handrails were introduced to these in late September 1942, and pistol ports were introduced in August 1943, when the cupola was introduced (discussed in Chapter 32).

The second new turret type was the soft-edge turret. Being constructed from two plates meant that the turret's structural integrity was far greater than that of the composite turret.

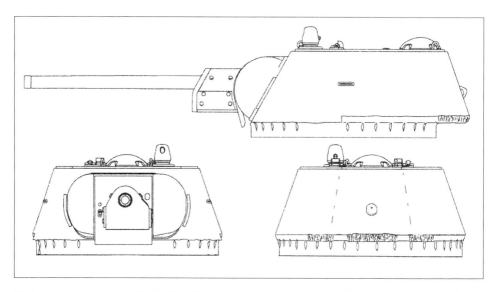

The hard-edge turret designed for the T-34. This turret was primarily used by UTZ 183 throughout 1943 and before T-34-85 production, UTZM up until early 1943, and Omsk 174 from September 1942 until early 1943. This turret would receive handrails, pistol ports, and a cupola before production ended.

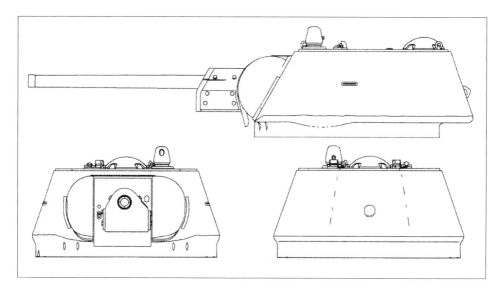

The soft-edge turret designed for the T-34. This turret was primarily used throughout ChKZ production, UTZM production from October 1942, Omsk 174 from December 1942, and Krasnoye Sormovo 112 with a cupola. This turret would receive handrails, pistol ports, and a cupola before production ended.

Opposite below: This T-34 was probably lost during Operation Little Saturn (16 December 1942–20 February 1943). These were the follow-up actions to the highly successful Operation Uranus, the encirclement of Stalingrad. This T-34 (UTZ 183 Hard-Edge Early) was likely manufactured in September 1942. The V-type waffle track was redesigned in mid-1942 so that every link had a waffle pattern on it. A dead crew member lies before the tank.

A T-34 (UTZ 183 Hard-Edge Early). The hull of the tank is identical to those being used by the earlier T-34 (UTZ 183 Standard Production Composite) tanks. There are no grab handles on the hull or turret. Some whitewash has been applied, but it seems to have been mostly removed. Notice the one open, one closed armoured cap for the driver's vision blocks.

The same tank on page 263. Notice the 122-mm howitzer behind this tank. Take note of the diamond divisional marking, which is clearer in this photo.

This turret's lower edge to the front of the turret had a noticeably softer edge to it on the underneath of the front sides of the turret. These turrets were not used extensively by UTZ 183, and the overwhelming majority of the turrets used were hard-edge. Soft-edge turrets were originally issued without pistol ports but were later introduced into the design in August 1943. The soft-edge and hard-edge turret were manufactured simultaneously from September 1942 until March 1944.

The turrets were not used by every factory, UTZ only using hard-edge turrets; ChKZ 100 only using soft-edge (and pressed turrets discussed on pages 299–301 and 312–314); Omsk 174 first issued hard-edge, but later moved onto soft-edge; and UTZM issued hard-edge and pressed turrets, then moved onto soft-edge turrets. Krasnoye Sormovo 112 did not issue the turrets until August 1943 and only issued soft-edge turrets, while STZ never issued the turrets due to the proximity of the Germans to the factory and the subsequent evacuation.

The description of the hull changes that follow concern those done at UTZ 183, but they were copied by or from other plants and will be discussed in the relevant section.

Opposite below: An interesting example of a rebuilt T-34. Much like the T-34 on page 259, this vehicle shows many features of different factories. First, the chassis is a Krasnoye Sormovo 112 production hull, with four long hull handrails, glacis handrails, rails over the engine deck, and splash bars around the turret ring. Secondly, the turret is from UTZ 183, being a hard edge turret, with V-type waffle tracks. Lastly, the wheels are an interesting mixture of items. Four of the road wheels are STZ cast wheels without reinforcements around the interior holes, and one UTZ cast spider-type road wheel. Notice the STZ style tow hooks, with a simple spike of metal welded to the glacis to prevent the tow rope coming from the hook.

Blown apart by a huge internal explosion, this T-34 (UTZ 183 Hard-Edge Early) was lost in fighting around Stalingrad in November 1942. The tank does not have handrails or exterior fuel tanks, the former being introduced in September, and the latter in October 1942.

T-34 (UTZ 183 HARD-EDGE MID)

As production of the T-34 continued, more ways of improving the tank were explored. Shortly after the implementation of the hard-edge and soft-edge turrets, handrails began to make an appearance on the tank's hulls. These were different from the handrails on Krasnoye Sormovo 112 tanks and were constructed by a rod of metal, attached to the tank on the hull sides by three brackets, but only by two brackets for those on the turret. In December 1942, another pair of handrails was attached to the engine deck.

On the hull sides, two pairs of long handrails were placed at the top of the hull. Onto the turret, a short handrail was placed at the rear of the turret, and two slightly longer handrails were placed on the rear turret sides. Unlike Krasnoye Sormovo 112, no handrails were placed onto the glacis plate or onto the mesh cover for the radiator.

It should be noted that early soft-edge-turreted tanks were also issued without handrails, although these tanks were incredibly rare as handrails were implemented at the same time that the first soft-edge turrets were implemented.

Minor variation can be found with the road wheel configuration. As the hard-edge turrets were introduced in September, thin-type road wheels were no longer issued to the tanks. From late 1942, the well-known 500-mm waffle-pattern track was introduced onto UTZ 183-manufactured tanks. These tracks had been used by Krasnoye Sormovo 112 and, to a much lesser extent, STZ since the end of 1941, only now becoming standard on UTZ 183 T-34s. Dropped from the production lines was the V-type waffle track. The last tanks that were issued this track did not have rear exterior fuel tanks.

A T-34 (UTZ 183 Hard-Edge Mid) manufactured in September 1942 before the introduction of fuel tanks. The tank was lost in the Battle of Stalingrad. Notice the radio, which was becoming more common in early 1943.

This T-34 (UTZ 183 Hard-Edge Mid) has a stove attached to the rear of the tank. This stove was used for cooking as well as heating the crew. This pattern on the stove was used from 1942 until the end of the war. Below this is what appears to be the corpse of a tank rider who was equipped with the DT machine gun (with flash hider) resting on the heater. One can also see a DP magazine resting on the rear of the turret which is wider and thinner than a DT magazine. The two UTZ box-type fuel tanks can be seen on the rear of the tank.

A collecting point in Kharkov for destroyed T-34s. Here, about twelve T-34s are scattered about and abandoned. Mixed among these machines are tanks from ChKZ 100, Krasnoye Sormovo 112, UTZ 183, and Omsk 174.

A close view of the previous photograph reveals one tank with a turret slogan, this being Московский колхозник ('Moscow Collective Farm'). This collective farm is known to have paid for (through a bond scheme) a column of tanks that fought at Voronezh in 1943. The T-34 on the left is a T-34 (112 with Handrails), The T-34 in the centre is a T-34 (Soft-Edge Mid), and the Moscow Collective Farm T-34 is likely a ChKZ 100 or Omsk 174 T-34, as these were the two factories that supplied the unit.

This T-34 (UTZ 183 Hard-Edge Mid) was blown up during fighting before Stalingrad. Notice the last road wheel is a cast spider-type road wheel. By the end of 1942, it would be replaced with another cast steel-rimmed type road wheel.

This T-34 (UTZ 183 Hard-Edge Mid) tank was lost in front of the T-34 on page 218. Notice the damage to the hull fillet. This was a known weak point on T-34s, hence why it was redesigned to come to a point.

In September 1942, a decree from the GKO stated that the minimum fuel allowance for the T-34 was to be increased to 380 litres, so every factory experimented with their own fuel tanks to this end.

UTZ 183 designed two rear-mounted fuel tanks that were box-shaped and had five sides as viewed from the side, with one long side that also followed the angled contour of the hull. Each fuel box could carry an extra 40 litres. These were first attached to tanks from UTZ 183 from October 1942 onwards and were also copied by Krasnoye Sormovo 112 and UTZM.

Due to the addition of the fuel tanks at the rear of the T-34, it is possible to date T-34s with handrails and no fuel tanks from late September–early October production. Minor changes were made to the rear cover for the fan. Also, because new exterior fuel tanks were implemented, it became necessary to attach new hardpoints and tubes for the fuel.

During the winter months, hardpoints were attached to the exhaust plate for attaching a heater. This was a large metal box that was a stove and allowed the crew to prepare a warm sleeping tent at the back of the T-34. A small exhaust pipe was on the side of this box, which was fuelled by wood or coal.

In November 1942, the rearmost road wheel was replaced. Originally a cast spider type was put onto the fifth position, but it was replaced with a fourth cast steel-rimmed type road wheel. This was done as supplies of rubber road wheels for UTZ 183 were running short, therefore the minimum amount of rubber was used. It should be noted however that all of the other factories were increasing the amount of rubber road wheels used.

This UTZ T-34 has taken several penetrations to the front of the tank. Notice also that the barrel has been pierced by a shell that came from in front of the vehicle, as discerned by the large exit hole on the rear of the barrel. The hull has two large penetrations near the driver's position. One can also see the engineer's escape hatch, which is open.

This T-34 (UTZ 183 Mid) has suffered a great explosion that has caused the left hull plate to pop out of its position. Notice the white paint. As we cannot see the turret, no name clarification has been given. However, most UTZ 183 T-34s were issued with the hard-edge turrets.

This T-34 (UTZ 183 Hard-Edge Mid) has suffered a hit to the left track, causing the tank to be disabled. The tank's turret has '2212' painted in white as a Soviet marking; however, the rear hull has German road signs painted on it. This tank was lost in March 1943.

A blown-up T-34 (UTZ 183 Hard-Edge Mid). Internal explosions were a common cause for lost vehicles.

A T-34 (UTZ 183 Hard-Edge Mid). While obscured by German soldiers, this tank is a hard-edge hexagonal turret that was produced in 1943. It was in October 1942 that UTZ 183 began manufacturing box-type rear fuel tanks. T-34s at this time were also given handrails. Unlike those at Krasnoye Sormovo 112, the handrails at UTZ 183 were bars with small pieces of metal with holes attaching them to the tank.

A notable yet subtle change was a small strip of metal attached to the glacis plate under the driver's hatch. This was introduced in late 1942 to stop spalls from entering the driver's compartment. A second smaller strip was placed just above the nose joint in late 1942. It is thought this was used for the ease of the driver to enter and exit the tank.

T-34s from UTZ 183 in the discussed configurations were present for most of the important winter battles of 1942 and early 1943. A handful of these T-34s would survive to fight at Kursk, but most were lost during the Third Battle of Kharkov.

T-34 (UTZ 183 HARD-EDGE LATE)

Between December 1942 and August 1943, not much was changed at UTZ 183 regarding the items used on their tanks. Small items were changed, but nothing at the magnitude previously discussed.

One such small change done was the removal of the middle diamond hinge that was attached to the exhaust and gear plates. This was done in early 1943 and is sometimes seen during the Third Battle of Kharkov. Additionally, more radios were issued to the tanks, and by the time the cupola was introduced in August 1943, nearly every tank had a radio.

A rather beat up T-34 (UTZ 183 Hard-Edge Mid). Notice that the handrails on the turret have been removed, leaving just the hardpoints. The air intakes for the radiator can be seen having been blown out of their position. This tank has been equipped with the box-type fuel tanks, as discerned from the hardpoint on the rear of the tank next to the exhaust.

The same tank as seen above. Notice that only the front road wheel is the rubber type. The rear of the turret appears to have a stripe of white between the two hardpoints for the handrail and covers the pistol port.

This T-34 (UTZ 183 Hard-Edge Mid) has had one road wheel replaced during its lifetime. Notice the UTZ box-type fuel tank on the ground next to the tank along with an exhaust shroud. The tank was likely lost at the end of March 1943, being photographed in April.

Two T-34 (UTZ 183 Mid) lost in the Third Battle of Kharkov. The tank in the foreground was likely destroyed by an aircraft or a very large mine. The box-type fuel tanks can be clearly seen, and the hull side interior can be seen resting up against the rear tank. On this, one can see vertical springs and the gears for the final drives.

The same tanks on page 274. Notice the dislodged gun mantlet. The tank's rear hinges have been reduced from three to two.

Two T-34 (UTZ 183 Mid) lost in the spring of 1943. The front of the first tank has taken some very heavy hits, which have completely removed the front MG ball mount. The markings on the hull and fender are German road signs.

In the summer of 1943, and especially after the Battle of Kursk, the Red Army was keen on standardising many items of the T-34. Most of the changes made at UTZ 183 between July 1943 and the implementation of the T-34-85 in March 1944 were these such changes. Many of these changes will be discussed after the cupola was added to the design and can be found in Chapter 32.

Before the cupola was added, very minor changes were made to the T-34s at UTZ. The toolset was updated, and a newly added wood saw was placed onto the hull's front left side just behind the gun-cleaning kit.

Most of these tanks were used from Operation Uranus in November 1942 until Operation Bagration in June 1944. However, they were outclassed by most German tanks and were eventually replaced with the T-34-85. Regardless, it should be noted that T-34/76s were still in large enough numbers to be common on the battlefield until the Battle of Berlin (April–May 1945).

The soft-edge and hard-edge turrets were used from mid-late 1942 until the end of the war. Late production tanks with command cupolas were the most common survivor in 1945, with most other types being lost to combat and never repaired.

Hexagonal-turreted tanks were used by other countries after the war. The East German National People's Army (NVA) used T-34/76s until the late 1960s, and the DPRK (Democratic People's Republic of Korea) is also known to operate some T-34/76s as recently as 2016. While the tank is hopelessly obsolete on the modern battlefield, in 1942, it was a spectacular update to the T-34 that resolved many of the tank's original design flaws. One turret that was issued in conjunction to the described soft and hard-edge turrets was a much rarer hard-edge turret with a central seam that ran around the centre of the turret. Not much is known about this turret type, other than it being an incredibly rare version. The turret was cast in three sections—turret ring and bustle, turret lower, and turret upper. It is likely that the turret was unsatifactory and weaker than the other turrets due to the vulnerability of the weld lines on the turret sides.

This T-34 (UTZ 183 Hard-Edge Mid) was lost at the Battle of Kursk. Take notice of the interior of the tank, with the V-2-34 engine in the centre, and the transmission in front of it.

Above left: This T-34 (UTZ 183 Hard-Edge Mid) appears to have two turret periscopes. This could mean that it is a command tank. Notice also the damaged headlamp.

Above right: This T-34 (UTZ 183 Mid) was lost during the furious fighting at Kursk. Notice the rear road wheel is a cast steel-rimmed type, which was very common after January 1943. A bracket for a UTZ box-type fuel tank can also be seen on the exhaust plate. Interestingly, the middle bolt for attaching the exhaust plate to the hull side has been reintroduced.

This T-34 (UTZ 183 Hard-Edge Late) was lost in the Battle of Kursk. The last road wheel is now a cast steel-rimmed-type road wheel, and a wood saw has been added to the tank. Shortly after this tank was manufactured, the command cupola was introduced, and rubber wheels were reintroduced on the third and fifth positions.

32

HEXAGONAL TURRETS WITH COMMAND CUPOLAS, 1943–1944

One major problem with the T-34 was that it always needed more space inside the turret to accommodate a third crewman. The simplest way to do this was by adding a command cupola. While this did not increase the volume inside the tank greatly, it allowed the commander to sit higher inside the tank still with armour protection and gave a major additional benefit: a cupola allowed the commander a greater, undisrupted view of the battlefield. In fact, the advantages of the cupola were sorely felt when comparing the work of the commander of German tanks compared to Soviet ones. Nonetheless, even with the addition of a cupola, the turret was still too small to have a third crewman inside.

UTZ 183 had been experimenting with cupolas on T-34 turrets since 1941. The T-34M was originally designed with a cupola, and even though this project fell through, cupolas were always on the agenda and so UTZ 183 began designing a cupola for the T-34/76. This design was never implemented because all the experiments with cupolas at UTZ 183 were for a three-man crew, which was not feasible with the hexagonal turret's limited internal space.

In the spring of 1943, it was then felt that a cupola was necessary as an improvement to the T-34/76's turret, so UTZ, ChKZ 100, and Krasnoye Sormovo 112 experimented with cupolas. Krasnoye Sormovo 112's cupola won the design competition, and it was therefore ordered that the other factories would incorporate this design into the production of turrets.

It was ordered in June 1943 that T-34s would be issued with the cupola, but it took longer to implement the cupola than expected, and it was only in July, after the Kursk battles that the cupola was introduced onto the battlefield.

Two methods of construction were used for cupolas: Krasnoye Sormovo 112, UTZ 183, and ChKZ 100 all cast their cupolas, whereas Omsk 174 used rolled plates to construct theirs. A cast cupola would be stronger but would also be slightly more time-consuming to produce and harder to repair.

The cupola had seven armoured vision ports around for the commander to look through. The top of the cupola could rotate and had a simple spring latch to lock the cupola facing forward. There were two doors to the hatch, with the front hatch door equipping a new MK-4 periscope for outward vision. This was first implemented in July 1943 and was very popular with the commanders of the T-34s. Even the pressed turrets were equipped with these cupolas. It was a cheap and effective way to give the commander a slight edge by placing him higher in the tank, giving him a better view of the battlefield.

Despite this, the cupola was only a stopgap in the T-34 design, as already by summer 1943, a new turret was being designed to accommodate a bigger gun, and, by extension, a third turret crewman, thus freeing the gunner from being the commander. Also, to look through the cupola, the gunner had to stand up on his seat to look through the vision ports, therefore costing precious seconds between visually spotting a target and sitting back down to train the gun on them.

That said, the pros outweighed the cons as the advantage of being able to look out over the battlefield and stop targets was a huge advantage over not having the cupola. Interestingly, experiments were conducted on whether a third crewman could fit inside a turret with a cupola; they showed they could not. Furthermore, tests were done on installing a S-53 85-mm gun into a hexagonal turret with a cupola, but these tests were not successful.

T-34 (112 SOFT-EDGE WITH CUPOLA)

It should be mentioned that Krasnoye Sormovo 112 went from producing the early style turret to the hexagonal turret with a command cupola without manufacturing the hexagonal turret with the two circular hatches like at other factories (except for STZ, who never produced the hexagonal turret). The cupola turrets were of the soft-edge type at Krasnoye Sormovo 112, but all types of hexagonal turrets (soft-edge, hard-edge, and pressed-type turrets) were given cupolas at other factories.

Krasnoye Sormovo 112 T-34s with command cupolas had an interlocking glacis plate, a rounded nose, and handrails on the glacis plate.

Later in 1943, major structural changes were also made at Krasnoye Sormovo 112, and the interlocking plates were removed. This was done at the same time as the nose fillet being redesigned from being rounded to coming to a point. These tanks retained the splash fillets on the upper glacis plate.

It should be noted that some Krasnoye Sormovo 112 T-34s with cupolas were not issued with any exterior fuel tank brackets. It is unknown why this was done, but many examples can be found lacking any form of brackets, be it drum or rear box type.

T-34 (UTZ 183 SOFT/HARD-EDGE WITH CUPOLA)

Krasnoye Sormovo introduced the command cupola first in the summer of 1943. This was swiftly followed by UTZ 183. UTZ 183 did not just introduce the command cupola, and changes were done to the layout and stowage of the tank.

While the cupola was added, the wheel set of the tank changed. The rear road wheel was once more the cast spider-type road wheel, and the third (middle) road wheel was changed to this type, too. This change was between August and September 1943, and further changes followed, mainly to wheel set. The second and fourth road wheels were additionally changed to cast spider-type wheels, so every road wheel was rubber-rimmed again.

This T-34 (112 Soft-Edge with Cupola) was manufactured in late 1943. Notice the glacis handhold and most interestingly the angled nose. This angled nose was a feature of some of the first T-34-85s manufactured at Krasnoye Sormovo 112, but some Krasnoye Sormoye 112 tanks were issued with the rounded nose.

A T-34 (112 Soft-Edge with Cupola) rolling down a street in a captured German city. This T-34 has the typical tow hook hardpoint in the centre of the gear plate.

Opposite above: This T-34 (UTZ 183 Hard-Edge with Cupola) was lost in the spring of 1944. Notice the wood saw placement next to the stowage box. Take note of the two types of road wheel on display. The first positions wheel is a cast spider type, compared to the second wheel, which had small holes close to the hub, known as a cast spider late type. An Sd.Kfz. 184 Elefant tank destroyer can be seen in the background.

This T-34 (UTZ 183 Hard-Edge with Cupola) was knocked out in fighting in early 1944. In the background, an Elefant tank destroyer, built on a Porsche Tiger chassis, and two Brummbär assault guns drive past. This tank was lost near the T-34 as above.

This T-34 (UTZ 183 Hard-Edge with Cupola) had a command cupola before the turret roof was blown off. The turret has a pistol port, indicating that it had a cupola. The main gun appears to have been hit by a shell.

Along with the new cupola and road wheels, next was the replacement of the box-type rear fender fuel tanks with ChKZ 100 designed drum-type fuel tanks in August 1943. These could carry up to 50 litres, and the exterior of the tanks could hold three drums. These proved to be more effective than the box-type tanks, being able to carry more fuel and being stronger structurally.

UTZ 183 never used the ChKZ 100 solid-bracket type hardpoints for the external fuel tanks. Instead, UTZ 183 used the strap-type bracket. This was a bent piece of metal, bent into an 'M' shape that cradled the tank. A strap extended over the top of the fuel tank to secure it down.

Minor changes were made to the periscopes issued to the tanks, with some tanks being issued two PT-4-7 scopes, while others, still late into production, were issued MK-4 periscopes like that in the cupola hatch door.

Lastly, at the same time as the wheel set was changed, the glacis plate nose fillet was redesigned as to not be rounded, but rather it was angled, and the lines of the glacis came to a point. T-34s in this configuration were produced until the introduction of the T-34-85 in early 1944.

The same T-34 (UTZ 183 Hard-Edge with Cupola) as on page 283. A soldier with a *Panzerfaust* stands in front of the tank. Notice the hole from an explosive charge on the side of the tank. However, observant readers will notice that the tank is lacking hull handrails. Handrail brackets are seen on pictures on page 283.

A 1944-manufactured T-34 (UTZ 183 Hard-Edge with Cupola). The vehicle was destroyed in combat, then used as a target for *Panzerfaust* training. Notice the pistol port in the turret and the angled nose fillet.

The same T-34 (UTZ 183 Hard-Edge with Cupola) tank as seen above and on page 282. The tank's turret side shows evidence of discharging of *Panzerfaust* rounds on the tank. Note also the debris around the tank including ice cleats, some track, a piece of tarp, a DT magazine, and some shells.

This T-34 (UTZ 183 Hard-Edge with Cupola) has been knocked out in fighting and moved to the roadside at a later point in time. In the movement process, the tracks have been pulled rearwards. This is an earlier example of a UTZ 183 tank with a command cupola as the nose fillet is the older rounded type. Note the red '33' marking on the turret side.

A close-up of an idler wheel of a T-34 (UTZ 183 Soft/Hard-Edge with Cupola). One can tell that it is indeed a cupola tank, and a T-34/76, as it has an angled nose fillet, and is lacking fillets on the glacis plate and hull sides for the turret overhang. A Russian Orthodox Church can be seen in the background.

33

ChKZ 100: 1942–1944

ChKZ 100 was ordered in July 1942 to begin manufacture of T-34s in a bid to make up the losses that had been made due to the proximity of German units to Stalingrad. The factory was originally called Chelyabinsk Tractor Factory (ChTZ) and is often known as 'Tankograd' ('Танкоград'). Interestingly, the same name is given to UTZ 183 and UTZM.

ChKZ 100 was experienced in the manufacture of the KV-1 tank, and it was therefore the only plant to manufacture both legendary tanks. Here, the C-2 high-speed tractor was dropped from the production line in favour of the T-34.

T-34 (ChKZ INITIAL PRODUCTION)

The first ChKZ 100 T-34 rolled out of the factory in August 1942. Like almost every plant, the first tanks were assembled from kits supplied from UTZ 183 to help set up the appropriate production lines and to give workers experience in assembling the new tank.

Shortly into production, changes began to be made. For example, in September 1942, the new hard-edge and soft-edge turrets were introduced into T-34 production, replacing the composite turrets previously used. ChKZ only used soft-edge turrets, and UTZ 183 only used hard-edge turrets—one of the few ways to identify the really early ChKZ tanks.

From the beginning of T-34 production at ChKZ 100, the factory received most of its items for production from UTZM. UTZM primarily issued hulls, turrets, and tracks, so it can sometimes be difficult to tell UTZM and ChKZ 100 tanks apart. One major difference between ChKZ T-34s and UTZ 183 T-34s was that ChKZ never used the hard-edge turrets, instead only using soft-edge and pressed-type turrets.

Once the new soft-edge turret was introduced, more general changes began to be made to production at ChKZ. For example, in September 1942, the new 'rod and bracket' handrails were introduced.

A very early example of a T-34 (ChKZ Initial Production). This can be deduced by the fact that the turret of this tank is a soft-edge turret. This was very rarely used at UTZ 183 but was common at UTZM and ChKZ 100. UTZM used pressed-type road wheels from the start of production, meaning that this can only be ChKZ 100. This gives a good insight to early ChKZ 100 production before mid-September. Notice the simplified drive wheel, which lacked return rollers. Also, the road wheel set was identical to UTZ 183. Shortly after this tank was likely made, handrails were introduced, and in October 1942, drum-type fuel tanks would be added.

A T-34 (ChKZ Initial Production), from either the 59th or 60th Tank Regiment, which was issued with tanks purchased by the 'Moscow Collective Farm' (Московский колхозник). These regiments were issued both T-34 (ChKZ Initial Production) and T-34 (174 Early Production) tanks, as seen on pages 268, 287, and 316. This tank displays the earliest features of ChKZ 100 tanks, such as a cast spider-type road wheel in the first position, with four cast steel-rimmed type road wheels. However, the drum-type fuel tanks are the clearest giveaway to its origin, in conjunction with the other features. This tank was lost in March 1943 but still retained the winter whitewash.

The same T-34 as on page 286. Notice the turret number and the slogan 'Moscow Collective Farm' (Московский колхозник). The positioning of the left side external fuel tank is indicative of ChKZ.

This T-34 (ChKZ Initial Production) was lost in the fighting for Stalingrad in December 1942. The tank has suffered two hull penetrations on the side, which blew away the fuel tank bracket. The strap for the drum can be seen at the rear right of the tank.

ChKZ issued initially the same V-type waffle track that UTZ 183 issued, as well as the newly designed 500-mm waffle track. From September, new tracks were cast at the plant. These new tracks were 500 mm wide and had the same pattern as that on the V-type track being manufactured at UTZ 183. However, the track had the same dimensions as the 500-mm waffle-pattern track, like that being used at Omsk 174, Krasnoye Sormovo 112, and UTZM, and therefore was thinner. This track was exclusive to ChKZ 100 and can be called the 'V-type ChKZ' track.

During this time, the rear-most road wheel was changed from a cast spider-type wheel with a rubber tyre to a UTZ cast steel-rimmed type, so-called for being designed at UTZ 183.

In October 1942, a decree from the GKO stated that the minimum fuel allowance for the T-34 was to be increased to 380 l. As such, ChKZ 100 implemented their famous drum-type fuel tanks. These could carry up to 50 l, and the exterior of the tanks could hold three drums. These were first implemented in October 1942, and therefore, ChKZ 100 T-34s can be found by their drum-type fuel tanks in the winter battles of late 1942 to the early summer of 1943. After August 1943, all other factories manufacturing the T-34 moved onto the drum-type fuel tanks.

The drum-type fuel tanks were essentially borrowed from KV-1s being manufactured at ChKZ 100. KV-1 tanks had been issued the drum-type fuel tanks since October 1941. The new KV-1S (introduced in September 1942) was issued four drums, whereas the T-34 was issued three.

ChKZ 100 drum-type fuel tanks were attached to the hull sides by a solid crescent moon-shaped piece of metal, with a strap and buckle to attach it to the hull. These can be called the solid-bracket type. This pattern of fuel tank hardpoint would be used by UTZM and Krasnoye Sormovo 112, and this should not be confused with the strap-type bracket as used by Omsk 174 and UTZ 183. This type was instead constructed using a single strap of metal bent around the drum and attached to the hull at each end of the strap.

A T-34 (ChKZ Intermediate) tank lost on 13 March 1943, two days before the Third Battle of Kharkov ended. The tank displays features indicating it was manufactured in October 1942, namely the single pressed-type road wheel on the first position, followed by UTZ cast steel-rimmed type. The turret is the soft-edge type.

The same T-34 (ChKZ Intermediate) as seen above. More early features are seen now, such as the wavy pattern exhaust shrouds, UTZ 183-style angled gear covers, a hull missing the middle bolt to attach the rear plate to the hull sides, and a middle diamond pattern hinge. The V Type ChKZ track is also clear.

A T-34 (ChKZ Intermediate) lost during the fighting around the ring of Stalingrad in November 1942. The pressed road wheel gives away its identity, along with the drum-type fuel tank brackets, just visible on the tank. In the foreground, an interesting mix of V-type ChKZ and split-type waffle track can be seen.

A T-34 (ChKZ Initial Production) with a single pressed-type road wheel followed by cast steel-rimmed road wheels. The track has been removed, indicating that this photograph was taken long after the vehicle was lost.

The earliest ChKZ 100 tanks had a stowage layout identical to UTZ 183, but this would soon change. On the left side of the T-34, next to the stowage box, a U-shaped tie-down point was placed horizontally on the hull side for tarpaulin stowage.

Later, in October 1942, a hardpoint was placed directly behind the gun-cleaning storage box for a tool kit. This tool kit was unique to ChKZ 100 and was used throughout ChKZ 100 tank production, so it is a key identification point on ChKZ 100-manufactured T-34s.

Above: The scene after an air attack during the Third Battle of Kharkov. A T-34 (ChKZ Intermediate) lies on its side, and two T-70s flank it. The split-type track can be seen, noticeably clean, but one can see silvery ends of the track where the metal has been rubbed clean. T-70s are very rare vehicles to see in photographs, but even more so when equipped with spoked wheels. The turret markings on the T-70 on the left is not identical on the side and the rear. The right turret side is a '44' in a circle, whereas the rear is '4Ф'. This translates to '4F'.

Right: The same T-34 (ChKZ Intermediate) as seen above. The split-type track can be seen more easily. The engineer's escape hatch can be seen on the forward underside of the tank. The turret is likely a UTZM pressed-type turret. A drum-type fuel tank can be seen on the left of the frame—a clear indication that this vehicle is a ChKZ 100-manufactured tank.

T-34 (ChKZ INTERMEDIATE)

During the winter fighting of 1942, new patterns of road wheels can be found on ChKZ 100 T-34s. On these intermediate tanks, the wheels would have been a mixture of UTZ cast spider-type wheels, the UTZ cast steel-rimmed type wheels, and the introduction of pressed-type road wheels. However, in early 1943, ChKZ 100's wheelset changed to all pressed-type road wheels.

A T-34 (ChKZ Intermediate) issued with a pressed turret. The first and last road wheels are the pressed type, whereas the middle three wheels are the cast steel-rimmed type.

A T-34 (ChKZ Intermediate) with a pressed turret. Notice the rearmost road wheel is a pressed-type road wheel. While the front road wheel is absent, it would also have been pressed. The pressed turret has red numbers painted onto the turret's upper right side, but due to the German inspectors, it is obscured.

This T-34 (ChKZ Intermediate) is equipped with a V-type ChKZ track. This track was the last V-type developed and was very similar to the standard 500-mm waffle-pattern track. It seems that only ChKZ 100 used this track. The tank also has pressed road wheels on the first and fifth positions. The tank was lost in the Ukrainian SSR in late 1943. The hull appears to have been painted with a German road sign.

A T-34 (ChKZ Intermediate) lost in the winter fighting of early 1943. Notice that at the bottom of the glacis plate, a small strip of metal has been placed This feature was possibly unique for ChKZ, but also could have been used by UTZM. It is thought that this was to help crew members get in and out of the tank. Notice also the '555' turret marking, likely painted in red. The track is the V-type ChKZ.

This T-34 (ChKZ Intermediate) was likely lost somewhere near Kharkov in March 1943. The tank displays a more unusual wheel set, with two cast steel-rimmed wheels that are not together. Notice some of the non-standard stowage, such as the oil drum which is tied down with cable. Interestingly, the radio port is plugged. Lastly, the track is an interesting mixture of V-type ChKZ and split-type track. It is likely that as the older V-type was phased out, the new 500-mm waffle-pattern track was gradually introduced.

Initially, the first road wheels on both sides of the tanks were the pressed type, with the next four wheels being the UTZ cast steel-rimmed type. In late October 1942, the rearmost road wheels were changed to a second pressed-type wheel. Then, in November 1942, this was changed to three pressed-type road wheels, with UTZ cast steel-rimmed type wheels on the third and fourth road wheel position. This was sometimes on the second and third positions.

T-34 (ChKZ STANDARD PRODUCTION)

From January 1943, all ChKZ 100 issued T-34s were given a full set of pressed-type road wheels. This would make them almost identical to UTZM manufactured tanks.

Photographs of ChKZ 100-manufactured T-34s in Kharkov in March 1943 can be found with the pressed-type road wheel in the first position and UTZ cast steel-rimmed type road wheels in the other positions. If not for the drum-type fuel tanks and the unique pattern of tarpaulin tie downs, it would be hard to distinguish these tanks from UTZ 183 tanks.

A T-34 (ChKZ Intermediate). The vehicle has a mixture of road wheels, with more pressed-type wheels than cast steel-rimmed ones. Initially, all road wheels were cast with rubber only on the first wheel, then with a single pressed wheel on the first position. After this, a second rubber-pressed wheel was placed onto the last position. It appears that the third pressed wheel was placed either in the second or fourth position before all road wheels were pressed.

A close up of the tank as seen above. Notice the damage to the drum-type fuel tanks.

A T-34 (ChKZ Intermediate) tank with a similar wheel set to the tank on page 295. Notice the bicycle on the rear of the tank. The exhaust shrouds are the sunken type, similar to that which UTZM manufactured.

In this early period of ChKZ 100 manufacturing, the tanks used multiple parts seen at other plants. For example, ChKZ 100 issued three distinct types of exhaust shrouds. The first type was that with smooth edges, as had been used since 1940. The second type was the exhaust shrouds issued at UTZM, with depressions made around the bolts on the shroud. The third and rarest type is the UTZ 183 waffle-type shrouds—these are by far the rarest, only seen on these early tanks.

As with all the factories, the most diverse period of hexagonal T-34 production was from its inception (in this case August 1942) to January 1943, when production had been streamlined at all factories. ChKZ 100 was no different, and after January, very little change occurred. The same basic changes that were made at UTZ and other plants were implemented, such as the removal of the central hinge for the exhaust plate.

It was only after the Battle of Kursk that further changes to ChKZ 100 production were made. These changes were only done to standardise the T-34 design between factories.

Like the tanks manufactured at UTZ 183, a wood saw was introduced into the tank's toolset. This was placed on the tank's right side, rather than on the left like at the other plants. This was due to the placement of the bracket for the tool kit being on the left side of the tank.

A T-34 (ChKZ Standard Production) lost in March 1943. This vehicle was likely factory fresh before being knocked out, as it was in January 1943 that ChKZ 100 issued pressed-type road wheels as standard. Interestingly, ChKZ 100 T-34s from all previous production runs can be found in action around March 1943. The rear of the turret is wet and reflecting the sun.

This T-34 (ChKZ Standard Production) suffered an internal explosion. Note that the turret is not on the turret ring. There is also some evidence of a slogan having been on the tank, but the paint has burned away, so it is hard to make out. A dead crew member can be seen on the right.

An East German NVA (*Nationale Volksarmee*)-operated T-34 (ChKZ Standard Production). The handrails on this tank are of the same pattern as T-34-85s. The rearmost tank in this line is a pressed-type turret.

This T-34 (ChKZ Standard Production) was knocked out in 1944 in the Ukrainian SSR. Notice that this vehicle has the unique toolbox that was issued exclusively to ChKZ 100 tanks—the bracket behind the gun-cleaning box was specifically designed for this.

T-34 (ChKZ PRESSED TURRET)

ChKZ 100 is well-known for being one of the plants that was issued pressed-type turrets. These were manufactured at UTZM but were mostly sent to ChKZ 100, making ChKZ 100 the most famous user, especially due to the Tamiya Models 1/35 scale model of a pressed turreted T-34, marketed as a 'ChTZ-made' tank.

ChKZ 100 produced a total of 5,095 tanks, but only 2,670 pressed turrets were manufactured, and these were all made at UTZM. Seeing as though nearly all UTZM's own tanks would be given pressed turrets in 1943, it is estimated that just under half of ChKZ 100 tanks would have been issued with the pressed turret.

A T-34 (ChKZ Intermediate) with a pressed turret, shown here as a monument in the 1960s. What is so important about this tank is not only its rare technical features but also the vehicle's history. In 1942, this is the tank that closed the ring around Stalingrad. It was knocked out in fighting at Mamayev and is now a monument to the success of Operation Uranus. The tank is now at Mamayev Hill, outside of Volgograd.

An early T-34 (ChKZ Pressed Turret). The pressed turret was larger than the soft-edge and hard-edge turrets and was noticeably plumper. This tank displays many features consistent with the ChKZ 100 tanks of early 1943, with a full set of pressed road wheels, Split UTZM track, and exhaust shrouds with sink marks for the bolts, again consistent with UTZM. However, UTZM did not issue drum-type fuel tanks at this point in 1943.

A T-34 (ChKZ Standard Production) with a pressed turret. Notice the three hinges on the rear plate and the exhaust shrouds with sinks for the bolts. This tank has a radio, as can be seen in the hull port. The gun has been knocked out of the cradle and has been pushed back inside the tank.

A T-34 (ChKZ Standard Production) with a pressed turret. The tank was likely hit with a HE round that tore away the hull right side fender and smashed the rear fan cover. Notice the exhaust shrouds and the solid brackets.

The same T-34 as seen above. Notice the pattern of the turret pressing and the sharpness of the lines. Other pressed turrets were not as crude as this example. The tank is equipped with a split-type track.

T-34 (ChKZ WITH CUPOLA)

In late 1943, ChKZ 100 began equipping tanks with command cupolas. The cupolas that ChKZ issued were cast in construction. Like at other plants, some of these turrets were pressed. These pressed turrets with cupola are highly unusual, and not many were made before the plant stopped production. Some evidence suggests that towards the end of T-34 production at ChKZ, hard-edge turrets were briefly introduced. These turrets were not common, and therefore, the overwhelming majority of ChKZ T-34s were issued the soft-edge or pressed turrets.

The last of ChKZ 100's T-34s were issued with angled nose fillets for the glacis plate. This was already standard at Krasnoye Sormovo 112 and UTZ 183. These final T-34s rolled out of ChKZ 100 in February 1944 after two years of manufacturing the T-34 and KV-1S. Shortly after, it began production of the new IS-1 heavy tank.

A T-34 (ChKZ with Cupola), which was attached to an assault gun division, knocked out in December 1943. Many T-34s (76s) were used in the command or reconnaissance role in assault gun or tank destroyer platoons. This vehicle was knocked out in fighting, alongside SU-85s and a SU-122 (seen on page 416). This vehicle still retains the rounded nose fillet, that was to soon be replaced. Split-type track can be seen on this vehicle, in conjunction with pressed-type road wheels and solid bracket-type fuel tank hardpoints, which indicate this tank to be from ChKZ 100.

A T-34 (ChKZ With Cupola) lost in the Ukrainian SSR. Take note of all the interior details. The tank suffered a catastrophic explosion, which obliterated the side of the tank.

The same T-34 as seen above. The turret is a hard-edge turret with a cupola.

A rare photograph of a pressed turret issued with a cupola. This ChKZ-manufactured tank is being inspected for shots done on an impromptu range. One soldier is painting a hit. A line of Panzer IVs is to the right of this photograph.

Two T-34 (ChKZ With Cupola)s also lost in the Ukrainian SSR. Notice the turret roof on the ground, where a cupola can be clearly seen. Loss of the turret roof was a common occurrence when there was an internal explosion.

The same tank as on page 304. After ChKZ 100 finished manufacturing T-34s, they moved onto IS-1 and IS-2 production. German graffiti, possibly a road marking, has been painted onto the turret.

Another T-34 (ChKZ With Cupola). Notice that the wood saw is once again on the right side of the hull. This tank has two turret periscopes, indicating that it is a command tank. Notice the turret penetration to the turret side.

34

UTZM: 1942–1943

The Ural Heavy Machinery Factory (UTZM), also known as Uralmash, began as a subsidiary plant to UTZ 183. The factory was based at Sverdlovsk and supplied armoured hulls for the T-34. It was also was involved in the simplification process that had taken place in late Spring 1942. However, the number of hulls reaching UTZ 183 from its other subsidiaries increased to such a point that it could reject UTZM's hulls.

It became feasible for UTZM to begin its own full-scale production from late summer 1942. As such, from August 1942, and between December 1942 and August 1943, T-34s and SU-122 assault guns on a T-34 chassis were manufactured in tandem at UTZM. The plant only produced these tanks for less than a year before switching to full production of SU-85 tank destroyers in August 1943.

UTZM only manufactured 719 T-34s between 1942 and 1943, making it the factory that produced the lowest number of T-34s during the war. However, UTZM's production is comparable with other factories if one includes the 638 SU-122s, increasing the total production from August 1942 until August 1943 to 1,357 tanks.

T-34 (UTZM INITIAL PRODUCTION)

UTZM began T-34 production in August 1942, and these were immediately different to UTZ manufactured tanks. They equipped their tanks with pressed-type road wheels, which were rubber-rimmed, unlike those at UTZ, which used cast spider-type wheels. This was likely due to UTZM receiving their shipments of wheels from a different subsidiary than UTZ. There is some photographic evidence to suggest that in August and very early September, UTZM tanks lacked the machine gun ball mount guard.

This is a T-34 (UTZM Initial Production), manufactured in September 1942 before the implementation of handrails or fuel tanks. ChKZ 100 was issuing their tanks with a mixture of road wheel types, and Omsk 174 was manufacturing T-34s with all cast spider-type road wheels at this time.

T-34 (UTZM STANDARD PRODUCTION)

In September 1942, the 'rod and bracket' style of handrails was introduced in UTZM T-34 production. Additionally, the plant issued tanks made between October 1942 until January 1943 with the UTZ 183 box-type exterior fuel tanks.

UTZM designed a new pattern of cast track, which was introduced in September 1942. Tanks began to be issued with the split-type track. While the toothed track links remained unchanged, the toothless track links were split down the middle of the track to create two separate halves for a link. Some SU-85s were equipped with this track.

UTZM manufactured the split-type track, but the track type was also used at ChKZ 100, making it harder to distinguish the two tanks apart. UTZM and ChKZ 100 tanks looked incredibly similar, and in many instances, the track and the placement of the toolbox on ChKZ 100 tanks are the only clue to a tank's factory origin. At the beginning of UTZM production, turrets were a mixture of hard-edge and soft-edge turrets, but during the early months of 1943, the hard-edge turrets were phased out.

The exhaust shrouds of UTZM and ChKZ 100 tanks were sometimes issued with a unique pattern compared to those being manufactured at UTZ 183 or the other plants. These new shrouds had small depressions around the bolts that attach them to the hull. Seeing as though UTZM and ChKZ 100 issued these, it is difficult to distinguish the two using this feature, although they were also used by post-war manufactured Czechoslovakian T-34s. These exhaust shrouds can be known as 'sunken type'.

A T-34 (UTZM Standard Production) tank. This tank has the box-type fuel tanks on the rear, originally developed at UTZ 183, but used at UTZM and Krasnoye Sormovo 112. This tank was knocked out by the 3rd SS Panzer Division *Totenkopf*.

A T-34 (UTZM Standard Production) lost in the winter of 1942–1943. Notice the crude red star in a circle painted on the turret and the German soldier inspecting a 76.2-mm round.

This UTZM-produced T-34 displays some very rare tracks. Notice on the left side track belt, the toothless link is two pieces that are separated by a gap. This track was only manufactured at UTZM and was intended to be used to widen the T-34 track by a further 200 mm. No evidence exists that this was used in the field. It is rare for the left and right track belts not to match in pattern.

T-34 (UTZM LATE PRODUCTION)

At first, SU-122s were the only tanks issued ChKZ 100 drum-type fuel tanks at UTZM, whereas standard T-34s were still issued the UTZ 183 box-type fuel tank. However, from late February 1943, UTZM began to distribute the drum-type fuel tanks on standard T-34s. The delay in T-34s receiving these fuel tanks was likely due to UTZM using up stocks of the older fuel tanks first.

UTZM was therefore the second plant to introduce the drum-type fuel tanks. It is interesting to see how close the tanks from these two factories tanks were to each other, making identification quite hard. UTZM's hardpoints for the exterior fuel tanks were also the solid-bracket type of hardpoints, being a single cast piece of metal that attached to the handrails on the hull rear side.

Between January 1943 and August 1943, the same basic hull changes were made to UTZM that were also made at UTZ 183 and ChKZ 100. This included the reintroduction of the middle bolt attaching the exhaust plate to the hull sides and the removal of the central hinge below the transmission hatch (used in hinging the exhaust plate away from the hull for engine removal).

A T-34 (ChKZ Standard Production). This tank was lost on the streets of Kharkov. Only ChKZ 100 was manufacturing drum-type fuel tanks for T-34 at this time in the war, but UTZM was manufacturing them for the SU-122. It was around this time that their T-34s were also issued the drum-type fuel tanks.

A T-34 (UTZM Standard Production), lost in fighting for Stalingrad. The turret roof has been blown off, as has everything in the hull, with the engine landing on the left and engine deck plates just behind the tank. An interesting note is that the tank only has two hinges at the rear of the exhaust plate, as well as five bolts connecting the plate to the hull sides. It is likely that UTZM was the first factory to make these changes.

A T-34 (UTZM Late Production) in mid- to late 1943. The T-34 ran into a truck. Notice the placement of the drum-type fuel tank, leaving space for the tarpaulin. ChKZ 100 also placed the fuel drum here with tarpaulin next to the drum. The turret markings are strange, the number '5328' is on the forward part of the turret, and a white square separated into three parts is on the second half of the turret. In this, various markings can be seen, including 'P', in two of the three sections, followed by '0' underscore '53'. A white square can be seen painted around the smoke extractor.

Here, the rear of the tank as seen above. The UTZM split-type track and the UTZM type 'depressed' exhaust covers, with depressions around the bolts, are clearly seen. Notice the turret markings are not featured on the right side of the tank's turret.

T-34 (UTZM PRESSED TURRET)

In the summer of 1942, a new pressed-type turret was designed at UTZM intended to overcome the shortcomings in production that were occurring. To put it simply, all factories were not receiving enough turrets for the number of hulls they were producing because composite turrets were made using a time-consuming process. This pressed-type turret was created using a 45-mm thick piece of metal, and then pressing it into a mould with a 5,000-ton press. This turret was, in fact, slightly longer and wider than other hexagonal turrets, and due to the nature of pressing, slightly stronger, too. Interestingly, the pressed turrets were issued pistol ports from the outset of production, unlike the soft-edge and hard-edge turrets, which did not receive pistol ports until the summer of 1943.

While UTZM was the first to try this new turret method, other factories received shipments of these new turrets, and it was not long before both UTZ 183 and ChKZ 100 began to issue them. The turrets had the same basic shape as a regular soft-edge T-34 turret, but with softer, rounded-off corners to the turret, plus a distinctive turret seam that dipped in the front half of the turret.

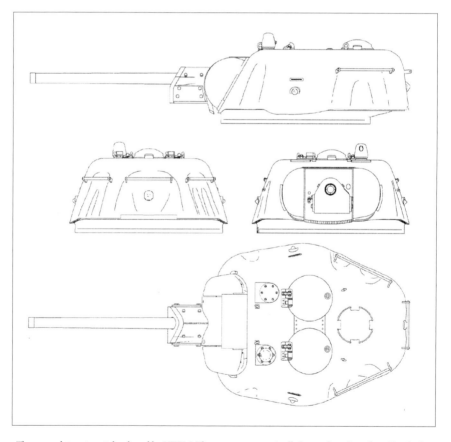

The pressed-type turret developed by UTZM. The turret was marginally larger than the soft and hard edge turrets and was also marginally stronger due to the method of production. The turrets always had pistol ports, and likely always had handrails. Towards the end of production, cupolas were added to the design.

A T-34 (UTZM Standard Production) with a pressed turret. The tank displays all the features from the first production run to receive pressed turrets, having pressed road wheels, and UTZ box-type fuel tanks. This is surprisingly rare on the battlefield as a lot of these turrets were sent to ChKZ 100. There is a corpse of a dead crew member in the foreground.

A T-34 (UTZM Pressed Turret) tank at Kursk. The Soviet soldiers appear to be burying one of their dead by the tank. Notice the split-type track, developed at UTZM, but also used at ChKZ 100. Compare this picture to the T-34 as seen above, which is the first type of UTZM T-34 with a pressed turret.

This pressed turret is often called 'Formochka'. This once again is a post-war name for the turret, and the correct term for these turrets is pressed. *Formochka* is the Russian term for the toys that children play with to form sand structures like shells and starfish. The turret is given this name due to its similarly rounded nature.

These turrets were issued to all the factories that manufactured the T-34 but is most widely associated with ChKZ 100 and UTZM. UTZM manufactured and issued these turrets and sent a large proportion to ChKZ 100, as mentioned earlier. That said, UTZ 183 and Krasnoye Sormovo 112 also issued these turrets, but these tanks were much rarer, and only appear to have been turrets equipped with a command cupola.

In total, 2,670 pressed-type turrets were manufactured. In addition to using them for their own tanks, many were sent to other factories. That said, nearly all examples of pressed turreted T-34s manufactured in 1942 are UTZM tanks, with the few others being ChKZ 100. During 1943, the pressed-type turret was far more common on ChKZ 100 manufactured tanks as more ChKZ 100 tanks were made than UTZM tanks and therefore more turrets were delivered there than used on UTZM tanks.

35

OMSK 174: 1942–1944

The Voroshilov Plant 174 was evacuated from Leningrad to Chkalov in late 1941 before
the factory moved again to Omsk in mid-1942. After the move to Omsk, the plant began
to produce T-34s. This factory was the last plant to produce T-34/76s before switching to
the T-34-85.

Before the war, Voroshilov Plant 174 was the main factory that manufactured the T-26 light
tank, producing an estimated 11,000 tanks. It was also Voroshilov Plant 174 that designed the
less famous, but just as important, T-50 light tank. Omsk 174 was also a repair factory, and
therefore many knocked-out T-34s were taken to it for rebuilds. This can explain why many
Omsk 174 features can be seen on T-34s.

The first T-34s rolled out of Omsk 174 in the summer of 1942. In the space of six months, the
T-34 had gone from being manufactured at STZ (with small numbers trickling from Krasnoye
Sormovo 112 and UTZ 183) to full production lines at no less than six factories. This would
be the greatest number of factories manufacturing the tank at any time.

Perhaps the most famous Omsk 174 T-34s are the T-34s paid for through a bond scheme by
the Moscow Collective Farm, which were fielded in the early months of 1943, and are often
misidentified as UTZ 183 made tanks. Famous photographs of several tanks exist in the early
months of 1943 that display an array of early features on Omsk 174-made tanks.

T-34 (174 EARLY PRODUCTION)

Omsk 174's tanks originally would have looked like the tanks being produced at UTZ 183,
with a mixture of cast spider-type wheels. Initially, the tanks were issued with composite-type
turrets, but the factory moved onto soft-edge and hard-edge turrets.

The defining feature of the T-34s manufactured at Omsk 174 in 1942 and 1943 was that they
retained the early pattern of drive wheels. These were later replaced with plain-type drive
wheels sometime in 1943.

The first major change implemented by Omsk 174 was that all road wheels were the cast-spider type. It is unknown when this was done, but it was before the addition of rear fuel tanks on the T-34s in October 1942.

In September 1942, Omsk 174, along with all the other factories, was ordered by the GKO to increase the maximum fuel stowage on the tanks. Omsk 174 chose a similar design to UTZ 183 with two rear-mounted 40-litre fuel tanks that were triangular. These fuel tanks were wider than UTZ 183's rear fuel tanks and had two pipes that exited the bottom of the fuel tank, running over the top of it to enter the vehicle. Omsk 174 used these fuel tanks up until 1944. The factory then moved onto the ChKZ 100 drum-type fuel tanks before the plant moved onto production of the T-34-85. Initially, all turrets were hard edge, but by winter 1942, soft-edge turrets were being used.

Omsk 174 also received a small number of early patterned turrets from factory number 70. These were the same turrets issued to 112. It received a negligible amount of the smaller turrets, but it is important to mention this as a tank can be mistaken for a rebuild due to the smaller turret on a 174 chassis.

This T-34 (174 Early Production) was serving in either the 59th or 60th Tank Brigade and was given the turret slogan 'Moscow Collective Farm' (Московский колхозник). Often mistaken for a UTZ 183 T-34, take note of the 174 box-type fuel tanks, and that the wheel set is all cast spider-type road wheels. This wheel set was short-lived, and pressed-type road wheels were soon used. The drive wheel, too, is the older style of drive wheel. The hull also appears to feature a German road marking.

T-34 (174 Early Production) knocked out in the spring of 1943. It is possible that this tank served in the 59th or 60th Tank Brigade.

Another 174 T-34 from the 59th or 60th Tank Brigade. This vehicle is slightly later than others from these brigades, as all the road wheels are pressed. Notice the hard edge turret and the 174 pattern fuel tanks. As with many tanks, one crewman did not make it out of the tank alive, lying dead on the glacis plate.

T-34 (174 STANDARD PRODUCTION)

One of the few ways to tell an Omsk 174 T-34 apart from other T-34 was the tow hooks on the glacis of the tank. These tow hook hardpoints were softer than those at the other plants, lacking a small 'spike' in the metal on the back of the hook. Other factories issued these two hooks but replaced them in mid-1942 with newer designs.

The tanks were also issued with pressed-type road wheels from November 1942 and the rod and bracket type handrails.

Omsk 174 did not drastically change the design of the T-34 between December 1942 and June 1943. During this period, the tanks were involved in the heavy fighting for Stalingrad (19 November 1942–3 February 1943), Kharkov (19 February–15 March 1943), and Kursk (5 July–23 August 1943).

Along with the hexagonal turrets, Omsk 174 also received the earlier pattern of cast turret from Factory Number 70 (which were also used by Krasnoye Sormovo 112). Omsk 174 received the turrets from Factory Number 70 pre-cut out and ready for vision blocks to be installed, but instead of the earlier and recognisable protruding style of vision ports, much simpler mountings were fixed into the turret by Omsk 174; therefore, most of the cut-out space for the block was resealed and flush with the turret with these much smaller vision ports unique to Omsk 174. Additionally, these turrets were given rod and bracket handrails. There is also some photographic evidence to suggest that turret pistol ports were not gas-cut out, despite them being cast into the original turret, thus leaving distinctive casting bulges.

A T-34 (Omsk 174 Standard Production). Notice the lack of the usual protruding vision port common to the early turret style. At Omsk 174, these turrets were received from Factory 70 and the vision ports issued at Omsk 174 were a simply slit protected internally with bulletproof glass. Note the rear fuel tanks and the stowage of the two DT-29 magazines on the turret side.

T-34 (174 Standard Production) '22'. This tank belonged to the same regiment as the two tanks below and on page 320.

This T-34 (174 Standard Production) was lost during the fighting for Kharkov in February 1943. The tank suffered a major internal explosion. A DT-29 machine gun magazine is balanced on the gun.

A T-34 (174 Standard Production) that has suffered a major internal explosion. The tank was lost during the fighting for Kharkov in 1943.

What is likely a T-34 (174 Standard Production). The transmission has been removed, leaving the two brake pads open.

T-34 (174 LATE PRODUCTION)

The handrails were redesigned in mid-1943, copying Krasnoye Sormovo 112's bent rod-type handrails. These were four long and bent handrails, so these tanks, especially after the cupola was introduced, are easily mistaken for Krasnoye Sormovo 112 tanks. Drive wheels were initially the early type used in 1941, but by summer 1943, newer, simpler types of drive wheels were being introduced.

When Omsk 174 began T-34 production, the rear transmission plate was attached to the rear gear plate by the typical three hinges. This was the case until the summer of 1943 when a new pattern of rear hinge was introduced. This new hinge was like that of a Krasnoye Sormovo 112 tank, but it was squarer, not to mention that the transmission plate sat on top of the gear plate rather than sitting over it like on Krasnoye Sormovo 112 tanks. These new hinges were very similar to Krasnoye Sormovo 112 hinges, and often tanks get mistaken for one another.

An interesting example of a T-34 (174 Late Production). This vehicle was lost after Kursk, captured by the 17th Panzer Division, and taken as a trophy to the southern German town of Augsburg, which was the location of one of the German MAN factories, which designed the Panther. Notice the technical features of this T-34, with bent rod-type handrails and the early drive wheel. Interestingly, the rear fuel tanks are the UTZ 183 type. The tank would have been initially given the Omsk 174 box-type fuel tanks.

The same T-34 (174 Late Production) as on page 321. The tank displays the new pattern of handrails issued to Omsk 174 T-34s around the time of the Battle of Kursk. The handrails in question are identical to those used at Krasnoye Sormovo 112, which were four long bent rods. For a short time, the diamond-shaped hinges were still being used at Omsk 174, but shortly after the introduction of the new handrails, the new Omsk 174 pattern rear hinges were also introduced.

A rather interesting T-34 (174 Late Production), lost shortly after the Kursk battles. Notice the handrails, in conjunction with the Omsk 174 pattern rear fuel tanks. The tank has had a minor repair, having the middle road wheel replaced with a cast one. The turret markings are of interest. Take note of the barrel damage.

T-34 (174 WITH CUPOLA)

In the autumn of 1943, T-34s were equipped with command cupolas, and these were manu-factured from a rolled plate, unlike those at Krasnoye Sormovo 112, UTZ 183, and ChKZ 100, which were cast. With regards to extra fuel stowage, Omsk 174 was relatively conservative, not issuing more than two drum-type fuel tanks or the two rear box-type fuel tanks.

The final production T-34/76s from Omsk 174 were nearly all OT-34s, the variant with the flamethrower unit in the hull that replaced the DT (to be discussed later).

Final design changes made before the implementation of the T-34-85 included a new angled nose fillet (rather than a rounded nose), but most interestingly of all, T-34/76 turrets were issued the T-34-85 wedge-type lifting points on the turret sides. These last T-34/76s manufactured can be called T-34 (174 Last Production).

A T-34 (112 Soft Edge with Cupola) in service with the East German NVA. Just visible are the small fillets on the upper hull to protect the turret ring.

A T-34 (174 with Cupola) that burned up. The first two handrails have been replaced with the rod and bracket-type handrail—highly odd on an Omsk 174 T-34 of this date. It was likely a local rebuild rather than being sent back to a factory.

This T-34 (174 with Cupola) is a slightly rarer example, being issued with a hard-edge turret with cupola. The hallmarks of 174 are clearly on display. Notice the straight sides of the command cupola, in conjunction with the pressed type road wheels. Interestingly, the fuel tank stowage has four 50-l fuel drums, two on the sides of the tank and two on the rear of the tank. The brackets at the rear were intended for the drums of chemicals for generating smoke.

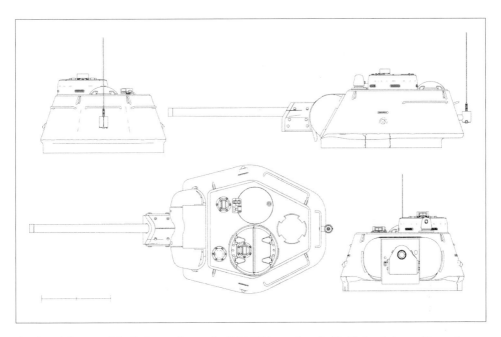

A technical drawing of the final type of turret that T-34 (76s) were issued with. Notice that one of the periscopes is the new MK-4. A radio is placed in the turret, but this was due to this example being an OT-34. The tank has T-34-85 lifting hooks, instead of lifting loops.

A column of T-34s on parade in Kiev in 1948. The rearmost vehicles are T-34 (174 with Cupola) tanks. Notice the straight sides of the cupola, a clear indication of Omsk 174 manufacture. The rears of the tanks lack the central hardpoint for towing that Krasnoye Sormovo 112 T-34s had. Also, the tanks are lacking external fuel tanks, but brackets are there.

A OT-34 (174 Last Production). This tank displays features that are exclusive to the last Omsk 174 T-34 (76s,) including the T-34-85 lifting hooks on the turret and the angled nose of the hull. The turret marking is 'C-6' (English: 'S-6'). The turret also has MK-4 episcopes instead of PT-4-7 scopes of earlier tanks. The vehicle would have only had two drum-type fuel tanks, one on either side of the hull.

An NVA-operated T-34 (174 Last Production) being used in the training role. The vehicle displays many unique features, such as the T-34-85 lifting hook on the turret. The vehicle has had 112-style splash guards mounted onto the upper hull, and due to the nature of being a training vehicle, the MG ball mount has been removed and a glass plate has been fitted over the front. This was likely for an instructor to direct a trainee driver.

36

SPECIALISED T-34/76s

FOG T-34S AND OT-34

As the T-34 became the Red Army's newest tank, avenues were explored in converting the basic tank for various roles. While experimentation was not as extensive as other Soviet tanks, such as the T-26, there were a few noteworthy designs. Almost every factory experimented with tanks that could perform multiple roles on the battlefield from as early as June 1940, but perhaps the most famous example was the OT-34, or 'Flamethrower T-34' (Russian: 'Огнеметный'—'О').

Designs for the OT-34 were discussed as soon as the first T-34s had rolled from the production line. After tests of A-34 No. 1 and No. 2 had been completed, these machines became testbeds for a multitude of experimental vehicles.

One such experimental vehicle mounted an ATO-41 flame unit. This flamethrower was mounted into the hull of the tank along with an internal tank of compressed air and another with the fuel, which replaced the position for the engineer, reducing the crew to three. The range of the jet of flame was between 65 and 100 metres. The necessary equipment could be attached to any standard T-34. The fuel was a mixture of 60 per cent mazut (a low-quality crude oil) and 40 per cent kerosene.

However, this flamethrower did not enter production on tanks until the last quarter of 1941, even though testing of the flame unit took place much earlier in January 1941. Once production began, the new OT-34 was fielded for the first time along with the KV-8 flamethrower tank in early 1942.

In early 1942, the ATO-42 flamethrower was developed. This increased the fuel capacity from 100 to 200 litres, and this was the type of flame unit used until 1945 in the T-34.

KhPZ 183 produced the first OT-34 tanks, but they did not manufacture many before the factory was evacuated in October 1941. Krasnoye Sormovo 112 also issued flamethrowing OT-34 tanks but not many. STZ also issued a handful of units between December and March 1942.

An OT-34 (UTZ 183 Initial Production). Notice the flame unit in the hull blister. Reinforced 550-mm-type track can be seen on this vehicle.

An OT-34 (UTZ 183 Hard-Edge Mid). This tank was lost in fighting around Kharkov in March 1943. The flame nozzle can be clearly seen in the hull blister position. The driver's hatch has a piece of rebar or railway track stuck into it. Note also the whitewash paint and the green '25' on the turret.

Omsk 174 issued the largest number of flamethrowing T-34 tanks. In fact, almost every T-34/76 issued in 1944 was an OT-34. As the 76-mm gunned tanks were obsolete by that stage, it was thought that these tanks could be deployed more usefully as flamethrowing tanks.

Both UTZ 183 and Omsk 174 also issued T-34-85s with the ATO-42 flame unit in the hull. While much rarer, these OT-34-85s were certainly used in combat.

In total, 3.3 per cent (around 16,000) of all T-34s manufactured were flamethrowing tanks. Another interesting attempt to create a flame-throwing T-34 was the adaptation of the FOG flamethrower system.

Experiments were conducted in late 1941 on mounting flamethrowers on the sides of T-34s as anti-infantry weapons. The idea was unlike the OT-34 which had a forward-facing flame unit, but rather the flame throwers would be mounted on the rear hull side of the tank, angled outward facing at about 60 degrees.

Two T-34s are known to have been equipped with the FOG system. One vehicle has three flame units on either side of the engine, and the other vehicle had four flame units. These units were protected by a sheet of rolled plate that stood vertically from the fender. The engineer controlled the flame units, with the ideal scenario having the flame units triggered when the tank was surrounded by enemy infantry.

There were some serious drawbacks to this design, and the FOG system was dropped. The FOG unit was very vulnerable, and burning oil could leak into the tank's engine bay. Of the two T-34s issued with the FOG flamethrower system, only one is known to have been photographed after its loss. The vehicle in question was manufactured at STZ and was given steel road wheels with internal shock absorbers. The tank was knocked out near Leningrad in January 1942.

This STZ manufactured T-34 is equipped with the FOG flamethrowing unit. Notice the additional armour on the hull sides that protects the four flamethrowers. Each flamethrower had its own canister of fuel. The flamethrowers used were converted infantry flame units.

The same tank as seen below. One can clearly see the exhaust cover for this generator. This is an incredibly rare feature, and this is the earliest version known. This tank can be called a T-34 (112 Simplified Rear Command Tank).

The same tank as seen above. One can see the Krasnoye Sormovo 112 rear plate, with the exhaust plate above the gear plate and the Krasnoye Sormovo 112 hinges.

COMMAND T-34s

Krasnoye Sormovo 112 issued a specialised command tank based on the T-34/76 chassis, likely of all types, but only one confirmed example exists that shows a T-34 (112 Simplified Stowage). These command tanks differed from standard tanks by having very powerful radio sets. This required a small gasoline engine inside the body of the tank not connected to the regular engine or electronics of the tank to power it. As such, the tank had an exhaust port on the hull's left side. This exhaust was identical in pattern to that used for the rear exhaust and was provided with the same cover. This was angled at 120 degrees to point rearwards.

The ammunition load of these tanks was reduced, and these tanks were usually issued to commanders of tank divisions or higher. Krasnoye Sormovo 112 was the only plant to manufacture these tanks, and they were very rare. When T-34 production moved to T-34-85 tanks, the number of command tanks increased to roughly 1 per cent (roughly 1,400) of the production output of Krasnoye Sormovo 112.

EMBARKED INFANTRY ARMOURED T-34

Perhaps the strangest T-34s ever fielded were those that were given firing points for embarked infantry. These tanks are very rare, and only two are known through photographic evidence.

In the late autumn of 1942, at least two T-34s from the 38th Army under the direction of Major Kazimirov were given thin armour plates on the fender for embarked infantry to shoot through. One tank was a Krasnoye Sormovo 112 manufactured tank, while the other was a UTZ 183 T-34 with a hard-edged turret.

The Krasnoye Sormovo 112 made vehicle had symmetrical armour on the left and right fenders. On the forward portion of the fender, a 5–10-mm plate was welded onto the side of the fender. The plate extended above the height of the turret ring, but not as high as the gun mantlet. Forward was a flat plate, with an angled plate above it. On the lower vertical plate, a square hole for a firearm was cut. A bracket was placed to hold the vertical side armour in place. There was a gap between this and a rear vertical plate. The rear plate was longer than the forward plate, but as high as the forward plate. It was cut at the rear to follow the angle of the exhaust plate, but due to the vertical nature of the rear-facing plate, it was extended past the rear exhaust plate. On the rear-facing plate, another rectangular hole was cut for small arms. There was another bracket to hold the side armour vertical on this rear plate.

The UTZ 183 tank was different. The vehicle was still symmetrical for the left and right fenders, but the conversion was more extensive. The forward part of the fender had simi-lar-shaped armour plates to the Krasnoye Sormovo 112 tank, but these were much shorter and had a roof. Therefore, the crew for this position had to enter this section by the rear. On the front left fender, the gun-cleaning toolbox was moved rearwards. There was no armour on the rear fenders, but attached to the exhaust plate was an armoured box, as wide as the T-34, and from the side was curved, somewhat like a nappy on the back of the tank. Rearward, there were three pistol ports for small arms. It is not known how infantry entered the vehicle.

The base tank used for the conversion for embarked infantry was a T-34 (112 handrails), and indeed, other than the new plates, everything is typical for the tank. The extent of the plates can be clearly seen, with a gap between the forward and rear sections for infantry to access this fighting area. Notice the bracket holding the armour vertical on the forward portion of the armour. At the rear of the armour plate, a square pistol port can be seen.

Another view of the T-34 with armour plates for embarked infantry. The view from both sides indicates that the plates were symmetrical. The pistol port at the rear of the plate can be clearly seen. The broken drive wheel can be seen, placed into the armour on the side of the tank. This was likely done by German forces. The tank's track is the 550-mm waffle type, indicating the tank to be pre-August 1942 in production.

The vehicles were used during the advance on Kharkov in early 1943, and of the two known, only one—the Krasnoye Sormovo 112 T-34—is known to have been photographed after combat. The vehicle was knocked out due to damage to the drive wheel, and the vehicle was abandoned in a small village. The fate of the other vehicle is unknown.

T-34T

One of the most well-known examples of using old, war-weary tanks was to convert them into recovery tractors or munition wagons. This was done during the Second World War, but it was more common after the war, especially in East Germany. The recovery vehicle T-34s manufactured from older tanks were known as 'T-34T', standing for 'Tank-34 Tractor' (Танк-34-тракторный), but other post-war versions existed. The most common examples were the Czechoslovakian VT-34 and the Polish WPT-34.

Wartime conversion to recovery vehicles was quite easy as all that was normally done during the war was the turret of a T-34 was removed to lighten the chassis, and often extra track, tools, and recovery equipment were carried. The turret ring was often simply kept open, with more storage carried inside the old fighting compartment. Often these vehicles were open-topped, but others were sometimes provided with a cover for the turret ring. These covers range from well-crafted metal roof plates with cupolas and hatches, to some examples having an engine access hatch cover welded over the hole and the crew entering or exiting the vehicle through this.

While rarer, ammunition carriers followed the same basic plan, with the turret being removed, but instead of towing equipment externally, extra ammunition boxes could be carried internally, inside the old turret ring. This conversion was not very common, but some examples were used by the Red Army, most notably, during the Battle of Kursk (July 1943), when some famous photographs were taken of a T-34T recovering a knocked-out T-34. Even some T-34Ts were captured or manufactured from captured T-34s and pressed into *Wehrmacht* service, known as the '*Bergepanzer* T-34'.

Some attempts were made to manufacture dedicated T-34 recovery vehicles. UTZM designed and produced in small numbers the AT-42. This was a tractor built onto the T-34 chassis, with a cab and stowage deck, like that of previous tractors, such as the C2 tractor or Komintern. Production was undertaken in 1944, and only a handful of vehicles, perhaps as few as fourteen, were finished.

After the war, more careful steps were taken to convert older tanks into recovery vehicles. In the USSR, it was far more common to convert assault guns and tank destroyers to recovery vehicles, due to them having a larger glacis plate for mounting towing equipment, and a larger interior space for tools. That said, conversions of regular T-34s were also done commonly.

There were two typical methods of conversion. The simplest method was to cover the turret ring with a thin cover, which normally also had a cupola placed onto this plate. This was mostly to protect the interior of the tanks from the elements. Secondly, after the war, it was common to see wooden cargo bays built into the tank. This was either done over the turret ring, built up on supports as to be level with the engine deck, or built onto the engine deck itself. These light wooden structures were effective as ammunition or support vehicles. This was commonly done in the NVA (*Nationale Volksarmee*), but also seen in the Soviet Union. These vehicles provided a good alternative to being decommissioned for worn-out vehicles, and many T-34Ts were in service until the 1990s.

A T-34T VTR of the East German NVA. The chassis is that of an Omsk 174-manufactured T-34-85. Over the turret ring, a new plate has been welded with new escape hatches. This example has a wooden cargo stowage box on the rear of the chassis.

An NVA T-34T. This conversion was normally done to T-34 (76s) that were no longer needed in a battle role but could perform a recovery role. This vehicle has a wooden cargo station built onto the engine deck. A metal plate was welded over the turret ring and an escape hatch cut into the top. Notice the caged headlight and the light on a long pole.

37

T-34/76 OVERVIEW

The T-34 changed drastically from June 1940 to April 1944. The tank became simpler, but it had many upgrades, too. By the time that the last T-34/76 rolled off the production line, an estimated 35,583 had been produced. This number is an estimate based on taking the lowest documented figure from each factory that manufactured the tank and adding them together. This number does not include the assault guns manufactured on T-34/76 chassis, nor any of the support vehicles and experimental tanks manufactured (this number does include OT-34s and command tanks).

When the first T-34 was rolled off the production line, the tank was equipped with a 76.2-mm L-11 gun in a small turret, with only one in five tanks being issued a radio. All the tank's road wheels were pressed type in design with rubber on every single wheel. The hull nose and rear were curved, with pin-type tow hardpoints. Furthermore, these early tanks were of an incredibly high standard of manufacture (at least, by the standards of Soviet industry).

As a comparison to the last T-34/76s manufactured, the final tanks produced were equipped with hexagonal turrets with a command cupola and the 76.2-mm F-34 gun. The tank had a five-speed gearbox, rather than the old four-speed gearbox. Tanks were issued, depending on the factory, with either UTZ cast spider late-type or pressed-type wheels, both with rubber only on the road wheels.

The track had been redesigned to improve grip and make the tank quieter. The hull nose and rear were now angled to speed up production, and overall, the hull was simplified. The transmission hatch was redesigned, as well as the driver's access hatch.

The hull MG blister was equipped with a cast cover to improve armour thickness and protect this position. More tanks were equipped with radios, and the external stowage was simplified. Tow hardpoints were simplified, as were the electronics of the tank. Finally, turret optics and periscopes were greatly improved.

All of this made an incredible tank, but one that was outclassed from its inception in a few ways by Germany's latest weapons, such as crew configuration. However, it was perhaps completely outclassed by Germany's late-war tanks, save for its relative ease of production, by the end of its production in 1944.

T-34/76 PRODUCTION

Factory Location	Factory Abbreviation	Factory Code	1940	1941	1942	1943	1944	Total
Kharkov	KhPZ	183	117	1,560	-	-	-	1,677
Stalingrad	STZ	-	-	1,250	2,520	-	-	3,770
Nizhniy Tagil	UTZ	183	-	25	5,684	7,466	1,838	15,013
Krasnoye Sormovo	-	112	-	173	2,718	2,962	557	6,410
Sverdlovsk	UTZM	-	-	-	267	452	-	719
Chelyabinsk	ChKZ	100	-	-	1,055	3,594	445	5,094
Omsk	-	174	-	-	417	1,347	1,136	2,900
Total per year		-	117	3,008	12,661	15,821	3,976	35,583

In June 1941, it is easy to argue that the T-34 was one of the most technologically and conceptually advanced tanks on the battlefield despite some shortcomings. The tank had excellent armour protection for the day—45 mm sloped on the glacis—coupled with the powerful 76.2-mm F-34 gun suitable for both anti-tank and infantry support roles. This outclassed Germany's heaviest tank in 1941, the Panzer IV, which was equipped with only 37 mm of armour and the low-velocity 7.5-cm KwK 37 L/24 gun, which was only truly suitable for infantry support roles.

However, the main disadvantages of the T-34 were twofold—the turret was too small and cramped for the crew to operate effectively and the nature of the Christie suspension meant that internal space was always dictated by the placement of the interior springs. These were features that were never truly rectified. However, it is worth considering that the T-34M would have eliminated both shortcomings, showing just how advanced Soviet tank designs were. In fact, far from Soviet industry being the stereotypically archaic and over-bureaucratic mess more typical of the late Brezhnev era, the necessities of war were the biggest factors in making Soviet tank designs so rudimentary. What is clear from the production change narrative so far is that engineers wishing to improve the tank pulled the design one way, but the necessities of the war pulled the design another, meaning that the tank was always a very imperfect product. In other words, the USSR had the capabilities to rectify design flaws and innovate, but they decided against it for military tactical reasons.

In 1944, when the last T-34/76 was manufactured, the tank was not the powerhouse that it once was. While the Soviets were more concerned with production rates, the Germans had been busy developing equipment to overtake the T-34 in both armour protection and firepower. The Panther, with its long 7.5-cm KwK 42 L/70 gun, and the Tiger, with its 8.8-cm KwK 36 L/56 gun, not only out-performed the 76-mm F-34 of the T-34 but was able to defeat the armour of the T-34 from distances upward of 2 km away.

In an odd way, it is perhaps to their overall benefit that the Soviets lost the technological advantage over the Germans during the Battle of Kursk. It was during this battle that the Panther was first fielded, along with the first large-scale use of the Tiger. While the Germans had the technological advantage, the Soviets had numbers on their side, which was a major factor in the Soviet victory. Germany, with its highly polished and technologically advanced designs, could never match the factory output of the USSR, with its rough, robust, and relatively primitive designs. Put simply, if the T-34 had been a more complicated design, such as with the T-50 or T-34M, Soviet industry would simply not be able to produce the tank in the numbers it did, and the results could have been devastating for the USSR.

Yet the T-34's production story does not end here. In the first half of 1943, especially after the success of Kursk, the Stavka was able to evaluate their tanks and tactics, as the strategic initiative had now fully swung in favour of the Soviets. The Stavka was more than aware that their tanks had lost their advantage over the Germans, and summer to winter of 1943 was spent evaluating all their front-line tanks. Not only did the T-34 get updated and redesigned, but other Soviet tanks were evaluated and halted. The KV, for example, had been in production for as long as the T-34 and was just as war-weary. Unfortunately for the KV series, the 1942 redesign, the KV-1S, had reduced the tank's armour thickness, and the tank had therefore lost favour with the Stavka because it was effectively an inferior product to the T-34. This tank would soon be replaced with the IS-1 heavy tank in 1944, but not before the KV-85 stopgap—itself a mix between a KV-1S hull and an IS-1 turret.

As for the T-34, experiments were conducted with the ZiS-4M 57-mm gun in a hexagonal turret, along with an 85-mm gun. However, tests definitively proved that the T-34 needed modernising, which ultimately required an entirely new turret to be designed. Again, as the Soviets had gained the strategic advantage, this was now feasible as they were not quite so desperate for tanks to be used for defensive purposes.

The T-34/76 was still fielded within front-line Red Army units until the last days of the war. To be sure, it was still a fantastic tank in many respects, being able to tackle the Panzer IV and the most common assault guns that were fielded by the *Wehrmacht*. However, the T-34-85 that followed proved to be an extremely potent tank and left the T-34/76 as a clearly outdated design.

38

TECHNICAL DESCRIPTION OF THE T-34/76 IN 1944

The necessity of increasing output and reducing production costs early in the war led to many changes, both large and small, in the way the T-34 was produced. Gone were hull rivets; the entire assembly was now constructed through welding alone. To the greatest extent possible, all the fine machining of armour plates was eliminated, and simple lap and butt joints were used. Where it was absolutely necessary, edges would be prepared by rough bevelling with an air chisel before welding. Welded turrets gave way to casting, increasing production while doing away with a large number of machining steps. Gone, too, was the machined driver's hatch, now replaced by a thicker casting.

Items considered luxuries or not absolutely essential were dropped. Even the 76.2-mm F-34 main gun was redesigned reducing the number of parts needed, but without affecting the weapon's efficiency.

From 1942 until the introduction of the 85-mm gun, the design of the T-34 essentially became frozen with only a handful of innovations being adopted. But despite these changes in the way the tank was constructed and equipped, the T-34/76 at the beginning of 1944 was in many ways the same as those of 1940 at least in terms of its general layout.

The glacis remained a nominal 45 mm thick, and its angles were unchanged. However, the lower hull, sides and rear armour were increased to 45 mm as well, which lowered the number of different thicknesses of plate needed to be produced for the tank. Visually, one of the most notable changes, instituted early in 1942, was the elimination of formed, rounded lower hull plate for the rear of the tank, now made from simple flat stock, the rectangular access hatch being replaced by a 550-mm-diameter circular cover. The hull roof and floor continued to be made from 20-mm plates. The hull's DT machine gun ball mount was given an armoured cover which gave better protection to not only the ball mount itself, but also the barrel and gas tube of the weapon.

In August 1942, the addition of a steel strip in front of the driver's hatch was ordered to protect the driver's legs from 'bullet splash'. These started to be installed in September at UTZ and slightly later at other factories. The rounded bow fillet or 'girder' was changed to a more angular version and became standard in most production late in 1943 and early 1944.

With these changes and the introduction of the 'Gayka' hexagonal turret, the T-34's weight increased to more than 28 tonnes. The suspension changed very little, though was now fitted with more robust cast swing arms.

The 500-mm waffle-pattern track, in several variations, were standardised across factories. Also standardised was the use of externally mounted 1-m-long drum-type fuel tanks. With these, the more common arrangement was two cylinders on the right rear side and one on the left.

Internally, the six fuel tanks had been increased to eight, with two tanks being added to the engine compartment just behind the firewall, though this may not have been accepted by all factories.

The driver's position was much the same. In front was the large hatch casting with two episcopes protected by movable covers and angled slightly outward to increase the field of view. A common practice was to keep one of the two covers closed in order to keep the driver from being completely 'blinded' should the glacis be hit by enemy fire or splashed with mud.

The seat itself had been simplified, now being made of an uncomplicated bent rod, angle iron, and sheet metal with slip-on padded covers. The instrument panel directly under the hatch now had only four gauges, which were, on the left, a clock followed by engine coolant and transmission temperature gauges and manometer. Another gauge panel was welded to the first suspension station sheet metal cover on the driver's left. It held the speedometer and tachometer.

The main wiring hub had also changed slightly, in most cases fitted with only the ammeter. The situation on the machine gunner/radio operator's was much the same. The 71-TK-3 radio had long given way to the 9R wireless set, and with that, a positionable mount for the antenna was added to the side plate. The design of the latches and the frame for the escape hatch were simplified, but other than those fittings, not much had changed.

The same order that called for the addition of external fuel cells in October 1942 also mandated increasing the number of main gun rounds from seventy-seven to 100. Exactly how this was accomplished is still a matter of some debate. Certainly, the eight ammunition boxes that made up the floor remained visually much the same as they had been from the introduction of the F-34, and the racks for ready rounds continued to hold just nine.

The two greatest improvements to the T-34/76 were the introduction of the hexagonal turret early in 1942 and the armoured cupola with five vision blocks for the commander/gunner from June 1943.

The first of these, at least to an extent, improved the intolerably cramped situation for the gun crew, though it was still an outdated two-man turret. The cupola gave the commander, who was previously nearly blind when the hatches were closed, a situational awareness nearly on par with what German tankers from the very outset of the war.

In some of these, turret racks for as many as six additional main gun rounds were positioned on either side behind the centreline of the casting, though these must surely have done little to improve the tight conditions.

Both the loader and commander were at this point provided with spring-loaded seats, the bottom of which automatically folded up when not in use. This was a boon for the loader especially in that he now had additional room when retrieving cartridges from the ready racks and floor boxes.

The firewall between the fighting and engine and fighting compartments was changed slightly, the steam relief valve now being accessible without removing the large centre panel. It was necessary to open this valve when filling the engine with coolant.

The situation with the V-2 engine, the performance of which had not improved—and in fact had become worse with demands for increased production—began to see a notable improvement in service life but only due to the front lines becoming more static, unlike in the early war. However, it still rarely attained the guaranteed mileage before having to be rebuilt.

The four-speed transmission had largely been superseded by a more efficient five-speed gearbox. Interestingly, UTZ, the factory that designed and tested the new transmission, may not have adopted it until late in the war, if at all.

All in all, the T-34 of late 1943 and early 1944 was a far more efficient weapon in terms of its production and deadliness than its overly complicated predecessor of 1940. Its usefulness would be even more improved with the introduction of the 85-mm gun and a new turret.

39

REPLACING THE T-34 ALTOGETHER?

By mid-1942, armour protection of the T-34 was becoming a major concern for the Red Army once again. As mentioned earlier, while the plated T-34 projects from Resolution 1062 were cancelled, in June 1942, Soviet forces had begun to encounter newer and heavier German guns, such as the 75-mm KwK 40 anti-tank gun. When all twelve T-34 (112 Full Plated)s were found to be totally ineffective, the GABTU (Main Automotive-Armoured Tank Directorate) issued requirements for two new tanks with armour protection as a major consideration. Both would be called 'universal tanks' and would be moderate upgrade packages for both the KV-1 and the T-34.

A design team at UTZ 183 worked on the T-34 update, and SKB-2 at ChKZ 100, which had just been ordered to manufacture the T-34, worked on the new KV tank (which would eventually lead to the development of the famous IS tank).

T-43

The design team at UTZ 183 essentially continued the work that had been dropped on the T-34M as they still held the documentation for the vehicle before it was dropped. While parts had been manufactured for the T-34M before the war, the tracks that were made were issued to T-34s in July 1941, but the five turrets that were cast do not appear to have been used at all. It is highly likely, but not confirmed, that the turrets for the T-34M were used on a testing range or were cut up and melted down to be used on standard T-34s.

However, the project started by UTZ 183 was not going to be called the T-34M but was instead named 'T-43', and just under a year of development was needed before the new T-43 prototype rolled out of UTZ 183 in March 1943. The T-43 weighed 34 tonnes; it was 8.1 m long, 3 m wide, and 2.6 m high. While the T-43 was a new design, it actually shared an estimated 70 per cent of the same parts as the T-34, such as the driver's hatch, engine, F-34 76.2-mm gun, optics, tracks, and wheels. However, the hull and turret shape were totally redesigned.

A front view of the first T-43 prototype. Many features are the same as the T-34s, but much is changed. The driver is on the tank's right, with a standard T-34s driver's hatch with armoured lids for vision devices. The turret is a three-man turret, with a cupola set to the left of the turret. One can see that only the upper hull to the turret ring is angled, past this, the plate is vertical. (*Maxim Kolomiets*)

The rear of the first T-43 prototype. The exhausts have been ducted to the sides of the hull to make for the placement of two UTZ box-type fuel tanks. There is the regular gear plate of the T-34 there, but at a sharper angle and with a central towing hardpoint. (*Maxim Kolomiets*)

The most important change was made to the suspension. Instead of the T-34's vertical spring 'Christie' type suspension, the tank was now equipped with torsion bar suspension. This greatly increased the space inside the T-43, which was the same width as the T-34, because the suspension was underneath the tank, as opposed to being part of the hull sides.

Additionally, a new turret was cast for the T-43 that looked like the later T-34-85 turret. Furthermore, the turret had a command cupola located on the left side, which allowed a third crewman in the turret. This was a huge improvement over the T-34 turret, which only had a crew of two, meaning that the commander also had to double up as the gunner. The original F-34 gun was retained, despite this greater room.

The glacis plate dispensed with the engineer's position, and the driver was moved from the left to the right of the hull. In the vacant seat to the left of the driver, ammunition racks were placed, making optimal use of space inside the still cramped chassis (although, as mentioned, it was relatively roomy compared to the T-34). The T-43's armour was noticeably thicker than the T-34's, but only the front half of the tank had sloped armour. After the turret ring, the armour changed from having a 30-degree angled plate to a vertical plate. This allowed for most of the fender (with all its stowage) to be behind the turret.

The glacis plate was 75 mm thick, angled at 60 degrees, and the hull sides were 60 mm thick, angled at 30 degrees. The turret's thickness was an impressive 90 mm. However, it should be noted that by March 1943, the Tiger had made its combat debut six months ago, and its 88-mm gun could easily knock out the T-43 from combat ranges greater than 1,000 m.

When testing was conducted on the T-43, it was found to be less manoeuvrable than the T-34 due to its weight, but it used the five-speed gearbox developed for the T-34S, giving more control moving over different obstacles.

Another frontal view of the first T-43 prototype. (*Maxim Kolomiets*)

A T-34 and the first T-43 prototype. While there are many differences, there is no doubt that there are similarities, too. Notice the driver's hatch on the right rather than the left, as well as the track, which is a T-34 track. (*Maxim Kolomiets*)

A rear view of the second T-43 prototype. (*Maxim Kolomiets*)

Another view of the second T-43. The F-34 gun was ultimately this tank's downfall as a higher calibre weapon was desired. (*Maxim Kolomiets*)

A second and moderately improved T-43 prototype was ready for testing later in 1943, which had a glacis plate that closely resembled that of the T-50 tank. The hull was now six-sided, with two extra angled plates making up the glacis plate. The driver's hatch was totally redesigned, but now the driver did not have a hatch he could escape through, and only had a smaller hatch to look through. This hatch was thicker than the older pattern of hatch, improving the chance that the hatch would not be penetrated. A new turret was cast for the second prototype, which had a rear-mounted command cupola. This turret closely resembled that of the T-34S.

However, what was required on the battlefield in 1942 was greatly different to what was required in 1943, meaning that the design of the T-43, having been drawn up in 1942, was arguably severely outdated. In fact, thicker armour was no longer as important as a tank with a gun capable of defeating the newest German tanks at moderate combat ranges of 500 m or more.

This need for a new gun was sorely felt in 1943, especially after the furious Battle of Kursk and the recapture of Kharkov. The Red Army was facing ever more German heavy tanks, and increasingly it was found that the 76.2-mm guns of the T-34 and KV-1 were no longer adequate weapons on the battlefield. After three years of war, the Stavka finally allowed design teams to begin work on new and improved designs for the standard T-34.

As a result, the T-43, while a vast improvement on the T-34, was not seriously considered as a viable replacement because the implementation of a new gun was deemed more important. Also, one must consider that thicker armour compromised the T-34's speed and manoeuvrability—two major factors in the T-34's success and preference over the KV series.

The second T-43 prototype (left) and the T-34S (right). On the T-43, notice the small driver's hatch that is on the right hull side. The cupola is at the rear of the turret, with an air extractor dome on the right turret side. The T-34S' turret was very similar to the second T-43 turret but was smaller. (*Maxim Kolomiets*)

The T-43 project was therefore dropped but not entirely forgotten as elements of the design were used on the T-44 tank, which was the ultimate wartime replacement for the T-34. The project would be revisited one last time when the new 85-mm gun was put into production.

However, one must be careful not to give the Battle of Kursk too much credit for influencing the development of the T-34 as the story of up-gunning the T-34 begins earlier in 1943—a story to which we now turn.

40

DESIGNING THE T-34-85

In January 1943, a single Tiger tank had been captured by Soviet forces in the Leningrad sector, and testing led to worrying results. The Tiger's 88-mm gun could effectively penetrate the armour of the T-34 from ranges exceeding 2 km, whereas the frontal armour of the Tiger could only be penetrated by a 76-mm round at point-blank range, and the sides of the tank could only be penetrated within 150 m. Tellingly, another Tiger fighting near Ssemernikovo Collective Farm on 15 March 1943 was hit with no fewer than eleven 76.2-mm shells, fourteen 45–57-mm shells, and upwards of 227 14.5-mm anti-tank rifle rounds without a major penetration.

It should be noted that there had been talks of attempting to re-introduce a 57-mm gun into the T-34 design around this time, also. The ZiS-4 that had equipped the ten tanks of the 21st Tank Brigade in 1941 had been redesigned to become the ZiS-4M in the spring of 1943. One T-34 (UTZ Hard-Edge) was issued with this new gun and was deployed in the 100th Special Tank Battalion at Kursk in July 1943. The tank never saw any action, and after Kursk, the project was once again shelved as even though the 57-mm gun was superior to the 76-mm gun in terms of armour penetration, it was deemed that a heavier gun was needed to defeat the frontal armour of the new German tanks.

In spring 1943, orders were issued on designing an 85-mm weapon for the T-34. Bureau Number 9 in Sverdlovsk presented the D-5T (the tank version) and D-5S (the assault gun version) 85-mm guns in May 1943, and Plant Number 92 presented the 85-mm S-53 gun in June 1943.

Outwardly, there were a few clear differences between the D-5 and the S-53 guns. The D-5T mantlet was short, with a flat face with four bolts placed around the gun. The S-53 had a much longer mantlet that had a rounded lip where the mantlet met the gun barrel. This mantlet was also attached by four bolts around the gun.

Both guns were extensively tested, but the D-5 eventually won the contest. Unfortunately, the D-5T was found to be too big to fit into a standard hexagonal turret. Therefore, it was necessary to design a new turret if this gun were to be issued to T-34s. In the meantime, a new assault gun platform on the T-34 chassis was designed, the SU-85, and this used the D-5S.

On the other hand, the design team of the S-53 gun was adamant that the 85-mm gun could fit inside a standard T-34/76 tank's turret, and trials were conducted with a T-34 (UTZ 183 with Cupola). After extensive testing, it was found that the S-53 gun was actually too large for this turret. Similar tests were conducted with a KV-1S, and even this turret was realistically too small for any 85-mm gun.[1]

However, after the Battle of Kursk, the need for an 85-mm gun was given top priority, and the project was therefore given more influence. Although the D-5S had already been accepted for production for the SU-85, the S-53 was reconsidered and given approval for mounting on the T-34 due to the political influence of the designer, V. Grabin (who also made the 57-mm ZiS-4), who presumably convinced the Stavka to accept his gun instead, even though the D-5T was simpler and more cost-effective to produce.

Once the gun designs had been finalised, the design team at UTZ 183 suggested that the first factory to begin manufacture of the new T-34-85 (the name given to the tank in Soviet documents) should be Krasnoye Sormovo 112, due to the relatively close location of Design Bureau No. 92. After much deliberation, this was agreed, and Krasnoye Sormovo 112 began to design a turret to accommodate this new gun. The project was called 'Object 135', and a new design bureau was set up to this end, but more than just a new turret was necessary for the introduction of the 85-mm gun.

The turret ring diameter was increased to its absolute limit as it was previously decided when testing the S-53 gun in a hexagonal turret that the most efficient way of equipping an 85-mm gun was to change the design of the hulls of the T-34 as little as possible. The diameter of the turret ring was altered from 1,450 to 1,600 mm. Due to not wanting to alter the hull as much as possible, the turret bustle and nose would have to be very high above the turret ring to clear the engine deck. This caused a bullet trap to be created between the upper turret and the hull.

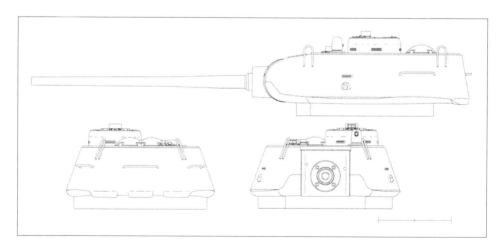

The Object 135 was the Soviet programme to design a new T-34 turret that could accommodate an 85-mm gun. The turret that was designed was longer and wider than the hexagonal turret, but still had a crew of two. While the design did succeed in accommodating an 85-mm gun, the design had serious limitations, such as bullet traps all around the turret ring.

The very first T-34-85 under testing during the late months of 1943. It is almost identical to T-34-85 (112 Initial Production) tanks. (*Maxim Kolomiets*)

This was, however, impossible to rectify due to time and design constraints. The turret was both lengthened and widened to accommodate the new gun, along with a turret ammunition rack. A new, shorter command cupola was placed on the upper left-hand side, and on the right-hand side was a standard T-34/76 round escape hatch with a lip to stop spalling.

The turret ring had one seat directly below the command cupola for the commander to sit in. The gunner's seat was now attached to the gun cradle, and the loader did not have a permanent seat, but he instead had a leather 'yoke' suspended by three straps that could be untied and stowed to allow for greater dynamic movement. It should be noted that the turret initially designed for the T-34-85 was designed to only accommodate two crew.

Since the S-53 gun was behind manufacturing schedule, the D-5T gun was placed into the turret of the tank, with the standard coaxial DT-29 machine gun.

The rear of the turret's bustle was now able to store ammunition for the main gun—something that had not been possible before. There was a four-tier wooden rack that could hold three shells per tier; therefore, a total of twelve rounds could be stowed in the turret bustle. A further three rounds were carried on the turret's left wall. This meant that the loader's job was made easier as on the T-34/76, ammunition was stowed on the hull walls as well as under the floor of the tank. This was still the case with the T-34-85, but now fifteen shells were immediately available to the loader. The early T-34-85s retained the radio in the hull with the engineer, and the ammunition layout was redesigned to accommodate the larger shells.

Due to the added weight of the new turret, the diameter of the suspension springs was increased from 30 to 32 mm. The suspension was strengthened to compensate for the added weight.

The prototype T-34-85 was trialled in November 1943, and while the tank's new turret had some major flaws regarding the bullet trap for the turret ring, it was hurriedly accepted for production. Soviet documentation called these tanks 'T-34-85'.

Stalin himself ordered that these new T-34s be ready for mass production by February 1944. However, teething problems with the S-53 gun meant ironically that to meet this deadline, initial production T-34-85s would have to be equipped with the D-5T 85-mm gun.

Surprisingly, in spring 1944, one last attempt was made at up-gunning the T-43 project to see if it was viable. A D-5T gun was placed in a T-34-85 turret manufactured at Krasnoye Sormovo 112, which was then mounted onto the first T-43 prototype's chassis. This prototype conducted tests, but it was still considered too dangerous to disrupt the T-34's production lines to implement this new hull. Additionally, by this time, plans to begin T-44 production at Kharkov's Factory Number 75 were underway, which doomed the T-43 entirely.

The first T-43 chassis, fitted with the D-5T gun, next to a standard T-34. There are interesting items to note on both tanks. On the T-43, it is interesting to make parallels with the front profile of the T-43 and that of the T-44, which bears a striking resemblance. The T-34 has a command cupola but has rear-mounted box-type fuel tanks, which is very unusual as the drum-type fuel tanks were in use at this point.

In a vain attempt to try to keep the T-43 in the spotlight, the first prototype was refitted with a D-5T 85-mm gun. Seen here, the turret was large enough to successfully install the weapon on the chassis.

41

KRASNOYE SORMOVO 112: JANUARY 1944–1946

T-34-85 (112 INITIAL PRODUCTION)

As the original factory to manufacture the T-34-85, Krasnoye Sormovo 112's T-34-85s are the most varied in type. The initial production T-34-85s were constructed of cast metal, with a very noticeable seam that ran along the bottom of the turret plate. This then very sharply curved upward at the gun mantlet. The turret upper sides were equipped with U-shaped lifting loops with two on each side of the turret. Of course, these early turrets were equipped with the D-5T gun as a stop-gap. These were produced from January to February 1944.

When these tanks first made it to the front lines, the troops who first used them, the 1st Guards Tank Army (who were fighting in the Ukrainian SSR), were very impressed with their new tanks. While the 85-mm gun was not as potent as the 88-mm and 75-mm guns of their German counterparts, it was able to penetrate 92 mm of armour at 500 m (90 mm being the thickness of frontal Tiger armour) and could destroy the Tiger from 750 m when shooting at its sides.

These early T-34-85s from Krasnoye Sormovo 112 had outwardly similar hulls to the T-34/76s being manufactured at the time. The tank was still covered in handrails, although the handrails on the engine deck and rear fan cover had been removed for turret clearance purposes. The two small handrails on the glacis were still present, however.

From April 1942, Krasnoye Sormovo 112's tanks had four long handrails along the hull. This was replaced when the T-34-85 began production with two short handrails forward of the centre of the turret ring and two further small handrails placed higher on the hull side past the centre of the turret ring. Above the second handrail, a fillet was placed on the upper hull to stop spalls from damaging the turret ring.

The interlocking hull and glacis plate had been previously removed on T-34/76s, and the nose fillet was either pointed or rounded, although rounded noses were quite rare.

At this point in time, both the hexagonal-turreted T-34/76s and the new T-34-85s were being manufactured at Krasnoye Sormovo 112. T-34/76s would continue to be manufactured there until stocks of those turrets ran out.

The prototype T-34-85. Notice the placement of the cupola of the tank, which is forward of the bend in the turret, to make it easier for the gunner, who was still the commander, to get into the cupola. (*Maxim Kolomiets*)

The front of the prototype T-34-85. The tank was almost identical to production tanks. (*Maxim Kolomiets*)

The rear of the prototype T-34-85. Notice the cooker on the back of the tank. (*Maxim Kolomiets*)

The top view of the prototype T-34-85. Notice the positioning of the command cupola, which is further forwards than those on most T-34-85s. This was because this early turret only had a crew of two, and not three. (*Maxim Kolomiets*)

A T-34-85 (112 Initial Production) armed with a D-5T 85-mm gun. On the hull, one can see the T-34/76-style handrails on the glacis plate, along with the solid bracket-type fuel tank brackets. The turret was designed for two men but would later be redesigned to fit three men.

T-34-85 (112 Initial Production) turrets, contrary to popular belief, were still only capable of accommodating two crewmen. Outwardly, there were differences from later turrets due to this fact. The command cupola on these early tanks was forward of the curve on the turret, whereas later turrets had the cupola moved rearwards of the curve on the turret wall to allow for the commander to sit behind the gunner, thus allowing for a crew of three.

The early T-34-85 turret also retained the single air extractor fan, which was at the rear of the turret and centrally placed. Forward of the cupola, these early T-34s retained the PT-4-7 periscope.

T-34-85 (112 S-53 GUN INITIAL PRODUCTION)

In March, the first S-53 guns began to be produced, and these equipped similar turrets as the stop-gap D-5T-gunned tanks. However, the turret layout was rethought when these guns were finally introduced. As such, the tank's crew was increased from four to five, with the addition of a dedicated gunner. This meant that the turret roof had to be redesigned to allow for more space inside the turret.

The cupola on the turret roof was moved rearwards of the curve on the turret side, allowing for clearance of the gunner's position. This change matched the layout of German tanks, with the commander behind the gunner, and the loader on the right.

A T-34-85 (112 S-53 Gun Initial Production). The T-34 was now equipped with the S-53 85-mm gun, but it still retained the U-shaped lifting hooks on the front and rear of the turret sides. Take note of the great changes made to the basic stowage of this tank.

The same T-34-85 (112 S-53 Gun Initial Production) as seen above. Notice the white triangle on the turret side—something common in June 1941 but far rarer in 1944.

The same T-34-85 (112 S-53 Gun Initial Production) as on page 355. Notice the white triangle painted onto the turret side—a feature more common during the battles in mid-1941.

The same T-34-85 (112 S-53 Gun Initial Production) as seen above and on page 355. This T-34 has a handrail on the transmission hatch—an irregular feature. The Krasnoye Sormovo 112 rear hinges and central towing hardpoint are clearly visible. Notice the track tool kit is now situated on the left rear hull once again. Notice the track stowage on the turret rear side.

Another T-34-85 (112 S-53 Gun Initial Production). Notice the curved-type fenders on display. The tank is painted in a worn whitewash, and no tactical numbers are seen.

The same T-34-85 as seen above. The turret is a totally unique type of T-34-85 turret, with a turret seam that dips in the turret centre. This is likely because Krasnoye Sormovo 112 was experimenting with casting patterns. No other T-34 turret like this has been observed.

The same T-34-85 as on page 357. Notice the missing front road wheel. This tank also has rearranged stowage, with the track tool kit being moved to the left rear fender.

Another T-34-85 (112 S-53 Gun Initial Production) lost in the Ukrainian SSR in March 1944. Notice the gun mantlet, with a longer gun sleeve, indicating the gun to be the S-53. There are U-shaped lifting hooks under the turret.

T-34-85 (112 S-53 Gun Initial Production)s were still issued the tall U-shaped lifting loops that were placed on the upper front and upper rear of the turret sides. Additionally, these tanks no longer had handrails on the glacis plate. They also had their track tool kit relocated to the left rear side of the tank; this was the original position of the toolbox in 1940, but sometime in 1944, this was relocated back to the right of the tank.

The old PT-4-7 periscope was replaced with an MK-4 episcope for both the gunner and loader. These periscopes had a much smaller exterior profile. Due also to the moving of the command cupola rearwards, the two internal extractor fans in the turret were also moved rearwards.

Some more complex electronics were reintroduced into the tank now that the production streamlining simplifications of 1942 were no longer necessary. The radio was also removed from the hull and placed into the turret (this being due to the new location of the commander) and thus the engineer was relegated to just operating the hull DT machine gun. Lastly, the lifting points on these early turrets were replaced with hook fillets, rather than the U-shaped lifting points.

T-34-85 (112 D-5T GUN MARCH 1944 PRODUCTION)

Briefly in March, D-5T 85-mm guns were issued again due to lack of S-53 guns, but stocks of the S-53 quickly caught up again. Around this time, the tank's fenders were redesigned to be as simple as possible. Rather than having a curved fender at the front, this was redesigned to be a simple angled piece, with a hinge at the top to allow for the fender to be moved out of the way for cleaning.

A T-34-85 (112 Standard Production) tank. Notice the strange placement of the rear fuel tanks. These brackets were designed for two 25-l fuel tanks, but here 50-l tanks have been put in their place instead.

T-34-85 (112 STANDARD PRODUCTION)

Once the S-53 gun was introduced, with the standardised lifting hooks, the T-34-85 was changed little at Krasnoye Sormovo 112 from then on. While new turrets were introduced at Krasnoye Sormovo 112, this standard type of turret was never removed from the production lines. These were the most numerous Krasnoye Sormovo 112 T-34s produced during the war because the turret was relatively simple to produce, and production was not negatively affected by the introduction of future upgrades.

Turrets, as described, are commonly collected together as T-34-85 Model 1944 by post-war enthusiasts, and the D-5T-gunned tanks are incorrectly called Model 1943s. These turrets were the most common manufactured at 112, but other patterns were used in smaller numbers.

Krasnoye Sormovo 112's type of turret was the most common type of turret seen on their T-34-85, but it did manufacture other, rarer types of turret later in production. Other than minor changes to some of the details, it remained relatively unchanged until the second half of 1945.

During the early part of 1945, more factories began production of the S-53 85-mm gun. The Imeni Stalina *Zavod* manufactured the ZiS-S-53 85-mm gun. This was a very similar gun to the S-53, but it was specially designed to be used with the T-34-85 turret. These guns were issued by all factories and incorporated with production runs including the regular S-53 guns.

The war was over when the picture of this T-34-85 (112 Standard Production) was taken somewhere in Germany. The vehicle took two hits to the rear of the tank during the fighting during the final days, both penetrated the exhaust plate on either side of the transmission hatch. Such wrecks littered the post-war landscape, many being scrapped in the weeks, months, and even years after the fighting halted. A white line can be seen painted onto the turret side, which was a semi-common scheme applied to identify the tanks as friendly to aircraft. Notice that the mantlet has been removed, revealing the casting behind the shield, along with portions of the S-53 gun. The drive wheel of the T-34 on page 379 can be seen on the forward left of this tank.

A T-34-85 (112 Standard Production) lost in the final days of the war, being inspected just after the war had ended. Notice the Krasnoye Sormovo 112 towing point in the centre of the gear plate.

A North Korean-operated T-34-85 (112 Standard Production). This tank was engaged by M26 Pershing tanks and came off worse. The Korean War was the swansong of the T-34 because this was the last time the T-34 was the main tank of an army fielded during a major war.

Another NKPA T-34-85 (112 Standard Production). Notice that there is a penetration on the glacis next to the blister position, which itself has been totally blown away. The driver's hatch and anti-spall strip have also been removed from the glacis.

Another view of the four T-34-85s knocked out by Pershing tanks in Korea as seen above.

A final view of the T-34-85s lost in Korea. Once UN tanks finally began to encounter the T-34-85s, the rapid North Korean advance was halted.

A Bulgarian-operated T-34-85
(112 Standard Production).
(*Stan Lucian Collection*)

A close-up of a T-34-85 nose fillet. (*Stan Lucian Collection*)

This T-34-85 (112 Standard Production Late) is on parade in Kiev in 1949. Notice the single door turret hatch and the mushroom-type air extractor domes. Also notice the star markings on the hull and fenders.

In January 1945, a new command cupola was designed for use of all T-34s; the change was as simple as the use of a single-piece hatch door with a periscope on the static portion of the hatch. This allowed for greater ease of access for the crew as the two-part hatch could be difficult to exit due to the limited cupola rim to grab onto.

Small changes were made during January and February 1945; this included the removal of the left-side turret vision ports on Krasnoye Sormovo 112 tanks.

Krasnoye Sormovo 112 also began to issue hardpoints on the lower glacis for track stowage. Contrary to popular belief, this was the first time such a move was made. Other factories followed suit, and this hardpoint became standard on T-34; it was even retrofitted on other tanks, including T-34/76s.

Another T-34-85 (112 Standard Production Late) on parade in Kiev in 1948. Notice the red star with white outline markings on the fenders. The fenders also have a white outline.

A Lithuanian-operated T-34-85. This tank has the new one-part turret hatch and split mushroom-type air filters. This can be called a T-34-85 (112 Standard Production Late).

This Bulgarian T-34-85 (112 Standard Production Late) has been issued a T-55-style headlight cover like most Bulgarian T-34s. Other than this, this tank is very typical of wartime-production T-34s.

T-34-85 (112 8-PART COMPOSITE)

In mid-1944, new eight-part composite turrets were manufactured at Krasnoye Sormovo 112. These were only manufactured in small quantities but were produced from mid-1944 until mid-1945. These tanks had a central seam running around the turret, a seam from the turret roof to the turret ring cutting though the pistol port, and another seam at the rear. These eight-part composite turrets slightly increased the volume inside the tank as the nose of the turret increased in volume. Outwardly, apart from the seam, the turret had a generally more bulged appearance, which is best seen through photographs than described. Additionally, the sides on later turrets were flattened off. A distinctive triangular indent can be seen on the turret's side below the cupola. It is unknown why this was done, but it is first observed at UTZ 183.

The eight-part turret was the rarest T-34 turret fielded, but with this in mind, the turrets were fielded with all major changes seen on other turrets—the older two-door cupola hatch, the newer one-door commander's hatch, and both mushroom-type split domes and regular air extractors. It was a Krasnoye Sormovo 112 eight-part turret that Fidel Castro posed with during the Cuban Revolution (the tank is currently on display in Havana), and interestingly, in 2016, a North Korean T-34-85 with an eight-part turret was paraded in Pyongyang.

A Second World War-operated T-34-85 (112 8-part Composite) photographed in May 1945. One can clearly see the seam that runs along with the turret and crosses in the centre of the turret. Earlier types of composite turret lacked the reduced section below the cupola. Note the turret marking, which is a white '346' with a diamond with perhaps some numbers in.

Another T-34-85 (112 8-part Composite) in Berlin, just after the war had ended. The distinctive turret seam can be clearly seen. The wounded major appears to be reading a newspaper. A German 37-mm Pak is being used by the Soviets as a rest.

This T-34-85 (112 8-part Composite) is currently on display in Havana, Cuba. The vehicle was famously ridden by Fidel Castro for propaganda purposes during the Bay of Pigs incident (1961). (*Anonymously donated*)

Another view of the rare T-34-85 (112 8-part Composite late) that has been buried as a bunker. Notice the mushroom-type domes on the turret roof, in conjunction with the turret seams, and the command cupola. (*Andrey Firsov*)

A very rare T-34-85 (112 8-part Composite Late) turret, being used as a pillbox. The chassis has been dug into the ground. This turret is very rare indeed and, additionally, had the older two-door command cupola. This turret is in modern-day Israel and was placed here by Israeli forces. (*Andrey Firsov*)

T-34-85 (112 HARD-EDGE-85)

In early 1945, new 'hard-edge-85' turrets were manufactured. These turrets had a welded front portion of the turret, which was identical to the earlier turret, but the rear of the turret was more akin to the hard-edge cheeks of the hard-edge hexagonal turrets. The turret armour extended slightly further below the turret bustle with the weld under the plate out of view.

The seam of the turret now ran under the bustle and was therefore safer than the earlier turrets. These turrets are found being used in the closing stages of the Second World War and are harder to find on the battlefield than their earlier counterparts.

Additionally, one must briefly mention the post-war names given to turrets. In many circles, this turret type is known as the composite-type turret. This is an accurate way to name the turret as the front and rear halves of the turret are manufactured separately and brought together in the construction of the turret. The authors however settled on this new name as composite turrets can also refer to the early hexagonal turrets manufactured at UTZ 183 in 1942, and additionally, the eight-part turrets are sometimes called composite turrets.

A Czechoslovak-operated T-34-85 (112 Hard-Edge-85). This photograph was likely taken in the 1950s rather than being wartime.

A Chinese Type 58. The base tank is a T-34-85 (112 Hard-Edge-85). Type 58s appear to be nothing more than T-34-85s with a handful of upgrades concerning the Type 54 HMG hardpoints, second turret cupola with Type 54 mount, and a new torsion bar-hinge system for the rear plate. Contrary to popular belief, the PRC does not seem to have manufactured T-34s, and there is no concrete evidence of Type 58 being an official name. The photograph is likely a tourist photograph for the sailor in the foreground, who was certainly not a crew member of the tank. Adding to this theory is that the tank is likely decommissioned, as can be seen by the triangular piece of metal that has welded the driver's hatch shut.

Three East German NVA T-34s in the 1950s. The tank in the foreground in a T-34-85 (112 Hard-Edge-85), whereas the machine behind is a T-34-85 (112 Standard Production). Notice the spare drive wheel balanced on the hull side. (*Jirka Collection*)

T-34-85 (112 STANDARD PRODUCTION LATE)

In April 1945, Krasnoye Sormovo 112 introduced the separated mushroom (also known as 'split') type air filters, with one forward and one aft of the command cupola. These air filters were taller than the twin rear air extractors, with a high dome over the filter. This was done on all the turret types being manufactured at Krasnoye Sormovo 112.

The mushroom-type filter turrets are often quoted as being post-war, but photographic evidence suggests that they were issued and fielded during the war, with photographs of one such tank in Czechoslovakia in May 1945. The mushroom air filters are features of both Krasnoye Sormovo 112 and Omsk 174 tanks. They were also used on all patterns of turrets still in production in mid-1945 at 112. This includes very rare examples of eight-part turrets. From hereon, all designations with the term 'Late' added as a suffix will refer to turrets issued with mushroom-type air filters.

T-34-85s manufactured by Krasnoye Sormovo 112 had become much more standardised than in the previous years, but one feature that was always a defining feature of Krasnoye Sormovo 112 tanks was the rear hinges that allowed for the rear plate to be opened. These hinges were much wider than other factories hinges (except for Omsk 174's), with the gear plate placed under the exhaust plate.

It is interesting perhaps that compared to the other factories that manufactured the T-34-85, 112 was by far the most diverse in casting patterns of turrets. The T-34-85 in general, however, was greatly streamlined compared to the T-34.

Krasnoye Sormovo 112 would manufacture in total 12,604 T-34s of all types and manufacture 7,488 T-34-85s when it ended production and reverted to ship-building in 1946. When production ended, all types of turret were manufactured, with 'hard-edge-85' turrets and the earlier style of turrets being the last turrets released for the tank. All these tanks had mushroom-type air filters.

This T-34-85 (112 Hard-Edge-85 Late) is seen just after the end of the Second World War in Europe. Notice the single extractor dome on the turret. Note also that the children are carrying a 'Free German Youth' (*Freie Deutsche Jugend*) flag.

A T-34-85 (112 Hard-Edge-85 Late) with cast spider-type road wheels. This tank was operated by the USSR after the war.

A Bulgarian T-34-85 (112 Standard Production Late). This tank also had the mushroom-type air extractors. Notice the low handrail on the rear of the turret, which is non-standard.

T-34-85 (112 Hard-Edge-85 Late) No. 629. Notice the split mushroom-type air extractors.

T-34-85 (112 Hard-Edge-85 Late) No. 629 of the East German NVA also has its number painted onto the fuel drums on the hull side. It is likely that in the post-war era, this was the standard method of keeping tanks with fuel tanks.

T-34-85 (112 Hard-Edge-85 Late) No. 629, with two Model 1956 steel helmets. Originally developed in 1944, Hitler personally hated them, so the design was shelved until the East German NVA required new helmets.

A post-war Soviet-operated Krasnoye Sormovo 112 T-34-85. Notice the rough casting and gas cutting of items such as the gun sleeve and the turret seam.

This Bulgarian-operated T-34-85 is an interesting example of non-Soviet paint schemes. Notice that the turret side and the upper right glacis plate have a red star with a white outline. Contrary to popular belief, red stars were not at all common on Soviet tanks but were seen somewhat more often after the war. This is not to say that wartime tanks did not have red stars or any Communist symbols painted onto the tanks.

42

UTZ 183: MARCH 1944–DECEMBER 1946

UTZ 183 was the second factory to begin T-34-85 production. In early 1944, the factory produced its last T-34/76 during T-34-85 production to use up stocks of the old 76-mm gunned turrets. These last T-34/76s would have been constructed with either soft-edge or hard-edge turrets, equipped with command cupolas, and UTZ cast spider late-type road wheels.

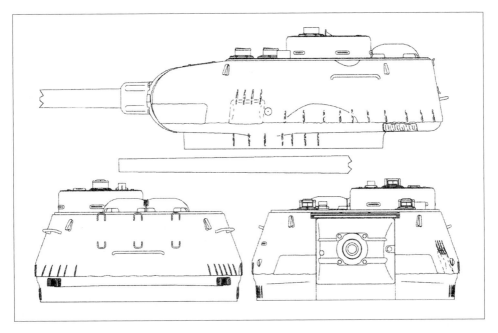

The turret that was designed by UTZ 183 to accommodate the 85-mm gun. This turret was based on the turret refined at Krasnoye Sormovo 112 and modified to suit UTZ 183's needs. The original turrets did not have a bulge for the turret traverse gear, though the electric motor had been present since 1940. The casting was much rougher than Krasnoye Sormovo 112, with more imperfections in the casting. This turret was also sent to Omsk 174 and was the base of their design.

T-34-85 (UTZ 183 EARLY)

The first T-34-85 began manufacture at UTZ on 15 March 1944. When UTZ 183 shifted to T-34-85 production, the factory had to adjust the hull and interior of the tank. Ammunition stowage needed to be changed, plus new electronics were necessary.

To further standardise T-34s, when UTZ 183 moved onto T-34-85 production, it introduced the handrails that were being used by Krasnoye Sormovo 112, which were bent and much smaller than the handrails seen on their T-34/76s. There were five on each side of the hull.

New fenders were also first equipped on UTZ 183 tanks when production of T-34-85s began. These new fenders were identical to the fenders being manufactured at Krasnoye Sormovo 112, so rather than being round, they were now made of two parts with a hinge so that the front fender could be stowed. The older style of fender was still used until stocks ran out, of course.

The road wheels were subtly changed, too. The casting pattern of the cast spider-type road wheels was redesigned to cope with the extra weight of the tank. These wheels were still ribbed, but instead of alternating between one full rib and one half rib, all ribs were full length from the rim to the axle. It is unknown when this was done, but late 1944 seems to be a likely time frame based on photographic evidence.

The turrets produced at UTZ 183 differed greatly from those at Krasnoye Sormovo 112 because these turrets were produced from five cast plates—four basic plates for the body of the turret, plus the roof plate. The four side plates consisted of the lower portion of the turret with the turret ring, then the upper turret plate. This consisted of an almost entire wraparound of the turret, except for two square pieces of armour on either side of the mantlet. These cheek cut-outs were a defining feature of turrets produced at UTZ 183.

An interesting example of a T-34-85 (UTZ 183 Early), lost during Operation Bagration in summer 1944. The turret markings of 'C-3/3' are typical of late-war Soviet markings. The vehicle was subject to a major fire that burned all of the rubber tyres away. Some 85-mm shells can be seen on the fender.

A T-34-85 (UTZ 183 Early) knocked out in the summer of 1944. The turret markings are a little white star, followed by 'Л-87.' (note the full stop is part of the marking).

An early post-war photograph of a T-34-85 (UTZ 183 Early), which was knocked out on the outskirts of Berlin in 1945. Notice that the tank has survived a hit that penetrated the hull to the right of the foremost fuel tank bracket. This was subsequently repaired. Notice the white stripe painted onto the turret. The tank was photographed with the T-34-85 on page 360. Lastly, notice the British Universal Carrier tracks piled up next to the T-34. The USSR was sent several thousand Universal Carriers during the war.

A burning T-34-85 (UTZ 183 Early) in Budapest, March 1945. The tank's vulcanised rubber wheels have caught fire, which was a very common fate for tanks with rubber parts.

The early turrets did not have a bulge in the turret side for the internal motorised turret traversing system, although this motor was present inside the tank. The command cupola was taken directly from the T-34/76s being produced at UTZ 183 before the switch to T-34-85s and had two doors for the hatch (one with an MK-4 episcope).

The basic turret shape and layout from hereon in did not change dramatically, but extra external fuel tank hardpoints were provided for the tanks. Three or four drums could be carried on either side of the hull, with two smaller 20-litre tanks placed on the rear transmission plate.

T-34-85 (UTZ 183 LATE)

In early 1945, UTZ 183 introduced the new command cupola designed at Krasnoye Sormovo 112. This was the new one-piece hatch door with a periscope on the static portion of the hatch. This new system allowed for greater ease of access for the crew because the old two-part hatch could be difficult to exit. Some variation is also observed with the placing of handrails and hardpoints, but the turrets at UTZ 183 were not redesigned drastically.

The turrets that UTZ 183 manufactured were also distributed to Omsk 174, who could not manufacture enough turrets for their own tanks. UTZ 183 tanks had an armoured rain guard on the turret which was noticeably thinner than that of Omsk 174 rain guards. Omsk 174 also provided their own cupolas, which were distinctively rolled.

A T-34-85 (UTZ 183 Late) knocked out in fighting in Berlin in Kurstraße. This photograph was taken shortly after the street had been cleared of debris.

Another NKPA T-34-85 (UTZ 183 Late). This vehicle was knocked out in 1951 while engaging UN forces.

Another NKPA T-34-85 (UTZ 183 Late). This tank has been through several rebuilds and has non-standard UTZ 183 wheels. The severe damage, such as the missing turret roof and hull floor, indicates that the tank was likely attacked by aircraft.

The victorious crew of a T-34 that survived the war. This photograph was taken in July 1945 in Germany. Notice that the tank did not escape unscathed and is equipped with two steel-rimmed road wheels, one on the first position and one on the fourth. The Soviet crews' uniforms are a mixture of button-up and zip overalls.

A Bulgarian-operated T-34-85 (UTZ 183 Late). Notice the single door turret hatch on the cupola. All T-34 cupolas could rotate in any direction, but there was a latch that was activated when the MK-4 scope faced forwards to stop it from rotating any more.

A T-34-85 (UTZ 183 Late). Notice the NKPA markings painted over with American graffiti. An M24 Chaffee is driving on the ridge above. The tank might have shrubbery camouflage.

An NVA T-34-85 (UTZ 183 Late) being used in the training role. Notice two NVA T-34 (76s) in the background, one being on page 326. The T-34-85 displays typical UTZ 183 features, such as the typical turret construction with small cut-outs in the turret cheek. The tank is missing rear hinges, and interestingly, the bolts for the Soviet wartime heater can be seen below the exhaust pipes. The rearmost T-34 is a good example of a rebuild, featuring the original rounded rear plate with a square transmission hatch. The turret is the Composite type, indicating that the vehicle is a survivor from early 1942 UTZ 183. The drum-type fuel tank has been added, being introduced at least six months after the tank's initial release.

T-34s manufactured at UTZ 183 were only ever issued with cast spider-type wheels and was the only plant to do so. Both Krasnoye Sormovo 112 and Omsk 174 used pressed-type wheels. Some UTZ 183 T-34s observed after the war have full sets of pressed type road wheels, but this appears to be post-production rebuilds. Additionally, when UTZ 183 began production of the T-34s replacement in 1947, namely the T-54, Those tanks also had wheels that were cast with ribs. These wheels were wider than T-34 wheels and not interchangeable.

In December 1946, UTZ 183 produced its last T-34-85 and moved onto T-54 production. The T-54 was a huge leap forward in technology, with torsion bar suspension on a new low silhouette hull. This tank was the replacement for the T-44, which was manufactured at Factory Number 75 in Kharkov, the original home of KhPZ 183. In total, UTZ 183 manufactured 28,952 T-34s of all types, including 14,432 T-34-85s.

Unlike UTZ T-34s which were a very diverse array of tanks, the T-34-85s were greatly streamlined. There was little variation beyond the cupola design from the beginning of UTZ T-34-85 production to the end of production.

When production of the T-34 ended, UTZ 183 still held the paperwork for their construction. Therefore, when Polish and Czechoslovakian factories began to organise the production of the tanks in 1950, the paperwork from UTZ 183 was sent to them. The last Soviet-produced T-34s came from UTZ 183 in 1946, but the last ever T-34s produced were made in the Czechoslovakian Martin factory in 1956 (see pages 467–469).

The same T-34-85 (UTZ 183 Late) as seen below. Notice the fuel tank hardpoints on the rear of the tank. The Austrian marking of a red circle with a white upside-down triangle can be seen. The tank has pressed road wheels, which are non-standard for UTZ 183.

An Austrian T-34-85 (UTZ 183 Late) with M-46 Patton tanks. Austria was in a unique position by being allowed to be independent very shortly after Soviet occupation. Therefore, it inherited some Soviet and some American tanks.

A parade in Kiev with a mixture of different T-34s from different factories. The T-34 on the front left is a T-34-85 (UTZ 183 Late), whereas the next tank along is a T-34-85 (112 Standard Production Late).

T-34-85 (112 Hard Edge Late) No. 626 at an East German NVA barracks. On the left of the frame is a ZSU-57-2 SPAAG (self-propelled anti-aircraft gun).

Opposite below: A Bulgarian-operated T-34-85 (UTZ 183 Late) with its crew of five posing in front of it. The commander stands on the right and can be distinguished by his binoculars. A slogan is written on the turret side, but this cannot be read due to the angle of the photograph.

A Romanian T-34-85 crossing a river with mounted infantry, likely during a training exercise. Note the soldier on the left of the turret appears to have a DP machine gun deployed on the turret roof using a bipod.

43

OMSK 174:
JUNE 1944–DECEMBER 1945

Omsk 174 was not only the last factory to produce T-34/76s but was also the first factory to stop the production of the T-34 in the post-war era. Furthermore, Omsk 174 T-34-85s were produced in the smallest numbers during the war.

T-34-85 (174 EARLY TURRET)

The last T-34/76 ever produced rolled out of Omsk 174 in September 1944, but T-34-85 production began earlier that year in June 1944. This crossover period was to use up old stocks of old T-34/76 parts. As such, T-34/76s made in June–September 1944 had a pointed hull nose, plus other T-34-85-specific features, except the handrails on the hull side, which appear to still have been T-34/76 handrails.

On the subject of hybrids, Omsk 174 was where most T-34s were sent for capital repairs and T-34/76s requiring major repairs were converted into T-34-85s. As such, many examples exist of T-34-85s with rounded noses or hull radio ports, indicating them to be a rebuild using a T-34/76 chassis (see page 393).

Omsk 174 produced 2,038 turrets for their tanks, but also accepted 2,081 turrets from other factories. The main provider of these turrets was UTZ 183, and therefore many tanks made at Omsk 174 were equipped with the UTZ 183 standard turrets.

One of the ways to tell an Omsk 174 turret from a UTZ 183 turret is what type of rain cover and command cupola it was issued. Omsk 174 also issued a new gun mantlet. The outward difference was that the gun mantlet had two bulges on either side of the gun sleeve. Not all T-34s from 174 were issued this mantlet, but it is a good way to identify a 174 tank. Additionally, Omsk 174 manufactured the command cupola from a rolled piece of armour plate, whereas UTZ 183 and Krasnoye Sormovo 112 cast their cupolas. Omsk 174 cupolas also had a small patch of armour on the right-hand side of the cupola.

A T-34-85 manufactured at Omsk 174 in the streets of Berlin after the fighting ended. One can see the distinctive Omsk 174 rain cover.

This T-34-85 (174 with 183 turret) was photographed in the late 1940s in Soviet service. The rain cover over the 85-mm gun has been removed, meaning that water can easily enter the interior of the tank. After the Second World War, the T-34 played an important training and auxiliary role.

Two T-34-85 (174 Early Turret)s. The tank in the foreground is an OT-34, as can be seen by the flame unit in the hull. The Omsk 174 tow hooks are clearly visible, and the Omsk 174 rain covers are seen. The T-34 in the foreground has a UTZ 183 supplied turret, and the second tank is an Omsk 174-turreted tank.

A T-34-85 (174 Early Turret) in Bulgarian service. Notice the ZiS-53 gun mantlet and the markings; it is likely a division in the circle, then the tank number behind it.

A T-34-85 (174 Angled Seam Turret) tank in Poland in 1947. Notice the front road wheel is cast spider late-type, whereas the others are pressed-type road wheels.

A Bulgarian-operated T-34-85 (174 with 183 Turret). The turret was supplied from UTZ 183, but the Omsk 174 rain cover can be seen.

The same tank as page 391. Notice the Omsk 174 type tow hooks and the T-55-style headlights.

A T-34-85 (174 with 183 Turret) in post-war Soviet service. Notice the faded turret numbers, which are typical of Soviet post-war tanks, and the unditching beam attached to the hull side.

This T-34-85 is a rebuild now serving in the 63rd Guards Tank Brigade in Prague 1945. Outwardly, it looks like a T-34-85 (174 with 183 Turret), which, to a degree, it is. However, notice the nose of this tank is not pointed, but rather is rounded, indicating it to have been a T-34/76 hull. Omsk 174 appears to have conducted most of the factory rebuilds, and this tank is exactly that. One such example still exists today in the private collection of Mr Alex Hall.

The Omsk 174-designed rain cover was much larger than that at UTZ 183 and had distinctive bolts that attached this cover to the turret roof. Post-war-produced Omsk 174 T-34s were sometimes issued with a new cupola that resembled that of an IS-2's.

The turrets manufactured at Omsk 174 were subtly different to those at UTZ 183. Rather than the cut-outs in the cheek being separate from the other plates used in construction like at UTZ 183, the entire nose section of the tank was manufactured from four plates with an upper and lower left and right cheek plate. The seam for the lower cheek cut-out attached to the turret ring, unlike UTZ 183 turrets that met the seam for the lower turret plate on the turret cheek itself. Tanks made at Omsk 174 and made with turrets manufactured at Omsk 174 can be called 'T-34-85 (174 Early Turret)'. However, turrets made UTZ 183 and Krasnoye Sormovo 112 were used in production at Omsk 174 and these tanks can be called 'T-34-85 (174 with 183 Turret)' and 'T-34-85 (174 with 112 Turret)' respectively.

The turret cheeks of Omsk 174 tanks were noticeably rounder than those of the UTZ 183 turrets due to the placement of the seam between the upper and lower cheek plate.

As the turrets that were made at Omsk 174 were issued alongside turrets that were sent from other plants at the same time, and therefore, dating tanks cannot be done by their turrets, apart from the Omsk 174-made angled seam turret, which was introduced at the end of the war.

A clear view of an East German NVA-operated T-34-85 (174 with 183 Turret). The rain cover on the turret roof is clearly seen. This tank has been updated to Model 1960 standard. The tank has hardpoints on the hull side for tool kits not standard during the war, along with a non-standard caged headlight, along with a Notek headlight. Note also the DDR emblem on the turret. (*Jiří Zahradník Collection*)

A T-34-85 (174 with 183 Turret). Notice the Omsk 174-type rain cover and, most importantly, the bulged gun mantlet. This tank has an infrared light on the hull side.

A T-34-85 (174 with 183 Turret) with a rare command cupola. This cupola was similar in design to that of the IS-2 heavy tank. Notice the non-standard handrail on the turret. Also note the parade markings on the fender: red stars with a white outline, and a white outline drawn on the fender.

A pair of NVA T-34-85 (UTZ 183 Late). This tank has undergone some of the German modernisations, such as the rear turret stowage bin and the rearranged hull stowage. Both of the T-34s here are from UTZ 183, and the different turret finishes can be seen, with the T-34 in the foreground having far heavier casting sinks, indicating it to be a later turret.

The same group of NVA T-34-85 (UTZ 183 Late) tanks as on page 395. The NVA received many T-34s after the creation of the DDR, and by the early 1970s, many of the vehicles had been relegated to the training role.

T-34-85 (174 ANGLED SEAM TURRET)

The angled seam turret was manufactured from April 1945 until the end of production at Omsk 174 in December 1945. As such, it saw very limited service during the war in the Western Sector of fighting, with one being photographed in Berlin. The angled seam turret had the seam run along the lower rear portion of the turret, like that on earlier Omsk 174 tanks, but the seam cut across the cheek of the turret from just past the pistol port to about halfway down the turret's cheek in a straight line.

These tanks were extensively fielded in the Korean War (1950–1953) and are often wrongly referred to as 'post-war turrets'.

T-34-85 (174 ANGLED SEAM TURRET LATE)

Towards the end of turret production at Omsk 174 in April 1945, the factory introduced the mushroom-type air extractor fans. Some sources claim that only Krasnoye Sormovo 112 issued these domes, but most angled seam turrets were issued these domes, meaning that Omsk 174 also issued them.

An NKPA T-34-85 (174 Angled Seam Turret Late). This tank was engaged by M26 Pershing tanks and did not come off too well. Notice the large penetration on the front road wheel.

Another view of the T-34-85 (174 Angled Seam Turret Late) as seen on pages 362 and 363.

A T-34-85 (174 Angled Seam Turret) in Bulgarian service. Notice the distinctive rain cover once again.

OPPOSITE PAGE:

Above: A Bulgarian operated T-34-85 (174 Angled Seam Turret Late). Notice the repair done to the turret's left-hand side, indicating that this T-34 saw service in the Second World War and took damage. The gun mantlet of this tank is also mounted straight; this is likely due to damage internally from the penetration. A single red star is the only visible marking.

Below: An East German NVA-operated T-34-85 (174 Angled Seam Turret). Tanks have always enjoyed a crowd, and even in post-war Germany, tanks were popular with children.

A pair of Bulgarian-operated T-34s. The rear tank is a T-34-85 (174 Angled Seam Turret). Take note of the turret markings, apparently consisting of a three-digit number ('632') and a white stencilled triangle. (*Stan Lucian Collection*)

These mushroom-type air extractors were only issued to the angled seam turrets at Omsk 174. This turret was being manufactured just in time to see service during the Second World War, with one example of a rebuilt T-34 with an angled seam turret in Berlin in April 1945.

Since Omsk 174 used turrets from other plants and the fact that Omsk 174 also used mushroom-type air filters, it can be hard to identify an Omsk 174 tank from a T-34-85 from Krasnoye Sormovo 112 using this detail. Instead, the easiest things to look for are smooth tow hook hardpoints, a heavy bolted rain cover for the gun mantlet, or the square-type rear hinges for the rear plate, which do not have angled cut-outs like Krasnoye Sormovo 112 hinges. All these features are Omsk 174 exclusives.

Furthermore, welding at Omsk 174 was rather crude; hence one can spot very rough weld seams compared to other factories. Some minor details of their tanks were simpler, too, such as the pistol ports that had a plain plug without any taper to it.

The factory stopped production of the T-34-85 in 1946 and was the first factory to do so. However, in 1947, SU-100 production began briefly at Omsk 174, lasting for a year, with 203 examples manufactured until 1948. Later, Omsk 174 moved onto engine production and was later involved in T-80 Main Battle Tank production. In total, Omsk 174 manufactured 5,867 T-34s of all types, of which 3,994 were T-34-85s.

A line of East German NVA T-34-85s. All of them, apart from one, were made by Omsk 174. From right to left, there is a T-34-85 (174 with 112 Turret), T-34-85 (112 Standard Production), T-34-85 (174 Angled Seam Turret), and finally two T-34-85 (174 with 112 Turret)s.

An East German NVA T-34-85 (174 Angled Seam Turret). Notice the bulged gun mantlet, indicative of 174 tanks.

An East German NVA-operated T-34-85 (174 Angled Seam Turret). Notice the German modifications, such as the Notek headlight on the glacis plate, and a protective cage around the Soviet light. Many of the stowage boxes are non-Soviet. Notice the bulged gun mantlet.

Two Bulgarian-operated T-34-85s. Both vehicles are T-34-85 (174 Angled Seam Type Late). Notice the pattern of the pistol port, which was a clear indicator of the factory of origin, along with the other features such as the tow hook pattern, turret seam, and rain cover. A simple red star is painted onto the turret side.

44

BATTLE: T-34-85s AT OGLEDOW

Perhaps the greatest testament to both the T-34-85's ability on the battlefield and improved Soviet tactics that had been developed since 1941 is the well-documented and well-celebrated Battle of Ogledow. This battle was also the first showdown between the new Tiger II and the humble T-34-85. Despite the fairly extraordinary detail of fighting against the Tiger II, the story is actually rather typical of late-war Soviet tank combat. Whereas compared to earlier engagements in the war (such as the assault on Kalinin), Soviet crews were both much more trained and experienced in modern war, tactics at both a divisional and army level had greatly improved, and the vehicles the Red Army was fielding were also vast improvements on earlier ones.

OPERATION BAGRATION

The Battle of Ogledow was a minor engagement in the greater Operation Bagration, the Soviet summer campaign conducted against Army Group Centre. Operation Bagration was meant to coincide with the Allied landings on Normandy, but instead, it began on 22 June 1944 (the third anniversary of the German invasion of the USSR), sixteen days after the Allied landings on 6 June 1944.

Operation Bagration was the brainchild of Marshal of the Soviet Union Georgy Zhukov and was planned to be the total destruction of German forces in the Byelorussian SSR. The Soviets fielded 3,841 tanks (mostly consisting of the new IS-2 and T-34-85) along with 1.5 million men for the offensive. The Germans, on the other hand, only had 118 tanks available in June 1944 in Army Group Centre.

The offensive was to be the first real Soviet attempt at 'Deep Battle'. This was a Soviet tactic developed during the 1930s that aimed at disrupting the enemy in every sector that it operated in and required full coordination with ground and air units. Deep Battle tactics were very similar to those of *Blitzkrieg*, aiming to disrupt the enemy not only on the front lines but

A T-34-85 (174 Early Turret) knocked out during Operation Bagration in July 1944. Notice the ZiS-53 85-mm gun mantlet and the turret marking, which is just barely in shot.

also to harass supply columns, destroy bridges in the enemy's rear, gain air superiority, and relentlessly attack the enemy wherever it may go.

Operation Bagration began on the morning of 22 June 1944, and within six days, the German Fourth Army had been completely destroyed. Minsk was also encircled and finally captured on 4 July 1944.

Due to the dangerous position that the largely unaffected Army Group North and South were now in, with their southern and northern flanks (respectively) dangerously exposed, both units had little choice but to also retreat. The Soviet advance cut of retreating German units in the Crimea, as well as in the Lithuanian SSR and Latvian SSR. Following the initial successes, throughout July and August, the Soviet 'steamroller' continued to move eastward. By August 1944, the Soviets had liberated huge areas and crossed the pre-June 1941 German–Soviet frontier; they were now fighting in Poland.

OGLEDOW

The village of Ogledow (Oględów) was a small Polish village built on sandy ground in a shallow valley about 100 km east of the Soviet–Polish border. On 11 August 1944, Soviet units, namely the 52nd and 53rd Guards Tank Brigade, advanced towards the village, fielding both T-34-85s and IS-2s.

German forces did not currently occupy the village, which stretched over two settlements running parallel to a river. The Soviets occupied the eastern side of the village, whereas it was thought that the Germans were to the western side of the village. Before the battle, it was already noted that two German tanks were bogged down and abandoned in the sandy ground. These German tanks had not been knocked out in fighting and were likely abandoned temporarily due to being bogged down. The German forces knew many Soviet tanks were approaching the village and therefore did not have enough time to recover them.

A German infantryman had been captured on 11 August, and after interrogation, he told the Soviets that there were two abandoned Panthers in the village and that the Germans intended to enter the village and recover their lost tanks. With this information, the Soviets decided to set up an ambush around the more passable terrain around the village in the form of farmers' fields. In the high August summer, farmers around this area had already collected hay in one metre high bundles and placed them around their fields. The Soviets saw an opportunity to strike the Germans, who were thought to likely move across these fields to reach Ogledow and recover their lost vehicles.

PRELUDE TO BATTLE

The Soviets decided that they should ambush the Germans, who were likely to try to recover their abandoned tanks. Therefore, several T-34-85s were set up for an ambush organised by Guards Junior Lieutenant Alexander Petrovich Oskin.

Cunningly, Oskin ordered the men of his unit to disguise their T-34-85s among the hay bales. However, after the first tank was camouflaged, Oskin realised that among the 1-m-high bales, a handful of tank-sized hay bales would be fairly obvious, so much of the night of the 12 August was spent piling up the other bales of hay to be the size and shape of his concealed tanks.

He placed his tanks about the field, not to bunch them together, and ordered radio discipline to be maintained. The plan was to simply let the Germans, who were expected to drive through their field to regain their lost tanks, drive up to the village, exposing their weak sides. Then, at ranges of up to 400 m, they planned to open fire on the unwitting Germans. The German forces were expected to travel south-east towards the Soviets, with the tanks placed to the south of their predicted path. The Soviet tanks were laid out facing north.

The Soviet T-34-85s were discussed under hay, and behind the hills to the west, pre-prepared artillery pieces were waiting for the Germans to advance. In all of this, no time was spared to inspect the captured German tanks bogged down in the sandy terrain.

DUEL IN THE FOG

On the morning of 13 August 1944, the T-34-85s lay silent, engines off, but electronics operational, as to use the electric triggers and turret traverse. However, the rumble of German vehicles broke the still silence of the morning. The village was also covered in a layer of mist.

The left flank of the 53rd Tank Brigade radioed to report the sight of German tanks but was ordered to hold fire. Eleven German tanks emerged from the fog, with half-tracks and infantry for support. These advanced further, but with great difficulty, losing traction on the sandy ground. The tanks were traversing the clearer ground near the village, but even here, they were travelling slowly. The German tanks were spaced out quite far apart, and by the time the first tank had passed the T-34-85s, the third tank was only just approaching the Soviet tanks.

At this moment, the order to open fire was given. The first tank to begin the attack was Oskin's. The barrel of his tank emerged from the hay it was under, then aimed and fired. Oskin managed to get multiple shots off at the first target, presumably the first German tank to emerge from the fog. The German tank's turret began to turn, but after the volley of hits, it was set alight. The after-action Soviet report from the commander in the field noted that Oskin's shells left clean black penetrations.

The second German tank was also hit at the same time as the first tank, and its fate was much the same.

The third German tank's turret began to traverse to face Oskin's tank, but it was noticeably slow. The vehicle then began to turn its body to increase the speed at which the turret and gun would find a target. However, its track was damaged by a shell and its wheels were jammed. Under heavy fire, and fearing for their lives, the crew of the German tank bailed out.

After this, the Soviet commander ordered indirect artillery fire on the Germans' locations. This had been agreed on previously. By the end of 13 August, the Soviets had repulsed the German advance. For the T-34-85s, the battle was over, but more fighting with IS-2s was conducted to the east, where another two German tanks were destroyed. After consolidating their position, reports began to come back on the tanks that had been engaged by the T-34-85s.

Three enemy heavy tanks had been knocked out, originally being reported as Panther tanks. Additionally, it was found that three tanks (instead of the original two) had been abandoned and were awaiting recovery by the Germans. Two tanks were lost in the soft ground in Ogledow, but another vehicle was lost in the marshy ground to the east and found later on by the Soviets.

Upon inspection of the abandoned and knocked-out tanks, something strangely concerning was observed. The tanks that were engaged were not Panthers, as had been thought, but were a hitherto unknown tank. One of the abandoned tanks had not been cleared out by the German crew, and so technical documents were discovered in the vehicle.

The Soviets found out that this new German tank weighed 68 tonnes, had a crew of five, was equipped with a powerful 8.8-cm KwK 43 L/71 gun, and had frontal armour up to 185 mm thick. It was found out that the tanks belonged to the *Schwere Panzer Abteilung 501*. Unbeknown to the crews of the T-34-85s, they had just had their first brush with the *Wehrmacht*'s new Tiger II—perhaps one of the most legendary tanks of the war. Not only had they successfully ambushed these new German tanks, but three had been delivered to the Red Army in almost perfect condition, having only been bogged down in the sandy terrain. It was therefore not long before Soviet officials were crawling all over the captured tanks, and one was immediately sent to Kubinka for evaluation.

CONCLUSION

The Red Army had just engaged the first 'super heavy' German tanks of the war and come away unscathed. They had successfully defended themselves against these tanks and ruined the battlefield debut of the Tiger II on the Eastern Front. This success was achieved by knowing the limitations of their own tanks and successfully analysing the battlefield situation. The planning for this engagement was well-thought-out, and preparations were done effectively to limit the ability of the German forces to predict Soviet positions. The layout of the terrain was also analysed, and correct decisions of troop placements and the successful predictions of German movements allowed for the upper hand to be gained.

Finally, the limitations of the T-34-85 were understood by their crews, who were evidently well-trained. While the 85-mm gun was a huge improvement over the 76.2-mm F-34 gun, Soviet crews knew it was of little advantage to engage a German tank head-on and rather waited for the correct opportunity to engage a German tank on their flanks. Even though the Soviets did not know that they were fighting Tiger IIs, lessons from engaging other heavy German tanks were put into practice. One must also consider that unlike the earlier assault on Kalinin, the Soviets had the upper hand and were not engaging in a suicide mission.

For his actions, Guards Junior Lieutenant Alexander Petrovich Oskin was awarded the title Hero of the Soviet Union. It should be noted that in the awards citation, Oskin is credited with knocking out all three Tiger IIs, whereas it is far more likely that his units collectively destroyed the tanks. Additionally, elements of the story were embellished, claiming that he 'crushed 80 fascists under his tracks' in the village itself, which does not appear to be the case. Embellishments such as these are common in awards citations throughout all armies in the Second World War.

45

SOVIET T-34-85 PRODUCTION OVERVIEW

Unlike the T-34/76, relatively few details of the T-34-85 had changed from the first production run to the last. While there were differences from one factory to another in turret shape and its construction methods, the T-34-85s were little different from January 1944 until January 1947.

Both the D-5T and the S-53 guns performed well on the battlefield, and the appearance of the T-34-85 is often considered a major reason for the downfall of the *Wehrmacht* between 1944 and 1945 because it was able to defeat even the heaviest (and rarest) of German armour, as was discussed earlier on page 351.

SOVIET T-34-85 PRODUCTION

Factory Location	Factory Abbreviation	Factory Code	1944	1945	1946	Total
Nizhniy Tagil	UTZ	183	6,583	7,356	493	14,432
Krasnoye Sormovo	-	112	3,079	3,255	1,154	7,488
Omsk	-	174	1,000	1,940	1,054	3,994
						25,914

When the T-34-85 entered production, unlike the T-34/76, it was not the most formidable tank on the battlefield. Tanks being fielded by Germany, and even the Soviet Union, were superior in armour thickness, gun penetration power, and crew communications, just to name a few factors. However, the Germans were lacking in numbers, whereas the Red Army, with its relatively easy-to-produce T-34-85, was certainly not. For example, only 492 Tiger IIs were manufactured during the war, whereas roughly 16,000 T-34-85s were manufactured by June 1945.

Testimony to the T-34-85's performance can be shown with the swift destruction of Army Group Centre during Operation Bagration in June 1944. The hard lessons of the early war had long since been learned, and a bloodthirsty, well-trained Red Army was ready to unleash the most ambitious attack they had conducted in the war.

New tactics, vast numbers, and guns giving the ability to successfully tackle the heaviest of German tanks in ranges upward of 500 m led to a brutal and swift victory. The handful of Tigers and other such heavy tanks available to the Germans could not cope with the vast number of T-34-85s that were being fielded.

Compared to the new German heavy and super-heavy tanks such as the Tiger II and Panther tanks, the T-34-85 was an inferior product. However, the T-34-85 was much easier to manufacture and fielded in vastly superior numbers. History, too, would favour a medium tank that was fast and manoeuvrable compared to the super-heavy tanks that, after the Second World War, were all but made extinct on the battlefield. It was clear from all states that many medium tanks were more desirable than a few heavy tanks, with the following conflicts, many of which the T-34-85 found itself in, demonstrating this.

Interestingly, a report on combat damage sustained from the First Belorussian Front in 1944 indicated that 33.4 per cent of tanks were knocked out by a single hit. This is a fair survival rate as the Panzer IV, the most common enemy tank, had a single hit destruction rate of 38.4 per cent.

While not the best tank ever designed, or the best quality machines ever produced, the T-34 and T-34-85 were exactly what the Soviet Union needed. Much has been stated in this book, and in other sources, about the flaws in the design. It is fair to say that a moderately good tank with a few flaws that could be mass-produced easily was the war-winning combination for the Soviet economy and technical doctrine.

The T-34's short term replacement, the T-44, was rolling off the production line from November 1944 (although it did not see combat due to logistical reasons) but was itself replaced in 1947 by the T-54 Main Battle Tank, which would become a staple of militaries across the world even until this day.

46

TECHNICAL DESCRIPTION OF THE
T-34-85 IN 1945

The T-34-85, in many respects, was a total redesign of the fighting compartment and turret of the T-34. This was done as quickly as possible, and while the T-34-85 was a superior machine to the T-34, it had some major issues with regards to bullet traps.

The glacis remained a nominal 45 mm thick and angles were unchanged. The lower hull, sides, and rear armour were 45 mm thick, and the hull roof and floor were 20 mm thick.

To accommodate a newly designed turret for the tank, the turret ring diameter was increased from 1,450 to 1,600 mm. In conjunction with this, the inner walls of the turret below the turret ring were marginally redesigned to allow for clearance of all of the turret interior.

Little changed for the driver, and he still had all of the tools and instruments available on late war T-34/76s. The engineer's position was rethought slightly. The R-9 radio was moved from this position back to the turret, giving the engineer one less job to do. Therefore, in the radio's place, extra machine gun ammunition racks were placed, with two 85-mm shells standing vertically in front of the second vertical spring casing.

The first two vertical spring in their partial casings in front of the driver and engineer was thickened from 30 to 32 mm to help support the added weight of the new 10-ton turret.

The fighting compartment's ammunition racks were completely redesigned to accommodate the new 85-mm ammunition boxes. On the left side of the fighting compartment floor, four boxes, each containing six shells, were placed widthways down the tank, whereas the right-hand side had a single ammunition box containing twelve shells that was placed lengthways. Another single ammunition box was placed widthways at the rear of the fighting compartment against the firewall and centrally. This created a gap to the left and right that allowed for the additional stowage of two shells vertically on each side. There were no wall-mounted racks in the hull like the T-34, but some tanks were retrofitted with a heater mounted on the left hull side in the post-war era. An electrical hub was placed centrally below the turret ring; this would attach to a metal-braced cable that gave electric power to the turret.

The engine and transmission stayed almost the same from the standard T-34, but, as mentioned earlier, a new air filter, developed for the IS heavy tank, the Multicyclone air cleaner, which provided nearly 100 per cent air purification for up to eight hours without maintenance, was fitted to T-34-85s as standard.

The T-34-85 was also given a smoke generator. This was placed with the transmission, and two pipes were placed at the rear of the tank, exiting the vehicle at the mesh radiator cover, and splitting left and right, as to produce smoke on either side of the tank, above the exhaust pipes.

Obviously, the greatest change to the design was that of the new turret. The turret ring was 1,600 mm and the general shape of the turret was a six-sided design, with a large bustle and cheek overhang. This created a bullet trap around the turret ring and compromised safety, but due to the unwillingness to redesign the hull, this was the only option open to engineers.

The new turret was 2.3 feet high and could accommodate a crew of three, though originally, only two crew were accommodated. Initially, a D-5T 85-mm gun was installed, but this was replaced with an S-53 85-mm gun. This had a cast gun mount that attached to the turret via two fillets on either side of the turret cheeks. On the left of this was the gunner's position, who had a folding seat that was attached to the electrical feed. In front of him was the gun elevation handle with an inbuilt electric trigger and a manual trigger attached to the breach of the gun. Above this was an electric safety switch that allowed access to both the 85-mm and DT-29 machine gun triggers.

On his left, mounted into the turret side, was an electric turret traverse. This had both a manual and an electric setting. A cut-out in the turret ring allowed for the gunner to see etched angles on the turret ring to tell him when the turret was facing forwards. This, interestingly enough, stated that forward was '030'.

Behind the gunner's position was the commander's position. Attached to the turret ring was a folding seat directly below the cupola. Mounted onto the turret's left side was the R-9 radio set, with an antenna mount forward of the cupola. The cupola was shorter than the T-34's cupola, and early versions had five vision ports and a two-part hatch. Later models had a single hatch.

In the bustle, there was an ammunition rack that could hold twelve shells. There were four racks, each able to hold three shells. To the right of the gun was the loader's position. The loader did not get a permanent seat but instead had a leather cradle that attached to the turret ring and the gun, giving him a seat in the centre of the three leather straps. To his right, on the turret side, were ammunition racks for three wall-mounted shells placed horizontally. The loader had a circular hatch, carried over from the T-34/76 for escaping through.

All three positions had an MK-4 episcope, and the loader had a side vision port. Both the gunner and loader had a pistol port.

The 85-mm gun had two liquid-based recoil dampers under the gun and had a vertical breach. The gun had a gun shield that could be stowed vertically while in transit and lowered for combat. The shield had a spring-loaded shell guide to help the loader get a shell into the breach.

The 9-R radio set was now standard and was much more compact and reliable than the 71-TK-3 set.

Exterior stowage was much the same as the T-34 in 1944. A gun-cleaning toolbox was placed on the front left fender, and a track toolbox was placed on the rear right fender. A wood saw was stowed on the hull left side, and ice cleats were stowed on the right fender.

Some T-34-85 snow cleats belonging to a Krasnoye Sormovo 112 T-34 (which also features a Czechoslovak turret and hull buzzer), as seen at Shiveringham Army Barracks. This is the original Second World War stowage.

A standard ZiS-53 cleaning rod on the T-34 at Shiveringham Army Barracks. This is original, but the items underneath are not.

The engineer's position of the T-34 at Shiveringham Army Barracks. Notice the DT-29 with telescopic sight, not standard on all T-34s. Notice also that some DT-29 magazines have a fabric outer ring, while others do not. This is standard across all DT-29 magazines seen in the Second World War.

The track toolbox at the Shiveringham Army Barracks. This is the tool used for changing the tension on the front idler wheel. Under this kit, spare track pins can be seen. The second part of the toolbox has grease nipples in the original Soviet paper and a cap for the armoured fuel tanks.

47

ASSAULT GUNS AND TANK DESTROYERS ON THE T-34 CHASSIS

Like all states, the Soviet Union was keen to use their tank chassis for other purposes other than a battle tank. These fall into two categories of vehicles: combat and non-combat vehicles. Combat vehicles include all types of tank, assault guns, or specialised assault vehicles for mine-laying or troop carriers. Non-combat vehicles include recovery vehicles, mobile cranes, ammunition carriers, and tractors. To an extent, most of these vehicles were experimented with or even fielded at one point or another.

Since the T-34's original order was only 2,000 vehicles, it was not until after the war started that such vehicles on the T-34 chassis were considered. Also, due to the Stavka wanting T-34 production to be disrupted as little as possible, all these designs came out after January 1942, and more importantly, after German defeats.

While the main focus of this publication is the linear T-34, it would be remiss to not discuss the other Soviet-produced combat vehicles made using the basic T-34 chassis. There were several successful attempts to utilise the T-34 chassis in the assault gun and tank destroyer roles that made it into mass production (as well as many other 'paper-only' projects that never left the drawing board which will not be covered in this book). Nonetheless, the first successful combat vehicle designed on the T-34 to be fielded was the SU-122 self-propelled gun.

48

SU-122

The SU-122 was the Soviet answer to the *Sturmgeschütz* series of German assault guns. The *Sturmgeschütz* III (StuG III) was designed around the Panzer III chassis, mounting a 75-mm KwK 37 L/24 gun. This gun was not designed for engaging tanks and was instead a mobile infantry gun. However, when the Germans encountered tanks such as the T-34 and KV-1, the StuG III was up-gunned with a long-barrelled 75-mm StuK 40 L/43 gun to engage tanks.

The Stavka was very impressed with the fighting capability of the StuG III and desired a Soviet-manufactured counterpart. While some StuG III and Panzer III tanks were captured and pressed into Soviet service, an indigenous design was needed because there simply were not enough captured vehicles to meet demand, nor were there enough spare parts for these captured tanks.

In April 1942, the Stavka ordered that design bureaus investigate adapting current chassis as assault guns. The Uralmash Plant Design Bureau (Russian: КБ завода Уралмаш) under the engineers N. Kurin and G. F. Ksyunin proposed a self-propelled gun called the U-34.

The basic design used the chassis of a T-34 tank, but instead of a turret, a fixed fighting compartment was proposed, with 60 mm of frontal armour. The design would have been two tons lighter than the T-34 and 700 mm taller, mounting the same F-34 gun as the T-34. This was clearly an emulation of the StuG III, which mounted effectively the same gun as its Panzer IV counterpart but in a superstructure as opposed to a turret.

This tank was proposed to be manufactured at UTZM in place of standard T-34s, but the T-34 was deemed too important. It took until October 1942 for a formal decree to be issued for design teams to design a new assault gun. Decree No. 2429ss was passed for assault guns to be designed, armed with 37-mm, 76.2-mm, or 122-mm guns.

The Uralmash plant began designing a 122-mm assault gun on the T-34 chassis. This tank was to be armed with the M-30 122-mm howitzer developed by Sverdlovsk plant No. 9, which also would later design the D-5S and D-5T 85-mm guns.

The first prototype, named U-35, was tested in November 1942 and competed against the SG-122, which was a Soviet-designed 122-mm gun on a captured Panzer III tank. Obviously, since the Soviets were manufacturing the T-34 chassis, and not the Panzer III chassis, the

U-35 was accepted for production as well and was renamed SU-122. It should be noted that the SG-122 was still manufactured, but small scale.

Production began in 1942, but the first tanks were delivered in 1943. The last SU-122s were manufactured in August 1943, and in total, 638 units were manufactured. In the same timeframe, UTZM also manufactured T-34 tanks and made 719 T-34s. Therefore, before SU-85 production, 1,357 vehicles were manufactured at UTZM.

The SU-122 used the same T-34 chassis that was being manufactured at UTZM in December 1942 through to August 1943. The tanks were issued with pressed-type road wheels, and some vehicles were issued with a split-type track.

The engine deck of the SU-122 matched that of the T-34, but the forward superstructure was completely redesigned. Instead of a turret, the glacis plate extended upward past the point that the T-34 glacis reached. This was 2.235 m above the ground. Mounted on the upper left glacis was a M-30 122-mm gun. To the left of the gun was a vision port for the driver, with a single armoured lid for a periscope. This was essentially a half-scale T-34 driver's hatch.

The upper hull walls were not angled as steeply as regular T-34s, and to attach it to the T-34's engine deck, small fillets were placed at the rear of this new armoured superstructure. On each fighting compartment side, there was a typical rod and bracket handrail, and on the upper portion of the fighting compartment, an exterior periscope was placed centrally on the plate.

This UTZM manufactured SU-122 is one of the last examples of the tank built before production switched to SU-85 tank destroyers. The vehicle has many parts borrowed from a T-34, but the vast majority of the forward and upper hull has been modified. The M-30 howitzer in its distinctive limited traverse mount is clearly seen. The fuel tank brackets on the SU-122 and later SUs were very different to T-34 brackets, supported the drum from below, rather than being parallel with the hull side. This SU-122 was lost during fighting in December 1943 and was lost alongside SU-85s and a T-34 (page 302).

The fighting compartment roof had the standard PT-4-7 scope, along with an air extractor fan, and a single large escape hatch at the rear of this superstructure. A small armoured cupola was provided for the gunner, but it did not have an escape hatch.

The SU-122 had some major flaws, one of which was that the 122-mm gun did not have an effective anti-tank round. Additionally, the crew compartment was not effective, and the gun created uncontrollable rollback when fired. The driver had very poor visibility, and escape hatches were lacking.

Due to these factors, and the changing requirement from an assault gun to a tank destroyer, the SU-122 was cancelled in favour of its replacement, the SU-85. In total, no more than 1,150 SU-122s were manufactured.

A handful of SU-122s were converted into SU-122Ts. This was the conversion to a recovery vehicle by removing the gun and installing towing equipment onto the glacis plate. This is how the only surviving examples are found today. A SU-122T was used extensively in Hungary, and today, it is at an army barracks at Budaörs, outside of Budapest. This relatively rare conversion for SU-122s was more frequently done to SU-85s.

A SU-122 with a gun is at Patriot Park Museum outside Moscow, which was a restored SU-122T, seen in Moscow ploughing snow before being donated to Kubinka.

49

SU-85

In the spring and summer of 1943, the Red Army was in desperate need of a tank that could engage German tanks at combat ranges over 500 m. In fact, as early as April 1943, a committee had been established at UTZM to begin design work for new Soviet assault guns and tank destroyers. It should not be forgotten that this was not a new concept for the USSR, and designs dating back to the late 1920s and early 1930s can be found, using various indigenous tank chassis.

In May 1943, Design Bureau Number 9 in Sverdlovsk presented to the ABTU the D-5T and the D-5S. The 'T' was intended for tanks, whereas the 'S' was intended for tank destroyers. The latter was an impressive gun, able to penetrate 92 mm of armour at 500 m, which was the same as the S-53 tank gun developed for the T-34. However, the S-53 was designed for a turret mount, and therefore, the gun could not simply be placed into a traversable mount that could move left and right, as well as the up and down. Therefore, work began immediately on developing a T-34 tank destroyer using the D-5S gun, along with other candidates from rival bureaus.

Before the D-5S was trialled, an older 85-mm gun designated 'C-31' was tested on an SU-122 chassis. However, it was found that it was impossible to simply jam a different gun onto the chassis, so a major redesign had to be undertaken. Ammunition storage, along with gun layout, also had to be designed from scratch.

The technical drawings for three new assault guns with 85-mm guns and a new assault gun with a 122-mm gun were submitted on 20 May 1943, and after deliberating over several designs, including the C-18-1 (essentially a ZiS-5 76.2-mm gun modified into an 85-mm gun), it was decided on 7 June to test all three designs at once, so the three 'SU-85s' with different guns, along with a modified SU-122 and a handful of other vehicles were tested simultaneously.

Testing began on 20 June, barely a month after the order was given for the designs, and ended on 25 June 1943. Of the three SU-85s tested, two were abject failures. The 'SU-85-I' featuring the C-31 had trouble with the breech of the gun, thus leading to failures after only sixty-two rounds were fired. The 'SU-85-IV' with the C-18-1 only fired thirty-nine shots before testing had to halt as the gun was so unfit for service that it was considered pointless continuing tests. The 'SU-122-III' with the D-6 122-mm howitzer was also found unsuitable and was dropped. Only the 'SU-85-II' with the D-5S gun performed well—in fact, superbly, firing 129 shots in testing—and was accepted for full production.

UTZM geared itself for mass production of the SU-85 with the D-5S and stopped production of the T-34 and SU-122 in July to set up production lines. The SU-85 was officially accepted for service on 1 August 1943, notably after the first four chassis had been manufactured.

The vehicle should be referred to as a 'tank destroyer' rather than an 'assault gun' as the latter are a platform for heavy artillery pieces to be more mobile, like the SU-122, whereas tank destroyers are anti-tank guns typically placed into a mount of limited traverse on a tank chassis without a turret (although official definitions differ from state to state).

The new SU-85 shared many features with the SU-122; in fact, it used the same chassis and a similar superstructure. Externally, only the gun, glacis plate, and turret roof differed majorly from the SU-122.

The D-5S gun was mounted into a slightly recessed gun mount on the glacis plate to the right of the vehicle. This had a protective rain cover and a cast mount for the gun. To the right was a standard T-34 driver's hatch. This greatly improved one of the major drawbacks of the SU-122 as the driver now had a much better field of view. The turret roof of the SU-85 was moderately re-arranged as to make escape hatches and vision devices easier to access with the placement of the 85-mm gun.

The SU-85 was first fielded in August 1943, and a steady stream of tanks arrived at the front from that point. At last, the Soviets had a gun that could cope with the thicker armour of German tanks. Crews were happy with the vehicle and lauded over the firepower of the gun. However, the vehicle was not perfect.

A SU-85 tank destroyer lost in September 1943, therefore one of the earliest examples lost. Take note of the D-5S gun, which was very similar to the D-5T.

An original wartime Soviet photograph of the crew of a SU-85. Notice the distinctive bolt face for the D-5S 85-mm gun, which was shared with the D-5T 85-mm gun on the early T-34-85s.

In late 1943, a list of new design requirements was made. These ranged from basic integrity changes of the vehicle, to battlefield survivability changes. Soviet intelligence had discovered that the Germans were designing new tanks with even bigger guns and even thicker armour. Therefore, the SU-85 had to adapt to the new threats.

Some of the important changes requires were as follows:

Increase the thickness of the frontal armour of the hull to protect against 75-mm guns.
Increase the firepower of the gun to fight new German tanks at long distances from 1,000 to 2,000 m.
Increase the amount of ammunition stowed inside the vehicle.
Install a defensive machine gun to protect against infantry.
Install on the glacis hardpoints for attaching spare tracks.
Install a command cupola with a MK-1U episcope and remove the PT-4-7 scope.
Improve the ventilation of the fighting compartment by installing two fans.

Some changes were easy to do, but some were far more challenging. In fact, some changes were so crucial that it was felt that a whole new vehicle would be required to fulfil specifications such as increased firepower, thus leading to the development of the SU-100.

However, from September 1944, some of these changes were made and a new vehicle was developed. The new SU-100 was intended to begin production, but not enough 100-mm guns were delivered. Therefore, some D-5S guns were put into the chassis of the SU-100. These hybrids were known as SU-85M. The chassis of the SU-85M was that of an SU-100, itself

Two SU-85 tanks advance in the closing months of World War Two. Notice the D-5S gun, which was almost identical to the D-5T used in early Krasnoye Sormovo 112 T-34-85s.

updated to the T-34-85 standard by improving the front suspension springs, and adding such features as smoke generators, and an angled nose fillet. Most important of all, the glacis plate was thickened from 45 to 75 mm.

The old roof bulge for the commander to the right of the gun was replaced with a command cupola, identical to the T-34-85's command cupola. This required a cone to be mounted onto the right hull side of the vehicle to allow for space for the commander and the cupola. The MK-4 episcopes were installed rather than MK-1U episcopes, and a second extractor fan was placed onto the turret roof.

These SU-85Ms were only manufactured as stop-gap vehicles from September 1944 until November 1944, after which sufficient 100-mm guns became available to meet production of the SU-100 hull. At the end of production, 2,644 SU-85s and 315 SU-85Ms had been manufactured.

Even though the SU-100 had been accepted for production and fielded from 1945, the SU-85 remained in front-line service until 1956. It saw active and wide-ranging service during the Second World War and was distributed to many Soviet satellite states such as Poland and East Germany.

SU-85T

After the end of the Second World War, the SU-85 was somewhat outdated. It was still a potent tank but its thin armour and 85-mm gun were no match for newer tanks on both sides of the Iron Curtain.

A SU-85T recovery vehicle in service with the East German NVA. This photograph was taken before much of the equipment was placed onto the glacis plate, which occurred later in the conversion run.

A SU-85T. Notice the towing equipment on the glacis plate of the tank. A Notek headlight can be seen on the glacis, next to the driver's hatch.

The SU-85 was used as a tank destroyer into the 1950s, but by this time, it had become sorely outdated. Therefore, many tanks were converted into recovery vehicles. The conversion was quite simple, and similar things were done to T-34s. The D-5S gun, so valued in 1943, was removed from the vehicle, along with the mantlet and all ammunition boxes and stowage racks. On the glacis plate, a simple plate was welded over the hole in the mantlet and towing equipment was then placed onto the glacis plate.

These converted SU-85 tanks were known as SU-85Ts. They were used extensively by many Soviet satellites, especially with the East German army, the NVA (*Nationale Volksarmee*). After the reunification of Germany, the *Bundeswehr* used the vehicle. SU-85Ts were only retired from German service in the 1990s.

Many other countries still use either SU-85Ts, T-34Ts (the T-34 conversion into a recovery vehicle), purpose-built T-34 recovery vehicles from Czechoslovakia or Poland (VT-34), and the PRC even used some indigenously converted vehicles.

50

SU-100

While the SU-85 was a total success, with the introduction of the Ferdinand tank destroyer and various heavy tanks at Kursk by the Germans, the Red Army felt the need to up-gun the SU-85.

The Red Army had tested higher calibre anti-tank guns in the past, such as the ZiS-6 107-mm gun, which was tested on a KV-2 in early 1941. However, only a handful of these 107-mm guns were manufactured before Leningrad was under siege and no longer able to produce the gun. This was not such a problem for the early war as the 76-mm F-34 was suitable for anti-tank duties, but by 1943, a higher calibre gun was required, but the only gun available for testing of a similar calibre was the 100-mm B-34 naval gun.

The UTZM design bureau was once again required to test guns, but this time on the SU-85 chassis. The prototype of this new tank destroyer was known as 'Object 138', and the programme began as early as September 1943, just one month after the inception of the SU-85 tank.

On 27 December 1943, the drawings were submitted and approved, then twenty-four hours later, Resolution 481 was passed, formally approving the project. The modified B-34 gun was named the C-34, and it was to be manufactured at Factory Number 94.

However, a second gun had been in the wings all this time—the D-10 100-mm gun. The D-10 was developed from the BS-3 100-mm field gun, which itself was an earlier successful attempt at creating a 'land only' version of the B-34 naval gun. It was almost the same dimensions as the D-5S 85-mm gun of the SU-85. Therefore, the gun was prototyped as the D-10S, and it proved to be a total success. Between February and April 1944, tests were conducted, and the vehicle was accepted into the Red Army as the SU-100.

Despite this success, there was still the question of whether the C-34 could be used on the SU-100. Therefore, a second SU-100 prototype was fitted with this gun, called the 'SU-100-2'. Testing was conducted in June 1944, somewhat delaying the delivery of the SU-100 (fitted with the 100-mm D-10S) to the Red Army. After extensive testing, the C-34 was found to be inferior to the D-10S after all.

However, as is so typical with Soviet bureaucracy, the SU-100 production did not start without any problems. As mentioned earlier, while SU-100 hulls were manufactured in August

A Soviet-manufactured SU-100 in the post-war era (perhaps the 1950s). The Soviet-made machines differed from the Czechoslovakian SD-100s by their command cupolas and lack of rear hull buzzer.

The same SU-100 as seen above. The cupola can be clearly seen to be the Soviet type with two hatch doors, as opposed to the SD-100, which had a single turret hatch.

1944, no D-10S guns arrived. The situation was so bad that eventually, 85-mm D-5S guns were fitted onto the SU-100 chassis, thus creating the SU-85M.

The SU-100 had a chassis almost outwardly identical to the SU-85, but with some moderate changes to the design. The glacis plate was increased in thickness from 45 to 75 mm; a cupola was placed on the front right of the turret roof. The roof did not have enough room to fit the cupola, so a distinctive small cone of armour to accommodate the commander was placed on the front right of the hull which bulged outwards.

Some minor changes were also made. Two extractor fans were placed onto the hull roof, along with an MK-4 episcope. Internally, racks for 100-mm ammunition were provided, along with all of the necessary optics.

SU-100s made their combat debut in January 1945. From the moment they entered the battlefield, they made a huge impact. Soviet crews were most happy with the SU-100 because of its ability to engage and destroy Tigers at a range of over 1,500 m. This was a huge morale boost to the Red Army as a whole.

After the war, in 1947, SU-100s were manufactured at Omsk 174. Some 198 were manufactured in 1947, and another eight were manufactured in 1948. Total Soviet production was 2,335 units, mostly being delivered from UTZM.

The glacis plate of the same SU-100 as page 425. Unlike the SU-85, the SU-100 (and SU-85M) used the chassis of a T-34-85.

After the war, the SU-100 was used extensively by the Red Army and was still the front-line support tank way into the 1960s. The vehicle was also sold to many countries after the war such as Cuba, Algeria, North Korea, Yemen, North Vietnam, Iraq, the People's Republic of China, and others. Czechoslovakia also manufactured 1,300 SD-100s under licence, of which large sales were made to many Middle Eastern countries such as Egypt and Syria, but also other countries such as Angola.

The licence-built SD-100 (the Czechoslovakian designation) was outwardly very similar to the Soviet-manufactured vehicle, but the vehicle had three main differences. First, a rear hull buzzer was placed under the rear left fuel drum. Secondly, command cupolas on Czechoslovakian SD-100 were the later single-door hatch, unlike all Soviet SU-100s, which had the two-part door. Lastly, some SD-100s were issued with the distinctive UTZ 183-style 'wavy' exhaust shrouds.

SU-100 and SD-100s can be found still in service with many states today. Most notably, the Russian Federation still uses SU-100s for parades, and therefore still lists them in army stocks. The Yemeni army also still uses SU-100s, as does the Vietnamese Army. In 2017, film footage emerged of the Vietnamese army on manoeuvres, still using the SU-100.

This Czechoslovakian SD-100 is in service with the Egyptian Army in the late 1950s. Notice the rear hull buzzer on the tank's left side—a clear indicator that the tank is Czechoslovakian. Notice too, the Czechoslovakian rear hinges. The exhausts are not typical of SD-100s, being long and curved away from the lower hull. This was likely to try to stop sand from being kicked up into them.

51

ARMOURED TRAINS AND BOATS
WITH T-34 TURRETS

While the focus of this publication is the linear T-34, other vehicles that used the T-34 turret should be briefly touched upon.

The Soviet Union had been producing armoured trains since its inception. It was not until the Soviet industrial age of the 1930s under Stalin, and when indigenous tank designs were being manufactured, that the question of mounting tank turrets onto trains became a reality.

Soviet armoured trains during the pre-war period generally were purpose-built, and the most common type was the PL-37 wagon. This wagon was an armoured train car, with a single central viewing port and a purpose-designed 76.2-mm gun turret on either side of this. Four water-cooled Maxim machine guns were also mounted on the train car.

One train in 1942 was rebuilt with some tank turrets on the top. Armoured train 'For the Homeland' was issued a KV-2 turret in place of one of the 76.2-mm gun turrets, and most interestingly of all, a T-34 turret with a 45-mm gun was placed next to this. This was clearly a rebuild, but a second unidentified train also had the same conversion.

Other armoured trains equipped the T-34 turret, but these turrets were also placed on the PL-37 wagon and replaced the purpose-built turrets on the train. These turrets retained their 76.2-mm F-34 guns.

Lastly, many river boats and fast attack craft were issued T-34 turrets. Notably, 1124, 1125, and S-40 class boats were issued T-34 turrets dating from late 1941 and 1942. The 1125 boats also had T-34-85 turrets on them and were used until the 1950s.

Most interestingly of all is a North Korean destroyer that featured a T-34-85 turret in place of the regular 4-inch guns, which was seen during the Korean War.

Soviet armoured train *For the Homeland*. Notice that the T-34 turret has a 45-mm gun instead of a 76.2-mm gun. Notice the camouflage on the turrets, a base of 4BO, with brown painted over it.

A captured Soviet armoured train in 1941. The turret was taken from a KhPZ 183 tank and is equipped with two periscopes. Take note of the turret pressing.

52

BEUTEPANZER T-34s:
A BRIEF OVERVIEW

Beutepanzer (English: 'trophy tank') is a generic name given to captured foreign tanks pressed into *Wehrmacht* service. With such a vast number of T-34s pressed into German service throughout 1941–1945, it would be difficult to give more than a brief overview in this book.[1] Nevertheless, the identification of these tanks can be made not only by their painted-on Swastikas, *Balkenkreuz*, and flags, but also their German-specific upgrades.

The German invasion of the Soviet Union left in its immediate wake a huge number of abandoned and knocked-out tanks. Most of the tanks lost in June and July 1941 were lost not due to combat, but mechanical failures or were simply abandoned due to lack of fuel or ammunition. In fact, estimates suggest that the Germans captured roughly 900–1,100 T-26s, 300–500 BTs, at least forty T-28s, and at least forty-five T-34 and KV-1 tanks in working order during Operation Barbarossa. This number increased as the German advance continued.

Initially, abandoned Soviet tanks were merely disarmed and either pushed into a ditch if they blocked a road or taken to a captured vehicle pool. There were a variety of reasons as to why the Germans did not immediately assimilate these vehicles into their ranks as with other vehicles (such as countless French vehicles captured in 1940). Firstly, the Germans expected a quick end to the war against the USSR, meaning that there was no pressing need for more tanks to be fielded. Secondly, it was logistically unsound to operate apparently mechanically poor vehicles, especially without more spare parts and munitions for them.

After the advance into the Russian SFSR, the Germans realised not only was the war not going to end as soon as they had hoped, but also that excessive losses of their own tanks could not be compensated for by their own production. As a result, many Soviet tanks were sent to Riga at the end of 1941 to be fitted with German equipment and painted in German colours for the front. This did not happen on a grand scale, however, and many tanks that could have been reused appear to have simply being left in the field to rot. Moreover, many *Beutepanzers* appear to have been merely repaired in the field for German use. Quite evidently, the German logistics system was not only stretched to capacity supplying the front but was also overwhelmed with the sheer number of Soviet tanks that they had to clear up out of roads.

Five *Beutepanzers* in the winter of 1942–1943. The tanks display a mixture of upgrade types, with some machines receiving limited German updates, whereas others have been completely overhauled. The T-34 in the middle has a Panzer III cupola, whereas the green T-34 has no updates whatsoever. The KV-2 in the background has been fitted with a cupola, also.

Two STZ-manufactured *Beutepanzers*. These two vehicles are unique as they were operated by Croatian forces. These two tanks were given to the Croats in July 1942, but as is apparent, they were knocked out.

All captured tanks pressed into German service were issued a new designation, and the T-34's was the T-34-747(r). Soviet *Beutepanzers* were quite uncommon on the battlefield, and a common misconception is that thousands of *Beutepanzers* were used by the Germans. While it is true that many French and Czechoslovakian tanks (typically light tanks for anti-partisan and policing duties) were pressed into German service, a relatively small number of Soviet tanks were used, which first started in late autumn of 1941.

It should also be noted that most Soviet *Beutepanzers* were either vehicles used for tractor purposes, such as the towing of guns, munitions, and other such things, or they were used merely as anti-partisan or policing vehicles. These roles were typically given to armoured cars such as the BA-6 and BA-10, but also some light tanks such as the T-26 and T-70.

The T-34 saw service with the Germans most commonly in its original role as a medium tank (and also as a tank destroyer), but anti-partisan or policing and other specialised roles are not unknown. They were issued to all-tank units and mixed in with German tanks. This had a few exceptions, with the most famous all-*Beutepanzer* regiment being *2.Kompanie/Panzer-Abteilung z.b.V.66*, created for the invasion of Malta. On 31 May 1942, it is reported that the unit operated nine T-34s, one KV-1, and a KV-2. This regiment had some strange-looking *Beutepanzer* T-34s as some photos from 1944 show that they had at least one L-11-gunned T-34 with the drive wheels and tracks removed and replaced with those of a Panzer I Ausf. F. Other examples of their T-34s show that they had new German cupolas, whitewash paint schemes, and new stowage.

A T-34 (L-11 Gun), formerly of *2.Kompanie/Panzer-Abteilung* z.b.V.66, now used for training of Czechoslovak volunteers. Notice the unique updates done to the vehicle, such as the Panzer I Ausf. F drive wheels and tracks. Initially, this unit was established for the invasion of Malta, but they were not used in this role and instead returned to the Eastern Front. (*Jirka Zahradník Collection*)

T-34-747(R) TECHNICAL FEATURES

The most basic of *Beutepanzer* T-34s would have had simple German markings added to them, perhaps with a new paint scheme (typically a whitewash of some sort), but more complex *Beutepanzers* are well-known due to the spectacular nature of their upgrade packages. Three additional general categories are therefore observed, but it cannot be overstated that these are arbitrary categories that not every *Beutepanzer* T-34 will fit perfectly into.

The most basic of upgraded *Beutepanzer* T-34s included a Notek headlight, a new paint scheme—typically whitewash, *Panzergrau* (Panzer grey), or *sandgrau* (sand grey)—along with some other minor adjustments, such as a German radio. Some examples also have their DTs replaced with German machine guns, new stowage with new wooden boxes, and mounts for the Stalhelm on the hull sides and turret.

More extensive overhauls can be identified by the addition of German cupolas in the turret. The new cupola was commonly a Panzer III cupola and was placed over the single hatch of the 1941 manufactured tanks. In later war tanks, this cupola would be placed over the left hatch, with the right hatch being cut down in size to accommodate the new cupola. The single hatch that early tanks were issued with was welded closed, but it was often removed entirely and replaced with two small access hatches placed on either side of the cupola. These tanks were usually issued with all new German stowage on the hulls that included custom wooden boxes on the hull side for fuel can placement, along with German tow ropes and toolset, and sometimes even a spare road wheel. Some tanks also had new stowage on the rear of the turret, such as a Panzer III stowage basket or a wooden box. A German jack was also commonly issued.

The most spectacular (and rarest) sort of overhauls was introduced after the Battle of Kursk. This involved the already described changes, but also included *schürzen* (side skirts of additional armour) as seen on at least one tank from *2nd SS Panzer Division Das Reich*. It should be noted that before the skirts were implemented, some tanks were issued just the Panzer III stowage bins on the rear of the turrets.

No *Beutepanzer* T-34s are known to have had their main guns replaced with a new German gun. However, Wolfgang Kloth, a former German tank commander who saw service in the 3rd Panzer Regiment (of the 2nd Panzer Division) mentioned one noteworthy main gun modification from around 1944 or 1945 during an interview at the 2008 AMPS (Armor Modelling and Preservation Society) international show:

> There was an interesting unit in Kurland; Panzerbrigade Kurland, and they only had captured tanks. They had a Sherman and a General Lee and two T-34s. They took Russian 87 mm [meaning 85 mm], and took it to the ship wharf, and reamed it to 88 mm. They shot 88 ammunition out of it. They were very inventive! Because up in Kurland, your back was against the water, you know.

Further information on this tank is lacking, and while it is known Soviet 85-mm AA guns were reamed to fire 88-mm rounds by the Finns, there are still some questions as to whether German 88-mm casings would fit in the chamber of a tank gun at all, not even considering the potential need for a major overhaul to the gun likely requiring a specialised factory, not a simple field workshop.

This *Beutepanzer* was likely captured in July 1942 and was given the Panzer III cupola. Notice the optimistically small cross, which often caused friendly fire incidents. It is likely this tank was used by *Panzer-Abeitlung* z.b.V. 66, based on the type of new stowage that other T-34s from that unit have been seen with. (*Will Kerrs Collection*)

This *Beutepanzer* has been painted *sandgrau*. The leather muzzle cover can be seen on this tank. This tank is likely a T-34 (ChKZ Standard Production). This tank is photographed in 1943, likely before the Battle of Kursk.

Three *Beutepanzer* T-34s and a STZ-3 tractor. These crews are likely training for the upcoming battles at Kursk. The tanks were all manufactured in late 1942, with the tank on the left having all pressed road wheels, indicating it is either an Omsk 174, UTZM, or ChKZ 100 tank. The tank in the foreground has its engine deck open, and just behind it appears to be evidence of non-standard stowage on the turret—possibly hooks with helmets.

PAINT SCHEMES

The T-34s that were pressed into German service were often extravagantly painted. As previously mentioned, regular German tanks were painted *Panzergrau* up until late 1942 to early 1943, after which they were painted a base of *sandgrau*, with crews than painting their own camouflage. This, too, was the case for the *Beutepanzers,* though many retained their original 4BO green.

Almost all *Beutepanzer* T-34s had some *Balkenkreuzs*, which were not at all standard across all tanks, although some types are much more common than others. Usually, these were applied as large as possible to reduce the risk of friendly fire incidents, although many examples exist of small (and perhaps ineffective) *Balkenkreuzs*. Additionally, many were usually applied to the same vehicle in different places, with common places being both sides of the turret, the turret roof, the turret rear, the front of the hull, the sides of the hull, and the engine access plate on the rear of the hull. Many tanks were also adorned with Swastika cloth flags either on the turret, turret hatch, or front of the hull to aid German pilots especially. The use of painted Swastikas, also of varying types, is not unknown to this end, either, but is far less common.

In addition to this, some tanks had rarer markings such as nicknames, slogans, 'kill rings' on the gun barrel, and divisional markings (not to be confused with mere graffiti on knocked out tanks). Some tanks were also given three- (or sometimes four-) digit turret numbers.

SPECIALISED 'BEUTEPANZER' T-34s

The *Wehrmacht* used several T-34 chassis to convert into specialised vehicles, but only a handful of examples of these conversions exist in photographs.

The *Munitionschlepper* had a wooden superstructure built up around the turret ring and was used to ship ammunition to the front lines. This was originally an STZ tank, with its turret removed and German towing equipment attached to the rear of the tank.

The Pioneer T-34 was similar to the *Munitionspanzer*, but this tank towed a trench digging device that was first used by an Sd.Kfz. 8. This vehicle could be the same as the previous two tanks, but it was likely that multiple tanks were used in such a capacity.

Perhaps the most heavily debated *Beutepanzer* is the *Flakpanzer* T-34. This was a T-34/76 that was fitted with a specially designed turret mounting a Flak 38 4 × 20 mm. The turret was open-topped with six sides to it. It sat above the turret ring on a platform of wood level with the engine deck. It was reportedly used by the 653rd Heavy *Panzerjäger* Battalion in July 1944. If this tank is real, it was certainly the only example made. The chassis was likely manufactured at UTZM or ChKZ as the glacis is lacking interlocking plates and all the road wheels are the pressed type. The tow hooks are not the Omsk 174 type hooks. The track is the 500-mm waffle type, which was used by all plants, but UTZM used the split-type 500-mm track as well as the 550-mm waffle-pattern track.

Two fakes that must be mentioned by virtue of their popularity are the T-34-85 photoshopped to be equipped with a Flak 38 88-mm gun, and the T-34-85 equipped with an 8.8-cm KwK

A very rare *Bergepanzer* Pz.kfw 474 (r). This is either a Soviet T-34T that was captured or a captured T-34 that was converted and then pressed into *Wehrmacht* service as a recovery vehicle. The vehicle itself is travelling through a German town in 1944 or 1945, though this could be the Western Front, meaning that this tank was facing the Western Allies.

36 L/56 gun from a Tiger. The former was photoshopped onto a *Beutepanzer* T-34-85 and originated from a Japanese modelling magazine that even stated that the tank was a 'what-if' (and the original unmodified photograph has since been found). In the case of the latter, this is impossible as the turret face and mantlet size do not match up and appears to be based on Wolfgang Kloth's story of the tank rebored to fire 8.8-cm ammunition.

BEUTEPANZER T-34 CONCLUSIONS

In all, *Beutepanzer* T-34s are often over-exaggerated in use and numbers. Relatively few T-34s were pressed into *Wehrmacht* service, and only a handful of captured T-34s were used by the Hungarians, Croats, Italians, and ROA (Russian Liberation Army).

What little is known about *Beutepanzer* T-34s is that they saw service from autumn 1941 until the last days of the war, with perhaps all types of T-34s being used, except those with the 57-mm gun. Their usefulness was hindered by the lack of spare parts, which generally were salvaged from other T-34s knocked out in battle.

Beutepanzers have fallen into the realm of mythology, with many claims of great usage, vast numbers, and great conversions. While it is true that some *Beutepanzers* were converted into other types of vehicles, only a handful were done.

53

PANZERATTRAPPE AND DUMMY TANKS

Panzerattrappe, or dummy tanks, date back in German service to at least 1927, when the limitations of the Treaty of Versailles meant that Germany was prohibited from manufacturing or operation of tanks. Therefore, the *Wehrmacht* had to use dummy tanks when it was trialling tank tactics. These were nothing more than cars with wooden frames on them to represent tanks.

Once Germany could manufacture tanks, turning a blind eye to the Treaty of Versailles, the *Panzerattrappe* became very useful training vehicles. The two primary roles of German *Panzerattrappes* were for driver training, and anti-tank training. After the invasion of the USSR, German troops began to be trained in anti-tank duties on these *Panzerattrappe* that looked like T-34s as well as other Soviet tanks. These tanks ranged in quality from a passable T-34 until inspected closely to some very dubious and inaccurate depictions. Generally, these were manufactured from wood and placed onto the top of *Kubelwagens* or other such German light cars. Carts and other simple wheeled structures were also used.

Most appear to have been manufactured at the local level, with no two *Panzerattrappe* being truly the same. It is unknown whether these vehicles were used in combat as actual dummy tanks, but some accounts from Poland claim that some were used to fool Polish units into thinking that the Germans had more tanks than they had. As for their use in the USSR, the information is apparently non-existent.

The *Panzerattrappe* seem to have been distributed around the *Reich*, with photos of T-34 *Panzerattrappes* being found in Antwerp, Berlin, and Warsaw.

Other wartime oddities include dummy tanks produced by the Soviets to confuse German reconnaissance planes into thinking there were more Soviet tanks than actually there. Most states conducted this type of warfare.

The myth of the T-34 and the notoriety of the tanks meant that it was ingrained onto the German soldiers' psyche, and every soldier was taught how to tackle them. Many infantry anti-tank schools were either equipped with *Panzerattrappe*, or sometimes simple murals were painted of the tank with directions on how to take out a tank. Weak points such as vision ports were highlighted.

This Pre-War T-34 (F-34 Gun) T-34 has been repurposed as an infantry training vehicle by the Germans. The tank has a crude German-built dummy turret replacing the original, and one can see that the hull side has magnetic mine blast marks. Many captured T-34s shared this fate.

The same training tank as seen above. Notice the mine that is stuck in place on the hull.

This *Panzerattrappe* could pass at a distance as a real T-34, but closer inspection reveals the wooden construction. Notice the wheel at the front, which is from the vehicle that hides under the wooden frame. The track is held together by wire and is nothing more than boards cut roughly to shape.

Another *Panzerattrappe*. This one is relatively more to scale than other types. Notice the details painted onto the wood, such as road wheels, bolts on the glacis plate, the MG blister, and radiator intakes.

A Soviet-made dummy T-34 during the Third Battle of Kharkov. This simple wooden and canvas structure was painted to look like a T-34 tank. The Germans also made dummy tanks, but typically made them look more realistic.

A T-34 painted on a wall. This is likely at a German training centre. Notice that weak points are highlighted. The tank is a representation of an L-11 Gun T-34, indicating that this was perhaps made early in the war.

54

T-34-85 REPLACEMENTS

With the production history of the T-34 now complete, it is only fitting to discuss the T-34's replacements. This chapter will begin with the failed T-34-85M project, followed by the T-44 (a top secret but only moderately successful project that was insufficient for Soviet needs), and the T-34's ultimate long-term replacement—the T-54, arguably the most successful tank of the post-war era.

T-34-85M

As discussed previously with the T-43, the armour thickness of the T-34 was always a serious concern for Soviet crews and engineers alike. While the emphasis switched from thicker armour to bigger guns in 1943, the following year, the Red Army had their bigger gun, so work was ordered in looking into increasing the T-34's armour again.

The order supposedly came from Stalin himself in February 1944, and UTZ 183 was ordered to begin work on a project known as 'T-34-85M', not to be confused with the T-34M. However, UTZ 183 were already preoccupied with the manufacture of the T-34-85, especially setting up production lines. Moreover, the design process of the T-44 began in March, so most efforts were focused on that project.

Nevertheless, design work on the T-34-85M began, and by May 1944, two prototypes rolled out of UTZ 183. The vehicles were issued with a 75-mm-thick glacis plate, with updated transmissions. However, to compensate for this extra weight, the floor plate was reduced in thickness from 20 to 15 mm. Additionally, the gear plate had its thickness reduced from 45 to 15 mm. A new small diameter drive wheel was issued also; this would later be used on the T-44.

The second T-34-85M prototype differed by having a totally redesigned rear plate. This rear plate now housed two 190-l fuel tanks that sat above the transmission. This gave the tank a distinctive rear, which resembled that of a BT-7 tank, with a raised mesh radiator above the radiator and having the exhaust pipes exit the vehicle through this mesh cover.

A front view of the first T-34-85M prototype. From this angle, it is hard to see what is different to a regular T-34-85. That said, close inspection will reveal that the MG blister is wider and thicker, and that the driver's hatch has extra strips of armour around it. The glacis plate is thicker at 75 mm, and a wider fillet is necessary. The handrail on the right side is larger, too. (*Maxim Kolomiets*)

A side view of the first T-34-85M prototype. From this side, very little is different from a standard T-34-85. Notice, however, that the front of the turret is slightly different, being thicker at the front. (*Maxim Kolomiets*)

The second T-34-85M prototype. This vehicle has some of the same upgrades as the first prototype, but now even more changes can be seen. Most obviously, the entire rear of the tank has been redesigned. Notice the small drive wheel, later used on the T-44. (*Maxim Kolomiets*)

A top view of the second T-34-85M prototype. From this angle, the redesigns are clearer. The rear of the tank has been greatly extended as to place more fuel tanks internally. Therefore, like the BT-7, the exhausts are now situated though the mesh radiator cover. (*Maxim Kolomiets*)

The rear of the second T-34-85M prototype. The project was dropped because the gear plate's thickness was decreased from 45 mm to just 15 mm, which greatly compromised the structural integrity and protection of the tank. The placement of the fuel tanks over the transmission was also undesirable. (*Maxim Kolomiets*)

Testing was conducted throughout May and June 1944, but the vehicle was rejected. The T-34-85Ms' problem was not that they weighed too much (as the tanks had the same basic weight as the standard T-34) but that the plate thickness reductions had drastically compromised the defensive integrity of the tanks in those areas. As such, Red Army evaluations found that the tanks were extremely vulnerable to mines, and any hit to the gear plate was guaranteed to penetrate. Additionally, although the weight stayed relatively the same, the tanks were less agile and had a high centre of gravity high. The running gear was inferior to the T-34's, and the drive wheel was less effective than the T-34's standard variant.

As it was, the T-44 was already going through trials, and while this would not enter production until very late 1944, the writing was on the wall—the basic T-34 chassis was unsuited to the modern and future battlefields and had to be totally overhauled, as decided in 1941.

T-44

The updating process for the T-34 has already been discussed, but along with up-gunning the T-34, prototyping began for a tank to replace the T-34 in the medium tank category altogether. This new design would incorporate many of the lessons learned from the previous two years of combat and was to specifically focus on internal space, placement of the fuel tanks, and the suspension. This new design was designated 'Object 146'.

The chassis designed for this tank was a radically modern design. The hull was a very low profile, with a sharply angled nose and no hatch on the glacis plate rather being on the hull roof to not make a weak point in the hull. There was no engineer's position and therefore no hull machine gun position. The suspension consisted of five pairs of road wheels borrowed from the T-34 tank coupled with torsion bar suspension. This allowed for greater internal space inside the tank.

The engine was the V-2-IC engine, and unlike earlier tanks, the engine and cooling system was placed sideways. It was deemed that the turret of this tank was large enough to mount either a 100-mm or 122-mm gun. The turret resembled that of a T-34, but was larger, with a different turret seam to those of T-34s.

While this tank appeared like the T-34, many things were different. Glacis armour was now 75 mm thick, with hull sides being 60 mm thick. As previously mentioned, the glacis was featureless, therefore presenting no weak points for the enemy to exploit. The prototype tank did have a small vision port that could open on the top left of the glacis, however. In standard production tanks, this would be replaced with a simple vision slit.

This new vehicle was designated 'T-44' upon its acceptance for production. While proto-typing of the tank was happening, the armament selected for the tank was the D-5T 85-mm gun. An 85-mm gun was selected due to the originally desired 100-mm gun not being close to readiness, and a 122-mm gun not being found suitable for the tank. A single prototype was made with a 122-mm gun, but this project was unsuccessful. As it happens, the S-53 gun as used on the T-34-85 was eventually used on the tank.

A T-44 photographed after the war. Take note of the T-34-esque turret on a very modern hull. The T-44 was essentially a secret project, even after the war, so to find private Soviet photographs of the tank is quite unusual. The turret markings are typical of post-war Soviet tanks.

Another T-44 in the early 1950s. Notice the slit on the glacis plate for the driver—a feature that was removed during the designing of the T-54.

All round, the T-44 was an improvement over the T-34, and the vehicle was accepted for production, with the first five tanks manufactured in November 1944.

The plant selected to manufacture this tank was the newly liberated Kharkov Locomotive Plant, formerly Factory Number 183, now renamed Factory Number 75. An order for 850 tanks was given, but since the factory had to be totally rebuilt, as well as having new production lines added, this process was very slow. Another reason for the slow production of this tank was the priority given to the T-34-85 and IS-2 tanks, which had reached their peak in production. Additionally, the T-44 was a secret tank; many officers and Red Army officials did not know of the tank's existence until after the war.

Most importantly of all was that the replacement for the T-44 was already being designed, so the order was cut short after a mere 200 tanks were manufactured. These tanks did not see combat in the Second World War, even though they were equipped to training units.

In 1966, to modernise the small number of T-44s in Red Army service, tanks were sent to UTZ 183 to be refitted with more modern equipment. This included a new V-54 engine, tracks and drive wheels from a T-54, as well as the waffle patterned wheels of the T-54-2. A mount for a 12.7-mm DShK was also placed onto the turret cupola. This modernisation was known as the T-44M. Other alterations were done later too, including the T-44S, which had a gun stabiliser, and the T-44MK, which was equipped with multiple radio sets and was a command tank.

This T-44 is equipped with a T-34 road wheel. Much of the equipment is identical to that of a T-34, including the gun cleaning toolbox, tracks, ice cleats, and other items. As only 200 examples were made, spare parts were not likely manufactured in large numbers, hence the replacement wheel.

A column of tanks used in training in the Soviet Union in 1962. A T-34 sits just out of fame to the left, but three T-44s sit in the centre of the frame. Unusually, the turret of the foremost vehicle is equipped with tactical markings beyond a three-digit number. A PT-76 amphibious tank can also be seen in this column.

T-54

In 1944, when the T-44 was being designed, a 100-mm gun was desired for the tank. This could not be achieved with the prototypes that became the T-44, so a new project was started instead. This new tank, the Object 137, would be designed from the outset to mount a 100-mm gun.

The prototype was issued a new water-cooled engine called the V-54, and the tank borrowed many features of the T-44. New wider track was designed for the tank, with a newly designed drive wheel with external spokes to take the track, much like German drive wheels.

A new turret, with a bustle, was designed and was equipped with the LB-1 100-mm gun. This tank eventually entered service on 1 January 1947 and took over the production lines at UTZ 183 (which had been manufacturing the T-34 up until this point). While the T-44 was an important stepping stone in the advancement of Soviet tank designs, the new T-54 tank was the tank the Soviets had long hoped for.

Some 1,940 examples of the T-54-1 were manufactured before the new T-54-2 entered service. This tank was equipped with a new turret that still had a bustle but was greatly reduced in size. This turret had a distinctive dome behind the gun and offset to the right that was a smoke extractor.

The T-54 and its successor, the T-55, became the most widely produced tank in the world, surpassing even the numbers of T-34s manufactured. Some 55,000 tanks were manufactured between 1947 and 1961, not to mention the numerous foreign copies such as the Type 59 from the PRC. However, the stories of these tanks are for another, more detailed publication.

At last, the Red Army was equipped with a medium tank that fulfilled the requirements of the T-34M from 1940, seven long years later.

A T-54-1. The early T-54s were issued with similar pattern wheels to the late T-34s, except thicker.

This T-54-3 is what ultimately replaced the T-34 as a frontline tank. With a more powerful 100-mm gun, a superior suspension system, and improved crew layout, it is often regarded as the most influential tank design made in the post-war era. A T-34 Model 1969 is behind it to the left, just in shot.

An NVA T-54-3. These vehicles would quickly replace all T-34s in front-line Soviet service, and once they became obsolete in the USSR, they were sold to other Communist states.

55

POST-WAR SOVIET UPDATES TO THE T-34

While T-34-85 production had ended in the Soviet Union in 1946, the tanks still played an important front-line role until 1960 and played a significant role in secondary and training duties post-1960. While this was happening, many small adjustments were made to the tanks to keep them as modern as possible, even though more modern tanks had been manufactured.

The immediate post-war updates were done in 1946 and consisted mainly of new hull hardpoints for tow ropes and other equipment. Most notably, a wood saw was added onto the tank, along with a German-style hull rack that featured a shovel and a coiled-up tow rope.

After the T-54 was introduced in January 1947, T-34s began to be fitted with the headlights of T-54s in place of the original light on the hull side. This type of light was later replaced with a glacis-mounted headlight cage identical to the T-54's headlights.

THE 1960 UPDATE

In 1960, a complete overhaul was conducted on the remaining T-34-85s left in Red Army service. This was also done to tanks in the NVA (*Nationale Volksarmee*) of East Germany and the Polish Armed Forces. This overhaul is commonly called the T-34 Model 1960, but Polish T-34s also updated along the same lines were called T-34-85-M1.

The V-2-34 engine was replaced by the improved V-34-M11 engine. New VTI-3 air-cleaners were installed with this engine, along with improvements to the cooling and lubrication system.

Internally, a heater was provided for the crew. This was placed on the left side of the hull, above the ammunition racks. This, however, did cause some minor issues with the crew, because if one turns the turret to the right, the gunner of the tank can get his legs caught between the seat and the heater. If one was not careful, serious damage can be done.

The stowage of the tank was totally rearranged. The stowage box that had been on the front left fender since 1940 was moved to the front right fender, and sometimes a second identical box was placed behind it. New stowage bins were placed on the fenders. These were small,

A line of East German NVA T-34s that have been updated to Model 1960 standard. The stowage has been completely reworked, as well as some addition to the tank. There are brackets for 200-l fuel drums on the rear of these tanks, as well as rear turret stowage bins.

One of the East German NVA T-34s but close up. Notice the relocated stowage box on the front left fender. This is a T-34-85 (174 Early Turret). Notice the shovel stowage, along with a Notek headlight on the glacis.

The same tank as on page 452. The turret marking is typical of East German T-34s, and there is a DDR emblem painted on the turret side but is mostly obscured by the soldier.

with lids that were angled, which made the boxes five-sided. These boxes were placed below the 50-l drum-type fuel tanks.

The NVA (*Nationale Volksarmee*) had some additional changes made to the tanks, that can be covered by the '1960 update'. The rear of the tanks was rearranged to allow for greater fuel tank placements. The two small twenty litre fuel tanks were moved down the rear plate and placed straddling the exhaust pipes. Above the transmission plate, two pairs of brackets were placed. These brackets held a single 100-l drum each.

The rear of the turret was additionally given a stowage bin. To fit this on correctly, the turret rear was given two vertical handrails that the stowage box sat between. Minor changes to optics were also done.

While different armies added or changed different pieces according to need, all these tanks fall under (perhaps wrongly) the Model 1960 classification. This change was mostly done to increase the T-34-85's combat range, but also gave some small updates for the crew with regards to optics and headlights. Without a doubt, though, the T-34-85 was still outdated on the battlefield even despite these updates.

A column of East German NVA T-34-85s. Notice the Notek headlight on the glacis plate. Some of the headlights are caged, whereas others are the Soviet type.

A T-34-85 (Polish Production) in East German NVA service. This tank has been updated to Model 1960 standard. Take note of the stowage layout.

THE 1969 UPDATE

By 1969, T-34s were seriously falling behind modern tanks. Therefore, T-34-85s in the Soviet Army were updated once again to what is called the 'Model 1969' standard. The most obvious, and often misquoted, change was the implementation of new road wheels. These new road wheels can be called the 'starfish' wheels but are more often incorrectly thought to be T-54 wheels. While the wheels do look like those of a T-54, they are not interchangeable, being much thinner, as well as having a different pattern of hub cap with five bolts unlike the six of the T-54.

A new exterior toolbox was fitted onto the hull side of the tank, the lid of which has an embossed 'X' for strength. Additionally, the optics of the tank were greatly improved. The driver and gunner were both given infrared scopes. There was an infrared light placed on the front right-hand side of the tank, and a T-54-type light on the right of the tank.

These tanks are commonly seen today. Model 1969 tanks were sold to People's Army of Vietnam (NVA) during the Vietnam War, and many monuments to the war display Model 1969 tanks. The annual victory parade in Moscow currently only has T-34-85s of the Model 1969 standard participating in the parade.

T-34-85 Model 1969s were also predominantly used in the numerous Arab–Israeli wars, the Angolan Civil War (1975–2002), the Rhodesian Bush War (1964–1979), and the Yugoslav Wars (1991–1995).

It is in this configuration that most T-34s that are still surviving countries today are in. As a rule of thumb, these are either the Soviet Model 1969 configuration or Czechoslovak-made tanks.

This T-34-85 Model 1969 is in service with the Soviet Army as a training vehicle. The base tank is a T-34-85 (112 Standard Production). One can see the new toolbox on the hull side, along with the 'starfish' road wheels.

A line of T-34-85 Model 1969s and T-54s. These vehicles are in Soviet use for training. The tank in the foreground is a T-34-85 (174 Angled Seam Turret).

Two Yugoslav T-34s. The tank in the background has elements of the 1969 update. Notice the toolbox attached to the hull side forward of the side fuel tank. The tank in question is a T-34-85 (174 Angled Seam Turret). Notice the rear plates hinges, typical of Omsk 174 type hinges.

A Yugoslav T-34 updated to Model 1969 standard. A T-55 style headlight can be seen, along with infrared lights on the hulls right side. The base tank is a T-34-85 (112 Standard Production). The turret marking is a typical Yugoslavian chassis number, which was issued to all Yugoslavian tanks. Most photographs from the breakup of Yugoslavia show these markings on Serbian tanks, which kept them.

A column of Bulgarian operated T-34-85 tanks. The crew of the tank have their Tokarev TT-33 pistols drawn. (*Stan Lucian Collection*)

This T-34 matches that of the one in the private collection of Mr Alex Hall in every feature. The tank is registered as number '18991', and 'Usorski' is painted onto the turret side, as is 'HVO', and 'LAVOVI'.

A modern-day photograph of the T-34-85 as seen above. The tank is now owned by Mr Alex Hall, who intends to restore the tank back to a T-34 with a 76 turret. Notice the bracket for the hull-mounted stowage box.

The most common T-34-85 tanks today in private collections are the ex- Yugoslavian T-34-85s updated to '1969' standard. Here, two T-34s are on display at the Capel Tank Show in Surrey. The T-34 in for foreground is a 174-manufactured T-34 owned by John Dale. The T-34 in the background is a T-34 (76) chassis with a T-34-85 turret owned by Alex Hall. The tank itself was a 174 chassis, repaired at 174 during the war.

56

THE T-34B AND OTHER YUGOSLAV UPGRADES

The last Soviet update was the so-called Model 1969 update, but international operators of the T-34-85 continued to upgrade it. Most of the post-1969 updates were small and entirely locally done. Perhaps the most noteworthy small update was done in Yugoslavia during the late 1960s.

Yugoslavia did attempt to manufacture a T-34-esque tank before the country decided to buy surplus T-34s. Called the 'Tenk Tip-A', this was an interesting mixture of T-34 and IS-3 design features, having a six-sided coffin-shaped hull, like the early war T-50 or later IS-3, using the T-34 running gear, but a new lozenge turret. The vehicle was designed from the outset to be an improved T-34-85, but the vehicle suffered from many issues, mainly stemming from Yugoslavia's lack of ability to manufacture complex vehicles such as tanks. Manaufacture of prototype tanks began without using blueprints. Prototyping began in 1948, and the prototypes were displayed in 1950. Only five were built, and none saw active service. The only surviving example can be seen at the military museum at Kalemegdan, in Belgrade, Serbia. In the meantime, Yugoslavia purchased many M36, M18, and M3 tanks from the United States.

Between 1966 and 1968, up to 600 T-34-85s were purchased by Yugoslavia from the USSR. The tank in Yugoslav service was known as the 'T-34B', so theoretically the 'T-34A' would have been the T-34/76. It should be noted that T-34B does not refer to the Yugoslav upgrade, and rather only refers to the base T-34-85.

The T-34s purchased by Yugoslavia were T-34s that were undergoing conversion from the 1960 to the 1969 standard, already having some of, or all of, the previously described changes. As a part of the sale, spare parts for the T-34 were arranged from the USSR, which consisted of new patterns of equipment.

From 1966, all T-34Bs were given a minor update to best suit the needs of the Yugoslav Army. Most notably, an M2 Browning .50-calibre machine gun was mounted onto the turret. For this, there were three mounts: One stowage mount was placed on the rear of the turret for stowage; a combat mount was placed on top of the twin air filter dome (or to the right of the single mushroom-type filter); and a stowage bracket was also placed forward of the cupola that was on a hinge to lay against the turret roof when not in use and would clasp the barrel of the machine gun when in the turret bracket for combat deployment. These mounts were all taken from American tanks in Yugoslav service, with an indigenously produced foot plate and tube for the combat mount.

This was the most striking change, but other smaller items were also altered. Onto the rear of the turret, new small rails were added for stowing equipment. The rear turret grab handle was moved to the lower portion of the turret rear.

Some examples of Yugoslav T-34Bs were issued with new fenders either side of the tank, but this appears to be a rare occurrence, and generally, most of the Soviet stowage was unchanged.

Yugoslavia also manufactured a single example of a T-34 mine-clearing vehicle. This tank did not have an official name but was in service with the Yugoslav Army until 1999.

Additionally, many T-34s were used for training, being issued with special equipment mounted above the gun to simulate the firing of the main gun. Evidence suggests that these vehicles carried special boxes on the fenders with much of the equipment being stowed in these boxes when not in use. These tanks were re-converted into fighting tanks by 1991.

The upgrade, as described, was standard for all Yugoslav T-34s, and once the breakup of Yugoslavia begun in 1991, the T-34B made up a significant part of the tank forces of Croatia, Bosnia, and Yugoslavia. Many of these former Yugoslav T-34Bs were given armour upgrades in the form of rubber sheets or tyres. With the Yugoslav Wars (1991–1995) being so recent, many of the surviving examples of T-34s in western Europe are T-34Bs.

Similar updates were done with T-34-85s in service with the Cypriot army. Interestingly, rather than placing an M2 .50-calibre machine gun on the rear of the turret, the mount was placed on the forward portion of the turret. Similarly, many Syrian-operated T-34s (though mostly Czechoslovak-production tanks) were given a DShK mount on the cupola.

The same T-34-85 owned by John Dale on page 458. The rear of the turret reveals this tank to be a Yugoslav T-34B. Notice the new hardpoints on the turret, along with a rear turret mount for an M2 .50-calibre machine gun, along with an air filter-mounted machine gun mount. (*Helen Pulham*)

The same T-34-85 owned by Alex Hall as on page 458. Notice the stowed M2 .50-calibre machine gun barrel stowage on the forward turret. Other than this and the rear turret adaptations seen on page 460, Yugoslavian T-34-85s differed little from Soviet-operated vehicles.

A Serbian T-34-85 updated to the Model 1969 standard, known in the Yugoslavian army as the T-34B. Rubber sheets on the turret side to improve its armour protection against RPGs have been placed. On the right are two Serbian M-18 Hellcats. The picture was taken in 1995 at a border town, currently in Bosnia and Herzegovina, called Brčko, right on the Croatian border. Notice a .50-calibre machine gun on the turret roof.

A Greek-Cypriot-rebuilt T-34. The turret is from UTZ 183, but the chassis is that of a Krasnoye Sormovo 112 tank. Two items are the giveaway: first, the solid bracket-type exterior fuel tank brackets, and secondly the rear plate, where the exhaust plate sits above the gear plate. Notice also the locally added mount for an American .50-calibre machine gun. (*Anonymously donated*)

A Greek-Cypriot T-34-85 (112 Hard-Edge-85 Late), as shown by the hard edge of the rear of the turret. (*Anonymously donated*)

57

POST-WAR PRODUCTION OF THE T-34-85

While the T-34 had been a valuable and celebrated tank during the war, towards the end of the conflict, the T-34's eventual replacements were being designed. The last Soviet T-34s rolled off from the production lines in December 1946 from UTZ 183 and were replaced with the T-54.

After the conflict in Europe had ended, there was much talk of peace among the occupied states of Europe. For the eastern side, however, one dictator was replaced with another, and once Stalin had taken control of all eastern Europe, he turned many states into satellites.

As previously discussed, Soviet-made T-34s were used extensively in the crew training role, but an even greater number were exported to the Soviet satellite states and allies. Three countries in particular who wanted the T-34 were Czechoslovakia, Poland, and the People's Republic of China (which became a Communist state in 1949 following a brutal civil war). While T-34s were supplied, it soon became apparent that it would be more advantageous to allow for each country to independently begin manufacture of the T-34, although whether the PRC intended to build the T-34 is debatable. The T-34 was selected over newer tanks for two main reasons.

First, if Poland and Czechoslovakia produced the T-34, but then attempted to overthrow their respective Communist governments, when the USSR stepped into intervene, the Soviets would have superior tanks—namely, the T-54.

Secondly, indigenous production allowed the USSR to keep large stocks of T-34 tanks for the secondary roles, such as training and as auxiliary tanks, instead of selling all their stocks off. A by-product of a larger Soviet stock was that when the T-34 became even more outdated towards the end of the 1960s and 1970s, the USSR could sell more onto other Communist countries while still keeping the T-54 in their stocks.

58

CZECHOSLOVAKIAN T-34-85s

Czechoslovakia fell under Stalin's control following the 1948 *coup d'état* by the Communists. Fearing the need for security, especially as the post-war order appeared threatened due to flashpoints between the Western Allies and the USSR, such as the Berlin Blockade (1948–1949), the subject of indigenous tank manufacture arose.

The Czechoslovak Army, both before and during the early part of the Communist regime, fielded 130 T-34s (supplied during the war to anti-German forces), 124 StuG IIIs modernised as StuG 40s (including new optics and a new 75-mm gun), and eighty Panzer IVs, along with other lighter and inferior tanks. Some attempts were made at designing their own armoured vehicles, but none of these were fruitful, even if some were promising.

As such, the Soviet government, therefore, decided to manufacture T-34-85s in Czechoslovakia, with an agreement being signed in July 1949. The T-54 was not selected as the Soviet government was only just beginning production itself of this classified vehicle, not to mention the previously described fear of anti-Communist revolutions.

Documentation was delivered from UTZ 183, and the plant chosen for production was the CKD plant in Sokolovo, situated in modern-day Czech Republic. The setup of production and subsidiaries took a long time, and while this process started on 1 January 1950, it was not until September 1951 that the first T-34-85s were produced. The plant also produced SU-100s (locally known as the SD-100) and ARV (armoured recovery vehicle) T-34s.

T-34-85 (CKD EARLY PRODUCTION)

The very first T-34s manufactured at CKD looked very similar to T-34-85s issued from UTZ 183. While the turrets of the initial tanks matched those of UTZ tanks, these early tanks had subtle hull changes. First, the headlight on the hull front right was put into a distinctive cage to protect the headlight from damage. Secondly, a rear hull buzzer was placed onto the hull's rear right side. Thirdly, a second buzzer was placed on the turret roof. The T-34s made at

A Bulgarian-operated T-34-85 (CKD early Production). The tank's nose plate is different from Soviet tanks, not having a nose 'fillet'; rather the nose is created using the glacis plate edge and the underside nose plate. The tank has the front fenders stowed, which was a unique feature with T-34-85 fenders. A caged headlight can just be seen.

the CKD plant were given cast spider late-type road wheels, making these early tanks near identical to UTZ 183 T-34s.

It was while at CKD that a new turret was designed to best suit the casting capabilities of the plant. The seam was now more flowing and without a cut-out on the turret cheek. The seam dipped at the centre of the turret cheek below the pistol port, then it levelled out towards the rear of the turret.

These tanks were equipped with some unique features. Some tanks were equipped with the Notek headlights, taken directly from German Second World War-era tanks, but this was not a common occurrence and only a local update. Also, the very rear of the tank had a buzzer. This was located at the rear left side of the tank, under the rear fuel tank, and was a cone-shaped object with a button. If this button was pressed, a buzzer sounded in the turret alerting the commander that the external troops wanted to communicate.

Following the initial production tanks with UTZ 183 turrets, there are main subtypes of Czechoslovakian T-34 tanks. The tanks can be categorised into 'T-34-85 (CKD 1951–53)', 'T-34-85 (Martin 1952–56)', and 'T-34-85 (Syrian Upgrade)'.

T-34-85 (CKD 1951-53)

Czechoslovakian T-34-85s were initially issued the diamond-shaped rear hinges for the rear plate and the gear plate, like that at UTZ 183. However, in 1953, the design was changed. The hinges on the rear plate were now almost identical to those used by Omsk 174, but rectangular and longer.

In the first year of production, a caged headlight would be placed onto the hull side, where the original Soviet headlamp was. This was essentially the standard Soviet headlight, but with a cage over the front to protect it.

Above: A Czechoslovakian T-34-85 (CKD 1951–53). The turret is unique to Czechoslovakian tanks. On the rear of the hull, one can see a rear hull buzzer, and the distinctive caged headlight can be seen on the hull side. Unusual covers can be seen for the MK-4 and radio port on the turret, this was Czechoslovakian-designed waterproofing for deep wading. The cupola had a tube that attached to it allowing for a depth of five metres to be achieved.

Left: A T-34-85 (CKD 1951-53) in Bulgarian service. Notice the typical Czechoslovakian cage-type headlight, indicating it is from an early batch.

A Bulgarian-operated T-34-85 (CKD 1951–53). Notice the rear hull buzzer—a clear indicator of the tank's origin. The turret, too, has the distinctive casting pattern, which is somewhat obscured by the Bulgarian officers. Notice that the rear fuel tank is not upright in its bracket, with the cap on the underside of the bracket. Additionally, the post-war Soviet-style tow rope bracket can be seen on the side of the tank.

T-34-85 (MARTIN 1952-56)

Production at CKD was coupled in February 1952 by production at Martin in modern-day Slovakia. The Martin plant had started off as a subsidiary of the CKD plant, supplying them with T-34 and SD-100 armoured hulls. However, it was soon decided that the entire Czechoslovakian T-34 production should be moved to Martin.

The move was done because the Soviet government was concerned that the CKD plant was too close to the west, and in the event of a war, it would be taken over within days. However, with the plant now further away, tanks could still be produced during a hypothetical war.

T-34s were manufactured in tandem between May 1952 and December 1953. CKD production ended in December 1953, and Martin's production continued until 1956.

There were immediate differences between the Martin tanks and the CKD tanks. The main difference between the two plants was that Martin issued pressed-type road wheels. Martin also did not use the caged headlight as it was replaced with the T-54 style of headlight. This new style consisted of two headlights in a small caged-off area on the glacis plate instead of the hull side. One light was a traditional light, whereas the other was a Soviet copy of the Notek light.

The rear hinges of the tank were redesigned. Originally, the hinges were the Soviet diamond-shaped hinges, but new ones were added, which were rectangular, with three teeth on the bottom hinge and two teeth on the top. This was done at both CKD and Martin sometime in 1953. These hinges were like those used by Omsk 174 except wider. This is how T-34s were manufactured in Czechoslovakia until the end of production.

Above: A Czechoslovakian-manufactured T-34-85 (Martin 1952–56). Notice the T-55-style headlights, typical of the Martin production, in conjunction with the pressed-type road wheels. This vehicle is currently located at the end of Mandela Way, in south London, and is affectionately known as the 'Stompie Garden T-34'. The vehicle regularly is painted in many strange and artistic schemes and is currently carefully and lovingly looked after by volunteers and members of the local community. (*Will Kerrs Collection*)

Left: This T-34-85 (Martin 1952–56) was being used by the Syrian Arab Army and has had some Syrian updates. Notice that, despite the fact that the vehicle is being operated in a desert environment, snow cleats can be seen. (*Andrey Firsov*)

East German NVA T-34-85 (Martin 1952–56) No. 645. Notice the distinctive turret shape and its seam, which dips in the forward part of the turret before rising to meet the mantlet. Pressed road wheels are a clear indicator that this is a Martin-made T-34. The vehicle has some 1960 updates, such as the rear turret stowage bin. Some 200-l fuel tanks can be seen on the rear too.

T-34-85 (SYRIAN UPGRADE)

Lastly, a notable upgrade to Czechoslovakian (and some Soviet) T-34-85s was done by Syria. The cupola hatch was redesigned and had a single circular cupola hatch, which had a mount for a 12.7-mm DShK machine gun. Attached to this was an oval mount with a hydraulic lifting arm for the DShK.

The Syrian T-34s were operated during the Six-Day War, and many were lost on the Golan Heights. This upgrade is often called the 'Model 1956', but this conversion was done by the Syrians, not the Czechoslovak Army.

Czechoslovakian production ended in 1956, after 2,376 tanks were manufactured (not including 1,300 SD-100s and all the support variant T-34s manufactured). These tanks are still currently being operated by many armies around the world, with some examples being used, or at least photographed, in the Syrian Civil War, although many of these tanks are misidentified as the Second World War tanks as the subtleties are often missed with the turret. Perhaps the most famous Czechoslovakian T-34 is the one on Mandela Way in London, which is now used as an art piece.

In 2019, Laos exchanged thirty T-34-85s with Russia for 'several dozen' T-72B1s. Russia wanted new T-34-85s for use on the 9 May Victory Day parades. The tanks supplied from Laos were all Czechoslovakian tanks; none were Soviet in origin. Therefore, most of the T-34-85s on parade in Moscow from 2020 onwards are actually Czechoslovakian rather than wartime Soviet-production examples.

T-34-85 (Syrian Upgrade). This tank was lost during the Six-Day War (1967). The DShK AA mount is clearly visible. No. 8 is likely an Israeli marking. The vehicle in the background is a BTR 152 Armoured Personnel Carrier (APC).

The same T-34-85 (Syrian Upgrade) as previous. Notice the turret seam, which is a clear indicator of a Czechoslovakian design, and the Hebrew graffiti.

A T-34-85 (Syrian Upgrade), photographed in 1971. Notice the rear hull buzzer. The turret slogan states 'Suleman Ahmad […]', but the last word is difficult to make out.

A T-34-85 (Syrian Upgrade). The DShK AA mount is clearly visible here. This is the same T-34 as seen above. (*Ed Okun Collection*)

Another T-34-85 (Syrian Upgrade). Take note of how the DShK AA mount was attached to the cupola. (*Ed Okun Collection*)

The same Syrian T-34-85 (Syrian Upgrade) as seen above. (*Ed Okun Collection*)

This T-34-85 (Syrian Upgrade) is missing the DShK AA mount, but the hinges can be seen for it. (*Ed Okun Collection*)

The same tank as seen above. Take note of the rear hinges for the rear plate, and the rear buzzer for infantry. (*Ed Okun Collection*)

59

POLISH T-34-85s

WARTIME USE

The Polish Armed Forces in the east had been an active military organisation since 17 August 1941, upon the re-establishment of Soviet–Polish relations and the declaration of the Molotov-Ribbentrop Pact being null and void. All Polish soldiers captured in the 1939 Soviet-German invasion of Poland were considered 'Soviet citizens' and were therefore recruited and pressed into Red Army service. However, after the front had stabilised somewhat after the Battle of Stalingrad, and after the emergence of the Katyn massacre, Soviet–Polish relations were once again severed.[1]

Between the summer of 1943 and the end of May 1945, two Soviet-controlled Polish armies had been formed—the First Polish Army formed in March 1944 and the Second Polish Army in January 1945.

Both units became ostensibly independent fighting forces, with their own tank divisions, supply logistics, artillery, and infantry. Yet the reality is that they were Soviet-controlled from the top down, and their equipment was often second-rate in quality. While T-34-85s were operated by these units in late 1944, before this, most of their tanks were T-34/76s, and these were often older types and rebuilds. It should be noted that not many tanks were fielded by Polish units during the war, and in May 1945, the Polish Army was equipped with only 199 T-34s. Interestingly, until May 1945, some T-60s were listed in the order of battle.

POLISH PRODUCTION

After the war's conclusion, the Soviet government installed a Communist Polish government sympathetic to them with no resistance whatsoever from the Western Allies despite the Polish government-in-exile residing in the United Kingdom. In fact, this installation had already been agreed upon between Churchill and Stalin, without the knowledge or permission of the other Allied states, let alone the Polish government-in-exile.

After the war's conclusion, the Polish Army was established from the ethnic Polish Armies that fought alongside the USSR. Those Poles who were fighting under the western Free Polish Army could not return home for fear of persecution from the communist government. The sad truth is that Britain, who had gone to war on Poland's behalf, had now abandoned its ally to appease Stalin, and this action would taint Anglo–Polish relations for years to come.

While Poland was in no immediate danger of western invasion, east–west tensions were already mounting shortly into the post-war era. Additionally, at Poland's south-east border with the Ukrainian SSR, there was trouble with Ukrainian partisans who were eager to unite all ethnic Ukrainian peoples into a new state, some of whom lived in Polish territory. Here, T-34s, including T-34-85s were deployed locally for policing. This minor unrest was ostensibly settled by 1946.

Between 1945 and 1949, the Polish Army was supplied T-34s coming from the Soviet Union, but in as early as 1948, the Polish authorities wanted to begin T-34 manufacture wholesale, so on 14 September 1948, a communication was sent to Moscow requesting to build the tank, starting with spare parts to prepare for full production. However, this was severely delayed due to mistrust between the government of Poland and Stalin considering the extremely chequered history of Soviet–Polish relations.

Eventually, from 1948, a factory was set up in the town of Labedy. The factory was named Bumar, and this factory was set up to manufacturing spare parts for the Polish fleet of T-34 tanks. Parts ranged from the mundane to the complex. Eventually, engines and transmissions were being manufactured in 1951.

Initially, like in Czechoslovakia, production was originally intended to begin in 1950, but this did not happen. This was mostly due to the inability for the Bumar factory to successfully and reliably manufacture parts for the T-34. Additionally, it took until 1951 for the licence to produce the V-2-34 engine.

It took until 1952 to begin the manufacture of the T-34 tank. Production of the T-34 in Poland lasted from 1952 until 1954, with a total of 685 tanks being manufactured. The tanks were like those produced in Czechoslovakia, and like Czechoslovakian tanks, the turrets were of a unique style that can be easily identified.

DIFFERENT BUT THE SAME

When T-34 production began at Bumar, as with Czechoslovakian T-34s, plans were shipped from UTZ 183, along with Soviet technicians. However, unlike the Czechoslovakian-manufactured T-34s, Polish T-34s were not a complete copy of Soviet tanks, with differences ranging from the method of turret construction to the internals of the tanks.

The turrets were of a similar shape to those made in Czechoslovakia, with a soft, curving seam that dips in the centre of the turret, and sharply angled towards the centre of the gun mantlet. However, Polish T-34s have a very straight seam from just below the pistol port to the mantlet. In addition, casting marks, typically horizontal lines, on the rear portion of the turret are clearly visible.

One subtle change to Polish T-34-85s was the command cupola, which had an outwardly different rotating ring for the hatch. The command cupola's hatch on all T-34s could rotate, and Polish manufactured tanks had a thicker rotating disk, sometimes with grooves like that of a vinyl record on them.

An East German NVA-operated T-34-85 (Polish Production). Poland appears to have exported their tanks to many other Communist states.

A T-34-85 (Polish Production) No. 774. Notice the subtle difference in the seam, which is more straight than Czechoslovakian turret seams, but still more 'wavy' than Soviet turrets. Horizontal casting lines are often seen on Polish manufactured turret sides.

An East German NVA T-34-85 (Polish Production). Notice the subtle changes compared to Soviet-made tanks such as the turret shape and the gun mantlet. A casting number on the gun sleeve is a clear indication of Polish origin, seeing as though they were the only ones to do this. Note the turret markings—a DDR emblem, with what appears to be a single white '2' on the rear. The tank is strangely whitewashed. (*Jiří Zahradník Collection*)

This T-34-85 (Polish Production) is in East German NVA service. Careful inspection of the turret reveals the command cupola rotating top has a slightly thicker rim to it, indicating its Polish origin. In addition, following careful inspection of the turret cheek, one can see the Polish straight seam from the turret cheek to the lower turret. Notice the very rare East German T-34/76 in the background.

Wheels used on these tanks were the cast spider-type road wheels, but with one difference between Soviet and Polish cast wheels—Polish vulcanised rubber tread has vertical lines that run across the rubber from rim to rim, whereas Soviet wheels are lacking this feature. Additionally, the cast gun sleeve at the end of the mantlet had casting numbers on them.

The nose of Polish T-34s was different from that of the Soviet tanks. Rather than having a fillet that the glacis and bottom nose plates attached to, the nose of the tank was made from the joints of the two plates. This gave the nose a pointed look, as the fillets of Soviet tanks (even the pointed fillets) did not follow the same angle as the glacis plates. The Soviet fillet was a 90-degree angle, whereas Polish and later Czechoslovakian tanks were at an angle of 60 degrees.

Smaller differences also included the stowage. The earliest Polish T-34s stowage matched that of the Soviet-made tanks, but most Polish tanks had a greatly altered stowage layout. Behind the first gun-cleaning toolbox on the front left fender, a second gun-cleaning toolbox was placed. This did not hold gun-cleaning tools, and other items were stowed in this box, sometimes elements of the deep-wading kit. There was also new tool kit placed onto the front right fender. Some other Polish T-34s sometimes carried a large toolbox on the hull right side, which was four-sided but followed the angle of the hull sides.

Polish-manufactured T-34s were generally distributed throughout Polish tank units, but some were exported. Photographs in this publication show Polish-manufactured T-34s in Bulgarian and Romanian service during the 1960s. Furthermore, it is known that at least one Polish-built T-34 was sold to North Vietnam and was captured by the Chinese in 1978, but details on Polish exports to Vietnam are lacking.

A T-34-85 (Polish Production) in the service of the East German NVA. Interestingly, the tank has been fitted with a whole new wheel set. Polish tanks were issued with cast road wheels, whereas this tank has pressed-type road wheels.

The same T-34-85 as on page 478. Readers with a keen eye will notice the slightly different turret cupola ring of Polish T-34s, the lack of a nose fillet, and the nose of the plate is actually the edge of the lower plate.

The same East German NVA-operated Polish production T-34-85 tank as seen above. Notice the casting numbers on the gun sleeve—a clear indicator that the tank is of Polish production.

The same East German NVA T-34-85 as on pages 478 and 479. Take note of the typical post-war stowage of the tow ropes.

A column of NVA T-34-85s. The tank in the foreground is a Polish-made vehicle, as discerned from the turret casting. The photograph was taken in 1970, but the NVA crew are wearing late 1940s Soviet tank crew hats with in-built earphones, which are not as large as the Soviet 1970s tank crew helmet earphones.

An NVA T-34-85 (Polish Production) covered in camouflage netting. The crew pose in front of the vehicle. The NVA was intended as a buffer force between the Western Allies and the USSR and was issued mostly obsolete equipment because it was only intended to slow a potential NATO invasion of East Germany, as to allow for the Soviet forces more time to prepare a defence or counteroffensive.

POLISH UPGRADE

Post-production, the Polish T-34-85s were subject to a rigorous upgrade package. This was known as the 'T-34-85-M1'.

Polish T-34s were designed to also be an improvement over the original T-34-85 design. During production, the tanks were re-designed to require one less crewman, which was achieved by omitting the engineer's position by having the hull machine gun be remote-controlled.

Fuel tank hardpoints were placed onto the rear of the tanks. These could hold an additional 200 l. This update was very similar to the one done by the Soviets and the East Germans.

A second modernisation was conducted in the 1970s. Tanks with this update were known as 'T-34-85-M2'.

The exterior of the MG position was noticeably different, with a large-rimmed face to the position; this was to allow for a waterproof cover to be placed over the MG position for deep wading. Polish T-34s were modernised to be waterproof, featuring watertight seams and the ability to place a waterproof cover over the mantlet.

The mantlet had hardpoints for a deep wading cover. This had plastic screens for the gun sight. This attached also to the barrel of the gun, which additionally required a cover over the muzzle.

A typical T-34-85 (Polish Production) in Polish service. This machine is likely a T-34-85-M1 (the Polish version of the Soviet Model 1960 update) due to the 200-l fuel drums attached to the rear, which also bear the same '1636' marking as the turret.

The same T-34-85 (Polish Production) as seen above. Take note of the location of the casting number on the turret '103'. This normally refers to a mould used for the turret.

This T-34-85-M1 (Polish Production) was purchased by the North Vietnamese Army (NVA) and served during the Vietnam War (1963–1975), then captured during the Sino-Vietnamese War (1978). The tank is still preserved today in the Beijing Tank Museum.

A Polish-production T-34-85 in service with the Polish Army sometime in the late 1950s. The tank is very unusual, as it has been painted in a three-tone camouflage. The turret markings are also strange, with a four-digit marking painted using dots. The Polish emblem is also on the front side of the turret. (*Przemysław Skulski Collection*)

A Polish-operated UTZ 183 manufactured T-34-85 that has been updated to the T-34-85-M2 standard. Technical features for the M2 standard include the waterproof cover over the gun mantlet, the metal ring around the MG position for the cover's placement, the numerous stowage bins placed onto the hull sides, T-55 style headlights on the glacis, and stowage for a deep wading snorkel on the hull left. This T-34 is being operated by a Polish airborne unit, as can be seen on the glacis of the tank. (*Przemysław Skulski Collection*)

A line of Polish T-34-85-M2s. Interestingly, notice the different track tension, with tank No. 321 having a much higher idler wheel than the other tanks. All of the vehicles have deep wading snorkels. (*Przemysław Skulski Collection*)

A monument made from a Polish T-34-85-M2. All of the technical features are typical of Polish production. Notice the deep wading snorkel on the hull side. Two gun-cleaning tool kits are typical of Polish production tanks, but the second box did not contain gun-cleaning kits and was likely stowage for more deep-wading kit. (*Przemysław Skulski Collection*)

The rear mesh radiator cover had to be covered with metal plates that could be removed when not in use. Additionally, the glacis plate had new headlights in a cage, not unlike that of the T-55. New equipment was carried on the hull sides, and brackets for the deep wading snorkel had to be put on the hull left side. Waterproofing had to additionally be done to the driver's hatch and the command cupola. This mostly consisted of rubber seals for the driver's hatch and a new rim to the cupola as to put a bag over the top of the cupola.

T-34s were operated by the Polish army until the 1980s. After T-34 production stopped, licences were gained for the production of the T-54. The Polish Army no longer uses T-34s in the training role, and most Polish T-34s are used in museums or podiums. A famous example of a Polish production T-34-85 is on display at the Imperial War Museum Duxford, which is incorrectly painted as a tank in Berlin 1945.

60

CHINESE T-34-85s AND THE 'TYPE 58'

In the 1950s, the People's Republic of China (PRC), a fledgling Communist state, was sold many T-34-85s (along with vast amounts of other materiel) by the USSR to replace their outdated and battle-worn tanks. The name 'Type 58' (almost certainly an unofficial name) typically refers to the PRC's upgraded T-34-85s featuring newly-added parts, such as a second command cupola, a heavy machine gun stowage system on the turret cheek, and torsion bar hinge system for engine access.

As this section shows, the history of T-34-85s in the PRC is shrouded in mystery. One of the greatest problems is that the most detailed sources on early Chinese tanks come from Chinese social media such as Weibo and Baidu Tieba (seeing as though military archives remain closed for research, and interviews with or memoirs by veterans or factory workers are very rare).

While they have the potential to shed significant light on the vehicles, one must be cautious when using such sources as just like western social media, fantastic studies are available (such as on the 'T-34 Interest Group' on Facebook), but likewise, dreadfully inaccurate information is rife.

Other sources, such as the memoirs of factory worker, Dan Ling, are also consulted, along with Chinese news reports, of course in addition to the usual analysis of the photographic record. Thus, this chapter will explore what is known about Chinese T-34-85s, as well as tentatively summarising claims made on Chinese social media about the history of them.

TANKS OF THE PLA AS OF 1 OCTOBER 1949

At the beginning of the 'end' of the Chinese Civil War in 1949, the Chinese People's Liberation Army (PLA) had only tanks in its stocks which were captured from the National Revolutionary Army (the NRA, the army of the Nationalist Government, the Kuomintang, KMT) during the Chinese Civil War (1946–1950).[1]

Quantitively speaking, most of the PLA's tanks are believed to have been Japanese-built tanks. Overwhelmingly, these were the Type 97 Chi-Ha, Chi-Ha Shinhoto, and Type 95 Ha-Go, but the

'A gift for the veterans', this picture is of PLA crewmen in the late 1950s with their T-34-85s and Type 58s. Notice that some of these tanks, the Type 58s, have been given the second turret cupola with the Type 54 ring clearly visible.

PLA also had some examples of rarer vehicle such as the Type 95 So-Ki, Type 91 So-Mo, Type 94 TK, Type 92 Jyu-Sokosha, and possibly other types, too, which are not known in photographic evidence. The Red Army captured an estimated 300,000 rifles, 5,000 machine guns, 1,226 artillery pieces, 369 tanks, and 925 aircraft from the Japanese during the Soviet Invasion of Manchuria (August 1945), and these are believed to have come into the hands of the PLA in the spring of 1946. Stalin's policy towards the CCP had been largely ambivalent at that time; the Nationalists were allowed to take control of the region, but simultaneously, the PLA's Eighth Route Army was allowed into Manchuria to harass the NRA and raid Soviet-controlled arms dumps for weapons.

Nonetheless, most of the PLA's Japanese tanks are believed to have been captured from the NRA during the civil war, who in turn captured them from the Japanese during the Second Sino-Japanese War (1937–1945). That said, if we are to believe CCP folklore, then the PLA's first tank, a Chi-Ha Shinhoto later known as 'Gongchen Tank' (功臣號), was captured directly from Japanese remnant forces in Shenyang, Liaoning Province, between October and December 1945.[2] However, one expects that this story is highly (if not totally) fictitious, and a means through which the CCP could distance itself from a narrative of having needing Soviet support to arm itself for the civil war.

The PLA also captured many of the NRA's M3A3 and M5A1 Stuart tanks, along with other American-supplied vehicles such as the LVT(A)-4, LVT-4, M3A1 Scout Car, and many others. These were originally supplied via Lend-Lease from the USA to the Chinese Expeditionary Force (CEF) during the Burma Campaign (1942–1945) but were retained by the NRA and used in the civil war. The CEF's M4A4 Shermans were all confiscated by the USA after the end of the Second Sino-Japanese War for fear that they may be used aggressively and not defensively, thus sparking a civil war (a war that came nonetheless).

Finally, the PLA fielded some rarer (but still outdated) vehicles such as a single M4A2 Sherman (apparently with a damaged main gun, which was missing its barrel), which was fielded by the United States Marine Corps' 1st Tank Brigade in Tianjin (Tientsin) and Beiping (the name given to Beijing when it is not a capital city, 'Beijing' meaning 'Northern Capital') from 1945–1947 during their repatriation programme of Japanese soldiers.[3] The tank was left behind by the USMC for the NRA to use, but whether it was reused by the NRA or not is unknown. A single photo shows the vehicle in PLA markings, missing its main gun but with a dummy barrel in its place, on a parade to mark the foundation of the PRC in Xuzhou, Jiangsu Province on 1 October 1949.

The PLA also operated a single T-26 (with P-40 AA mount) on the 1 October 1949 parade in Beijing (which was most likely captured during the Huaihai Campaign (6 November 1948–10 January 1949) from the Nationalists along with two wrecked T-26s). An estimated eighty-three T-26s (mostly models pre-dating the AA mounts) are thought to have been supplied to the NRA by the USSR in 1937, along with many other vehicles and weapons. The T-26s were used by the NRA throughout the Second Sino-Japanese War (with some being lost to the Japanese) and during the civil war (with some being lost to the PLA). A photograph exists which shows a T-26 (with P-40 AA mount) with the identification number '568' belonging to the 1st Group of the 3rd Regiment of the NRA having been captured by the PLA on 11 August 1946 at the Battle of Lanfeng (not to be confused with the earlier and more well-documented Battle of Lanfeng in 1938), with reports suggesting that five tanks—a mixture of T-26s and Vickers Mark E Type Bs—were captured during the battle.

While there also evidence such as this to suggest that the PLA captured plenty of T-26s during the civil war, it is unclear how many were in service by late 1949. On the one hand, with the exception of the one on parade, the others may have been destroyed during the civil war. On the other hand, exemption from the victory parade may suggest that far from being destroyed, they were used for training duties. The NRA is believed to have evacuated all of its remaining T-26s at Shanghai to Formosa (Taiwan), but exactly how many is unclear.

Finally, the PLA is reported to have operated some Vickers Mark 'E' Type Bs in 1949. Twenty were sold to the KMT by Vickers (along with other Vickers tanks) in batches between 1933 and 1935 (with the final delivery being made on 21 October 1936), four of which featured an extended turret with the Marconi G2A radio. While it is often thought that the KMT lost all these tanks to the Japanese in the Battle of Shanghai (13 August–26 November 1937), it is reported that the 2nd Regiment of the NRA still operated fourteen at the end of the Second Sino-Japanese War in 1945. Whether this is true or not remains unclear, but if true, then these were then captured by the PLA in northern China in various battles during the civil war, with one such time believed to be on 11 August 1946 at the Battle of Lanfeng, as detailed above. To further substantiate this claim, a photograph exists of several Vickers Mark 'E' Type Bs, purportedly being reviewed at the Armoured Corps School at Xuzhou by the PLA.

Despite this impressive array of tanks, most of these tanks were seriously outdated, except for most of the American vehicles. Therefore, PLA decided that it was in dire need of more modern and potent tanks if the fledgling state was to be able to survive and to achieve its ambition of conquering Formosa (Taiwan). As such, the PLA turned to its 'Communist ally', the USSR, for arms deals.

SOVIET ARMS SALES, 1950–1955

Relations between the CPSU (Communist Party of the Soviet Union) and the CCP (Chinese Communist Party) were frosty due to Stalin's decision to remain uninvolved directly in the Chinese Civil War, with some evidence suggesting Stalin favoured the Nationalists under Chiang Kai-shek for both practical and ideological reasons. Furthermore, the CPSU and CCP had various ideological differences, although these would become more pronounced when Khrushchev came to power in the USSR. Nevertheless, under the Treaty of Friendship, Alliance and Mutual Assistance (1950), the USSR agreed to supply the PRC with all the assistance that a new Communist state would need to prosper (although this fell short of nuclear weapons technology, despite persistent Chinese demands).

Therefore, in the years 1950–1955, the PRC purchased a huge variety of weapons and military equipment of all types from the USSR to replace their outdated weapons. Over 3,000 vehicles are reported to have been supplied to the PLA from the USSR in the years 1950–1955:

> 1950—300 T-34-85s, sixty IS-2s and forty ISU-122s (to be clear, the original model armed with the 122-mm A-19S, not the later ISU-122S with the 122-mm D-25S), which were organised into ten regiments (thirty T-34-85s, six IS-2 heavy tanks, and five ISU-122s in each).
>
> 1951—ninety-six T-34-85s, and sixty-four SU-76s, which were organised into four regiments.
>
> 1952—312 T-34-85s, and 208 SU-76s, which were organised into thirteen regiments.
>
> 1953—480 T-34-85s, and 320 SU-76s, which were organised into thirteen regiments (based on a total number of forty regiments at this point).
>
> 1954—649 T-34-85s, 320 SU-76s, twenty-two IS-2s, ninety-nine SU-100s, sixty-seven ISU-152s, and nine ARVs (at least two of which were based on the ISU chassis, the others likely being based on the T-34).
>
> 1955—No figures are available, but there were reported shipments in 1955. Based on varying estimates for the number of T-34-85s in China, 127 T-34-85s might have been included in this shipment, but this is not confirmed.
>
> Seventy-two additional ARVs and engineering vehicles were also supplied in this period.
>
> Total 1950-1954: 1,837 T-34-85s (some estimates suggest as many as 1,964 by 1955), eighty-two IS-2s, forty ISU-122s, sixty-seven ISU-152s, ninety-nine SU-100s, and 704 SU-76s. This gives a total of 2,829 tanks, (excluding ARVs and engineering vehicles) organised into sixty-seven regiments between 1950 and 1954, although some estimates suggest that 3,000 armoured vehicles were sold to the PRC between 1950 and 1955. No T-34/76s are known to have been supplied to the PRC, even though many were supplied to North Korea.

These T-34-85s were a huge mixture of tanks from different factories including Krasnoye Sormovo 112, Omsk 174, and UTZ 183. Exact variants that can be seen in photographs include: T-34-85 (112 Standard Production); T-34-85 (112 8-part Composite); T-34-85 (112 Hard-edge-85); T-34-85 (112 Standard Production Late); T-34-85 (112 8-part Composite Late); T-34-85 (112 Hard-edge Late); T-34-85 (UTZ 183 Early); T-34-85 (UTZ 183 Late); T-34-85 (174 Early Turret); T-34-85 (174 with 183 Turret); T-34-85 (174 with 112 Turret); T-34-85 (174 Angled Seam Turret); and T-34-85 (174 Angled Seam Turret Late).

Two Chinese T-34-85s. The T-34 on the left is likely a T-34-85 (112 Hard Edge Late), whereas the tank behind is a T-34-85 (174 Angled Seam Type Late). These tanks are at a local repair centre and are being dismantled. The T-34-85 on the left has the loader's seat hanging from the turret's rear handles. The vehicle behind is having the DT-29 removed from the turret. Some Chinese-made tools can also be seen on the hull side of the rear tank. The markings are typical of Chinese T-34s, with a large '8-1 star' with a three-digit number in white behind it.

A propaganda picture of Chinese PLA T-34-85s. The foremost tank is a T-34-85 (174 Early Turret); notice the Omsk 174 rain cover. This photograph was likely taken during training exercises in the 1950s or early 1960s. Notice also the '8-1 star' marking on the turret, which shows the yellow border of the red star to be broken and not totally enclosed. The tank in the middle appears to have a rather long whip antenna.

The only T-34-85 variants not supplied to the PRC were variants with the 85-mm D-5T, the T-34-85 (112 S-53 Gun Initial Production), and Czechoslovakian and Polish variants. That said, the PRC captured some Polish-built T-34-85s from Vietnam during the Sino-Vietnamese War (1979), which are present in Chinese museums today, but these were never pressed into service with the PLA.

CHINESE MANUFACTURE?

While sources on early PRC tanks are sketchy (and usually very untrustworthy), there is a suggestion across various modern Chinese sources that the T-34-85 was intended for production in China before the T-54 (under the designation 'Type 59') was accepted instead. The basic story changes from source to source, but the general details are more or less as follows.

In 1954, the PRC asked the USSR for permission to produce the T-34-85 indigenously by 1958. This is because it was felt by Chinese leadership that the PRC should be self-sufficient in producing its own materiel, as well as maintaining it. The USSR agreed to this request, seeing as though they had superior replacements for the Soviet Army in production anyway. The PRC eventually managed to translate all the documents of the vehicles provided to them

A Chinese-operated T-34-85 (112 Standard Production Late) sometime in the 1950s. Notice the wear on the tracks where the road wheels have ground away the rust and dirt, leaving the silvery track inside. The vehicle appears to have three white numbers on the turret right, just barely in shot, but does not have an '8-1 star'.

and therefore began to organise license-production of the T-34-85 in the same year. However, production was slow to start.

The simple fact is that the PRC was unprepared for any form of large-scale industry in the years following the Communist victory in 1950 because industry across the country was in many respects never ready for serious tank production (beyond a few workshop conversions and light repairs to tanks and armoured cars). One must also consider that this was compounded by China having been in a near-constant state of war or emergency since 1916 and having fought both a bloody war against the Japanese from 1937–1945, as well as a civil war from 1946–1950. In fact, this issue of industry was so great that it was one of the driving factors in Mao Zedong's implementation of the Great Leap Forward in 1958.

Despite the poor state of Chinese industry, some workshops had managed to produce a set of tracks in 1955. By May 1956, a gearbox was also successfully made. Finally, in February 1957, a prototype V-2-34 diesel engine was made, meaning that the PRC was ready to organise production lines for the T-34-85 and was due to begin manufacture of the tank in 1958 with the designation 'Type 58'.

However, as the trials for manufacturing T-34 parts had gone on for so long, negotiations for the licenses and relevant documents to produce the T-54 had come to fruition and the T-54 was accepted for production instead. The story differs at this point between sources, but it is

An interesting example of a local repair centre repairing Chinese T-34-85s. The T-34-85 on the right is a T-34-85 (174 with 183 Turret), whereas the T-34 on the left is a T-34-85 (112 Standard Production Late). With the two factory types of tanks on display, subtle production and post-production features can be seen. One example is how Krasnoye Sormovo 112 T-34-85 has a white painted driver's hatch and loader's hatch interior, whereas the Omsk 174 T-34-85 has the a green interior of the driver's hatch and loader's hatch.

suggested that this deal came just before either a completely Chinese-made T-34-85 prototype was produced, or just before trials of Chinese-made prototype T-34-85 were complete (evidence for which is lacking) or even just after a short production run of Chinese-made T-34-85s had been complete (evidence for which is also lacking). However, once production of the T-54 (perhaps best described as such instead of Type 59, seeing as though Soviet-supplied kits are believed to have been used at first) began, Chinese production of the T-34-85 was abandoned and only replacement parts were made for their repair facilities. Nonetheless, to satisfy army demands, the remaining Soviet-supplied T-34-85s were given an upgrade package starting in 1958 known as the Type 58.

Whether this story of the PRC producing T-34-85s is true or not remains a mystery. However, it is the author's belief that sources with this story have at best simply confused various true events, and at worst circulated pure rumours and inaccuracies.

CHINESE MANUFACTURE DEBUNKED?

It is quite possible that the closest the PRC ever came to production of the T-34 is the production of replacement parts (and perhaps this has been interpreted as evidence of full-scale production), but even this cannot be confirmed.

The PRC had tank repair facilities as early as 1946 set up in Beijing (Beijing North Vehicle Group (北方车辆集)), but others were also set up later including Baotou (Inner Mongolia, where the Type 59 was later produced), and Harbin First Machinery Factory (Factory 674 in Heilongjiang Province, north-eastern China).

Although one must be exceptionally cautious when using oral histories for their factual content, according to the memoirs of a factory worker, Dan Ling, in 1952, Factory 674 was organised to produce tanks with 3,000 workers employed in the complex. Thirty Soviet Russian advisors, some ranking as high as *Polkovnik* (colonel), were also stationed there and helped run the workshops on a day to day basis. Despite being intended to produce tanks, all that the factory did at that time was repair T-34-85s damaged in Korea. The damage often concerned repairing large holes in the glacis plate. The Chinese workers at this factory sometimes only had two hours of sleep and worked overtime frequently, with tanks coming in and out at night, but according to memoirs of one worker, they did so willingly because they genuinely believed that they were building a new socialist society that would bring them prosperity. Surely such a facility would surely have needed spare parts produced in the PRC (including tracks, engines, lights, electronics, gearboxes, and so on)?

The reality is that no assertion can be made either way with current evidence. Evidence against the production of replacement parts is as follows. First, close examinations of photos (of various eras) does not reveal that there were any Chinese-made replacement parts of items (such as tracks, road wheels, etc.) with their own unique patterns, although many photographs are too poorly composed to see fine details. Secondly, extant examples in museums are not necessarily original vehicles in so far as many have undergone restorations or modifications while on display in museums and therefore cannot be necessarily trusted as accurate sources to make analyses of. Thirdly, one must consider that in the 1950s, the Beijing repair station suffered shortages of machinery, equipment, and even water and electricity to run the facility, let alone to produce replacement parts (although the Chinese certainly had the capacity to make parts by the end of the 1950s, (especially direct copies of parts) as seen with the Type 59 MBT).

Therefore, it is possible that Soviet-supplied vehicles may well have been used until they were broken beyond repair, with the Beijing repair station used for less complicated repairs such as mending damaged gearboxes and engines without replacing them outright. It is also possible—if not incredibly likely—that the USSR supplied replacement parts. However, positive evidence for the latter two possibilities is lacking.

Evidence supporting the production of replacement parts is thus:

First, one must not discount the possibility that the Chinese-made replacement parts were exact copies of the original Soviet parts (meaning that these parts would not show up in photographic evidence). This is not an unreasonable suggestion as the Type 59 MBT had identical parts to its Soviet counterpart, and to distinguish between a Type 59 and T-54 and T-55, one must look at a variety of technical features such as location of weld points, the turret ventilation dome, and so on. Even despite the poor conditions in the Chinese repair centres, these are likely to have improved by the 1960s, meaning spare parts production may have begun around that time, although it is doubtful that T-34-85 parts would have been produced this late. In fact, a declassified CIA report dated 22 November 1963 on Factory 674 reports:

> The facilities in this plant would not lend themselves to the manufacture of heavy immobile objects, such as large castings. This plant is more adaptable to the casting, machining and finishing of small parts. The actual assembly of these parts could be performed in this plant or these parts could be shipped to other plants for assembly.

Secondly, there is some photographic evidence that Chinese electronics, especially radios, may have been fitted, although this was likely as part of the Type 58 upgrade. One must consider, however, that these may have been parts produced for the Type 59 MBT.

Therefore, it is very possible that Chinese replacement parts were made but merely do not show up in photographic evidence due to their similarity to Soviet parts (or perhaps even their rarity).

Whatever the case may be, it is a dubious assertion that the production of replacement parts is evidence of an attempt (whether ultimately abortive or successful) by the Chinese to produce the T-34-85 in full production runs for the following reasons.

First, most sources, both Western and Chinese, suggest that an agreement with the USSR was made as early as 1956 to produce the T-54 MBT in the PRC. The first batch of these Type 59s was produced in 1958 using Soviet-supplied kits and were accepted into service in 1959, hence the designation 'Type 59'. Thus, it makes no sense for any work on full-scale T-34-85 production to take place in the PRC as late as 1957. Whether the PRC intended to produce the T-34-85 back in 1954 remains unclear.

Secondly, one must consider also that the story has too many variations and inconsistencies between sources, and that they all appear after certain video games sparked interest in early PLA tanks.

Finally, tank historian Yuri Pasholok reports that all the Type 58s and T-34-85s he studied while in the PRC had Soviet serial numbers.

The story of the T-34-85 in the PRC is inextricably bound up in the history of Chinese tank projects of the 1950s, such as the 59-16 and 130 light tanks, but hard facts on these vehicles remain as elusive as those on the T-34-85 in the PRC. This problem is only compounded by distortions and sheer inventions in light of recent video games sparking interest in such vehicles. Without further evidence, this story of Chinese production of the T-34-85 is perhaps best regarded as nothing more than a rumour.[4]

THE TYPE 58 UPGRADE PACKAGE

The so-called Type 58 project is another source of mystery and myth about Chinese T-34-85s.

What is clear is that many (but not all) Chinese T-34-85s were fitted with a fairly standardised set of upgrades, chiefly concerning adding a second command cupola, a heavy machine gun stowage system on the turret cheek, and a torsion bar hinge system for accessing the engine. Photographic evidence suggests that throughout the 1950s and 1960s this set of upgrades, widely known today as the Type 58, became increasingly common.

The difficulty with understanding this set of upgrades is that no official military documents are available to corroborate stories told in Chinese internet sources, and period photos are too few and not detailed enough to show all the characteristics. It is also clear that some other upgrades took place on a local scale, meaning that these, too, must be separate and separated from those associated with the so-called Type 58 design. To complicate matters further, many Type 58s in Chinese museums today have been modified and often inaccurately restored for display purposes, which means that some technical details are not original.

The year 1958 is the commonly cited date for when the package was adopted, but this is clearly part of an ex post facto rationalisation for the modern name 'Type 58'.[5] It was certainly adopted no earlier as photographs of the 1957 National Day parade in Beijing show regular T-34-85s and no Type 58s. In any case, photographic evidence suggests that the design was definitely around sometime in the early 1960s.

Regardless of these issues, the sum of photographic evidence suggests that the main upgrades definitely consisted of the following:

> A hardpoint for stowing a 12.7-mm machine gun. This was always on the right cheek of the turret, which appears to be a copy of the stowage mount as seen on the rear of the T-55 and Type 59 turrets.
>
> A distinctive second 'cupola' in place of the original loader's hatch. The original hatch was removed, and a simple metal cylinder was placed over the hatch hole. Some of these cupolas had crudely made vision slits (apparently without optics or even simple glass) although others did not feature vision slits (meaning these are more accurately described as 'superstructures'). On top was a crude hatch door, and a mount for a 12.7-mm Type 54 (the Chinese production variant of the Soviet DShK), apparently a copy of the T-54's mount. When stowed on the hard-points on the turret's side, also a copy of the T-54 design, the Type 54 machine gun would face the rear and would also have a tarp placed over it to prevent damage. Some 'Type 58s' also had a small 'V' shape (as viewed from above) piece of metal welded at the front, connecting both cupolas. There is no evidence for a continuum of designs evolving over time—our scant evidence implies a lack of absolute standardisation of this detail.
>
> A new rear transmission-rear hull plate hinge system. This was an exterior rod type, and essentially strengthened the joint when opening the rear of the tank for inspection. The circular

A Type 58 converted from a T-34-85 (112 Hard Edge). Notice the second cupola in the turret, and the turret side mount for stowing the Type 54 HMG while in transit. This tank is likely decommissioned and used for soldiers to take souvenir photographs with, as can be discerned from the removed optics in the driver's hatch and the general subject matter of these photographs.

transmission hatch also had a small metal stopper (in some cases, two pieces) welded onto it to stop the hatch swinging down and hitting this torsion bar. Chinese SU-100s and T-34-based ARVs were also given this hinge upgrade.

There are other details that may have been included in the upgrade, but these could also have come from repairs, more localised upgrades, or museum restorations:

New optics and headlamps. While Type 58s are often seen with factory original headlamps, one period example shows a new headlamp mounted on top of the DT mount, which does not have a DT fitted. Another example in a museum shows that some Chinese T-34-85s and Type 58s have been fitted with a T-55-style headlamp cage on the top right of the hull, but this is believed to be a museum addition.

Removed Type 54 stowage points, either partially or totally. Close inspection on such vehicles reveals weld beads where the mounts originally were. Therefore, this is believed to be part of various museum restorations. For example, one Type 58 in the Korean War Museum in Dandong, Liaoning Province, has had these hardpoints and its second cupola removed to make the tank

The same Type 58 as page 496 and below. The soldier is operating a radio that appears to be attached to the interior of the tank via a cable coming from the second cupola.

The same Type 58 as seen above, though this time, the soldier is in the second cupola.

appear like a Korean War-era T-34-85, although it retains the rear transmission-rear hull plate torsion bar-hinge system. Other examples in museums are noted.

New fenders, fuel tanks, and handrails. While it is not unreasonable to assume that the Chinese would have produced replacements for these, many T-34-85s and Type 58s in museums have seemingly cheap and handmade features such as fenders, fuel tanks, and handrails, which are all more likely as part of a museum restoration job. It is conceivable that some of these were done locally during their time in the PLA, but not proven.

Removed engine covers, sometimes welded over with single plates. When tanks are put into museums, it seems to be standard across the PRC that their engines have been removed (presumably for security reasons). As such, some museums have either totally removed engine covers (and in some cases, the exhausts, too) and either left them open, or welded simple metal sheets over to prevent the tanks from rusting [although an alternative explanation for this is discussed below].

One museum example also shows that the Type 54 ring has also been removed, which was likely done by the museum for an unknown reason.

Some internet sources also suggest that the Type 58 upgrade included a new Chinese-produced diesel engine, but this cannot be confirmed.

To be sure, tanks may have repaired using Chinese-produced parts and therefore appear to be upgrades, but whether these replacements would have been specifically part of an upgrade 'package' or not is unclear.

Many pictures exist of Chinese tank crew and soldiers posing with T-34-85s and Type 58s as souvenir photographs. Note that this one has retained the radio antenna, and the '8-1 star' can also be seen on the turret side.

A view of a Chinese soldier leaving the driver's hatch of a Type 58. Notice the Tokarev TT-33 (or more likely, Type 54) pistol on his side.

A line of Chinese T-34-85s. The foremost machine was manufactured at Omsk 174, as can be discerned by the rain cover.

A Chinese soldier poses in front of a Type 58 as a souvenir photo.

The Type 58 upgrade was given to all subtypes of T-34-85s supplied to the PRC. However, not every individual vehicle seems to have had this upgrade, as many standard T-34-85s can be seen in the PRC today with no evidence of ever being Type 58s (such as weld points on the turret for the Type 54 stowage mounts or the rear engine access plate torsion bar system). Furthermore, there are some T-34-85s that only appear to have been given the rear engine access plate torsion bar system, but no new cupola or Type 54 stowage points on the turret (or evidence of the turret modifications having been there). There is no proven theory as to why this is the case, but it is plausible that not enough Type 58 parts were produced, so a small number of T-34-85s only had some Type 58 upgrades, and some fewer none at all.

The history of the so-called Type 58 is incredibly sketchy. According to one Chinese internet source, the Jinan Military Region is believed to have been the first region to upgrade T-34-85s in this manner. The reason was simple; it was felt that the vehicle needed greater anti-aircraft protection. As a result, work began to install a mount for a 12.7-mm machine gun on a new cupola. The machine gun chosen was an upgraded version of the Type 54 featuring a set of high-altitude sights known as the Type 58 (although this detail is also likely an *ex post facto* rationalisation of the Type 58 name). Other military regions are believed to have copied the design, and while a tempting explanation for the lack of absolute standardisation of Type 58s, and, indeed, not all T-34-85s being upgraded, this story remains entirely uncorroborated by reliable sources.

OPERATIONAL SERVICE OF PLA T-34-85s

The general operational service of T-34-85s and Type 58s in the PLA is also somewhat mysterious due to a lack of reliable sources. Nonetheless, the following is what can be pieced together.

1950–1966

The T-34-85 saw service in the Korean War with the Chinese People's Volunteer Army (PVA). However, their tanks were so rarely encountered in the war that there are no American records of having encountered them at all. However, tank historian, Steven Zaloga, has suggested that US reports were poorly kept and often lost during the end of the war, which may explain this lack of evidence. The fairly well-known story of T-34-85 '215' is, of course, mythical, and on par with CCP myths such as 'Gongchen Tank', or 'Comrade Lei Feng'.[6]

On the subject of the Korean War, all of North Korea's tanks are believed to have been supplied by the USSR in February 1950, when a military advisory group was sent along with small arms, aircraft, artillery, and other military equipment types—enough to equip eight field divisions and other combat units consisting of 100,000 men.

It should also be made clear that the Type 58 was never fielded in the Korean War because the package did not exist at that time.

By sheer numbers, the T-34-85 formed the bulk of the Chinese armoured divisions until being replaced over time by the newly built Type 59s and Type 62s starting from the 1960s. However, this was a process that took thirty years.

1966–1980

Reports throughout the mid-1960s from the CIA Imagery Analysis Division of aerial surveillance photographs widely report the use of the T-34-85 across the PRC in even small military installations.

Nonetheless, Chinese photographic evidence seems to suggest that the mid-1960s saw the first T-34-85 and Type 58 begin to be gradually phased out of service and were instead used as gate guardians, training vehicles, and in other lesser roles. This is likely due to the replacement of T-34-85s with Type 59s and Type 62s. However, it also reported that the Type 58 could not return to repair facilities at Baotou due to the outbreak of the Cultural Revolution in 1966 (although no specific reason is given), which might contribute to the abandonment of stocks of T-34-85s.

According to one Chinese internet source, during the 1960s, the PLA transferred many of its Second World War-era vehicles for militia anti-tank training purposes, and such efforts were accelerated in 1969 as a result of the Sino-Soviet border conflict. Despite this, dummy tanks of varying quality (some were made from mud, some from scrap metal, some from real tank wrecks, and some were real tanks) were more common for training purposes.

While it is believed that the 'Type 58' never saw combat, T-34-85s (or, possibly, Type 58s) were reportedly issued to the tank regiment attached to the 54th Army Corps (likely the 11th Armoured Brigade) during the Sino-Vietnamese War (1979). However, these T-34-85s are not believed to have seen active combat during the war.

1980–1990

In the 1980s, the PRC's economy had significantly improved and it was able to produce more MBTs to replace the T-34-85. Nonetheless, a CIA report from 10 February 1986 reports that the PLA had 9,000 tanks, of which 3,000 were T-34-85s and the slightly more modern Type 62 light tanks and Type 63 amphibious tanks (no distinction is made by CIA reports about the Type 58).

One Chinese internet source reports that in 1981, the 28th Army conducted exercises in Yuncheng, Shanxi Province, simulating a Soviet attack on the area. This exercise prompted major reforms of the PLA, with a desire for infantry fighting vehicles, gunship helicopters, and the need to retire older vehicles such as the T-34-85. As a result, most T-34-85s and SU-100s were retired shortly after.

Regardless, the 1980s saw a huge expansion of Chinese tank production, and thus many T-34-85s were phased out en masse. The fate of a retired T-34-85 or Type 58 was one of the following: sent to a museum or memorial; cannibalised for parts for the few T-34-85s which remained in service; test vehicles for new technologies such as an automatic fire extinguisher, laser ranging devices, and night vision sights (features which would be used on the Type 69 MBT); sent to scrapyards and possibly destroyed; or even abandoned on the spot by the side of a road in at least one case.

1990–Present Day

The Type 58 and the remaining few T-34-85s are believed to have only been totally retired in the 1990s, when some were still stationed along the Soviet (later, Russian) border. The vast majority remain in museums, scrapyards, or on PLA weapons testing ranges. Nonetheless, there have been some interesting non-military uses of the T-34-85, such as being used as bulldozers by construction companies, with one photograph apparently showing two T-34-85s that had their turrets removed and replaced with commercial bulldozer windscreens. Details on these vehicles are sketchy.

One well-documented non-military use is a Type 58 converted into a firefighting vehicle. The *Liaoshen Evening News* reported that firefighting engineer and captain of Shenyang Firefighting Squadron (1969–1983), Chen Songhe, was inspired to create a firefighting tank by a chemical fire in the 1970s:

> Once, a truck full of gas tanks was on fire, and two gas tanks exploded in the air. The heat radiation [forced] the firefighters to slam [onto] the ground. I saw with my own eyes that the fragments of the cylinder that exploded later would flatten trees more than three meters high [up to] twenty or thirty meters away. While fighting the oil fires, the firefighters generally could only stand outside the danger [zone] because of their outdated equipment. [However,] If a tank rushes into the sea of fire, you are not afraid.

In 1994, Chen obtained official permission for the project and went to a tank repair centre in Shijiazhuang (Heibei Province) where he found many old T-34-85s. The Type 58 in the best condition was chosen, and testing showed that even this old vehicle could still reach 60 km/h. The vehicle was converted and tested by 1996. It features two 1.5-m-long water cannons, one 50 mm and another 100 mm in diameter, in place of the main gun. However, the tank did not have an internal water supply, so it had to have a support vehicle pump water into it. To control the worst effects of the heat, the tank tracks were sealed together, and water sprinkler systems were added to the side of the hulls in order to control the immediate outside temperature. A dozer blade was also added to the front of the tank to tackle obstacles and push down walls. Since then, more firefighting tanks have been built using more modern chassis such as the Type 69.

CONVERSIONS?

There is no evidence of Type 58s receiving any additional major upgrade packages, but small changes (such as track stowage hardpoints) are noted, probably being done on nothing higher than the divisional level. There is no evidence at all to suggest that the PLA investigated any means of converting their T-34-85s into other vehicle types such as self-propelled guns or tank destroyers, although ARVs, tractors, and training vehicles are likely but unproven. There is, however, absolutely no evidence that the Chinese designed, or even considered production of, a vehicle even loosely based on the T-34 design—such designs are modern inventions deriving from a certain video game.

The only known Chinese T-34-85 combat variant is a flamethrower tank. The design seems rather simple—a pair of Chinese-produced flamethrower systems (not dissimilar from the Soviet TPO-50) are mounted on either side of the turret in boxes attached to brackets. One Chinese internet source reports that in November 1955, to test the PLA's combat capabilities, especially regarding amphibious landings, the PRC organised a field exercise at the Liaodong Peninsula. Here, it was found that one of the greatest weaknesses of the T-34-85 was its inability to deal effectively with bunkers. A Soviet adviser offered to sell the PRC OT-34-85s, but this was rejected by Defence Minister Peng Dehuai. Instead, the PLA developed its own design. This featured twelve TPO-50 flamethrowers, with six mounted on either side of the turret in boxes. While it is reported that it passed trials, the design seems to have been rejected, and the prototype remains intact at Oriental Oasis Park in Shanghai to this day.

Strangely, one Omsk 174-produced SU-100 at the Tank Museum, Beijing, had its exhaust system totally removed and welded over, but a new exhaust system was fitted above the engine access hatch consisting of two near-flat exhausts poking out of the top of the plate. The glacis also has eight small hardpoints for track stowage. At least one other SU-100 and a T-34-based ARV standing in a museum are known to have the exhaust change. According to a Chinese internet source, one serious problem with the T-34-85 is that owing to the Sino-Soviet split, the PRC was unable to receive spare parts for repairs for the vehicle (which, if true, further suggests that the PRC never produced its own replacement parts).

The air filter and exhaust systems were in dire need of replacing by the mid-1960s. One problem was that the fighting compartment would fill with exhaust gases meaning that the crew would suffer from carbon monoxide poisoning. Another was that water would enter the tank, especially when fording rivers or other water obstacles.

The Nanjing Military Region hit upon a crude but effective solution. The original exhaust system was removed entirely, welded over, and replaced with a new system at the top of the engine deck extending from the cooling grilles. They also installed a set of water-fording equipment. In 1967, one vehicle was successfully tested with this design, so by 1968, all their Type 58s (and likely other T-34-based vehicles) had been modified. However, in September 1969, the region was transferred a batch of Type 62s, so their Type 58s were transferred to Wuhan. Many museum examples also have their original exhausts removed and welded over without any new exhausts put in. It is suggested that exhaust fumes left the vehicle via the radiator grilles. These explanations for the exhaust changes remains to be proven.

The mysterious 'Type 63/65 self-propelled anti-aircraft gun' (an unofficial name referring to the vehicle's main gun) is often regarded as a Chinese design, but evidence suggests that it was more likely a one-off (or short series) improvised vehicle made by the North Vietnamese Army. Put simply, the vehicle is a T-34-85 that has had the turret replaced with a crudely built, open-topped, box-shaped superstructure housing a Type 65 AA gun, essentially a twin-barrelled Chinese copy of the Soviet 37-mm 61-K AA gun. The superstructure features a small hatch at the rear and also has a few handrails on it. The hull also has some modifications such as some welded plates to protect the turret ring, a hinged turret lock on the rear, some stowage boxes welded to the hull, and what appears to be a strange fuel tank bracket above the left gear cover. This specific tank was captured by the Army of the Republic of Vietnam's 4th Infantry Regiment during the 1972 Easter Offensive and was then given to the USA and was sent to Aberdeen Proving Grounds for testing. Today, it is on display at the Air Defence Artillery Museum in Fort Sill, Oklahoma.

The Type 63/65 SPAAG. This example was on display at the Aberdeen Proving Grounds, as pictured. The chassis is from a T-34-85 made at UTZ 183. There also non-standard stowage bins on the side, although parts are missing from it. The tank has been repainted in a somewhat inaccurate scheme. While the crude construction indicates that the vehicle is of an improvised construction, there is some evidence to suggest it may have been built in a small series because a photograph exists, which shows a similar vehicle featuring a 57-mm S-60 gun. (*Don S. Montgomery via Wikimedia*)

It is believed to be North Vietnamese-built not only because of its crude design and because similar improvised NVA SPAAGs are known to have existed. Three seemingly unique SPAAG conversions are shown 'moving to the front' in a wartime photograph on display at the Vietnam People's Air Force Museum in Hanoi. This included a T-34-85 SPAAG closely resembling the Type 63, but instead featured a 57-mm S-60 AA gun (perhaps indicating a short production run of the design). Two different SU-76M SPAAG conversions are stood next to the vehicle, both of which had new superstructures differing from each other. One featured a 23-mm ZU-23-2, and another featured a 37-mm 61-K. Further details on all of these vehicles are lacking, but it must be concluded that all were North Vietnamese Army improvised SPAAGs as opposed to Chinese-built and supplied. North Vietnam's T-34-85s and SU-76s are believed to all be Soviet-supplied.[7]

According to an article on Weibo, when the USSR handed over the Lushun Naval Base to PLA control in 1955, it left behind three SU-100T ARVs; these vehicles were very popular with the PLA. Interestingly, at the Museum of the War of Chinese People's Resistance Against Japanese Aggression in Beijing stands an SU-85 that has been converted into a unique ARV. Special features include winches, a redesigned radio station, replacement of the periscopes, and a firing port for small arms. It is believed that this conversion is unique and was done by the PLA after being inspired by the SU-100T, but being an SU-85 chassis, the vehicle most likely came from the handing over of the Lushun Naval Base as none are known to have been sold to the PRC as part of the mass arms sales described earlier in this chapter.

MUSEUM RESTORATIONS CONSIDERED

Today, many remaining Type 58s are on display at many Chinese museums, along with a few standard T-34-85s (and some aforementioned hybrids). As mentioned, these examples should not be taken as entirely accurate representations of the Type 58 because of the many (and often obvious) inaccurate restorations that they have undergone.

For example, one Type 58 at the Korean War Museum in Dandong, Liaoning Province has been mostly re-converted back into a T-34-85 by the removal of the new cupola and Type 54 stowage mounts, but the distinctive rear transmission-rear hull-plate hinge remains, giving the tank away as a Type 58.

A T-34/76 stands alongside this tank, which is a serious rebuild using odd parts, such as T-34-85 modernisation wheels (almost certainly acquired in recent years, as they were made in 1969 at the height of the Sino-Soviet Split), T-55 style tracks, T-55 sprockets, non-standard (probably handmade) engine deck handrails, and a T-55 searchlight cage on the glacis plate (next to the driver's hatch). Most tellingly, the tank has a T-34/76 pressed turret's gun mantlet, but the rest of the turret is a soft-edge turret, which indicates that the tank is an inaccurate museum restoration using recently acquired parts. Both vehicles have clearly been modified by the museum to look like authentic Korean War era tanks. A SU-100 is also present at the museum.

All in all, the story of Chinese T-34-85s remains obscured and will only fully understood once archival documents are made available for all to evaluate. The use of various Chinese internet sources is particularly problematic, but the assumption that such sources are totally unreliable is unwarranted. Nonetheless, one must be careful accepting what they suggest as fact, hence the tentative presentation of such information in this chapter.

Two Type 58s at Jianchuan Museum Cluster. On the left is a T-34-85 (UTZ 183 Early), and on the right is a T-34-85 (174 Angled Seam Turret) that has clearly been converted into a Type 58 as discerned from the second cupola. The markings and colour scheme are not original, and are not faithful to period types, having been painted as part of a restoration done by the museum. (*'Tyg728' via Wikimedia*)

T-34-85 (174 Angled Seam Turret Late) No. 406 in the Beijing Tank Museum. On the right is a V-2-34 engine that has been cut away for visitors to view inside. On the left are two IS-2 tanks. The markings of these tanks are totally accurate. The hull of the tank may be a Type 58, as it has the rear transmission-rear hull plate torsion bar-hinge system. (颐园新居 *via Wikimedia*)

A Type 58 that was hand-colourised in the developer's studio. This is a fairly typical thing that was done with Chinese photographs of the period. Notice the Type 54 stowed in the turret side bracket and, most interestingly, a second headlight perched on the end of the hull MG blister. The hand-colourisation has been digitally edited to show more of the tank's technical features.

A rare Omsk 174 SU-100 No. 421 of the Chinese PLA in the Tank Museum, Beijing. There are eight small hardpoints on the glacis plate for track stowage, which are likely a PLA upgrade. A SU-76M is in the background. (*Anonymously donated*)

The rear view of SU-100 No. 421. Strangely, the original exhausts have been removed and welded over. Just above the gear plate, two new exhausts can be seen. The tank also has the rear transmission-rear hull plate torsion bar-hinge system most commonly seen on Type 58s and most T-34-based vehicles in the PLA. (*Anonymously donated*)

A Soviet-built T-34T armoured recovery vehicle in the Tank Museum, Beijing. At least eighty-nine ARVs were supplied to the PRC by the USSR between 1950 and 1955, most of which were based on the T-34 chassis. The others were based on the ISU chassis.

T-34-85 No. 406 in the Tank Museum, Beijing. While the turret appears to be an unmodified T-34-85 turret, close inspection of the rear (not in shot) shows that it has the rear transmission-rear hull plate torsion bar-hinge system like a Type 58. It is possible this tank is a museum rebuild, but it is also possible that it was only given a partial Type 58 upgrade.

A rear view of T-34-85 No. 406. Note that the exhaust pipes have been removed; this was done during engine removal when the tank was given to the museum. Also note the rear transmission-rear hull plate torsion bar-hinge system which is more typical of Type 58s. Note also the missing bolts on the transmission plate. Type 58 No. 404 can be seen in the background.

61

BATTLE: MAJOR GENERAL DEAN'S 'TANK HUNTING' AT TAEJON

Having discussed the post-war production and upgrades of the T-34, it is worth exploring a post-war battle that the T-34 was involved in. The Battle of Taejon (14–21 July 1950) is perhaps one of the most celebrated American encounters with North Korean armour during the Korean War (1950–1953) and is a telling example of how using appropriate tactics are more important than having the most modern and technologically advanced vehicles.[1]

COLD WAR TURNS HOT

Following the end of the Second World War and the withdrawal of Japanese occupation forces, the Korean Peninsula was split between a Communist north propped up by Soviet and PRC interests, and a democratic south propped up by American and other western interests, with both the Soviet Army and US Army occupying half of the peninsula each. The 'two Koreas' were given autonomy in 1948 forming the Republic of Korea in the south, and the Democratic People's Republic of Korea in the north. At this time, a large force of western (mostly American) advisors and soldiers helped govern and were also involved in training the fledgling Republic of South Korea Armed Forces (ROK Armed Forces), and the North's 'Korean People's Army' (NKPA) was likewise funded and trained by the Soviet Union. The latter was given many ex-Soviet tanks, including scores of T-34s (mostly T-34-85s, but some T-34/76s). Contrary to popular belief, the NKPA did not receive many modern weapons such as AK-47 assault rifles—in fact, far more common were SKS and Mosin Nagant 1898 rifles, and PPSh-41 and PPS-43 submachine guns were also supplied in large numbers.

In this context, tensions on the Korean Peninsula grew towards the end of the 1940s. Both the north and south wished to be reunited as a nation-state, but the north wanted a Communist Korea, whereas the south was chiefly interested in a western-style government. This tension boiled over on 25 July 1950, when the NKPA crossed the '38th parallel north' (the border between north and south Korea) and invaded the Republic of Korea.[2]

The NKPA's advance south was swift, as the ROK Armed Forces could not (or, in some cases, would not) hold the NKPA back, especially due to their lack of training and anti-tank weapons.

A GLORIOUS LEADER

Major General William F. Dean was an American officer who had served in Europe during the Second World War. In October 1947, Dean was sent to Seoul as a military governor in charge of policing, rice collection, railroads, and telegraph operations until the elected Korean government took over on 15 August 1948. Following this, Dean withdrew to Japan and was made commander of the 24th Infantry Division in October; he remained stationed in the southern Japanese islands until 1950. However, on 25 June 1950, a duty officer informed him that the North Koreans had just crossed the 38th parallel north, sparking what Dean thought was the beginning of 'World War III'.

The 24th Infantry Division was only a mere occupation force, and despite having seen a great deal of combat in the Second World War, most of its battle-hardened veterans had been reassigned, meaning that they made up only 15 per cent of the total men. To make matters worse, the division only had two-thirds of its wartime strength, with infantry regiments consisting of only two battalions each, and artillery battalions only two batteries each. Furthermore, they only had Second World War-era equipment such as 2.6-inch bazookas and M24 Chaffee light tanks. Worse still, the Division was in training at the time, but this was a troubled affair because all the units within the Division were scattered across the southern Japanese islands.

After a flurry of contradictory orders, on 30 June, Dean was ordered to ship out to Korea as commander of both the 24th Infantry Division and the overall command of a land expeditionary force, the so-called 'Task Force Smith'. This would be the first American force to face the NKPA, but it was only at battalion strength, with the 21st Rifle Battalion, some artillery, and a medical battalion initially sent. On 3 July 1950, Dean arrived in Taejon (125 miles south of Seoul) where he set up his headquarters.

THE NORTH KOREAN ATTACK

The main NKPA attack at the west, where Dean was stationed, was coming from the main road and railway lines which ran parallel through Suwon, Osan, Chonan, Taejon, Kumchon, Taegu, and Pusan, which had previously been used by the Japanese during their invasion of Korea. The main road was also being used by fleeing civilians, as well as retreating national police officers and some South Korean military units. East of this, mountains prevented a flanking movement except for on the extreme east coast, but to the far west, the flank was exposed south of Pyeongtaek.

South Korean military headquarters was set up next to Dean's in Taejon, who stated that their army was fighting hard beyond the eastern mountains, and sometimes brought back a captured 'armoured vehicle' to prove it. However, Dean felt that not enough was being done to hold off the NKPA until major US reinforcements could land in Korea. So, to stop the retreat of South Korean units, Task Force Smith began to rally at Osan, just north of Pyeongtaek, to provide them with a boost of morale. Despite this gambit, South Korean HQ still continued to make excuses for the retreat, such as a lack of artillery, lack of anti-tank weapons, or having been outflanked. One particularly good suggestion from the second chief of staff, Lee Bum Suk, that they should let enemy tanks pass through their lines and then dig ditches behind them to prevent them from retreating, was ignored, even though NKPA tanks were almost always unsupported by infantry.

By 4 July, the newly arrived US 34th Regiment took up positions on the main highway at Osan, and an attack came the following morning with disparate reports suggesting that NKPA tanks were advancing. Not long after, retreating witnesses began to reach Taejon, reporting that forty NKPA tanks drove directly at poorly camouflaged US artillery emplacements with both forces exchanging point blank fire. The result was that four tanks were knocked out by direct fire from the artillery, and four more by infantry counterattacks. Over the next few days, remnants of Task Force Smith slowly withdrew to Pyeongtaek with about half their original strength. However, they had to scuttle their artillery pieces as they could not be withdrawn safely.

Despite the US retreat, Dean ordered a major delaying action which ultimately meant that his left flank was defended only by 500–1,000 dissident, non-Communist North Koreans known as the 'Northwest Youth Group', effectively a guerrilla force. The delaying action was fought just north (and just outside of) the town Chonan by the 34th Regiment under Colonel Robert R. Martin. However, American forces were quickly overrun. A retreating officer reported that Colonel Martin personally led a counterattack with a 2.6-inch bazooka in hand, which he used to force NKPA tanks to retreat. However, Martin was killed shortly after by another tank that came around a corner around 25 feet away and fired a shot from the main gun, which blew him in half, after which resistance collapsed.

More delaying actions were fought until 20 July, when NKPA tanks began to assault Chonan. Put simply, American forces in Korea were not large or strong enough to stop the NKPA's advance, and it was not long before the NKPA was approaching Taejon. As a result, Dean officially moved his command south-east to nearby Yongdong, but he personally remained in Taejon to oversee the defence and delaying action. US forces in Taejon had no armour or anti-tank guns available at first, and only had a small number of 2.6-inch bazookas and 3.5-inch M20 'Super Bazookas' to hand. All that was there to stop the NKPA was the American 34th Infantry Company—a force of under 150 men. The situation was dire but delaying the NKPA for as long as possible until UN forces could land was imperative.

5.30 A.M.–9 A.M.: TANKS IN THE STREETS

The morning of 20 July was shattered by the rumble of at least five NKPA T-34-85s advancing through the streets of Taejon (behind US front lines) at around 5.30 a.m. Of particular note were three T-34-85s with 'tank riders', which had gone behind US lines by entering the city from the north-west shortly after dawn. These tanks drove into the centre of the town and the 'tank riders' disembarked and began raining down sniper fire from rooftops throughout the course of the battle. Additionally, the tanks they disembarked from began to cause havoc.

Two of the tanks turned into a vehicles compound (where the 34th Infantry Regiment had established its command post) and began to open fire, destroying some vehicles and killing around three men. After this, these tanks turned around and began firing on other suitable targets while on the move. Only after the initial firing stopped could US soldiers in the compound scramble to find a 3.5-inch bazooka and return fire, but they were too late as the tanks had rumbled out of range. Instead, the soldiers fired a white phosphorus round at some NKPA snipers in a nearby building, thus causing a great fire to spread throughout Taejon.

Unimpeded, the two tanks advanced to an intersection where several medical jeeps were parked to assist some wounded soldiers. One of the T-34-85s approached the vehicles and engaged the jeeps, killing all but two who were at the scene. One man in particular was laid out on a stretcher, and unable to move, the T-34-85 ran him over. A bazooka was fired at one of the two T-34-85s, but the round did not penetrate, so the tank continued its advance.

One T-34-85 then drove to the nearby train station, where it began to destroy wagons of supplies. However, the tank threw a track and its crew bailed. The escaping commander was killed by small arms fire, but the fate of the others is unknown.

Back at the intersection, two other T-34-85s were knocked out from bazooka fire. The first was hit with a rocket, which caused a 3-sq. foot piece of armour from the glacis to fly off, and the second was destroyed by a penetration to the turret roof.

A North Korean-operated T-34-85 (174 Angled Seam Late). Typical of the wrecks scattered across the Korean Peninsula, the T-34 was an equal match to the M4 Sherman and M24 Chaffee but was not capable of facing the M26 Pershing or Centurion tanks fielded in the Korean War or most AT weapons. Notice a teddy bear stuffed into the driver's hatch—clearly an American addition to the vehicle.

Only at 6.30 a.m., an hour later, Dean was informed that NKPA tanks had been seen in the city. Seeing as though he felt he had no officer's work to do, he set off from his HQ with his personal aide, Lieutenant Arthur M. Clarke, and his Korean translator, Jimmy Kim, to go 'tank-hunting'.

Dean's team came to the intersection where the two T-34-85s lay knocked out, with various US ammunition carriers burning behind them. Dean reports that a seemingly undamaged fourth T-34 (in addition to the two at the intersection and the one at the railway station) tank was found in a field near some housing built for dependents of American soldiers during the American occupation. However, as the team approached the tank, they were fired upon with a high explosive shell, although its source was unclear. After retreating back to the intersection, Dean found a 0.75-ton lorry with a 57-mm recoilless rifle reversing back towards the two knocked-out T-34-85s. Dean got the driver's attention and directed him towards the tank in the field. From a suitable firing position, the gunner missed all four (or five) of his shots, being either too nervous or inexperienced with the weapon. As the weapon was out of ammunition, the lorry drove away.

After this incident, the party returned to their command post where they ate breakfast. Later that day, it was discovered that the tank had already been disabled, but Dean suggests in his memoirs that it showed no signs of damage.[3]

DEAN'S SECOND ATTEMPT

Later on, Dean went looking for more T-34-85s to destroy, and on their way, the team picked up a bazooka gunner who had only one round left. Not much longer after, they found two T-34-85s behind the burning ammunition carriers at the intersection (implying four T-34-85s were on that road, including the two knocked-out ones from earlier). The party advanced towards the tanks but had to withdraw due to machine gun fire apparently coming from the tanks' turrets. Reassessing the situation, the team advanced again from behind some buildings on the side of the street where they were protected by the smoke of the burning ammunition carriers and the cover of ruined buildings. This move allowed them to get far behind the tanks, within 10 or 15 yards of the street, but while they were sneaking up on them, the tanks had managed to turn around in the narrow street and began to move back the way they came. Not wanting to miss the opportunity, the bazooka gunner fired at the tank from a range of 100 yards, but was so nervous that he missed, with the round falling far too short.

Probably unaware of the party's presence, the tanks rolled past, getting within a mere twenty yards of them. Dean drew his .45 pistol and began firing at the second tank in sheer frustration, with rounds plinking off the armour.

With no more anti-tank weapons to hand and exploding shells from the burning ammunition carriers landing close, Dean's party withdrew. Clarke was ordered to take measurements of the tracks and armour thickness of the knocked-out tanks, and then to call in an airstrike on the retreating tanks if possible. It was then around 9 a.m., and it is believed that four of five tanks that entered the city had been destroyed.

12 P.M.–2 P.M.: HOT PURSUIT

Later, at around 12 p.m., a single T-34-85 rumbled through the town from the south going towards the frontlines at the north and west of the town. It passed by Dean's HQ and an artillery battery, not firing at all on either, but instead made its way up to the frontlines as directly as possible. Once it reached its apparent destination, it turned around and passed by the HQ again, still not firing. Dean concluded that this was likely a diversion so that the NKPA could make a major assault.

Following this, Dean began chasing the tank along with Clarke, Captain Richard Rowlands (a division liaison officer), and a South Korean Army ordnance officer, along with 'some casuals' from the regimental command post consisting of cooks, clerks, or messengers. A bazooka gunner was also found *en route* to where the tank was last reported, along with his ammunition carrier, and the team killed some enemy snipers along the way and prepared some Molotov cocktails just in case they needed them.

The team found the tank roughly half a mile south of their HQ parked at an intersection of a business area, which had two-storey buildings all around. The team entered a store that was a block away from the tank and moved through it to enter a building that was only a few yards away. However, NKPA infantry had seen the team and began to fire at them with rifles, their location possibly having been given away by a local elderly woman who pointed them out. As a result, the team withdrew and began searching for another point to attack the tank from.

Shortly after, they found a building in the corner of the intersection and Dean and the bazooka gunner made their way upstairs by clambering through an open window, leaving the rest of team scattered throughout the building downstairs. Once inside, Dean peered out the window into the street, only to find that he was staring right down the barrel of the tank from a distance of around 12 feet. Dean then signalled the bazooka gunner to come over to the window and fire at the tank's turret ring.

The first shot hit the target and the backblast shook the entire building - plaster was sent cascading down from the ceiling, and fumes filled the room. From the tank, Dean recalled hearing 'the most horrible screaming I'd ever heard', and no fire was returned from the tank or any nearby NKPA infantry. Dean ordered another shot, and then another, after which the screaming stopped, and smoke filled the street. Clarke later recalled:

> I remained by the corner of the building in front of the tank to use my Molotov cocktail on it if it began to move. The first rocket hit the tank, and the occupants began to scream and moan. The second round quieted most of the screaming and the third made it all quiet. We all then withdrew to a better observation post and observed the tank burning.

Dean also recalled that he had totally lost track of time, so after making his way back to the command post, it was almost evening.

6 P.M.–12 A.M.: THE ORDER TO RETREAT

Even despite the intense anti-tank combat, the battle raged on, but various US officers were killed or captured, and ineffective counterattacks were being organised using kitchen staff, military police, clerks, and messengers. Worse still, NKPA sniper fire was also still pinning down US artillery batteries, preventing them from being used. As a result, the order to withdraw was given at 6 p.m., but the retreat was piecemeal, with many never making it out of the city.

At dusk, Dean began his own personal retreat using various HQ vehicles which they drove in convoy to the east of the city. Here, they found that the rear of a column of lorries escorted by M24 Chaffee light tanks (which had just arrived at the battle) had been ambushed, with US infantry on one side of the road intensely battling NKPA infantry on the other. Dean's convoy began to drive through at great speed, dodging small arms fire and zigzagging to avoid burning lorries. In the confusion, Clarke, who was riding with Dean in a jeep, told him that they had missed a turn, but they decided to continue on and make the turn later. The jeep, now separated from the convoy, continued down a road towards Kumsan with sniper fire raining down on them from all sides. Eventually, they pulled over to rally with a handful of scattered soldiers but began taking heavy sniper fire. After a brief exchange of shots, Dean and Clarke, along with a handful of wounded, began to escape on foot into the pitch-dark night away from the city.

Dean escaped into the countryside with the small party, surviving on what little provisions they could find or acquire from locals. Over thirty-five days, the small party was scattered, leaving Dean alone save for another young infantryman he picked up (and later lost), as well as various local guides. Eventually, Dean employed two young locals to help him find his way back to US lines but was turned over to the NKPA by them for the equivalent of $5 (around $50 in today's money). Dean was a prisoner of war until 1953.

AFTERMATH

While American casualties were high, the NKPA had lost an estimated ten T-34-85s in the town to infantry armed with only bazookas. Estimates on the number of T-34-85s knocked out vary from account to account, but it is believed that in total, US forces managed to knock out eight tanks in or near Taejon by 11 a.m. (six by bazookas and two by artillery fire), and another two were knocked out in the afternoon. Only one of these tanks was knocked out under Dean's direct leadership.

This battle clearly demonstrated that NKPA tank crews used a mixture of effective tactics such as delivering 'tank riders' behind enemy lines to cause havoc with sniper fire, and some ineffective tactics such as advancing into urban areas without infantry support. One might speculate that had the Americans been led by a less experienced veteran, or had they more experienced bazooka gunners, the results would have been different in those respective cases.

The Americans recaptured Taejon later in 1950, and when it was recaptured, all of the tank wrecks from the battle were still around the city. American soldiers who had heard of the battle painted a slogan on the tanks: 'Knocked out 20 July 50 Under the supervision of, MajGen W.F. Dean'.

This T-34-85 (UTZ 183 Early) was knocked out in fighting for Taejon in Korea, July 1950. Unfortunately, due to a lack of photographs, it has been difficult to connect tanks in photographs with certain parts of the story.

One of the T-34-85s knocked out at Taejon, 20 July 1950. This is a T-34-85 (UTZ 183 Late), as seen by the typical UTZ 183 features such as the cast spider late-type road wheels, the strap-type fuel tank brackets, and the one-piece command cupola. Notice the 2.6-inch bazooka hit to the wood saw. (*United States Army Military History Institute*)

62

EPILOGUE: THE BEST TANK OF
THE SECOND WORLD WAR?

With regards to the raging debate on whether the T-34 was a 'good' tank or 'the best tank of the Second World War' (whatever these terms may mean), the reader should have seen from this book that the production history of the T-34 was complex and it made the vehicle heterogeneous. In other words, one T-34 from one factory would differ in quality from another—likewise for tanks made at different times (e.g. 1941 and 1943).

While it is true that the T-34's construction quality was sometimes abysmal (especially STZ-made tanks, and tanks made in 1942–1943), this was, for the most part, a result of circumstances of the war—chiefly a shortage of materials—and the need for high production figures led to a simplification of the design and rushed production. One is quick to add here, as a side note, that the intention here is not to defend the Soviet mode of production—i.e. a command economy propped up by state terror—by suggesting that it was on par in terms of production output and/or quality with any western liberal democracy and that the war explains all of the shortcomings of the Soviet economy. This is patently not true.

However, the point is that the design quality of the T-34 not only improved as the Second World War continued, but was always quite high. Indeed, the popular culture (and 'pop' history) conception of Soviet tank designers, engineers, and military scientists all as totally ill-educated, inexperienced, and incompetent proletarians is very much a hangover from the height of the Cold War and should be discarded once and for all. True, Stalin's Purges saw the imprisonment and execution of many talented and experienced skilled workers, and, indeed, many new workers, the *vydvizhentsy*, were therefore promoted to positions far beyond their rapid education courses should have permitted, but there were nonetheless many talented and skilled workers working in Soviet industry.

The T-34-85, for example, was of a much higher quality than its mid, early, and pre-war predecessors, with even small features such as the new multi-cyclone air cleaner and 9-R radio, not to mention the higher quality of finished hull and turret parts.

Furthermore, the four battles sections should have suggested to the reader that the use of sound tactics is more important to military success than the quality of one's equipment (whether modern and technologically advanced or, conversely, highly outdated and perhaps even rudimentary).

On the subject of the 'best tank of Second World War', the reader should note that every tank was built to fit a specific need at a specific time and was designed to fit a specific manufacturing process, thus the use of the term 'best' is problematic. Additionally, 'best' implies that there is some sort of universal tank design that all design bureaus across the world should be striving for. The implication is that there would be some sort of technological design convergence. While this may initially seem to be true in the case of the development of the 'Main Battle Tank' (MBT), this vehicle type came into existence in a very specific context at the height of the Cold War, where the anticipated use would be in Germany.

One might argue that in more modern warfare, which has most recently been guerrilla warfare and insurgencies in the Middle East, such a vehicle class is inappropriate. One can see this in the Syrian Civil War (2011–present) in which the Syrian Arab Army's (government forces) T-72s are being hammered by rebel rockets, thus necessitating some extreme and improvised applique armour upgrades. In other words, there is no ultimate tank concept, and therefore no 'best tank of the Second World War'. Every vehicle was designed to fit a specific geographical, temporal, military, and production context.

In fact, the T-34's initial design context is often overlooked. To be sure, it was a pre-war design aimed at being a high-quality stop-gap vehicle while other designs were worked on such as the T-50 and T-34M. However, due to the outbreak of war in 1941, it was suddenly made the Red Army's main tank. As a result, it was simplified throughout its production to become easy to mass-produce, and the design was updated and upgraded to make it more combat viable as time went on. Indeed, the T-34's origins were humbler than its wartime (and, indeed, post-war) legends presuppose.

Furthermore, one might wish to compare the T-34 to tanks of the same classification. However, one must remember that terms such as 'medium tank' are just arbitrarily applied categories, mostly for bureaucratic simplicity and also differ in definition from state to state, thus meaning that it might be highly inappropriate to compare one tank to another just because they come under the same category.

For example, the T-34 was built as a general-purpose vehicle (as clearly discerned by the focus on a compromise between speed and armour, and the adoption of the multirole 76-mm gun), whereas the German Panzer V (Panther) is understood to have been a tank-killer of sorts. The M4 Sherman, Panzer III and IV, and Matilda tanks might be more somewhat more appropriate comparisons, being designed and produced roughly contemporarily and fitting the same 'general tank' role, but if one were to make such comparisons, one must remember the crucial details: they were built by different states with different factories, different resources, different military doctrines and war necessities, different front lines, and different military and production experiences, and any given version of these highly heterogeneous tanks is not representative of the vehicle series as a whole.

For example, one cannot imagine using the M4A3(75)W Sherman to talk about all Shermans, or the Panzer IV Ausf. D to talk about all Panzer IVs, in just the same way one cannot use the T-34 (UTZ Final Early Turret) to talk about all T-34s. Thus, the single T-34 which was tested at Aberdeen Proving Grounds in 1943 in the USA is not adequate proof of 'the T-34 being trash'—although one hastens to add that much (not all) of the critique on both design and production flaws in the reports were valid not just to that specific and individual vehicle, but to Soviet production as a whole—and instead a much broader overview, considering the sum of all technical and combat evidence, is needed to make any valid assessment of the T-34.

Such an investigation would require an inconceivably large amount of materials to be delved through and understood, and this could take more than a lifetime. Nonetheless, the results of such an investigation are easy to predict. As Boris Kavalerchik ('Once Again About the T-34', p. 187) summarises: 'Any piece of equipment, including tanks, has its own virtues and shortcomings.'

APPENDIX

TECHNICAL DRAWINGS

T-34

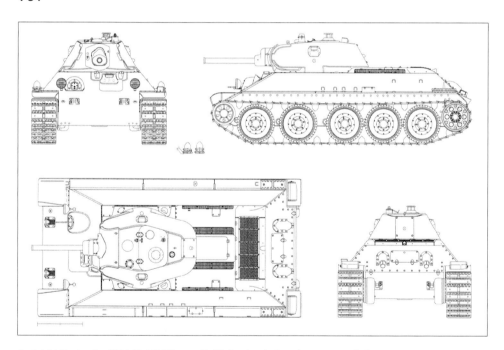

An Initial Production T-34 (A-34) (Chapter 8). Notice the glacis and nose are made from one piece.

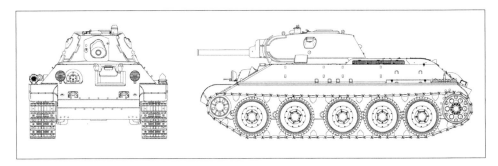

A T-34 (L-11 Gun Last Production) (pages 80–93). There is no POP periscope in the turret hatch, and many of the improvements of the April Report have been implemented.

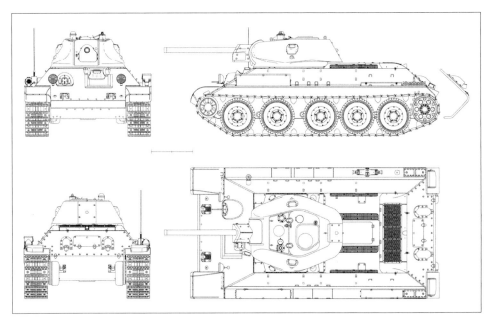

A pre-war T-34 (F-34 Gun) (pages 94–104). Notice the large gun cleaning toolbox and, in this case, a four-bolt rear turret hatch.

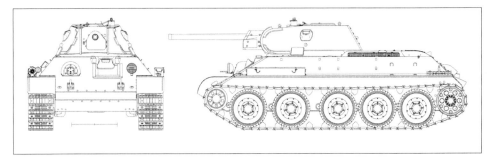

A T-34 (KhPZ 183 8-Bolt Turret) (pages 119–127). The gun-cleaning toolbox has been reduced in size, and the track toolbox has been moved from left to right. Note one jack and a hull-mounted jack block.

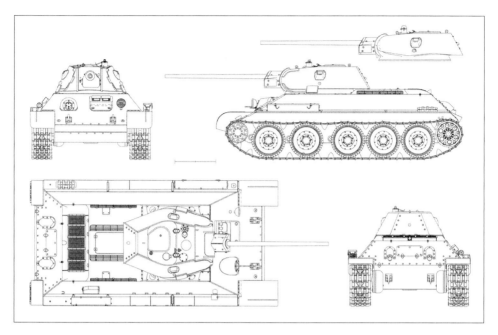

A T-34 with ZiS-4 (Chapter 18). Both an eight-bolt turret and a cast turret have been depicted with the gun, both of which exist in photographic evidence. The track is the V-type 41 track, and the chassis lacks hardpoints for fuel tanks.

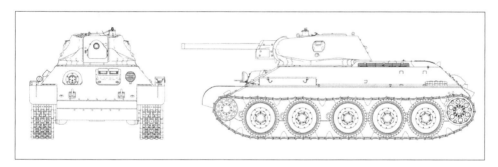

A T-34 (KhPZ 183 Last Production) (Chapter 17). There are no hardpoints for fuel tanks on the hull sides, and the driver's hatch is of a new pattern that is cast. The track depicted is V-type waffle track, introduced in summer 1942, whereas the tank was manufactured in October 1941.

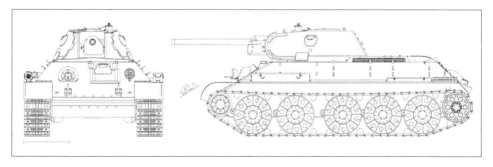

A T-34 (STZ Cast Wheels) (pages 172–174). The fuel tank layout is typical of STZ T-34s from September to December 1941. Note the STZ tow hooks.

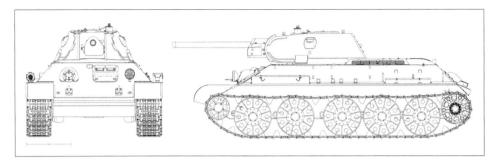

A T-34 (STZ Interlocking Hull) (pages 174–179). Fuel tanks have been reduced to four, and the shovel stowage has been moved back to the left hull side.

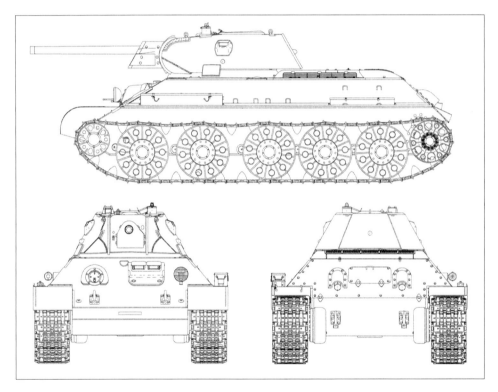

A T-34 (STZ Welded Turret Back) (pages 192–198). The road wheels are the later pattern, with reinforcing rims around the cut-outs. No fuel tank stowage is provided, and much of the rear plate has been redesigned for simplicity. Note the chiselled gun recuperator armour designed at the Barrikady Gun Factory.

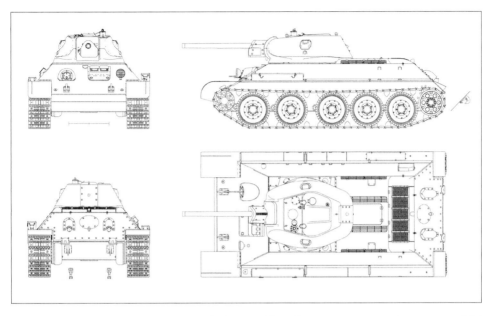

A T-34 (112 Simplified Stowage) (pages 204–208). The rear of the tank is unique to Krasnoye Sormovo 112 and did not change much at this factory once implemented. This depiction is without fuel tanks, but some simplified stowage T-34s retained a single fuel tank at the rear left of the tank.

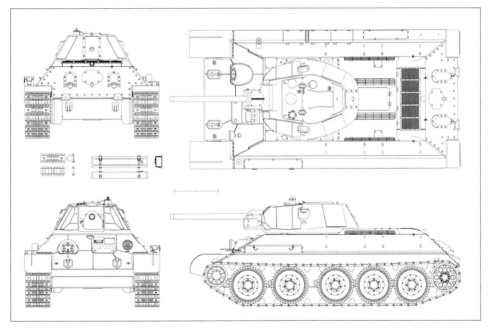

A Plated T-34 (112 Early) (pages 222–228). A seven-part glacis plate is depicted—the most common glacis plate. The turret has the standard turret plate arrangement, but this changed a lot throughout plated production.

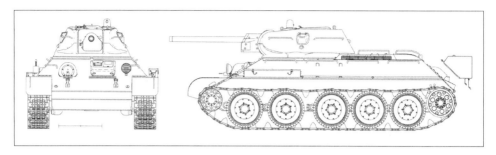

A T-34 (112 with Handrails) (pages 212–219 and 268). Handrails cover the tank, and exterior fuel tanks were provided. Fillets were placed around the upper hull around the turret to protect it from enemy fire.

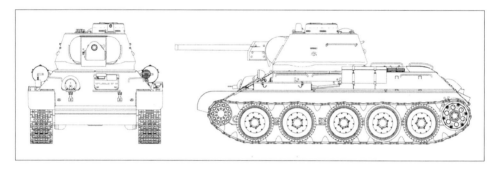

A T-34 (112 Soft Edge with Cupola) (pages 279–280). Drum-type fuel tanks were used at this stage in production, and a wood saw was provided. Also, the glacis plate did not interlock with the side plate. Krasnoye Sormovo 112 only issued soft-edge turrets.

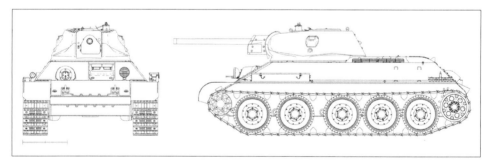

A Plated T-34 (UTZ 183 Early) (pages 162–164). The glacis plate is typical of UTZ 183 T-34s. The drive wheel is still the early type, but the later ribbed-type drive wheel was also used.

Opposite below: A T-34 (UTZ 183 Early Production Composite) (pages 238–246). The wheel set has changed to be a single pressed-type road wheel, with four cast spider-type road wheels. These were a mixture of thin-type and regular thickness wheels. An additional plate on the glacis is depicted but was very rare on these vehicles. Additionally, the rear plate is rounded here.

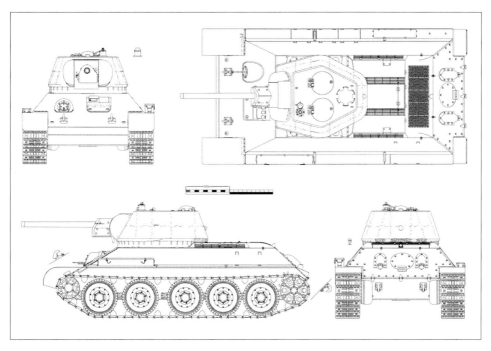

Above: A T-34 (UTZ 183 Initial Production Composite) (pages 234–238). This example has an angled rear plate, but many retained the rounded rear plate. The composite-type turret has an air extractor fan dome with six cut-outs. The MG blister is unamplified, and the mesh radiator cover is tied down with leather buckles.

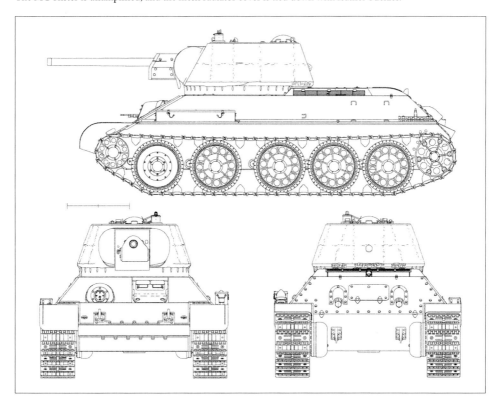

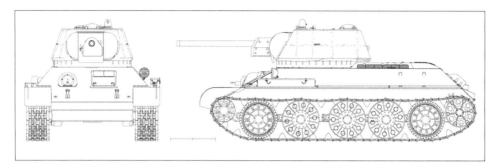

A T-34 (UTZ 183 Standard Production Composite) (pages 245–258). The wheel set is standardised, with three inner cast steel-rimmed type road wheels, flanked either side by a cast spider-type wheel. The track is the V-type waffle track. The turret air extractor dome has four cut-outs, and the periscope is a PT-4-7. The MG blister is amplified.

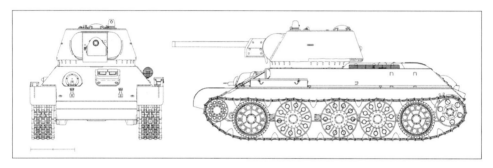

The profile of a T-34 (UTZ 183 Hard-Edge Early) (pages 258–265). A new turret is on the chassis, and the drive wheel is the simplified type. This drive wheel lacked return rollers for the track teeth.

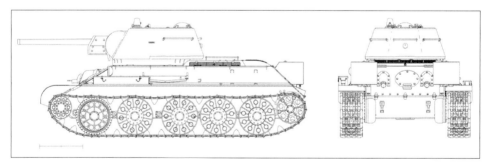

A T-34 (Hard-Edge Late) (page 277). Handrails cover the tank, and a wood saw is placed onto the hull side. The tracks depicted are the rare V-type waffle track, but the 500-mm waffle-type track was the norm.

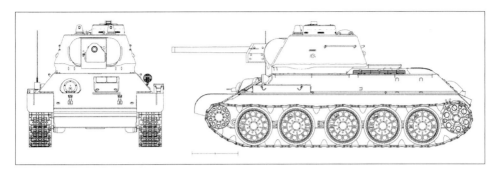

A T-34 (Soft-Edge with Cupola) (page 281). All of the road wheels are the cast spider late type. The track is a Finnish-made type. The tank would have drum-type fuel tanks.

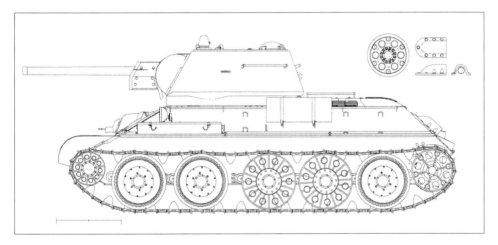

A T-34 (ChKZ Intermediate) (pages 289–299). Before October 1942, all of the wheels were cast, with the first wheel being a cast spider type, but from late October through until December, pressed-type wheels were introduced, then slowly made standard. Exhaust shrouds are the sunken type. A bracket for a toolbox is between the fuel drum and the gun-cleaning toolbox.

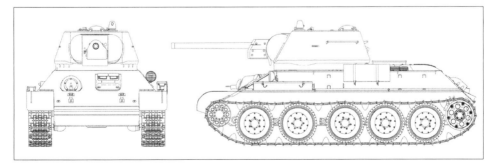

A T-34 (ChKZ Standard Production) (pages 294, 297–301, 310, and 434). All road wheels are the pressed type. The ChKZ 100 T-34s changed little until the introduction of a command cupola.

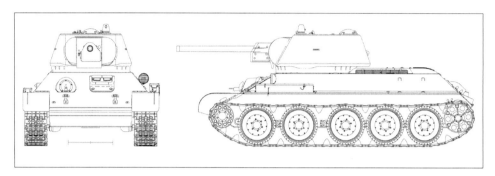

A T-34 (UTZM Standard Production) (pages 307–310). The wheels are the pressed type, and the track is the split-type track. Handrails were introduced in September and UTZ box-type fuel tanks in October 1942.

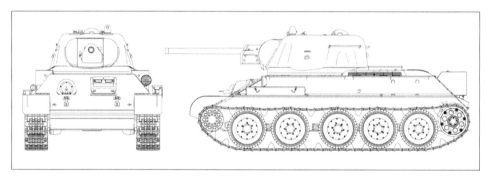

A T-34 (UTZM Pressed Turret) (page 313). The pressed turret was issued between all of the plants, but UTZM made it and issued it first. It was marginally larger than the soft-edge turrets and slightly stronger.

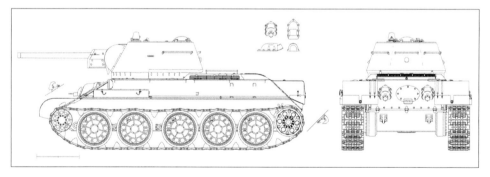

A T-34 (174 Early Production) (pages 315–317). The cast spider-type road wheels and Omsk 174 type fuel tanks were common. Notice the distinctive tow hooks that were of a much earlier pattern than what was being used elsewhere. For the most part, these would not be redesigned and are a defining feature of Omsk 174 T-34s.

Opposite above: An OT-34 (174 with Cupola) (pages 324–326). The tank displays many features commonly associated with Omsk 174, including the bent handrails, smooth tow hooks, and the Omsk 174 pattern of rear hinges. OT-34s from Omsk 174 had the radio placed in the turret as no crewman sat behind the MG blister (where a 200-l tank of propellant was placed instead).

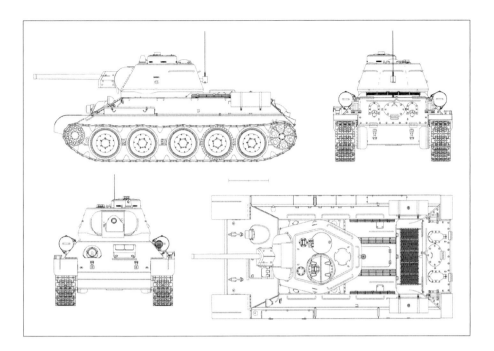

T-34-85

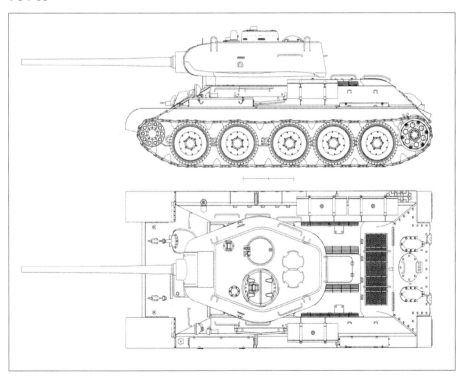

A T-34-85 (112 Initial Production) (pages 351–354). The command cupola is forward of the bend in the turret as the turret was designed for two crewmen, not three. The tank still retains many features that would soon be dropped, such as the glacis handrails. The turret has a PT-4-7 and an MK-4 episcope. The track toolbox was moved temporarily back to the left hull side.

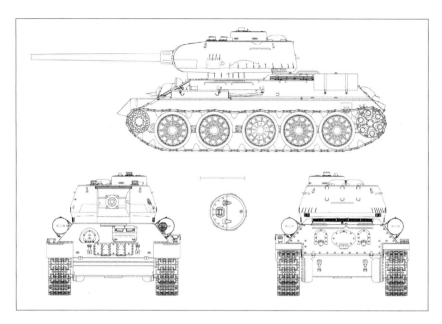

A T-34-85 (UTZ 183 Late) (pages 380–396). UTZ 183 T-34-85s did not go through major changes. Depicted is the wider 90-mm cupola with a single hatch door. The middle road wheel is a cast spider-type, whereas the other wheels are cast spider late-type wheels.

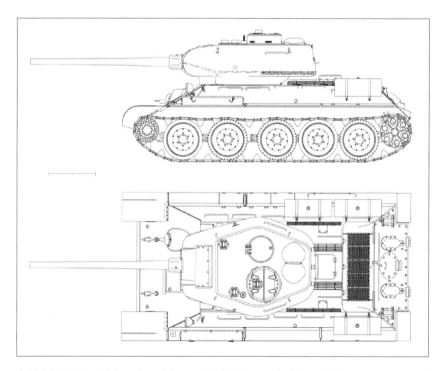

A T-34-85 (174 Angled Seam Turret) (pages 396–402). Depicted with two different patterns of road wheels, and the distinctive Omsk 174 rain cover. These turrets were used in the Second World War but were only seen at the very closing stages of the conflict.

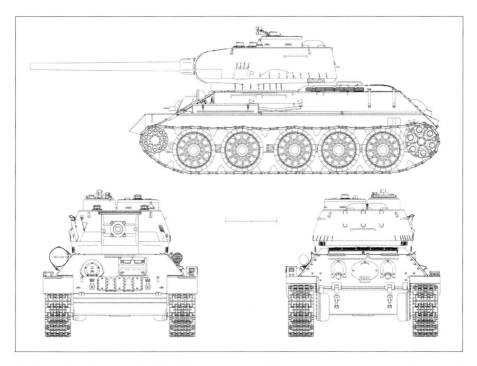

A Chinese Type 58 (pages 495–500). Chinese upgrades include a second cupola, equipped with a Type 54 mount, a set of Type 54 stowage hardpoints on the turret cheek, and a torsion bar lock for the rear plate. All models of Soviet T-34-85s were converted but depicted is a UTZ 183 T-34.

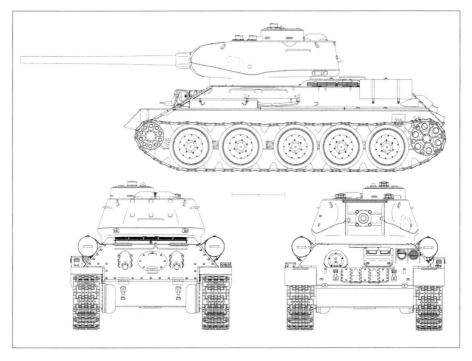

A T-34-85 (Martin 1952–56) (pages 467–469). The distinctive T-55 headlights on the glacis plate can be clearly seen, along with the unique turret castings, hull buzzer, and rear hinges. CKD T-34s differed by having a caged headlight and cast road wheels.

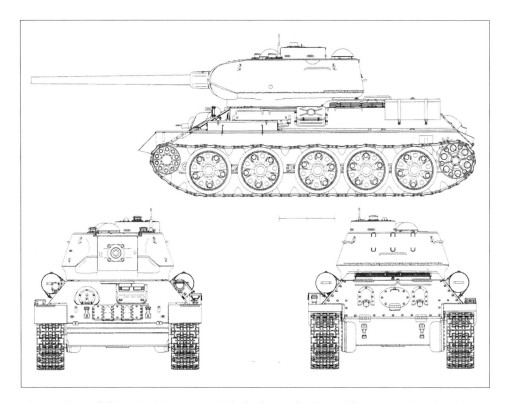

A T-34-85 (174 Angled Seam Late) (pages 396–400) that has been updated to Model 1969 standard. The basic changes include the new 'starfish' road wheels, infrared optics, and new stowage bins. Sometimes, tow rope stowage was placed on the hull side next to the tool kit, and sometimes another drum-type fuel tank was added.

OPPOSITE PAGE:

Above: All of the following tracks were used between April 1940 and December 1942: 1. Initial Production 550-mm track, KhPZ. 2. Reinforced 550-mm type, KhPZ, STZ and 112. 3. Reinforced 550-mm late type (seen in late 1941 and 1942), KhPZ, STZ and 112. 4. Double chevron V-type (T-34M track), KhPZ. 5. V-type 41, KhPZ and UTZ. 6. 'V-type 42', UTZ. 7. V-type waffle, UTZ, ChKZ. 8. 550-mm waffle pattern 1941, STZ and 112. 9. 550-mm waffle-pattern 1942, UTZ (rare), STZ and 112.

Below: All of the following tracks were used between August 1942 and the end of T-34 production in 1956: 10. 500-mm waffle-pattern (Initial production), 112. 11. 500-mm waffle pattern (Standard from October 1942 until the end of T-34 production) UTZ, 112, ChKZ, UTZM, 174, Brumar (Poland) CKD and Martin (Czechoslovakia). 12. 500-mm waffle pattern, 174. 13. 500-mm waffle pattern, 112 (October 1943–December 1944). 14. V-type ChKZ, ChKZ. 15. V-type ChKZ split type, ChKZ. 16. 500-mm split-type, ChKZ and UTZM. 17. 500-mm split late-type, ChKZ and UTZM. 18. 500-mm waffle pattern, 112 (T-34-85). 19. 500-mm waffle pattern (reinforced toothless links, very rare). 20. Finnish casting for toothed links.

T-34 TRACK TYPES

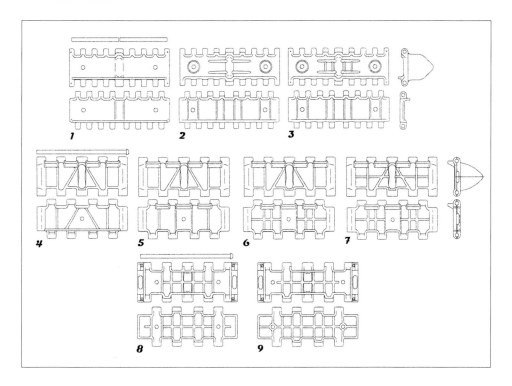

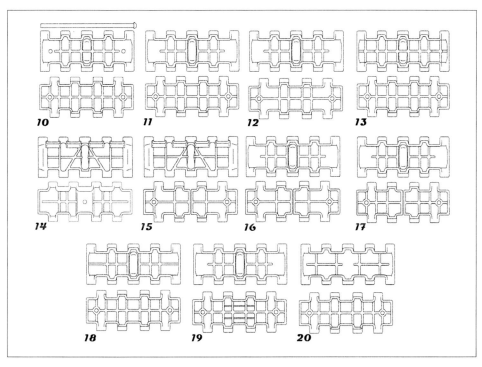

ENDNOTES

CHAPTER 3

1   Our summary of the Spanish Civil War's outbreak is evidently a gross simplification, but a more nuanced exploration would be irrelevant to the purpose of this section, explaining how the Spanish Civil War influenced Soviet tank design. For a 'pop history' of the Spanish Civil War, see Beevor, A., *The Battle for Spain: The Spanish Civil War 1936–1939* (London: Phoenix, 2006). For a concise but more academic history, see Payne, S. G., *The Spanish Civil War* (Cambridge: Cambridge University Press, 2012). For a concise pro-Soviet (albeit 'pop history') perspective, see Preston, P., *The Spanish Civil War: Reaction, Revolution and Revenge* (London: William Collins, 2016). Pro-Nationalist histories, such as those by Ricardo de la Cierva, have not been reproduced in English.

2   Delving into a deep historiographical discussion on Stalin's decision to intervene in Spain is not the purpose of this chapter either. For the 'anti-Nazi collective security thesis', see Payne, S. G., *The Spanish Civil War* (Cambridge: Cambridge University Press, 2012), pp. 149–159. See also Kowalsky, D., 'Operation X: Soviet Russia and the Spanish Civil War', *Bulletin of Spanish Studies* 91 (2014), pp. 159–178, for a historiographical discussion on Soviet involvement, as well as a concise but academic overview of Soviet operations in Spain.

3   Such discrepancies in the story of the Battle of Seseña are also common in secondary sources, too. One can compare the accounts in Beevor's *The Battle for Spain: The Spanish Civil War 1936–1939*, Zaloga's 'Soviet Tank Operations in the Spanish Civil War' (*The Journal of Slavic Military Studies* 12, 1999), and various internet sources to see immediate discrepancies in the sequence of events, levels of detail, and the actual events themselves. Our telling of the battle is based on the one written by Artemio Mortera-Peréz in *Los Medios Blindados en la Guerra Civil Española: Teatro de Operaciones de Andalucía y Centro 36/39* (Valladolid: AF Editores, 2009), pp. 88–97, which uses not only Soviet accounts of the battle, but also first-hand accounts from Nationalist soldiers. However, one is quick to note that his re-telling of events, while authoritative in terms of its use of sources, is tinged with pro-Nationalist sentiment. Moreover, his use of oral history sources is problematic for the usual reasons associated with oral history.

4   The exact value of 500 pesetas is difficult to pin down, but it was undoubtedly a huge sum for most Spaniards at the time, especially as wages were exceptionally low for soldiers and agrarian and industrial workers alike. It is thought that during the civil war, 500 pesetas would be around three month's wages, as Nationalist militiamen were paid around 5 pesetas a day, and this does not appear to have changed during the war. However, this does not account for the huge devaluation in the currency that took place during the civil war and changes in purchasing power, especially as some goods became more or less available (although this was more of a problem on the Republican side). For comparison, soldiers from Republican International Brigades were paid 30 pesetas a day, with 20 pesetas going to the family of the soldier. For another (but perhaps inappropriate) comparison, 500 pesetas is approximately equal to 892 euros in 2017, which is more than a month's minimum

wage today (currently 600–650 euros). Figures calculated using 1937 as the base for a basic purchasing power calculator at measuringworth.com/calculators/spaincompare/

5 The 'Chevrolet BC' (also known as the AAC-1937 or AAC-37) was a heavy armoured car produced by the Republicans at Factory 22 at Unión Naval de Levante factory in Barcelona in 1937–1939. The same complex had built an earlier 4 × 4 light armoured car series known as the 'UNL-35', which was heavily influenced by Soviet designs such as the FAI (although the UNL-35 was a major improvement).

The design was clearly based on the BA-6 armoured car, but differed in its details, as can be seen by close inspection of the engine deck (especially engine deck hatches), and the rear of the vehicle, which has different angles, too. The Republicans designed a small turret, somewhat resembling a BAI turret, which housed antiquated Soviet 37-mm guns (250 of which arrived in April 1938) as used on vehicles such as the T-18 and BA-27, and usually had a coaxial machine gun. However, it is also clear that various Soviet turrets from BA-6s, BT-5s, and T-26s were salvaged and placed onto the chassis, but these were much rarer.

Due to Nationalist air raids, production throughout 1938 was staggered, and only around 100 were built in total. Many were captured and reused by Nationalist forces and remained in service in the post-civil war era.

Some were still operated by Republican units when they retreated into France in 1939 and these were confiscated by French authorities at the border. It seems as though a handful were used in combat by the French in May 1940, but these were quickly captured (others perhaps were captured in depots, according to photographic evidence). In turn, these were reused by German forces as a policing vehicle near Leningrad in 1941 (some having received modifications, such as turrets removed or replaced with AA machine gun mounts) until they were all destroyed or captured. It is sometimes wrongly stated that they were used as an infiltration vehicle due to their resemblance to the BA-6; this claim originates from Zaloga, S. J. and Grandsen, J., *Tanks Illustrated No. 16: Operation Barbarossa* (London: Arms and Armour Press, 1985), but is an entirely baseless claim.

On the subject of salvaged turrets, at least one Nationalist-operated Hispano Suiza MC-36 (a pre-civil war armoured car series) had its original turret replaced with a Soviet one (whether from a T-26, BT-5, BA-3, or BA-6 is unknown) and was photographed on a victory parade in Seville on 17 April 1939. During the civil war, it is reported to have been the command car for *Agrupación de Carros del Ejército del Sur* and was used in the post-civil war era.

6 In fact, the T-26 is believed to have remained in Spanish service until at least 1961 with one unit in Barcelona. While the tank was regarded as an excellent design during the civil war, the Spanish felt that they should keep the vehicle in their stocks to make up numbers. Spain was something of a pariah state following the civil war, so they had little opportunity to buy arms from abroad. More modern tanks were received in 1943 from Germany including twenty Panzer IV Ausf. Hs and ten StuG IIIs, but these were too few to replace the T-26 altogether. The Spanish also attempted to design indigenous tanks to replace their older vehicles with projects including the Verdeja No. 1 (a project which took place between 1938–1945) and Verdeja No. 2 (1941–1950), but these were unsuccessful projects, the former being too outdated on its conception, and the latter due to a lack of funding. As a result, most T-26s are believed to have been phased out in the mid–late 1950s, following vast American arms sales through the Madrid Pact of 1953 including thirty-one M24 Chaffees, twenty-eight M37 105-mm HMCs, thirty-eight M41 Walker Bulldogs, and several other troop transporters and engineer vehicles.

7 At this juncture, it is also worth briefly mentioning that partly as a result of the experience in Spain it was decided that the T-26 was in serious need of a deep modernisation or complete replacement, too. Moderate attempts were made to thicken the tank's armour from 12–20 mm, this being the bare minimum required to stop 20-mm rounds for piercing the tank. However, from late 1937, more serious attempts were made at improving the T-26. The T-46-5 prototype (also known as the T-111) was not only a major attempt at improving the T-26 but was also the USSR's first shell-proof tank design—a feature also required of the T-34. These developments ultimately led to the T-50 light tank, which was going to be the Red Army's main tank if it were not for the outbreak of war against Germany in 1941, as explained on pages 67–70.

CHAPTER 4

1 Rivals using this political context against each other was an exceptionally common occurrence. For more examples, see Clark, K. and Dobrenko, E., *Soviet Culture and Power: A History in Documents, 1917–1953* (London: Yale University Press, 2007), pp. 322–335. The chapter consists of letters to Stalin about releasing people from, and sending people to, the 'Gulag'.

CHAPTER 7

1　The T-34 also replaced some medium tanks in the Red Army such as the T-24 and T-28. The T-24 was accepted for production in 1929, but only twenty were manufactured at the KhPZ. These tanks spent most of their early career waiting for their main armament, which finally arrived in 1932. However, by this time, the T-28 tank was already being designed, so the T-24 project was cancelled and the constructed T-24s led a very active career training crews. T-24s were later intended to be dug-in bunkers during the most desperate months of Operation Barbarossa in 1941 featuring a T-28's front turret section mounted onto the turrets, as well as being fitted with various Maxim machine guns.

　　The T-28 was designed in 1932 and put into production in 1933. The tank was somewhat of a copy of the British Medium Mark III, which was measured illegally by Semyon Alexandrovich Ginzburg in 1930. The tank had three turrets, one with a 76.2-mm KT-28 (or L-10 gun from 1938), and in the two smaller turrets, a single DT-29 machine gun was placed in a ball mount. Some 503 T-28s were manufactured between 1933 and 1940. They were in service with the Red Army until 1944, but most were lost in 1941.

CHAPTER 10

1　In fact, both the US and Britain had conducted tests of the T-34 and KV-1 using vehicles supplied to them by the Soviets as part of a 'reverse Lend-Lease'. The so-called Aberdeen Assessment, as we have called it, or 'Assessment of the T-34 and KV Tanks by Workers from the US Aberdeen Proving Ground, Business Representatives, Officers, and Members of the Military Committees Who Conducted Tests of the Tanks', to give it its full title, is a rather long document prepared by the USA in 1943.

　　On 3 June 1942, written orders were sent from Moscow to Lieutenant-Colonel Kozyrev, at UTZ 183 to prepare three T-34s for shipment within a month. One tank was to be sent to the US. UTZ 183 was chosen because it was the factory that produced the highest quality of tanks at the time, but one must remember that this was a period during which the T-34 was at its lowest overall production quality ever. The three tanks produced for the shipment were the absolute latest in terms of production changes, meaning that they were T-34 (UTZ Final Early Turret)s, and they were prepared for shipment by being cleaned thoroughly inside and out. Three layers of paint to prevent corrosion, for example, was given to them, which was non-standard. Technical manuals and drawings were also prepared along with the shipment. In August 1942, a T-34 and a KV was sent to the US, and another T-34 and KV were sent to the UK in June 1943 after severe delays of ten months.

　　Testing of the T-34 and KV began in the USA at Aberdeen Proving Grounds, the US equivalent of Kubinka Proving Grounds, on 29 November 1942, testing all things from the gun, armour, electronics, and driving performances of both vehicles. The British undertook similar trials.

　　Reports were made by both the US and UK, but they remain to be fully published as far as the authors of this book are aware.

　　The best summary and scholarly discussion of the Aberdeen Assessment can be found in Kavalerchik, B., 'Once Again About the T-34', *The Journal of Slavic Military Studies* 28 (2015), pp. 186–214.

2　POP episcope appears not to have an official name, and POP itself seems to be an acronym for 'Panoramic Periscope'. The only documentation about the device comes from January 1941, when they were ordered to be removed. In this document, it was referred to as 'all-round vision device' (Russian: 'универсальное зрение').

CHAPTER 11

1　Not much is known about the T-50's combat debut or performance on the battlefield because they were lost so early on. Despite this, it was undoubtedly the most potent light tank available to the Soviet Union in 1941, and indeed, years to come. What is known, however, is that the T-50, both in 1941 and in the present day, often gets confused with the T-34. The silhouettes of the tank are similar, but the T-50 was much smaller, had a smaller gun, torsion bar suspension, and higher ground clearance of the hull. The Finnish Army captured and took into its ranks a T-50, which they even named the vehicle *Little Sotka*, while the T-34 was named *Big Sotka* (Sotka being a species of waterbird), thus indicating how contemporaries often thought the two tanks looked the same.

CHAPTER 13

1　Calibre is an artillery measurement, by taking the bore diameter, and multiplying it until one reaches the barrel length, so 76.2 mm × 40 = 3,048 mm (3.048 metres).

CHAPTER 40

1   The Object 238 (commonly, but wrongly, known as the 'KV-85G') was an attempt to place an 85-mm S-53 gun into the turret of a KV-1S as a stopgap heavy tank before the new IS-1 entered service. Trials were conducted but it was found that the turret was too small to effectively use the weapon. However, at that time, the IS-1 turret was being tested on a KV-1S chassis. This KV-1S/IS-1 hybrid testbed entered comparative trials and was suddenly accepted for service as the KV-85 with some minor modifications, such as the hull DT being removed.

CHAPTER 52

1   An in-depth exploration of *Beutepanzer* T-34s goes beyond this book's aims. Moreover, an excellent book was recently published specifically on them. See Vollert, J., *Panzerkampfwagen T 34-747(r): The Soviet T-34 Tank as Beutepanzer and Panzerattrappe in German Wehrmacht Service 1941–45* (Erlangen: Tankograd, 2013).

CHAPTER 59

1   The Katyn Massacre (April–May 1940) was a series of mass executions of members of the Polish intelligentsia, especially the captured army officer corps, by the Soviet NKVD (Secret Police) outside of Smolensk, with an estimated 22,000 victims. The graves were discovered by the Germans in 1943, at which point the Polish government-in-exile demanded an immediate International Red Cross investigation, following which Stalin severed ties with them. Although some (chiefly Russian or pro-Communist) historians deny Soviet involvement (or that this event even took place) there is exceptionally strong evidence to suggest that the Soviets were responsible. Irrespective of this debate, the discovery of murdered Poles certainly impacted Soviet-Polish relations.

On the Katyn massacre see Sandford, G., 'The Katyn Massacre and Polish-Soviet Relations, 1941–43', *Journal of Contemporary History* 41 (2006), pp. 95–111, and Sterio, M., 'Katyn Forest Massacre: Of Genocide, State Lies, and Secrecy', *Case Western Reserve Journal of International Law* 44 (2012), pp. 615–631.

For a typical pro-Soviet or pro-Communist denial of the Katyn massacre, see Furr, G., 'The "Official" Version of the Katyn Massacre Disproven?', *Socialism and Democracy* 27 (2013), pp. 96–129.

CHAPTER 60

1   It is not necessary to reproduce a history of the Chinese Civil War for the purpose of this section. See Westad, O. E., *Decisive Encounters: The Chinese Civil War, 1946–1950* (Stanford: Stanford University Press, 2003) for a concise but academic history, which combines political, international, and some military perspectives, and remains one of the better works on the war in English. See also for a concise bibliography on the Chinese Civil War.

For a more focused military history, see Chassin, L. M., *The Communist Conquest of China: A History of the Chinese Civil War 1945-49* (Cambridge: Cambridge University Press, 1965).

For a thematic study on the decline of the Kuomintang regime (with a much broader temporal scope), see Eastman, L. E., *Seeds of Destruction: Nationalist China in War and Revolution, 1937-1949* (Stanford: Stanford University Press, 2002).

N.B. Most English language publications on the Chinese Civil War are either political histories (typically with a disproportionate focus on US involvement, seen to some extent in Westad's *Decisive Encounters*) or are oversimplified 'pop-histories' that serve only as an introduction (see Lynch, M., *The Chinese Civil War 1945–49 (Essential Histories)* (Oxford: Osprey Publishing, 2010) for an example). The most detailed studies on the Chinese Civil War tend to be only available in Chinese, but one must be selective and cautious due to the influence of the CCP on Chinese historiography, especially regarding the earliest works.

2   'Gongchen Tank' is a famous piece of PRC 'folklore' within the PRC, but the story has not been picked up on by western historians despite the tank standing today in a museum in Beijing. That said, it is almost certain that the story is a typical CCP myth which is totally fictional. For an account of 'Gongchen Tank', see Will Kerrs' retelling at tanks-encyclopedia.com/ww2/china/gongchen_tank

3   This is also a vehicle that is little commented on by western sources. It was only recently that a photograph showing this tank was discovered and the story was pieced together. See Will Kerrs' article at tanks-encyclopedia.com/ww2/china/m4a2-sherman-in-chinese-service/

4   We include the supposed story of Chinese production of T-34-85s very tentatively - In fact, we were very close to dismissing it entirely. However, we include it (albeit with major caveats made clear) because it is a story that has gained some considerable traction on 'the Chinese side of the internet' through forums (although

no concrete proof has been put forward to support it). One must also consider that stories of the Chinese production of T-34-85s have proliferated following the release of a video game featuring many fake tanks, or real tanks featuring fake or ahistorical guns, engines, radios, and so on. For a typical example of the 'Chinese T-34-85 production' story, see tieba.baidu.com/p/4908818042?pn=2

5   There is a debate as to whether the designation 'Type 58' is an unofficial name or not. Modern Chinese sources only use the name 'T-34-85' and state that it is difficult to declare with certainty that Type 58 was ever officially used, referring either to regular T-34-85s, or upgraded T-34-85s. Chinese museums use the modern western designation 'T-34/85', although this is not positive confirmation that the name was never used.

One source reports that the name came from the 12.7-mm Type 54 machine gun being upgraded in the late 1950s to feature high-altitude sights, with such upgraded models being known as Type 58 (although this is unconfirmed), and these were installed as part of the Type 58 upgrade. Other sources say that the name comes from the package being created in 1958. Others, still, suggest that it is because the T-34-85 was intended to be locally produced in the PRC in 1958. These claims are unconvincing.

It is the authors' belief that Type 58 is an unofficial name made up in recent years, given that there is absolutely no available evidence to support its official use. Thus, any attempt to explain the name Type 58 such as above are merely ex post facto rationalisations. Regardless, for the sake of differentiation, tanks with the upgrade package can be referred to as Type 58, and those without as T-34-85.

For updates on this vehicle, follow Will Kerrs' article at tanks-encyclopedia.com/coldwar/China/Type-58.php

6   The PRC make quite bold claims about their use of armour during the Korean War. Perhaps the most famous story is of T-34-85 No. 215, of which variations exist, but is generally as follows:

T-34-85 No. 215 and two other T-34-85s belonging to the 2nd Tank Division of the 2nd Tank Regiment (of the PVA) were deployed along with elements of the 200th Infantry Regiment on 6 July 1953. Their task was to fortify positions on Hill 346.6 (known as 石砚洞北山 to the Chinese) against the advancing American 7th Infantry Division.

Upon arriving at the hill on 7 July, the T-34-85s were tasked to find and destroy three M46 Patton tanks reported in the area. The T-34-85s took up ambush positions around the hill, but unfortunately, the Americans were able to hear their engines roar as they were approaching, thus ruining the element of surprise for the PVA. The Americans began to barrage the Chinese positions with artillery and as a result, '215' was inadvertently entrenched between two artillery craters and was unable to get out.

The Chinese were met with a serious dilemma. Would they abandon the tank and lose a large part of their firepower or would they concentrate manpower on digging the tank out? In the end, the crew of 215 spent half the day attempting to dig the tank out with help from infantry but were unsuccessful. It was only until the day got dark when the crew gave up and instead decided to make do with their current situation by camouflaging the tank with mud and foliage.

The following day, the Chinese began their assault, and three American M46 Pattons appeared to fend off the Chinese infantry. Upon revealing themselves the Pattons immediately came under fire from 215. At a range of approximately 1,450 m, the first Patton was reported to have been taken out with a single armour-piercing shot which caused an ammo rack explosion. The second Patton was seemingly also reported to have been taken out with a single shot at approximately the same range. The third Patton, however, was taking cover behind a hill that prevented 215 from hitting it. As such, 215 fired twelve high-explosive rounds at the hill that exposed the Patton. A couple of these shells supposedly hit the Patton and crippled it.

Having somehow not attracted any attention, 215 waited for night to fall, at which point it began revving its engine in such a manner as to make it sound as though the tank was reversing away. A PVA artillery unit then rescued 215 from the crater and the tank escaped down a road.

At this point, 215 encountered another column of three Pattons. Cunningly, the crew waited in a nearby woods until the column was close, and then somehow stealthily joined the column as the second tank. No. 215 stayed with the column until the convoy reached a US checkpoint, at which point 215 destroyed the Patton behind it (thus trapping the rearmost Patton), chased down and destroyed the leading Patton, and also proceeded to destroy a number of US bunkers and supply lorries. No. 215 escaped and the crew were celebrated as heroes, with the tank still standing today in the Tank Museum, Beijing.

Undoubtedly, this story is untrue because there are no records of these Pattons being lost at this stage of the war (although in a private conversation with the authors, Steven Zaloga advises that US records were poorly kept). In fact, the story fits in well with other CCP myths such as 'Gongchen Tank' and the more famous (although non-tank related) story of 'Comrade Lei Feng' and should therefore be dismissed as fake.

7   The North Vietnamese Army's first armoured unit is believed to have been formed in October 1959 consisting of an estimated thirty-five T-34-85s supplied to them by the USSR. Exact numbers of the T-34-85 supplied to the NVA are difficult to trace, but it can be tentatively assumed that they were supplied perhaps around 90-180 as ballpark figures. Similarly, the number of SU-76s is difficult to trace, but it can be assumed that they had even fewer of these than they did T-34-85s, although when the first batch of these arrived is unclear.

A declassified CIA Intelligence Memorandum dated May 1969 reports that thirty T-34-85s and twenty SU-76s were delivered in 1965 (with another thirty of the latter in 1967), but this is not all of the T-34-85s and SU-76s received. These tanks saw little service because they were so old, hence why some were converted to SPAAGs.

One T-34-85 regiment saw service at the Quang Tri Offensive in 1972 near the DMZ but was reportedly destroyed by American B-52 bombers.

The NVA also received an unknown number of SU-100s, some of which are in museums today, although some are still apparently in service.

All of the old Soviet vehicles are believed to be Soviet-supplied, as there is no evidence that the PRC supplied the NVA with any of their SU-100s, SU-76s, T-34-85s, or Type 58s. Furthermore, many of the NVA's T-34-85s are T-34-85Ms, a Soviet-only upgrade. Some NVA T-34-85s were also Polish-built.

More commonly seen NVA tanks include the T-55 and PT-76, although photos of captured American armour (including the M41 Walker Bulldog, M24 Chaffee, M113 APC, and others) are often circulated on the internet for their spectacular nature.

For some tentative remarks on the NVA's armour during the Vietnam War, see Green, M., *Armoured Warfare in the Vietnam War: Rare Photographs from Wartime Archives* (Barnsley: Pen and Sword Military, 2014).

For more on the Type 63/65 SPAAG, see Will Kerrs' article at tanks-encyclopedia.com/coldwar/vietnam/type-63-65-spaag/

CHAPTER 61

1   Our story here is not a comprehensive retelling of the Battle of Taejon and is instead focused on General Dean's tank-hunting operations on 20 July 1950.

One source for this story is Dean's autobiography—Dean, W. F. and Worden, W. L., *General Dean's Story of his Three Year's Captivity in North Korea* (London: Weidenfeld and Nicolson, 1954). This is an account of Dean's entire time in Korea in (more or less) his own words. However, one must consider that throughout the book Dean frequently notes that he is unsure of certain details of events. For example, Dean notes that he remembers nothing of stopping for a meal during the battle save for what he was later told by others who were with him (see pp. 22–23 of the autobiography). As such, the details in the book are sketchy and sometimes do not fit neatly with other eyewitness accounts—such is the nature of oral history sources.

A fuller account of anti-tank actions throughout the battle can be found in Chapter 11 of Appleman, R. E., *The U.S. Army and the Korean War: South to the Naktong, North to the Yalu: June–November 1950* (Washington: Office of the Chief of Military History, Department of the Army, 1961). This book was written with military records as well as interviews of soldiers involved in the fighting, thus providing a fuller account of the battle than Dean's 'autobiography' by using a far greater range of primary sources. However, it is less detailed on specific engagements.

Our retelling is a composite using both books, although some details are contradictory. We advise the reader to read both books to understand the issues at stake. One may be more inclined to believe Appleman's account due to its more scholarly nature, and methodological issues in using Dean's 'autobiography'.

Finally, some other secondary sources, chiefly internet sources, suggest that Dean destroyed up to three tanks himself using grenades and pistols, but this is not the case.

2   The build-up to the Korean War is far more complicated than many books on the subject can provide, hence our very brief contextualisation.

For a concise but wide-scoped (both temporally and thematically) study of the Korean War, see Sandler, S., *The Korean War: No Victors, No Vanquished* (Lexington: University Press of Kentucky, 1999).

For studies sympathetic to North Korea, see the two-volume series by Cumings, B., *The Origins of the Korean War: Liberation and the Emergence of Separate Regimes 1945-1947* (Princeton: Princeton University Press, 1981) and *The Origins of the Korean War: The Roaring of the Cataract, 1947-1950. Volume II* (Princeton: Princeton University Press, 1990).

For a wide-ranging bibliography, see Sandler, S., 'Select Bibliography of the Korean War', *OAH Magazine of History* 14 (2000), pp. 6–9.

One will also find no shortage of 'pop' history books on the Korean War, most typically dressing the conflict up as a 'forgotten war' or 'America's first major defeat'.

3   Appleman (p. 163) reports that at around 5.30 a.m., a tank passed by the 34th Infantry Regiment's command post and a roadblock because it was mistaken for a friendly tank until it was too late for the vehicle to be engaged by anti-tank fire. Later, this tank was knocked out by 155-mm howitzer fire after exiting and re-entering the city at the south-west edge of Taejon although this is uncertain. This may in fact be the 'undamaged' tank that Dean saw in the field, but this is unclear because one might expect 155-mm howitzer fire to leave some damage. As mentioned earlier, Dean's and Appleman's accounts are sometimes contradictory.

BIBLIOGRAPHY

BOOKS AND JOURNALS

Appleman, R. E., *The U.S. Army and the Korean War: South to the Naktong, North to the Yalu: June-November 1950* (Washington: Office of the Chief of Military History, Department of the Army, 1961).

Baryatinskiy, M., *Russian Armour Volume 4: T-34 Medium Tank (1939–1943)* (Shepperton: Ian Allan Publishing, 2006).

Beevor, A., *The Battle for Spain: The Spanish Civil War 1936–1939* (London: Phoenix, 2006).

Dean, W. F. and Worden, W. L., *General Dean's Story of his Three Year's Captivity in North Korea* (London: Weidenfeld and Nicolson, 1954).

Garthoff, R. L., 'Sino-Soviet Military Relations' in *The Annals of the American Academy of Political and Social Science* 349 (1963), pp. 81–93.

Green, M., *Armoured Warfare in the Vietnam War: Rare Photographs from Wartime Archives* (Barnsley: Pen and Sword Military, 2014).

Harmsen, P., *Nanjing 1937: Battle for a Doomed City* (Oxford: Casemate Publishers, 2015); *Shanghai 1937: Stalingrad on the Yangtze* (Oxford: Casemate Publishers, 2015).

Kavalerchik, B., 'Once Again About the T-34' in *The Journal of Slavic Military Studies* 28 (2015), pp. 186–214.

Kenez, P., *A History of the Soviet Union from the Beginning to its Legacy* (Cambridge: Cambridge University Press, 2017).

Kolomiets, M., Т-34: Первая полная энциклопедия (Moscow: Эксмо, 2009).

Kotelnikov, V., *Russian Piston Aero Engines* (Marlborough: The Crowood Press Ltd., 2005).

Krylov, N. I., *Glory Eternal: Defence of Odessa 1941* (Moscow: Progress Publishers, 1972).

McLellan, D., *Marxism after Marx* (London: Macmillan Press Ltd, 1998).

Michulec, R. and Zientarzewski, M., *T-34 Mythical Weapon* (Mississauga: Airconnection, 2007).

Mitter, R., *China's War with Japan 1937–1945: The Struggle for Survival* (London: Penguin Books Ltd, 2014).

Mortera-Peréz, A., *Los Medios Blindados en la Guerra Civil Española: Teatro de Operaciones del Norte 36/37* (Valladolid: AF Editores, 2007); *Los Medios Blindados en la Guerra Civil Española: Teatro de Operaciones de Andalucía y Centro 36/39* (Valladolid: AF Editores, 2009); *Los Medios Blindados en la Guerra Civil Española: Teatro de Operaciones de Levante, Aragón y Cataluña 36/39, 1ª Parte* (Valladolid: AF Editores, 2011); *Los Medios Blindados en la Guerra Civil Española: Teatro de Operaciones de Levante, Aragón y Cataluña 36/39, 2ª Parte* (Valladolid: AF Editores, 2011).

Payne, S. G., *The Spanish Civil War* (Cambridge: Cambridge University Press, 2012).

Porter, D., *Soviet Tank Units 1939-1945* (London: Amber Books, 2008).

Pulham, F., *Fallen Giants: The Combat Debut of the T-35A Tank* (Stroud: Fonthill Media, 2017).

Restayn, J., *The Battle of Kharkov: Winter 1942–1943* (Winnipeg: J.J. Fedorowicz Publishing, 2000).

Sandford, G., 'The Katyn Massacre and Polish-Soviet Relations, 1941–43' in *Journal of Contemporary History* 41 (2006), pp. 95–111.

Skulski, P., *T-34-85: Camouflage & Markings 1944–1945* (Sandomierz: Mushroom Model Publications, 2015); *T-34-85: Camouflage & Markings 1946-2016* (Sandomierz: Mushroom Model Publications, 2018).

Suny, R. G., *The Soviet Experiment: Russia, the USSR, and the Successor States* (Oxford: Oxford University Press, 1998).

Vollert, J., *Panzerkampfwagen T 34-747(r): The Soviet T-34 Tank as Beutepanzer and Panzerattrappe in German Wehrmacht Service 1941–45* (Erlangen: Tankograd, 2013).

Werlich, R., *Russian Orders, Decorations and Medals Including Those of Imperial Russia, the Provincial Government, the Civil War, and the Soviet Union* (Quaker Press: Washington, D.C., 1981).

Westad, O. A., *Decisive Encounters: The Chinese Civil War, 1946–1950* (Stanford: Stanford University Press, 2003).

Zaloga, S., *BT Fast Tank: The Red Army's Cavalry Tank 1931–45* (Oxford: Osprey Publishing, 2016); *KV-1 & 2 Heavy Tanks 1939-45* (Oxford: Osprey Publishing, 2013); 'Soviet Tank Operations in the Spanish Civil War' in *The Journal of Slavic Military Studies* 12 (1999), pp. 134–162; *Spanish Civil War Tanks: The Proving Ground for Blitzkrieg* (Oxford: Osprey Publishing, 2010); *T-26 Light Tank: Backbone of the Red Army* (Oxford: Osprey Publishing, 2015); *T-34/76 Medium Tank 1941-45* (Oxford: Osprey Publishing, 1994); *T-34-85 Medium Tank 1944–94* (Oxford: Osprey Publishing, 1994); *T-34-85 vs M26 Pershing: Korea 1950* (Oxford: Osprey Publishing, 2011).

Zhiwei, Z., 中國人民解放軍戰車部隊 *1945–1955 (The Tank Division of the Chinese People's Liberation Army 1945–1955)* (Taipei: Humanism Print, 2017).

WEB SOURCES (ACCESSED BETWEEN FEBRUARY AND DECEMBER 2018)

burbuja.info/inmobiliaria/temas-calientes/920573-cuanto-cobraba-miliciano-y-brigadista-trataban-brigadistas-a-camaradas-espanoles.html

chinesearmory.blogspot.com/p/pla-t-3485-type-58.html

grinnols.livejournal.com/1152.html

jczs.news.sina.com.cn/2004-09-27/1114230763.html

mzensk1941.narod.ru/index/t_34_76_quot_dmitrij_donskoj/0-48

m.v4.cc/News-1856769.html

news.china.com.cn/txt/2005-10/14/content_5998254.htm

net-maquettes.com/de/pictures/char-t-34-brem/

t34inform.ru/publication/p01-13.html

tankarchives.blogspot.com/2017/03/first-soviet-tanks.html

tankarchives.blogspot.com/2014/01/tank-inscriptions.html

tankarchives.blogspot.com/2016/11/christie-m1931.html

tankarchives.blogspot.com/2013/07/king-tigers-at-ogledow.html

tankarchives.blogspot.com/2013/04/aberdeen-t-34-and-kv-1-test.html?fbclid=IwAR1HfhaDvb8n15w-Gj0DDwU-oMMc51rF0wSx8GDLAKk-4V6wBo5yELMqjDk

tanks-encyclopedia.com/ww2/china/chinese-tanks-1925-1950/

tankfront.ru/ussr/tbr/tbr021.html

tankfront.ru/ussr/names/colums/moskovskiy_kolhoznik.html

tieba.baidu.com/p/4908818042?pn=2

toledogce.blogspot.com/2015/10/los-t26-en-sesena.html

usacac.army.mil/CAC2/CGSC/CARL/nafziger/939RXAJ.PDF

waralbum.ru/301767/

web.archive.org/web/20170728072510/http://www.aviarmor.net:80/tww2/tanks/ussr/

wwiiafterwwii.wordpress.com/2016/07/03/su-100-tank-destroyer-post-wwii-use-in-the-middle-east/

zhihu.com/question/36633152

zhuanlan.zhihu.com/p/25056122

OTHER SOURCES

Album of T-34 Photos and Data (An original T-34 technical manual from 1940 written for the manufacture of the T-34).

Andrew, M., *Tuo Mao: The Operational History of the People's Liberation Army* (PhD dissertation submitted to Bond University, Faculty of Humanities and Social Sciences, 2008).

China Builds a Better Tank … the Israeli Way [redacted] (A declassified CIA report dated 10 February 1986; available online through the CIA library: cia.gov/library/readingroom/document/cia-rdp86t01017r000605590001-5)

Harbin Tank Repair Factory, China (A declassified CIA report dated 22 November 1963; available online through the CIA library: cia.gov/library/readingroom/document/cia-rdp78t05439a000300020037-0)

Intelligence Memorandum: Communist Military Aid Deliveries to North Vietnam During 1968 (A declassified CIA report dated May 1969; available online through the CIA library: cia.gov/library/readingroom/document/00011747).

Makarov, A., 'Ask AJ—"Please help me to figure out the rear exterior fuel tanks of the T-34. When were they first used? Did their design differ from manufacturer to manufacturer and when were they finally replaced by the side-mounted cylindrical fuel tanks?"—Milo Jones', *The Armor Journal Issue 1* (2014), pp. 22–25.

Tank/Assault Gun Facility Tai-Yuan, China (A declassified CIA report dated 1 May 1966 by the Image Analysis Division; available online through the CIA library: cia.gov/library/readingroom/document/cia-rdp78t05161a000900010081-1). This is one of countless examples of a CIA IAD report from the mid-1960s about the widespread Chinese use of the T-34-85 in this period.